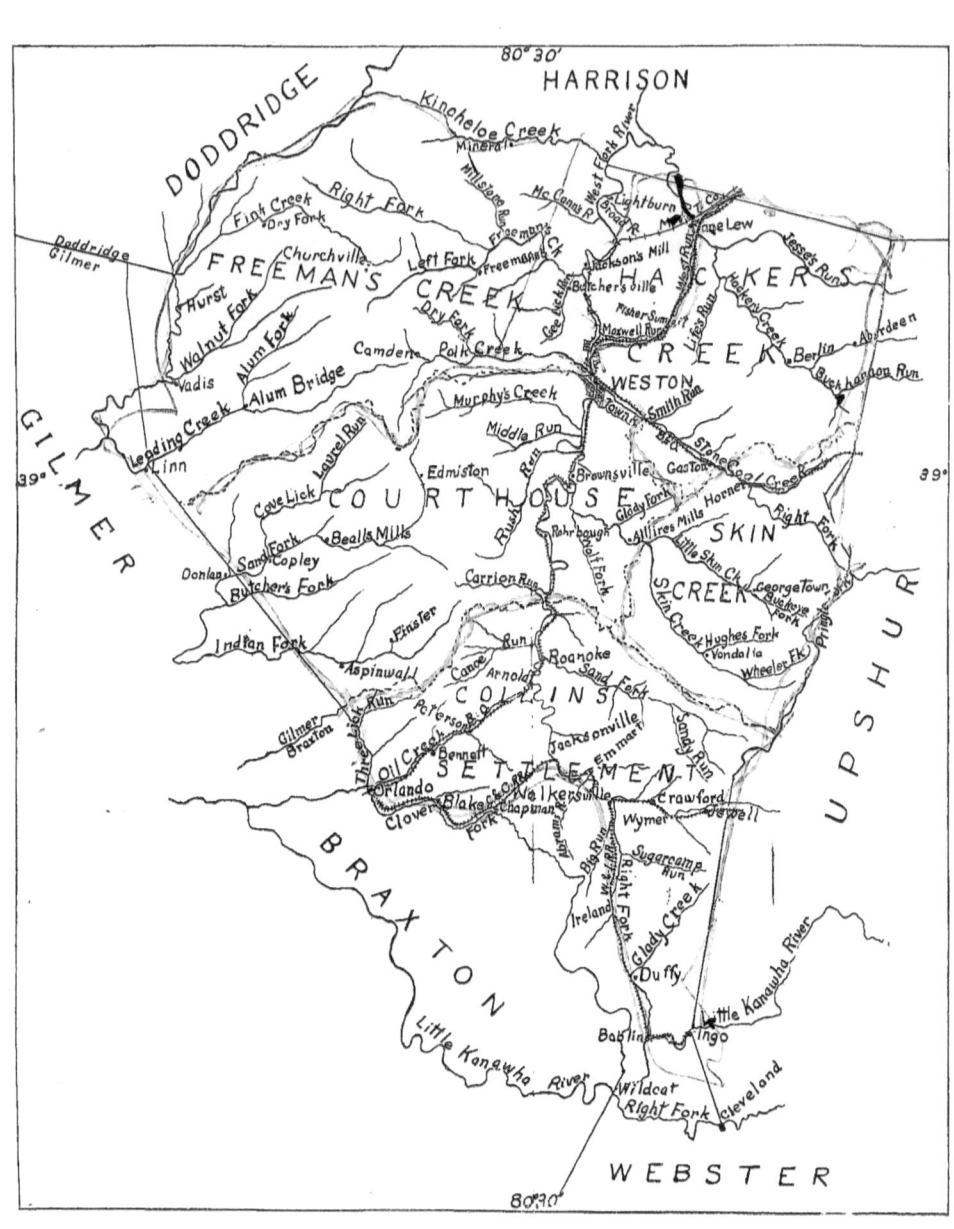

A HISTORY
OF
LEWIS COUNTY, WEST VIRGINIA

BY

EDWARD CONRAD SMITH, A. M.

Sometime Teacher of History and Civics in
Weston High School.

Southern Historical Press, Inc.
Greenville, South Carolina

This volume was reproduced
from a personal copy located in
the Publishers private library

All rights reserved. No part of this publication may be reproduced,
stored in a retrieval system, transmitted in any form, posted
on the web in any form or by any means without the
prior written permission of the publisher.

Please direct all correspondence and book orders to:
SOUTHERN HISTORICAL PRESS, Inc.
1071 Park West Blvd.
Greenville, SC 29611

Copyright 1920 by:
   Edwatd C. Smith
ISBN #978-1-63914-646-8
Printed in the United States of America

TO
MY FATHER
Whose life has been devoted to the upbuilding of Lewis County.

"The annals, and records, and life, of quiet neighborhoods are historically important by their vital connection with the progress and science of the nation and of the world."

—JAMES MORTON CALLAHAN.

PREFACE.

The purpose of this volume is to trace the economic, social and political life of the people of Lewis County from the time the first settlers came to the Hacker's creek valley to the present. Believing that the group is more important than any of its component parts, it has been my aim to deal with the development of institutions rather than with family history, to present as fully as possible a record of the whole county rather than tales of illustrious pioneers and their descendants. In order to accomplish this purpose I have selected from a great mass of material those incidents which I thought would best depict the life of the county, and I have tried to arrange them in order so as to show cause and effect, advance and retardation, of development.

It is hoped that this volume will fill a long felt want. It is a rather remarkable fact, in view of the importance of Lewis County and its influence on the life of Virginia and West Virginia, that a history of the county has never been published in permanent form. There have been published at various times important works relating to certain periods, and to certain matters affecting the history of the county. The first of these was "Chronicles of Border Warfare," by Alexander Scott Withers, which treats of the history of the frontier to the Treaty of Greenville, 1795. The same period has been treated lately by Lucullus Virgil McWhorter, in his volume entitled "Border Settlers of Northwestern Virginia." Both works are extremely valuable for a study of the early history of the county. About 1884, Hardesty's "Political and Geographical Survey of Lewis County" was published, which contains a historical sketch of the county very hastily and carelessly written.

Many writers have contributed sketches and recollections to the county papers at different times. Under the pseudonym of "Ancient", John Strange Hall wrote a series of articles for the Weston Independent depicting customs, personages and institutions of the 'thirties. George F. Oliver contributed to the Weston Democrat a series of articles in which the author makes a comprehensive survey of conditions in Weston and Lewis County as they were in 1844. In 1917, John R. King wrote a series of articles for the Weston Independent which throw considerable light on the manners and customs of western Virginia in the period just before the Civil war. Within the past few years, Roy B. Cook, a native of the county, has made valuable contributions to the same paper in an extended "Pioneer History of Lewis County," and a collection of documents, annotated, on "Lewis County in the Civil War."

I first began a systematic collection of materials on Lewis County history in 1915. Though the work has been greatly interrupted at times, I never quite lost sight of my original intention to write the story of development of Lewis County.

Every effort has been made to guard against errors in statement, but I am conscious that some errors may have escaped detection. The necessity for depending upon traditional accounts in the absence of records for a part of the early period has made the task of sifting evidence somewhat uncertain. In all possible cases I have attempted to verify the traditional accounts by the records.

I have drawn the materials for this volume from many different sources—from old letters and account books, from public documents, from old newspapers and from personal interviews with participants in the affairs of the county, as well as from books and pamphlets of earlier investigators.

It would be impossible to mention here the names of all those who have assisted in various ways in the preparation of this work. Cordial thanks are due to the publishers of the Weston Independent and of the Weston Democrat for free access to their files; to Mr. Roy R. Hale for lending his file of the Lewis County Record; to officials of Lewis, Harrison and Monongalia counties for valuable assistance in my search for records; to Miss Mary Strange Hall for a scrap-book containing the writings of her father; to Mr. Stark A. White for an article on the Baptists of Lewis County; and to all those who have accorded me personal interviews. Mr. E. G. Davisson has made valuable suggestions concerning the subject matter and has given much valuable material. Miss Edna Arnold has criticised portions of the manuscript.

EDWARD C. SMITH.

Weston, West Virginia,
January 1, 1920.

CONTENTS.

CHAPTER I
The Physical Basis for Development..................13

CHAPTER II
The Aboriginal Inhabitants..................22

CHAPTER III
The Beginning of Settlements..................30

CHAPTER IV
Lewis County in Dunmore's War..................44

CHAPTER V
Lewis County During the Revolutionary War..................51

CHAPTER VI
The End of the Indian Wars..................70

CHAPTER VII
The Beginning of Law and Order..................84

CHAPTER VIII
Economic Beginnings..................98

CHAPTER IX
Life of the Pioneers..................111

CHAPTER X
The Extension of Settlements—Skin Creek..................128

CHAPTER XI
The Collins Settlement 136

CHAPTER XII
Freeman's Creek District 143

CHAPTER XIII
Progress in Older Settlements 150

CHAPTER XIV
The Formation of Lewis County 162

CHAPTER XV
The Beginning of Weston 176

CHAPTER XVI
Progress Under the New Regime 197

CHAPTER XVII
Early Transportation 215

CHAPTER XVIII
The Irish and German Immigration 230

CHAPTER XIX
Territorial Losses 239

CHAPTER XX
The Great Business Boom, 1845-60 246

CHAPTER XXI
The Development of Education 268

CHAPTER XXII
The Seccession from Virginia 281

CHAPTER XXIII
Military Operations 297

CHAPTER XXIV
The Political Reconstruction...316

CHAPTER XXV
The Weston State Hospital...327

CHAPTER XXVI
Economic Development After the War...............................335

CHAPTER XXVII
The Coming of the Railroad...352

CHAPTER XXVIII
Twenty Years' Progress, 1880-1900....................................368

CHAPTER XXIX
The Oil and Gas Development...380

CHAPTER XXX
The Twentieth Century 397

APPENDIX A:
Sketch of Col. Charles Lewis...414

APPENDIX B:
Justices of the Peace Under Virginia..................................416

LIST OF ILLUSTRATIONS.

Map of Lewis County, W. Va..............................Frontispiece

The Jackson Homestead and Mill..................................160

Presley M. Hale 288

Stonewall Jackson 313

The Weston State Hospital..328

Lewis County in 1872 336

Map of Weston (From Mitchell's Geography, Edition of 1873)..344

The Copely Well...384

Judge Henry Brannon 400

CHAPTER I.

THE PHYSICAL BASIS FOR DEVELOPMENT

Lewis county is a homogeneous geographical division lying in central West Virginia. Save for a narrow strip along its western border which is naturally so like the remainder in soil, climate and natural productions that it may almost be said to be a part of it, and for a small district in the extreme south, the county occupies the upper valley of the West Fork river. On the east is Upshur County, including the more elevated valley of the Buckhannon river, on the south and west are Webster, Braxton and Gilmer counties with the more rugged hills and the narrower valleys of the head streams of the Little Kanawha; and on the north is Harrison County alone geographically united with Lewis County but politically distinct because the whole region is too large to form one county. The area of Lewis County is 391 square miles.

With the exception of a negligible strip on the east the county includes the whole upper valley of the West Fork river and its tributaries. The main stream is formed by the junction of two forks of the river at Walkersville. From there the course of the river is generally north, and that of the tributaries generally northeast or northwest according to whether they empty from the west or east. The river is not navigable except for floating logs, although declared a navigable waterway by Secretary of the Treasury Gallatin as early as 1805. The principal left hand tributaries in Lewis County are Hacker's creek, Stone Coal creek, Skin creek, Sand fork and the Left fork. The principal right hand tributaries are Kincheloe creek, Freeman's creek, Polk Creek, Rush run and Right fork. Among the principal streams leading into the Little Kanawha or its tributaries are Fink creek, Leading creek, Sand fork, Indian fork and Clover fork and both forks of the Little Kanawha river. As a rule the smaller streams have a rather rapid fall. In nearly all cases they have V-shaped valleys with flood plains of varying width depending more upon the character of the geological formation than upon the size of the stream.

In general the surface is rough and broken. Steep slopes and low mountains, winding ridges and bold spurs, low-gaps and winding valleys abound throughout the county. Below Weston the river valley broadens considerably and the terrace formation becomes one of the conspicuous features of the topography of the country. The elevation of the bottom lands is about 1,000 to 1,100 feet above sea-level, and that of the hill-tops is from four hundred to six hundred feet higher. The lowest point in the county is on Leading creek just above Linn, where the elevation is about 775 feet and the highest point is near Cleveland where one of the hills reaches 2,000 feet.

The climate is mild and healthful. The winters are rather long but not so cold as in the higher altitudes toward the east and south. Extremes of very hot and very cold weather, though not uncommon, rarely continue for a long period. The average active growing season for crops is five and one-half months between the last killing frost in the spring and the first in the fall. The precipitation is 46.85 inches, well distributed throughout the year, but heaviest in spring and summer when most needed for growing crops.

The soils of the county have been, for the most part, developed from the decomposition of shale and the thin beds of sandstone in the upper coal measures. Clay and clay loam are the principal kinds of soils found. As a general rule they are fertile or respond readily to treatment. On account of the character of the bed rocks and the sluggishness of the West Fork river the contour of the county is smoother than that of surrounding regions and the soil is more favorable for stock raising. For that reason, Lewis County is regarded as one of the three or four leading grazing counties of West Virginia.

Millions of years ago Central West Virginia was the bed of a great sea which scientists have called the Appalachian sea. The bed of the sea was some ten thousand feet below the present level of the valley at Weston. Streams flowing into this sea from a range of mountains which lay on the east toward the present Atlantic coast brought sediment into it and gradually filled it with sand and clay. Tiny animals like the corals lived on the bottom of the sea and their shells became built up layer by layer, until the deposit was several feet in thickness; then another layer of sand and silt was deposited in the sea covering the shells, which were cemented together by pressure. The sea became filled up until it was a swamp. Then giant ferns and other plants, growing a hundred fold more luxuriantly than any of the terrestrial plants in existence today filled the swamp with verdure. The dead plants covered the surface, raising its level many feet. A sudden subsidence of the soil—one of the inexplicable cataclysms of nature—made the layer of vegetation the bottom of the sea, and other layers of silt were deposited upon it, until the sea was filled and again became a swamp. Again the giant ferns of the carboniferous age grew, and flourished, and decayed. Then at long intervals there were alternate subsidences and fillings, alternate deposits of silt from the rivers and decaying vegetable matter from the carboniferous forests. As layer followed layer the heat of the earth and the pressure of the deposits below changed the silt into solid rock, and the vegetable deposits into coal, or oil, or gas according to the amount of heat present in the earth. Then came a mighty upheaval of the earth and the whole surface underwent a violent change. The bottom of the sea became a great mountain range. In the small section which is now Lewis County was a plateau several hundred feet above our valleys. The water which fell upon the surface was carried off. Rivers were formed which bore silt with them into other seas. After thousands of years the rivers accomplished the tasks set by nature for them. The surface was reduced almost to the level of the sea, and made almost as smooth as the top of a table. The streams coursed their sluggish way to the ocean by many a meander. Not much silt was carried because the rapidity of the flow was insufficient to hold it in suspension. There came finally another upheaval. Again the water courses had to descend a great distance in order to reach the sea, and again they became swift enough to carry silt in great quantities. They have now cut down several hundred feet below their original level, and the process is still going on and will continue many centuries before it is again completed. The streams, in cutting down to the new levels hold to some of their old meanders, and the valleys have serpentine curves much as we may imagine the streams were curved in long past ages.

The principal mineral wealth of the county is the result of the growths of the carboniferous ages. The coal is found in layers or strata in practically all sections of the county. The strata do not run perfectly level but rise and fall, and are bent downward into synclines and upward into anticlines. The erosive action of the streams has exposed many of the veins so that it is possible to mine coal on the surface. Others lie at varying depths below the floors of the valleys. The beds of vegetable matter which have been changed into liquid and gaseous forms through having been subjected to extreme heat and pressure are found near anticlines as oil and natural gas. These deposits have been stored in porous rocks, or "sands", far beneath the surface. It is reasonable to suppose that deposits existed nearer the surface, which have been gradually exposed by erosion and have escaped. Gas is found at a depth of about 2,000 feet, near Weston, and oil has been discovered in the extreme western part of the county at a somewhat lower depth. Some of the rocks of the county contain iron, but not in a form suitable for working. Limestone is also found in some sections in discontinuous beds or veins. There are traditions in nearly every part of the county that lead once existed in the vicinity. As evidence it is said that old pioneers used to go away from their homes, and after following a path unknown to other residents of the community and impossible to trail successfully, they returned with lead to replenish their stores. All trace of these mines died with their pioneer discoverers. There are stories of how some of the aged men have given directions for finding the mines to their sons, but they have been unable to discover any trace of the lead. The lead mine traditions may be set down as a myth. No geological formation can account for the presence of lead in this section. The traditions are probably pure invention or they rest upon the fact that some of the early settlers in their trips to Winchester returned with lead which they did not care to divide with their neighbors.

Long before the advent of settlers into this region the surface was covered with dense forests. In all but the wilder portions of the county the trees were deciduous, but beginning at Duffy and extending through the "shoestring" section conifers are found, with undergrowth consisting of dense thickets of laurel and holly. This type of forest growth is found also in some of the rougher land of the county—land which is stony and otherwise unfit for clearing. White oak and tulip poplar are the species of trees of greatest commercial importance. Other trees of more or less value are oaks, maples, beeches, hickory, chestnuts, walnut, elm and ash. The shell bark hickory, the chestnut, the black and the white walnut and the beech were valuable sources of food, which could easily be stored. Acorns were also valuable in fattening hogs. Practically all the valuable timber which once covered the slopes of the hills and valleys of Lewis County has been either felled by the lumberman or deadened and then burned to make way for agricultural operations.

The first settlements were made in clearings in this primeval wilderness. All the disadvantages of clearing land from which the larger growth had not been removed were felt by the pioneers. Wild animals which threatened the lives of the settlers' families or their livestock roamed through the forests. The fierce panther prowled in the thickets ready to spring without notice upon the luckless settler who passed in his way. Another of the denizens of the forest which impeded the march of civilization is commemorated in the name given to Wild Cat run. The wildcats had no hesitancy in attacking the livestock of the settlers or even man himself when they were defending their young. Wolf Fork commemorates another undesirable inhabitant. The gaunt gray wolves haunted the hills and valleys in packs, and woe to the pioneer who became lost after nightfall, or to the pioneer's live-stock which strayed too far from the humble cabin from which the owner guarded his property with jealous care. Underfoot glided noiselessly the deadly rattlesnake which gave notice of his presence only at the last minute and the still more deadly copperhead which struck without any notice at all. Both reptiles were man's implacable enemies; and the settler made unrelenting war upon them. Most of Lewis County youths of the twentieth century have never seen a live rattlesnake because of the utter extinction of the species. The copperhead still persists in all parts of the county and is a source of danger on every rocky bit of farm land. Into the vast expanse of primeval forest which covered the slopes of all the hills in western Virginia the hardy pioneers made their first settlements, after the last of the wars with the French.

The wilderness was not inhospitable. The Indians were able to live and thrive without any of the comforts of civilization, and the rugged race of Virginia backwoodsmen had been steeled to endure hardships in their ceaseless battle with the forest. They had quickly learned the ways of the savages in conquering the wilderness dangers. Some indeed became the superiors of the Indians in woodcraft. The forests of Lewis County were capable of supporting a considerable population. On every hand there are abundant evidences of the number of wild animals from which could be derived an abundant supply of meat. The Indians every fall came all the way from central Ohio to hunt. The supply was so great that the white men, who killed without thought for the future, did not exhaust the supply for nearly a century. The names which the early settlers gave to the natural features of the county show how great the supply was and how much importance it was in the lives of the pioneers. Buffalo lick, Buffalo stamping ground, Bull run, Calf run and perhaps others prove the presence in the county of small droves of buffalo or individuals met with by the hunters in their first incursions into the unknown wilds. Traditional accounts state that buffaloes destroyed the first corn crops planted on Hacker's creek. Bear run commemorates probably a hunt in which one or more of the tribe of Bruin went down before the rifle of some early hunter. Two streams by the name of Elk lick prove the existence of that noblest of all big game animals of the North American continent. Local place names telling of the presence of deer, an animal which furnished the most important part of the subsistence of every pioneer family, are legion. Deer run, Deer camp, Doe lick and Buck run are some of the larger streams. Every locality has its "lick", a spring where the deer went to drink. Skin creek was named from an enormous number of deer skins which were obtained by four hunters in a single day; and Carrion run is said to have derived its name from the stench arising from the carcasses of deer killed in a great hunt, which had been skinned and left where they fell. Goosepen run, Turkeypen run, Turkey Scratch run and Pigeon Roost run commemorate the presence of wild geese, wild turkeys, and wild pigeons, the last named of which formerly existed in the county in such enormous flocks that the sky was darkened for hours. Raccoon run and 'Possum hollow were named for two humbler beasts of the chase which have not yet become extinct. Beaver and otter, though never numerous, furnished employment for the earliest trappers.

All the larger streams abound in fish of superior size and flavor—pike, bass, catfish and many smaller and less important varieties which were caught easily by gigging. Turtles were then plentiful, and the pioneer learned from the Indians the trick of digging them out of their winter retreats in the swamps. Frogs were also plentiful, and were much sought after. Mussels would have proved an important source of food, but the settler evidently did not relish them.

From early summer until late in the fall there were always luscious wild fruits to tempt the settler. Wild strawberries, glistening white in the dew, grew on the hill tops early in June. Before they were gone the red service-berries ripened on bushes standing everywhere through the woods, the sticky-sweet mulberries beckoned from a thousand trees, and wild raspberries grew wherever a little rotting wood gave the ground extra fertility. Next came blackberries and huckleberries and elderberries and wild gooseberries and wild cherries. All varieties of wild grapes ripened in the autumn; and in the thickets about the bases of the hills pawpaws grew in abundance. Persimmons ripened after the first frost and hung on the trees until midwinter.

Chestnuts, hickory nuts, black walnuts, butternuts and hazelnuts ripened in the fall and furnished a never-failing food which could be stored and used through the winter. Acorns furnished abundant food for the fattening of hogs.

The pioneer's medicine chest could be filled from the products of the woods. Ginseng, yellowroot and snakeroot were specifics for a great variety of diseases. Skull-cap and bone-set, when gathered and steeped properly, proved efficacious in preventing or checking colds. The fat of the skunk was considered a cure for rheumatism when it was rendered under the proper conditions and phases of the moon. The smoking of "field balsam" and jimson weed was said to relieve asthma. Peppermint, wintergreen, pennyroyal and pinnikinnick leaves, sassafras roots and the branches of the spicewood bush were used in steeping teas.

CHAPTER II.

BEFORE THE WHITE MEN CAME

Unlike most other portions of the American continent Lewis County and West Virginia were not occupied by the Indians at the time the first explorers traversed the region. The whole expanse east of the Ohio river, rich as it was in game, held not a single permanent human habitation. There were Indians to be found in West Virginia during the summer and autumn months when they came from their camps and villages in the Scioto valley and elsewhere for the purpose of hunting, but at the approach of winter they always returned to their permanent homes.

Indications in many parts of the county point to a large aboriginal population of more or less permanence. Village sites, artificial mounds, burial places and other evidences of habitation are the reward of the antiquarian in almost any part of the county where he undertakes his investigations. On the present site of Cleveland just across the right fork of the Little Kanawha river in Webster County there were ten or twelve earth mounds, five feet in height and about twenty feet in diameter. They were thought to have been of Indian origin, but what part the mounds played in the social, industrial or religious life of the Indian is unknown. Excavation has failed to reveal any trace of their use as burial mounds. Just across the river from Jacksonville, in Collins Settlement district, there is an old field which, tradition says, is the site of an Indian village. There are to be found even now many arrow heads and broken pieces of flint which have been only partly worked into proper shape, indicating that a maker of arrow heads lived there in the days before the white men came. Near Round Knob school house on Big Skin creek there is a similar village or camping site. The remains of an important village were found at Arnold, and nearby another mound. Near the mouth of Canoe run there was also a mound.

It is on Hacker's creek, however, that the most important archaeological discoveries have been made. Seven Indian village sites have been found in the main valley of the stream, besides one on McKinney's run and another on Jesse's run. Temporary camping sites and scattered Indian graves have been unearthed all through the valley. On practically every elevated knoll or considerable tract of high bottom land the first explorers found a space which had been cleared for a village and nearby a burial ground where the dead had been laid to rest, from immemorial centuries. The locations which have been identified are Minor Hall's residence within the corporate limits of the town of Jane Lew, a second bottom at the mouth of Jesse's run, two locations within a short distance of each other on the farm of the late John Alkire, the original John Hacker settlement about one mile below Berlin, the old Cozad farm in the same vicinity, and two sites in Upshur County, one at the mouth of Rover's run and the other several miles further up the stream.

At the last named location there was a trace of Indian habitation of great interest to the antiquarian. When cleared in 1821 the site was covered with a growth of young sugar trees about twelve inches in diameter indicating that the place had in very recent times been occupied by Indians. The remains of a great ash-circle one hundred eighty feet in diameter are to be seen at the present time. It consists of a clear space sixty feet across surrounded by a heavy deposit of ashes in a belt sixty feet wide. The inside circle is thickly strewn with fragments of bone, mussel shells, pieces of broken pottery, flint more or less broken, and stone implements and ornaments. When first cleared the field is said to have been literally covered with fragments of shell and bones, evidently the votive offerings of a tribe which had either been exterminated or driven away.

In a mound close by the ash circle were found a flint spear head, a broken arrow point, a small piece of steatite paint-stone and a single bit of charcoal. A finely carved stone pipe made from brown sandstone has been picked up nearby. A perforated steatite "banner stone" in almost perfect condition was plowed up near the same place many years ago. An effigy-like figure of Indian origin was found on the crest of a hill adjacent to Bear knob. Three stone heaps each about three feet high by eight feet in diameter and surrounded by a curbing are located near the Lewis-Upshur line. One of them was removed some years ago revealing a small bed of ashes about one foot below the original surface. Nothing else was there save a small flint spear head, which showed traces of having been subjected to heat. It is claimed that a fragment of an engraved sandstone tablet was picked up near the site of Berlin, together with a fine "chungky" stone, and a small copper pendant. Grooved stone relics were seldom found, though mysteriously pitted cup-stones have been picked up in every glen in the valley. A grave opened in 1890 near one of the village sites below Berlin contained a fine stone bird-head pipe and a polished slate gorget; in another, was a well-made celt, slightly damaged at the poll; and in still another, a clay pipe and a broken clay vessel containing part of the shell of a turtle. Not all the relics found in graves, in mounds or scattered singly throughout the valley were of aboriginal make. Besides the copper vessel mentioned above there was found in one of the graves below Berlin a small fragment of bright blue home-spun woolen cloth. Iron and steel tomahawks and a clay pipe stem of undoubtedly European manufacture have been discovered in other Indian remains in various parts of the valley. These trinkets must have been taken as booty in wars with the English settlers of Virginia or else have been secured in trade either from the English settlers in Virginia or from the French in Canada who reached the region of Lake Huron as early as 1615. Probably they were obtained from the latter source. It is hardly supposed that the mounds, burial places, etc., were built by the later tribes who were merely hunters in the valley and who therefore would hardly undertake any considerable works. They must have been constructed within comparatively recent dates by a tribe who made their permanent homes in West Virginia. It may have been shortly after the first permanent English and French settlements in America, or it may have been at a considerably later time.

The Iroquois, or Five Nations, of New York (who became the Six Nations by the accession of the Tuscaroras of North Carolina in 1713) began a series of wars against the surrounding Indians about 1650, and within a century they conquered the mighty tribe of Hurons living to the west of them and had overrun all the territory as far west as the Illinois and Mississippi rivers and as far south as Alabama and Mississippi. West Virginia was included in the early conquests of the New York tribe. There were traditions among the Indians of long and bloody wars fought between different tribes. Several battles were fought among the West Virginia hills during which the streams are said to have run as with blood. It is possible that the Iroquois found a strong tribe occupying West Virginia whom they had to exterminate because they could not drive them out. The ash circle found on Hacker's creek is said to be very uncommon among the American Indians, and it may be that it was built by a tribe different in civilization from most of the other tribes found east of the Mississippi. All attempts to solve the riddle have been futile. The permanent aboriginal inhabitants of West Virginia will probably remain undetermined.

Very different is the case of the Indians who made their hunting trips to West Virginia in historic times.

According to Indian tradition the Iroquois in 1713, leased to the Shawnees and the Delawares the rights to hunt and fish in the district now embraced in West Virginia. These two tribes had left their settlements along the upper courses of the Delaware and Susquehanna rivers in Pennsylvania upon the approach of the whites and had taken up their residence in Ohio with their principal seat at Old Chillicothe. From there it was a journey of only a few days to the magnificent hunting grounds of West Virginia. The Shawnees often came in considerable bodies bringing their women and children with them and remaining from early fall until the near approach of winter compelled them to return to their villages. While the tribe was on one of these annual hunts it is claimed that Tecumseh, the greatest Indian military genius who lived within historic times, was born on Hacker's creek. The date of his birth is supposed to have been 1768, one year before the first exploration of the valley by the whites. The place is unknown, but it is said that the chieftain declared it to be one of the village sites of the valley, either about one mile below the present site of Berlin or at the mouth of Jesse's run. Both these sites were occupied as camping grounds by the Indians within a few years before the first settlement by the whites, as is attested by the finding of brass buttons and other perishable objects of European manufacture among the rubbish heaps left by the earlier occupants.

The Indians came to the Hacker's creek hunting ground and to others farther east by way of trails leading up the Little Kanawha river from its mouth, and thence across the divide to the waters of the West Fork. The principal trail in Lewis County followed Leading creek from its mouth to its source and then crossed over to Polk creek, down that stream to its mouth, up Stone Coal creek, thence across Buckhannon mountain and down Saul's run to the Buckhannon. Many years after the coming of the whites the Staunton and Parkersburg turnpike followed this trail except where the course was changed for political or industrial reasons. The Indians also reached Lewis County by coming up Sand fork and crossing to Rush run, and by crossing from the head of Oil creek to Indian Carrying run whence it is only a few hundred yards to the West Fork river. This is the only spot where the Indians, within historic times, portaged from the watershed of the Little Kanawha to the West Fork. The streams navigable for canoes are not more than three or four miles apart and the watershed is low. The old portage is now used by the Baltimore and Ohio railroad. At the Indian Carrying place there probably stood an Indian house of poles and bark or other light construction, mentioned in some of the older land office records. An Indian canoe which probably was brought over the carrying place was found moored to some willows near the mouth of Canoe run by some of the first white men to visit that section, and this circumstance gave the name to the stream. Settlers on Canoe run and Carrion run have a tradition that these streams were also used by the Indians in crossing from Sand fork to the watershed of the West Fork, and the name of the latter stream is declared by some to be a corruption of "carrying run". Freeman's creek was a short cut used by the Indians on their way to the Hacker's creek settlement. During the later years of the Indian wars it became necessary to station a body of men at the mouth of the creek to intercept them. Down Kincheloe creek came Indians who had come up Hughes river and crossed the divide. The Indians never came to the region by canoes during historic times, on account of the danger that their retreat might be cut off by a small body of men near the mouth of the Little Kanawha. During their war with the whites they never followed the streams in the vicinity of the settlements, but made their way along the ridges and benches from which they could observe the country and be comparatively safe from ambush.

The so-called "Seneca trail" by which the Indians reached the settlements on the upper reaches of the Tygart's Valley, Shaver's Fork, the upper course of the Greenbrier and the South Branch of the Potomac, passed through the southern part of the county. Sometimes the Indians followed the Little Kanawha through the "Shoestring" and at other times they came down the Left fork of the West Fork river, crossed to Abram's run and thence to Knawl's creek, a tributary of the Little Kanawha. The Buckhannon and Bulltown turnpike followed the course in later years.

Persistent traditions exist in several sections affirming the presence of white men in Lewis county before the coming of the permanent settlers. Several trees in the Lost creek valley were found by the first explorers to bear the letters "T. G." cut into their bark. The explorers believed that the man who carved the initials had been lost; or rather by a method of reasoning, which antedated the teachings of present day philosophy by a century and a half, they concluded it was not the man who was lost but the region through which he wandered; and the stream has borne the name of Lost creek ever since. The letter "G" was found carved on a beech tree beside a spring on what is now Gee Lick run. The identity of the person who did the carving has remained a mystery, and the spring and the stream has been called G (or Gee) Lick from that time. It is quite possible that captives may have been brought here by the Indians while on their hunting trips, but why they should have carved their names on trees is another question. At any rate no impetus to settlement or advancement in geographical knowledge has ever been made by the mysterious "G" and "T. G."

There are legends also of buried treasure in two different sections of the county. In a cave at or near the head of Stone Coal creek a Buckhannon dentist found, in 1867, a group of strange inscriptions which are supposed to relate to a rich mine near Indian camp in Upshur County near which buried treasure might be found. The inscription had been revealed to him by one Calvin Smith, a squirrel hunter, previous to setting out for the west. The inscription reads: "Was fought for the rich minds swartus cnancu 1555 riten snath done while the batel." The legend in explanation of the story is that an Indian wearing arm bracelets of silver arrived at Jamestown shortly after the first settlement. He offered to pilot a party to the place where he found the silver for his jewelry. A large group ranged about "Swartus Cnancu" (who, by the way, is not mentioned in Virginia history as being an immigrant) and they proceeded to the wilds of what is now Upshur County. After digging 1555 pounds of treasure they were set upon by the savages, and a great battle was fought, during which the white men blasted great stones to cover the opening, and Snath escaped to write inscriptions to guide them to the place in case of a return. It is said that much digging after buried treasure has been done by citizens of the vicinity, but needless to say, none of it has ever been unearthed.

Near the head of Canoe run there is a stone bearing a turkey's claw which, when looked at in a certain way, points to the spur jutting out from the low ridge opposite the mouth of the run. A legend in the community says that the marker indicates buried treasure. On the slopes of the knob a great deal of digging has been done in search of this treasure at various times.

NOTE—Most of the important archaeological discoveries on Hacker's creek were made by L. V. McWhorter and are more fully described in his "Border Settlers of Northwestern Virginia." The McWhorter collection of relics occupies a notable place in the State Museum at Charleston.

CHAPTER III.

THE BEGINNING OF SETTLEMENTS

The western frontier of Virginia from its earliest settlement by the whites was constantly changing, constantly pressing forward. The Virginians moved westward as immigration increased the need for new land. The early Scotch-Irish settlers in Pennsylvania were disappointed with the system of land tenure there, and they moved southwestward into the valleys which lie between the Blue Ridge and the Alleghanies and made new settlements for themselves in the wilderness. One of these settlements was in the Shenandoah; another and a more important one for the history of central West Virginia is on the South Branch of the Potomac. All along this stream and its tributaries by 1750 there was a thriving settlement composed of frontiersmen who, inured to hardship and privation and scorning the perils of the wilderness, had laid the foundations for a new commonwealth west of the mountains. The total population in 1754 was estimated at 10,000 whites and 400 blacks.

Soon the more daring residents of the South Branch began to make new settlements west of the divide. By 1753 pioneers had reached the upper valley of the Tygart's Valley river; the next year the Echarlys built their homes on the Cheat river; and by 1758, a party of settlers had located on the present site of Morgantown. The Indian forays following Braddock's defeat in the French and Indian war broke up all these settlements, and even endangered the pioneers in the valley of the South Branch. There were many bloody massacres in that outpost of English civilization in America during the years that followed.

The treaty of 1763 brought peace with the French

and their Indian allies; but the peace was not followed by the immediate reoccupation of the hills and valleys west of the Alleghanies. His Majesty, King George III, desiring to close the lands of the west to settlement until the Indian title could be extinguished by purchase, issued a proclamation, 7 October 1763, which forbade any of the colonial governments to grant the lands west of the mountains to settlers. The daring frontiersmen, fearing neither the displeasure of the distant king nor the dangers of the primeval forest, prepared to press farther into the wilderness. Their western progress was delayed for a small space by the conspiracy of Pontiac, who fell upon the exposed settlements of the Trans-Alleghany section with fire and tomahawk. For two years the frontier was ravaged by bands of Indians, until finally they were subdued by an invasion of their own country.

It is one of the vagaries of fortune that the white man's civilization should have been brought to the borders of Lewis County by deserters from the troops fighting against the Indians. Two of the soldiers who had enlisted for service in the western wilderness against the French and their savage allies were John and Samuel Pringle, brothers. While stationed at Fort Pitt, in the year 1761, they deserted the service, and with two companions fled to the wilds of the lower Monongahela. Subsequently they went to the upper glades of the Youghiogheny where they remained until the next year, when the party ventured to the nearest settlements at Looney's creek in search of supplies. Their companions were recognized and arrested, but the Pringles managed to escape. They soon entered the service of John Simpson, a trapper who frequented their former haunts in the Youghiogheny glades. Hunting parties from the South Branch were destroying much of the game, and also making the two deserters uncomfortable from fear of capture, and the three men determined to go farther west, where Simpson could obtain more furs, and where the Pringles would be more secure from detection.

It was not to be supposed that the Pringles, who had refused to subject themselves to their military superiors, would long obey the orders of a trapper like Simpson. After a violent quarrel in the wilderness they parted company. Simpson continued west along the Indian trail from the crossing of the Cheat to the West Fork valley. He encamped one night near the present site of Bridgeport, and gave his name to the creek which flowed past his camping ground. Pressing on, he reached the mouth of Elk creek, where he built his cabin on land now included in the city of Clarksburg. He continued his residence there until the coming of permanent settlers again impelled him to go farther into the wilderness in his search for fur-bearing animals.

The two Pringles, fearing the punishment of the English military law far more than the fury of the savages, did not turn back toward the settlements, but continued up the Tygart's Valley and Buckhannon rivers to the mouth of Turkey run, where they took up their abode in a hollow sycamore tree. Probably fearing detection from the Indians who had a village in the vicinity, they did not build a cabin, but continued to live in the hollow sycamore for three years. Late in the autumn of 1767 they found that they had remaining but two charges of powder. The younger brother braved the danger of capture, and visited the settlements on the South Branch to obtain a supply of ammunition. There he learned that the war with the Indians had closed some years before, and that the deserters would be safe in returning to the settlements. He returned at once to his brother with the news. They determined to abandon the old sycamore and go to the South Branch.

The lure of their old home among the pleasant dales of the Buckhannon was too great to be resisted. The next year they led a party of prospective settlers to their old camping ground, who were so well pleased with the country that they resolved to build their homes there. In the spring of 1769, a number of men came to the Buckhannon valley to make clearings, put out their corn crops and build cabins for themselves, preparatory to removing their families there. The names of the permanent settlers, many of whom were later intimately associated with the history of Lewis County, were John Jackson and his sons, George and Edward, John Hacker and Alexander and Thomas Sleeth.

With residents on or near the present sites of Clarksburg and Buckhannon in 1764, it seems impossible that the exploration of the territory now embraced in Lewis County could be long delayed. Simpson seems to have confined his hunting trips to the vicinity of his cabin, and the Pringles were either indifferent woodsmen, or they feared discovery by the Indians, for they seem never to have ventured far from their hollow sycamore. It was almost five years before there is a record of any white men in Lewis County. After the coming of the permanent settlers to the Buckhannon river valley, in 1769, explorations of the surrounding regions quickly followed.

Within the party there was formed almost immediately a rude sort of division of labor; the homeseekers—men who had families—preferred to work on their claims; others, for the most part wild youths, untrammeled with the responsibilities of life, preferred to rove through the hills in search of game. Those who had commenced their clearings were supplied with an abundance of fresh meat through the efforts of the hunters; and the latter secured their corn from the small patches which had been put out by the more industrious settlers. The hunters probably never cultivated much corn even after they were married, leaving the task for the most part to their wives.

While on one of their hunting trips the party, consisting of William Hacker, Thomas Hughes, Jesse Hughes, John Radcliff, William Radcliff and John Brown, came upon the headwaters of a stream flowing in a westerly direction to which they gave the name of

Stone Coal creek. They believed it led directly into the Ohio; but after following it several miles they discovered that it emptied into a stream which seemed to flow north. They followed it some three or four miles probably, in order to ascertain its true direction and named it West Fork. They then returned to the settlements by a different route (probably by way of Hacker's creek). They gave such glowing accounts of the land they had seen that others came to see for themselves and were so impressed with its superiority over the land along the Buckhannon river that some of them determined to make their homes in the more western valley.

The first permanent settler in Lewis County was John Hacker. He had made his claim near the present site of Buckhannon, and during the absence of Samuel Pringle in the South Branch settlements he had cleared part of the land. Upon the return of Pringle, Hacker learned that the land had previously been claimed by him. Hacker willingly consented to give up his claim in favor of the older claimant on condition that Pringle should clear an equal amount of land which Hacker had selected on the stream which now bears his name. In one of the most beautiful sections of the valley, about one mile below the site of the present village of Berlin, Pringle cleared some land near an old Indian camping ground, and John Hacker built his cabin there, probably in the fall of 1769 or early in 1770. John Radcliff and William Radcliff followed in 1770, and made settlements on the creek not far from Hacker's cabin.

The families of most of the settlers did not accompany them at once. They waited until the winter of 1770-71, when they could have corn which had been grown the summer before. When they came to the Buckhannon valley in 1769 they planted their corn and hoed it once or twice; then some of them returned to the South Branch settlements to assist their families to move to the west. While they were gone, the buffaloes invaded their clearings and totally destroyed the crops of several settlers. They were then compelled either to do without corn meal for a year or to delay moving their families to the new settlement for another year.

The pioneers of western Virginia were not to be deterred by obstacles. If there were no bread, then their families would eat meat. The movement of settlers was hardly checked at all by the lack of corn. Jesse Hughes, who was afterwards to achieve fame in the border annals second only to Lewis Wetzel, having chosen a tract of land near the mouth of Jesse's run, (known as Jesse Hughes' run in the earliest records) on his first visit to Hacker's creek in 1769, built his cabin and settled there after his marriage to Miss Grace Tanner, in 1770 or 1771. The records of the Monongalia County court show that a grant was made to him in 1781 of "400 acres on Hacker's creek, to include his settlement made in 1770."

The settlement on Hacker's creek was well begun by the close of 1771. The next year there was a rush of settlers to the valley and the surrounding country. John Whendy settled at the mouth of Whendy's run, a tributary of Hacker's creek; Francis Tibbs and Daniel Veach are known to have made settlements on the creek, which must have been only temporary on account of the absence of further records and also the fact of their having assigned their claims to others. Robert Lowther built his cabin at the mouth of Hacker's creek, and his son, William, who afterward became the most prominent leader on the northwestern frontier, settled near the home of Jesse Hughes for a year or more, and then moved to the vicinity of Clarksburg. The danger of Indian attacks did not force a grouping of the settlers as was the case later, and we find that hardy pioneers had made settlements which were the basis of later claims to land on the right fork of Freeman's creek, on

Gee Lick run, then called the left hand fork of Freeman's creek; on Polk creek, "beginning at the road that comes from Gee Lick," and not far from the present Polk Creek school house; and on Stone Coal creek before the year 1774. These settlements were all abandoned at the beginning of the later Indian wars, and even the strong Hacker's creek settlement was temporarily broken up during the year 1778.

It was not necessary for the immigrants who came after 1771 to delay removing their families until they could clear their land, build their cabins, put out a corn crop and wait for it to mature. They loaded their possessions on pack horses and, with their wives and children, walked from the South Branch to Hacker's creek. They depended upon the settlers who had previously come to the country for sufficient supplies to tide them over the spring and summer until their own crops were harvested. So many were the new immigrants that the settlers were unable sometimes to provide for them, and there was at one time not more than one-third enough corn for the needs of the population. The year 1773 is known in border tradition as "the starving year." The older settlers divided what must not have been a large crop of corn with the newer comers, but the supply was totally inadequate for their needs. There must have been great suffering if one of the newest of the immigrants had not risen to the occasion and shown the stuff he was made of. William Lowther, whose ability was later to be rewarded with the title of colonel and the command of the forces of northwestern Virginia, "roamed amidst danger and alarm, killing venison, elks, Buffalo and Bear, and thus he supplied all their wants." According to a later chronicler, "his name is transmitted to their descendants hallowed by their blessings." Still another account states that he was associated with Jesse Hughes in hunting for the settlement. The supply of game lasted until the crops matured, and there was never afterward any danger of starvation among the settlers in Lewis County.

The increase of population the next year was probably as great as in 1772; for there were many who preferred not to move to a new settlement until it had become permanent on account of the discomforts incident to life in the wilderness without any great supply of bread, without aid in raising their cabins and without neighbors. The most noteworthy of the new comers to Hacker's creek during the year were the Wests, father and two sons, who emigrated from the South Branch. After the removal of young Lowther to the settlements farther down the West Fork they assumed the lead in the Hacker's creek settlement, and later built for protection the fort which bore their names The settlements on Freeman's creek received a slight accession, and some tracts on the West Fork river below the mouth of the creek were cleared at this time. There was a considerable body of settlers below the site of West Milford and also at Clarksburg and Bridgeport. The settlements on the Buckhannon river had been extended to include homesteads on Saul's run and Fink run not far from the Lewis-Upshur line.

Within two or three years after the coming of the homeseekers the whole of Lewis County had been pretty thoroughly explored, and the settlers had got their bearings with regard to the surrounding country. Most of the streams in the vicinity of the Hacker's creek settlements had been traversed and named. Tomahawk claims had been made by adventurous hunters in all the most favored locations. The low gap between Rush run and Sand fork had been discovered and hunters had penetrated the hollows of Court House district —a territory which was not to support any considerable population for eighty years.

Tradition credits William Lowther, Jesse Hughes and his brother Elias with the first actual exploration of the Little Kanawha river. In 1772, it is said, the three men traveled up the West Fork river and, having crossed to the Little Kanawha by way of Sand fork, they descended the river to its mouth where Parkersburg now stands. The return trip was made by way of Hughes river, which they first discovered and named. By another account the discovery is said to have taken place in 1774, when the two Hughes brothers, after reaching the mouth of the Little Kanawha, proceeded down the Ohio river and took part in the battle of Point Pleasant while Lowther went to Fort Pitt.

The most remarkable of the explorations by members of the Hacker's creek colony was made by the first settler, John Hacker, soon after his arrival in the western wilderness. His first crop of corn was one of those which had been destroyed by buffaloes during the absence of the settlers in the east. His anger was so aroused by the devastation that he followed the trail of the three animals which led southward from his corn field, bent upon killing them and making their hides pay for the destruction. The herd was a small one—two full grown animals and a young calf—and they had proceeded leisurely southward toward their winter quarters. Hacker pitched his first hunter's camp at the mouth of Curtis run on Little Skin creek; the following night he encamped on Crane Camp run, which at first was called Crane's Nest camp; the third camp was a shelter in the rocks on what is now Hacker's Camp run; and the fourth was at Buffalo lick, now Hacker Valley, where he shot and crippled a buffalo cow. He followed a short distance further where he killed the wounded cow. Primitive vengeance was appeased. One of the destroyers of the corn crop had paid with its life for the destruction wrought; and the first settler of Lewis County took the robe and some choice meat and returned by the same route he had come. At each of the spots where he camped he made a tomahawk entry, that is, he cut his initials on a tree nearby. The only one of the "settlements" which he afterward claimed, however, was the one on Little Skin creek, which he gave to his son.

The character of John Hacker can not be judged from the single incident of the buffalo hunt. He was from the beginning one of the leaders of the community, generally being one of the first to introduce improvements. He brought to the west the first buhrstones, which he is said to have rigged up to run by water power, and which furnished a better quality of meal for himself and his neighbors than they could secure by the ordinary method of crushing the corn with a pestle in a mortar. He remained in the settlement throughout the Indian wars with the exception of a short time when Hacker's creek was deserted by all its inhabitants. His son William was given an education sufficiently good to enable him, according to tradition, to prepare a history of the Indian wars which later became a part of Withers's "Border Warfare." He served under General George Rogers Clark in his campaign against the British posts of Kaskaskia and Vincennes. When the Indian wars were over, 1795, he was chosen to represent Harrison County at the peace conference held at Greenville. His house was always open to the itinerant preacher, and there is a tradition that the first religious services held in Lewis County were held there.

A circuit preacher, writing about 1790, has this to say of John Hacker: "I believe this man could read, but not write; and yet he was a magistrate and a patriarch in the settlement. * * * He was a man of good common sense, and I think an honest man, and a good Christian, and among the first that took in the Methodist preachers. His house had long been a preaching place and the preachers' home, and also a place of refuge in time of danger."

It is unfortunate that all the settlers were not men of the character of John Hacker. Being far from the influences of organized society, without the ordinary restraints of the law, left to their own whims and caprices, the settlers were frequently guilty of outrages against others which would not be tolerated in a modern society. The necessity for presenting a united front to the Indian was the greatest restraint placed upon them. Wanton murder of Indians in time of peace was rather common; and murder of white men also occasionally took place. Instances are numerous of white men turning renegades and leading the Indians back to the settlements in order to gratify their spite against some of their neighbors. Such an occurrence took place at Bush's fort on the Buckhannon river, and it was so serious in its consequences that it resulted in the temporary abandonment of the settlement. How many murders attributed to Indians were really the work of white men will never be known. Minor crimes, like fraudulent entry of land, fraudulent claim for pensions, and theft were too common among the first settlers to excite much surprise. . Laziness and lack of respect for women were not uncommon traits. When John Radcliff and Elias Hughes moved to Licking County, Ohio, after the Indian wars, they are said to have given over to their wives the cultivation of their small corn patches while they roamed the woods, and it is probable that more than one of the small clearings on Hacker's creek was cultivated in the same way.

There is probably more truth than poetry in the humorous statement credited to Adam O'Brien, one of the eccentric pioneers of central West Virginia, as to his reasons for coming to the west. "He said he was a poor man, and had got behind hand and when that's the case, there is no staying in the settlements for those varmints, the sheriffs and constables. * * * That after the king's proclamation for all surveyors and settlers to remove east of the big ridge, from all the western waters, there was no people on the west side except those who had run away from justice and here they were as free as any buck a-going." There were many men like the Pringles who had reason to keep away from civilization. The frontier has always been rough and wild and disorderly until the permanent settlers, men with families and possessing considerable property have displaced the first comers.

Though the earliest settlers would hardly be eligible for admittance to polite society nowadays, it must not be forgotten that the services they rendered in the development of Lewis County were of the highest importance. They fought Indians in time of war, and drove them back. They held the western frontier of the Virginia commonwealth while the people of the eastern part of the state were repelling the British. They risked their lives in order that they might hold their settlements. Their clearings became the nucleus of further settlements. The homely comforts they had built up, the first beginning of institutions which they developed, their mills, their schools, their churches, in fact everything which added to the economic, social and political growth of the country, were all used by the later comers. Without the early beginnings made by the pioneers, it may be doubted whether conditions in the new country would have attracted the homeseekers.

Besides those who felt more comfortable on the western side of the wilderness there were three other principal classes. The first was made up mostly of younger men who were attracted by the magnificent hunting. To such as these existence for a long time in one place was unthinkable. The second class was composed of homeseekers who had been unable to buy farms further east, and who came west where good land was to be had for little or nothing. According to Adam O'Brien, it was necessary only to cut his initials, A. O. B. on some trees, cut down a few saplings and plant a handful of corn, and he had secured the right to four hundred acres of land, "though it afterwards cost him a great deal of hard swearing." The third class were men of initiative and energy who came west to secure large tracts of land and to make their fortunes.

Probably a combination of all these reasons was responsible for the rapid increase in population. The great movement of 1769 when, in a single year, settlements were made at the present sites of Morgantown, Wheeling, Buckhannon, Hacker's creek, and within the boundaries of Monroe, Greenbrier and Fayette counties, and in Kentucky, was not a spasmodic effort. In the year before, the Iroquois had ceded all their lands south of the Ohio river to the English government. Though the land was not formally opened to settlement, the pioneers on the South Branch disregarded previous proclamations of king and royal governors and rushed into the new territory intent on securing the choicest locations. The garrison at Fort Pitt made a pretense at expelling the settlers west of the Alleghanies during 1769, but there is no record of a single man's being sent back. The westward movement was inevitable, and it could not be long delayed by artificial barriers to settlement.

The royal authority could at least refuse the settlers full title to the lands if it could not prevent their coming. Not a single patent was issued until 1779 for any land west of the Alleghanies, and it was not until 1781, the year of the defeat of Cornwallis at Yorktown, that claims in the West Fork valley were adjusted.

The settlers took possession of four hundred acres each by reason of having made a settlement, and some of them took advantage of the right to pre-empt 1,000 acres additional, under the provisions of the Virginia act which applied to land on the western slopes of the Alleghanies. They held their claims without much dispute—as the pioneers generally respected the claims made by others. Another basis for claim to land was a corn right. A law of Virginia provided that a settler who planted a corn patch might have one hundred acres of land for each acre in his patch. Much land in Lewis County was originally granted on the basis of early corn rights. Another and very inferior sort of title was a tomahawk improvement, under which the conditions of the law were partly fulfilled by girdling a few trees near a spring, and cutting the initials of a settler on a tree nearby. No title could legally be maintained on a tomahawk improvement, but, in general, the settlers did not invade the claims made by others, but were careful to acquire all previous rights before claiming the land as their own. The settlers who came to Lewis County had their lands recorded for the first time in 1781, when a special commission was appointed by the court of Monongalia County to investigate land claims, to settle disputes, and to issue certificates to the rightful claimants.

CHAPTER IV.

LEWIS COUNTY IN DUNMORE'S WAR

The movement of settlers into northwestern Virginia, which in 1772 and 1773 promised to people the country within a few years, was rudely interrupted early in 1774 by Dunmore's war. The war resulted early in victory for the whites; but the final results of this war and of others which followed it in quick succession, upon the settlement of Lewis County and its later history can hardly be estimated. For twenty years, with only a short breathing space, the pioneers were subjected to all the horrors of Indian warfare, whole settlements were broken up, and many outlying families were completely destroyed.

The renewal of the Indian wars had been foreseen by English statesmen, who had advised against a settlement of the interior of the country until the lands between the Alleghanies and the Atlantic were completely occupied. The prospect of securing cheap lands, coupled with other reasons which have been enumerated, had resulted, as we have seen, in a considerable immigration even before the ban had been lifted, and before satisfactory arrangements had been made with the Indians. From the time of their first coming—that is, from about 1765 in the region around Fort Pitt—there had been hostilities between the Indians and the settlers at widely separated points. The wanton aggression of the borderers in murdering every Indian they could find alone, and the action of the Indians in repaying the debts with interest led to bitter feeling on both sides, until finally open war broke out with all the horrors usually attendant upon frontier conflicts with savages. The rapid advance of the settlers caused the Indians to fear lest the hunting grounds of their forefathers should be completely destroyed.

The land really belonged to the whites. The Indian title to the lands south of the Ohio had been extinguished by several treaties: with the Iroquois at Lancaster, Pa., in 1744; with the Shawnees at Logstown, on the Ohio, in 1752; and a renewed cession by the Iroquois, the real owners of the country, at Fort Stanwix, New York, in 1768. The last named treaty was, as we have seen, the immediate cause of the large immigration in 1769 and the following years. The Ohio Indians, lessors of the territory for hunting purposes, had not given their assent to the provisions of the treaty of Fort Stanwix, and they regarded the settlers as trespassers on their territory.

Almost from the beginning of the settlement on Hacker's creek some of the more reckless pioneers killed without thought of mercy all Indians whom they could find unprotected. Bald Eagle, a chief who was well regarded by both his own people and the whites, and who often took part in the hunting parties arranged by the settlers, was foully murdered at some time between 1770 and 1772 by Jacob Scott, William Hacker (a brother of John Hacker) and Elijah Runner. No motive for the crime seems to have existed save a wanton desire to kill. The body was placed in a canoe and allowed to drift down the Monongahela until it reached Province plantation where it was decently interred by Mrs. Province.

An even more atrocious crime took place at Bulltown, on the Little Kanawha river, now in Braxton County. The place had been occupied about the time of the coming of the whites by Captain Bull, a Delaware chief from New York, who had led five Indian families to western Virginia. He was regarded by the settlers as being friendly to the whites, who often resorted to his town to secure supplies of salt, and who often hunted with him. It was rather to the advantage of the pioneers to cultivate the friendship of Captain Bull, and most of them thought highly of him and his people. Unfortunately, in 1772 the family of Adam Stroud, a settler on the Elk river a few miles south of Bull's village, were all murdered in the absence of the husband and father, by a band of Shawnees. The trail of the murderers led in the direction of Bull's village; and without determining whether or not his people were guilty, a party composed of William Hacker, William White, John Cutright, Jesse Hughes and another man whose name is not known, constituted themselves a court of inquiry to wreak vengeance for the murder. All the Indians at Bulltown, with the exception of Captain Bull, who was then absent beyond the Ohio, were treacherously slain and their bodies thrown into the river. Upon their return to the settlements the five avengers stated nonchalently that they had been out hunting. Later, when the fact of the massacre had become generally known and suspicion was cast upon them, they at first denied all knowledge of the killing and then came out boldly with the story that they had killed the five Indian families because they were the murderers of the Stroud family. As proof of their assertion they declared that they had found clothing belonging to the Stroud family in some of the houses in the Indian village. None of the clothing was ever shown to the other settlers if it had, in fact, been found. Under the circumstance of nearby residence, the finding of the clothing there is not strange. At best it would be insufficient to convict the Indians of more than theft. The intentions of the party were suspected by the other settlers before they ever went to Bulltown, and they prepared a general remonstrance against the killing of the Indians. There is no record, however, of any action having been taken by the community as a whole after the murder. The settlers probably did not care particularly whether peaceful Indians were killed or not—

but as a matter of policy they disapproved of such murders as likely to bring down upon the heads of the settlement the vengeance of the relatives of the dead tribesmen.

While the five were at Bulltown, they learned that a party of thirteen Indians, who had come from beyond the Ohio on a hunting trip, were then at Indian Camp on the upper course of the Buckhannon river. They secured the assistance of Samuel Pringle, James Strange and others from the Buckhannon river settlement and made preparations for an attack against the hunting party. Just before daybreak the whites arrived outside the cave in which the Indians were asleep, and posted themselves so as to command the exit. When it had become sufficiently light, at a preconcerted signal a volley was poured without warning upon the unsuspecting Indians. So effective was the first fire that only one warrior, badly wounded, succeeded in escaping from the cave. He was dispatched by another shot. According to tradition, the bodies of the Indians were left unburied.

There was no immediate retaliation against the participants in the wholesale slaughter of these Indians. In other centers of white settlement there were Indian reprisals on detached cabins and lonely settlers. An intermittent guerrilla war was fought for another year in which both whites and Indians were killed. The whites on the Kentucky border suffered most.

War was inevitable within a short time, the character of the whites and Indians being as it was. The only question was how long the embers of conflict would smoulder before breaking out into the blaze of a general war.

The event was precipitated by an attempt to settle a problem which had nothing whatever to do with the Indians. Lord Dunmore, then the royal governor of Virginia, had land claims in the vicinity of Fort Pitt which would not be valid if Pennsylvania acquired title to the region as that colony threatened to do. He wished to secure the northwest for Virginia and also to divert the attention of the Virginians from the tyrannous acts of George III by a popular Indian war.

The war did not continue long. The Indians had little time in which to organize attacks against the settlements in the Monongahela valley before two Virginia armies reached the Ohio river. General Andrew Lewis with the southern army met the main army of the Indians under Cornstalk at Point Pleasant. After an all day battle he retained possession of the field at great cost. The Indians, being unable to sustain heavy losses, retired in disorder to the western side of the river. Lord Dunmore, with the northern army, advanced to within a few miles of their principal villages, and could have easily destroyed them. He refrained from attacking them, however, because he wished to secure peace, although the Virginia soldiers clamored for a further prosecution of the war.

The peace negotiated by Lord Dunmore was exceedingly advantageous to the settlers. His moderate conduct in not destroying the Indian villages was calculated to win their admiration; and the prowess of the Virginians at Point Pleasant gave the Indians a wholesome respect for the "Long Knives," as they were called. The Indians agreed to give up all their lands south of the Ohio river. In order to prevent further trouble which would follow settlement of the frontiersmen north of the Ohio, the British Parliament passed an act the same year which added all the territory north of the Ohio river to the province of Quebec.

The horrors of Indian warfare were not visited upon the Hacker's creek settlements in 1774, although other settlements in the vicinity suffered. The settlers in northwestern Virginia at first took no precautions of any kind, believing that they were too far from the Indian country to be molested. An attack led by the Cayuga chief Logan on the settlement at the mouth of

Simpson's creek disillusioned them. Following the raid, the settlers in the vicinity of Clarksburg immediately erected Nutter's fort, which afforded protection as well to the Hacker's creek and Buckhannon settlements.

Local tradition, not well substantiated, says that Jesse Hughes and Elias Hughes, who afterwards became famous as scouts, were members of General Lewis's army at Point Pleasant, and Elias Hughes was reputed long afterwards to be the last survivor of the battle.

The effects of Dunmore's war upon the settlements in Lewis County were more deeply felt than is indicated in chronicles of raids and reprisals. In the first place the westward movement received a decided setback. At the first outbreak of hostilities some of the settlers left their cabins and took refuge in the settlements on the South Branch. Some of them even sold their claims intending never to return. After the close of the war most of the former residents returned and with them were a few new homeseekers who took up their abode in the older settlements or made new settlements in locations which had been neglected before.

Among the new comers were John Schoolcraft, who built his cabin on Stone Coal creek at the mouth of Smith's run; Robert Burkett, who claimed land on Sand fork of West Fork; Elijah Williams and Lewis Duvall, who lived on Freeman's creek; Charles Washburn on Stone Coal creek; and Henry Flesher on the present site of Weston. The last named settlement was made in 1776. Tradition states that his home was built near the present site of Whelan's store, a few yards from the corner of First and Main; his barn stood near the corner of Center avenue and Second street; and his threshing floor later occupied the site of the court house. The settlement of John Schoolcraft on lands adjoining those of Henry Flesher, was made a year earlier. The lands farther up Stone Coal creek were more desirable than those at the mouth on account of the swampy nature of the latter location. An old river channel and a deep hollow about where Bank street now is must have further decreased the desirability of the lands for farming purposes.

CHAPTER V.

LEWIS COUNTY DURING THE REVOLUTION

Before the effects of Dunmore's war in retarding emigration to the west had ceased to be felt, the settlements were profoundly influenced by events which were taking place along the Atlantic seaboard. "The shot heard 'round the world" was distinctly audible in northwestern Virginia. Just how great an influence the American Revolution had upon the course of development of the region can only be surmised. Certain it is that if there had been no Indian wars after the battle of Point Pleasant the whole of northwestern Virginia would have reached a mature development much earlier than it did. One of the first results of the commencement of hostilities between the colony of Virginia and the mother country was the legal recognition of the existence of settlements west of the Alleghanies. Under the royal government no settlements were allowed there, hence it was not deemed necessary to provide any form of civil government for the district. For several years prior to the Revolution the Trans-Alleghany region was known as the District of West Augusta. It was a shadowy geographical division with no very definite boundaries or political status. There were no courts in the settlements, no justices of the peace, no recognized officers of the law. With the exceptions of the garrisons at Fort Redstone and Fort Pitt, both of which are now in Pennsylvania, there was no form of governmental authority until the very beginning of the Revolution when a court was held at Little Washington.

The settlements on Hacker's creek and on the West Fork river at first were examples of pure anarchies.

When the Indians at Bulltown were murdered, the settlers prepared a remonstrance. If there had been a horse stolen or a white man murdered and the crime had been fixed upon one of the settlers, it may be imagined that the whole neighborhood would have risen as one man and applied lynch law. Doubtless the knowledge that some such action would be taken, coupled with the necessity of uniting to combat the common danger from the Indians, prevented much disorder.

One of the first acts of the Commonwealth of Virginia was that defining the boundaries of the District of West Augusta and providing for the creation of three counties from it. One of these counties was Monongalia, including all the region drained by the Monongahela and its tributaries nearly as far north as Pittsburgh. Justices were appointed for the new county, among them being William Lowther, who had saved the settlers from starvation in the "starving year" of 1772. A county government was immediately set up with the county seat at Fort Redstone, far over the present boundary in Pennsylvania. Notwithstanding the distance of the Hacker's creek settlers from the seat of government there was an advantage in being in the new county. It meant that the people were to receive such help in solving their problems as the government of the state could give them. The settlers were also given the right to name their own officials and to take a part in the government of the state as a whole. One of the first acts of the county court was to designate Morgantown and Bush's fort (on the present site of Buckhannon) as voting places.

There were responsibilities as well as advantages connected with membership in the Commonwealth of Virginia. When it became apparent to the British government that the people of the colonies meant to fight, they sent their agents among the people of the frontier trying to induce them to take the side of the king and promising to protect them from the Indians in case of war. How much they underestimated the character of the Virginia backwoodsmen—the "shirt men", as they contemptuously called them—can be seen in a study of the history of the time. Practically all the frontiersmen were staunch patriots. Some of them were Tories but they soon moved to the vicinity of Detroit where they could be under the shelter of the British guns.

Failing in their efforts to induce the frontiersmen to side with them, the British officials in Canada sent their agents among the western Indians to urge them to break their treaties with the Virginians and again fall upon their settlements with tomahawk and scalping-knife, and to drive them completely out of the Indian domain. It was the idea of the English king and his advisors not only to send civilized armies against the seacoast districts of the colonies but to take them in the rear, compel a division of their forces and make easier the task of subduing them.

The English agents were not at first successful in inducing the Indians to lay aside the pipe of peace and make war upon the Virginians. The memory of the prowess of the "Long Knives" at the battle of Point Pleasant and in a dozen smaller encounters was a potent influence in causing the Indians to hesitate before again going on the warpath. Although the Tories, who had been compelled to flee from the settlements through fear of their neighbors, went among the Indians adding their appeals to those of the British agents, they secured only a lukewarm promise from some of the tribes to fight the settlers. Two years after the outbreak of the Revolution the British agents lacked the acquiescence of the Shawnees, the ablest warriors of the northwest, when two unfortunate circumstances led that tribe into the field. The first was the murder of their sachem, Cornstalk, who had been held as a hostage by the whites; the other was the arrival of Burgoyne in Canada with a large British force designed to march against the colonies in the vicinity of the Hudson river. Here was proof positive of British assistance; and the Shawnees and all the other Indians northwest of the Ohio, as well as the Iroquois farther north sent war parties against the frontiers.

The frontier line of defense in western Virginia proved a strong one. It stretched from Fort Pitt, at the confluence of the Monongahela and Allegheny rivers, along the Ohio to Wheeling and Moundsville, and then turned inland from the river forming a great semi-circle which passed through Morgantown, Clarksburg, the Hacker's creek settlements and Charleston, and again reached the Ohio river at Fort Randolph on the battleground at Point Pleasant. From there the line of defense included the few settlements which had been made in Kentucky.

The Indians fell upon the settlements in 1777, murdering alike the fighting men and the defenseless women and children, leading some into captivity to suffer the tortures of the gauntlet and the stake, and destroying all the property of the settlers they could find. The frontier was lurid with the flames of burning crops and houses during all the remaining years of the Revolution and for long afterwards. In the bloody "year of the three sevens", they besieged Wheeling fort, killing many of its defenders in ambuscades, they plundered homes and murdered settlers on Rooting creek in Harrison County, near Coon's fort on the borders of Harrison and Marion, on the Little Kanawha river, and very late in the year in the Tygart's Valley. Fortunately the Lewis County settlements escaped being attacked during the whole season.

The exposed position of the Hacker's creek settlement on the very edge of the Virginia frontier, and on the route from the Indian towns to the Tygart's Valley region made it impossible for the attack to be long delayed. Beginning in 1778 and continuing almost every year thereafter there were one or more Indian attacks against the Hacker's creek pioneers. An examination of the history of the period of the Indian wars shows that more attacks were directed against the Hacker's creek settlement than against any other settlement in northwestern Virginia.

It is apparent from an examination of the records of the period that most of the settlements in what is now Lewis County except those on Hacker's creek, the Flesher settlement at Weston, and some of the clearings farther down the West Fork were abandoned. Some of the settlers returned to their former homes east of the mountains and others gathered around some of the numerous forts which were built at centrally located points in the Trans-Alleghany region. The only large fort anywhere on the West Fork until the outbreak of the Revolution was Nutter's fort at Clarksburg; as soon, however, as it became apparent that the western Indians would attack the exposed settlements others were built. Powers' fort stood on the present site of Bridgeport; Richards' fort was about two miles below the present site of West Milford at the mouth of Sassafras run; Bush's fort stood near the present site of Buckhannon; and West's fort was within the present corporate limits of Jane Lew on the slight rise where Minor Hall now lives.

West's fort was probably a small stockade of logs enclosing a large log building constructed to protect from the elements those who had taken refuge within the stockade. The builders probably set the logs on end deep into the ground and then tamped loose earth around them to make the stockade substantial. Loopholes between the logs afforded opportunity for the garrison to command all approaches to the walls and all the cleared space around the fort within range of their rifles. At the same time they were protected from the fire of their besiegers by the logs composing the walls. None of the rifles at that time could pierce the heavy wall of logs, though artillery would soon have sent them splintering down. Since none of the Indian parties had cannon, and would have been unable to transport them without building roads if they had, the settlers were safe within the walls. Few of the frontier forts succumbed to the attacks of the savages. There was danger that the food supply might not hold out, or that the powder might be exhausted, but, if these were sufficient, the only danger was that the savages might set fire to the fort.

The stockade was called West's fort because built by Edmund West and his two sons, Edmund and Alexander, assisted probably by some of the neighbors. The Wests had come to Hacker's creek from Accomack County, Virginia, in 1773, and the senior West had settled at the old Straley farm about one mile above Jane Lew. Alexander West later became one of the greatest scouts on the border, and saw service in one or more attempts to carry the war into the Indian country. He has been described by McWhorter as being "a tall, spare-built man, very erect, strong, lithe and active; dark-skinned, prominent Roman nose, black hair, very keen eyes; not handsome, rather raw-boned, but with an air and mien that commanded the attention and respect of those with whom he associated." Beyond the fact that he took the lead in building the fort, little is known of the character of Edmund West, Sr. By a peculiar turn of fortune, the builder of the fort was later taken by surprise outside its walls and put to death by a body of Indians under circumstances of the most shocking brutality.

The settlers on Hacker's creek and vicinity were not terrified by the prospect of another Indian war. A large number stayed on the frontier, and many others made new settlements in the time of the worst savage fury.

The Hacker's creek bordermen did not supinely trust to the walls of West's fort to keep away the Indians, but went out into the open, stalked the Indians on nearly equal terms, formed parties in pursuit of them

LEWIS COUNTY DURING THE REVOLUTION

and oft-times inflicted greater damage upon them than they themselves had suffered. Among the settlers were many whose names are written large upon the tablets of history of northwestern Virginia. John P. Duvall, Jesse Hughes, Elias Hughes, Thomas Hughes, Alexander West, George Jackson, William Lowther, William White and John Cutright are all men who achieved more than local prominence as scouts or military leaders in the wars against the Indians in northwestern Virginia. Greatest of all without the shadow of a doubt was Jesse Hughes.

Jesse Hughes was born probably on Jackson river in what is now western Virginia, about the year 1750. With his parents he moved to the South Branch of the Potomac, where he lived until he joined the party which followed Samuel Pringle to examine the land in the vicinity of the sycamore in the Buckhannon valley. He became a hunter at first and roamed the wilds, becoming acquainted with every feature of the geography of the section. In 1771, he married and settled on a clearing at the mouth of Jesse's run. It will be remembered that he was one of the men connected with the massacres at Bulltown and the Indian camp. He first became prominent on the border in the year 1778, from which time he was one of the mainstays in the protection of the settlements. His pony was constantly kept tied in the lean-to adjoining his house ready for instant use in warning settlers of the near approach of Indians. His vigilance saved many lives.

Jesse Hughes is described by McWhorter as being rather tall and slender. He could not have weighed more than 145 pounds at any time in his life. His countenance was hard, stern and unfeeling; his eyes were cold, cruel and vicious—"like a rattlesnake's", according to the statement of a contemporary. "No Indian, no matter how peaceful, nor how good his record, was safe in his presence." He murdered young and old alike, under circumstances which would hardly be equalled in bloodthirsty ferocity by the worst savage. An old woman who knew him said he was desperately wicked, superstitious, cruel and vindictive. He is said often to have given way to abuse of his family. So uncontrolled were his passions, and so bad his reputation among his own people that he never attained leadership in the community.

He is said on one occasion to have decoyed an Indian almost to his own door by promising to go hunting with him, and then shot the unsuspecting savage from ambush. At another time, while he was on his way down the Monongahela in a canoe he saw an Indian boy playing with some white children. Only the interference of his companion kept him from taking the Indian boy into the canoe and then drowning him in the river. He was one of the most terrible enemies of the Indians to be found anywhere on the frontier.

He could trail with any Indian that lived on the border, and, though not a dead shot like some of the other settlers, his skill in stalking Indians and game caused him to have a better record at the end of the day than any of his fellows. Though he was by far the best trailer on the frontier, though he was more than a match for the Indian in cunning, though he seemed to have an intuition as to the plans of the Indians, and though his plans for following them were nearly always adopted, he was never placed in command of any important expedition. He served for a short time as ensign of a company of scouts, but seemed never to have had any of the men under him. The ability to command men is not usually possessed by men of his temperament. His temper was too fiery, his passions too fierce for him to retain the respect which was necessary to keep frontiersmen attached to a leader. Yet it is said that he had many friends, and that he was generous to those who had gained his confidence.

During the year 1778, the settlers collected within the forts early in the spring, and only went out in large groups to work the fields of the different farms in turn. At least two Indian attacks were made on West's fort during the year. Early in May the male population were working in a field near the fort, when the report of firearms at the edge of the clearing broke the stillness. Jonathan Lowther, a brother of William Lowther, and Thomas Hughes, father of Jesse and Elias Hughes, fell at the first volley. The other men of the party, all of whom had incautiously come to the field without their arms, ran to the fort for safety, with the exception of two, who were cut off by the Indians. They escaped by running to Richards' fort, where they gave the alarm. The Indians had already been in that community and had murdered one of the settlers on his way home from Hacker's creek. The settlers were too weak to pursue the Indians, who left Hacker's creek at once after taking the scalps of the men they had killed.

The Indians probably lost more by the attack than they gained; for the murder of the elder Hughes intensified, if possible, the hatred of the Hughes brothers for the Indians, and caused them to take an oath "to fight Injuns as long as they lived and could see to fight them"—an oath which was only too well carried out.

The Indians made a bolder assault on West's fort early in the next month. Three women who had gone out from the fort for the purpose of gathering greens in the field adjoining, were fired upon by one of a party of four Indians who were lying in ambush. The shot failed to take effect, and the women ran screaming toward the fort closely pursued by one warrior. He overtook a Mrs. Freeman, and thrust a spear into her back with such force that it penetrated completely through her body. Though fired at several times from the fort, he then coolly secured the scalp and carried it away with him. Jesse Hughes and others happened to be outside the fort at the time without their guns. As Hughes and John Schoolcraft were proceeding cautiously toward the fort they noticed two Indians standing by a fence, closely watching the fort for an opportunity to kill some of the refugees. Hughes and Schoolcraft passed on without attracting their attention. Later when a party went out of the fort for the purpose of bringing in the body of Mrs. Freeman, Hughes went to the spot where he had seen the Indians. At that moment from a point farther in the woods there came a sound like the howling of a wolf. Hughes answered it. The sound was repeated. This time the party located it, and running to a point of land they saw two Indians. Hughes fired once, but succeeded only in wounding the Indian. Others in the party wished to stop and finish him, but Hughes called to them to leave him alone and follow him in pursuit of the unwounded warrior. By doubling on his track like a fox, the Indian succeeded in eluding his pursuers. Meanwhile the wounded warrior had also got away, and Hughes was forced to return to the fort without a scalp hanging from his belt.

The garrison of the fort at this time had lately been strengthened by the addition of Captain Stuart and a company of Virginia militia, most of whom had come from the South Branch, but a few had volunteered from Randolph County. Some of his men pursued the war party and overtook them on Salt Lick creek, where they wounded one of them and the remainder dispersed upon the approach of Captain Stuart and the main body of his force. Stuart returned to West's fort and thence marched to Lowther's fort where he detached part of his men. He then returned to guard the fords of the Tygart's Valley river.

These two attacks were typical of all that followed. Without artillery the Indians could not hope to capture log forts, particularly if they were well built. It was opposed to the Indian temperament to sit down before the walls of a fortified place and wait until the garrison could be starved into surrender, while their own numbers were constantly being diminished by the fire of the beleaguered whites. No large bodies of Indians came east of the Ohio river. Attacks on the settlements in the Monongahela valley were more in the nature of raids planned with the idea of capturing prisoners, cutting off detached families or killing small bodies of whites whom they could surprise, than large expeditions to destroy all of the settlements. Most of the attacks were made by very small bands. It was but natural that women and children should be made the objects of attack, and that the vengeance of the savages should be visited upon those who were innocent of any harm to them.

The number of settlers was insufficient as yet to allow the formation of a large army, which should carry the war into the villages of the Indians beyond the Ohio, and purchase peace with the lead from their rifles. They had to content themselves with defending as best they might their lonely oases of settlement in the western wilderness.

Other forays of the Indians into the West Fork valley, though they did not result in the death of any of the other members of the settlement on Hacker's creek, caused severe losses to the neighboring settlements around Richards' fort. The continual danger from the Indians kept the Hacker's creek settlers idle within their fort or engaged in distant scouting expeditions, with the result that their crops were neglected. It may have been that the crops were set fire to by the Indians in the fall, and were destroyed. At any rate there was an acute shortage of grain at the beginning of the succeeding winter. Numerically the settlement at West's fort was not strong enough at that time to sustain the defense of so important a section of the frontier, exposed as it was to the first assault of every war party that came up the Little Kanawha valley. Discouraged at the prospect of another campaign like the last, and lacking requisite supplies to satisfy their wants through the coming growing season, they abandoned their homes on Hacker's creek. Some of the inhabitants went to

Nutter's fort, and some to Bush's fort on the Buckhannon, in both of which places their numbers were a desirable reinforcement. The more timorous returned to the South Branch where they would be safe from Indian molestation. The Flesher settlement at the mouth of Stone Coal creek seems not to have been abandoned at this time, and it remained during 1779 the only habitation of a white man within the present limits of Lewis County.

The opening of the year 1779 found practically all the settlements in better condition than ever before to resist the raids of the Indians. For one thing they had been consolidated. The detached farms had been abandoned. The settlers had also received considerable accretions in strength from adventurous young men who came west to engage in the war where they would not have to bother with discipline and commanding officers, and also from militiamen from east of the Alleghanies, who, like Captain Stuart, had been ordered to the forts in the valley of the West Fork. Most of the militiamen were rather indifferent Indian fighters, and some were court-martialed later for desertion. They afforded much strength, however, not only in the addition to the small numbers of the settlers, but also in the encouragement they gave the frontier guardians of Virginia that the authorities of the state had not utterly forgotten their danger, but were doing all they could to send relief, while themselves carrying on the war with the British troops on the Atlantic seaboard.

Active measures were soon afterwards taken by the state authorities to reduce the number of raids and the amount of damage done by the Indians. Vigorous efforts were made to watch the Indians and to warn the settlements of their approach. Several companies of spies were formed, among them George Jackson's company on the Buckhannon in 1779 and William Lowther's at Nutter's fort. From that time forth small parties scoured the woods in the vicinity of the Indian trails.

Sometimes the scouts would go down the Little Kanawha from the Buckhannon settlement to the mouth of the river, and return the same way, but the usual route was to proceed overland to Wheeling, then drift down the Ohio to the Little Kanawha, from which point they would return, closely examining all the trails along the river for signs of Indians. This system of scouting had been found to be most successful through a long period of warfare with the Indians, and by 1779, it was working well. The vigorous action of Colonel Lowther in pursuing the Indians after each attack had the effect of making them wary, keeping them from the settlements and reducing the amount of damage done. The largest number of men which he commanded in pursuing the Indians at any one time during the Revolution was about twenty-five.

During 1779, the Shawnees and other tribes were engaged elsewhere, chiefly in expeditions to regain the Illinois country which had been captured by George Rogers Clark, and in defending their villages, some of which Clark had captured and burned. During the winter of 1779-1780, several of the settlers who did not want to lose all their improvements and have to commence again in the wilderness ventured back to Hacker's creek, and in the spring they moved, as usual, into West's fort. They had not been there long when a party of Indians laid siege to the fort, and, contrary to their usual custom, remained there several days. The inhabitants were too few to sally out with any hope of success, their supplies were nearly exhausted and they were in despair of being relieved. Jesse Hughes determined, if possible, to secure aid from the Buckhannon settlements. It was an extremely hazardous undertaking, for the Indians had posted sentinels on all sides to prevent the escape of the garrison; but Hughes crept out in the dead of night, and, after proceeding cautiously for several hours, he passed far beyond the last outpost of the savages. In order to inform those still within the fort of his being clear, he gave the prearranged signal of the hoot of an owl. The Indians, probably understanding the counterfeit nature of this particular bird's cry, and knowing that help must be near, broke camp at once. The next morning Hughes led a party from Bush's fort back to Hacker's creek, and conducted the residents of West's fort in safety to the banks of the Buckhannon. Here they spent the remainder of the year. During their absence West's fort was set on fire by Indians, and completely destroyed.

Two days after the arrival of the garrison from West's fort there occurred perhaps the only battle on the West Fork, which was fought in the open, and which was yet not an ambuscade. A small party of settlers who had returned to some of the houses on Hacker's creek to remove their furniture, came unexpectedly upon a party of Indians in the woods not far from the Buckhannon. The Indians were equally surprised. They fired first and Jeremiah Curl, an old man, was hit under the chin. He refused to take flight, and called to the others that they were able to whip the Indians. An Indian rushed at him. Curl took aim and pulled the trigger; but the powder in his gun had become wet with blood from his wound and it failed to ignite. It happened that he was carrying a gun belonging to another of the party in addition to his own, and, taking quick aim with it, he brought the warrior down. Alexander West, who was one of the swiftest on foot of all the frontiersmen, pursued the Indians, and succeeded in wounding one of them before the others took refuge behind trees and made the conflict too unequal for him to maintain unaided. The war party was pursued the next day by about fifteen whites who could be spared from the fort, and they succeeded in recovering several stolen horses and other plunder with the loss of only one man slightly wounded.

The savages continued to lurk about Bush's fort all summer, and they succeeded in killing one of the Buckhannon settlers and taking his niece prisoner. They also infested the settlement around Richard's fort, stealing horses, killing live stock and committing other depredations. Horses were the special objects of their thieving propensities. Cows and sheep were often killed by the Indians in order to reduce the already extremely small number of domestic animals in the frontier communities.

The winter season of 1780-81 was, as usual, free from Indian forays, most of the savages being snug and warm in their log houses beyond the Ohio. During the seasonal lull the Hackers creek settlers again ventured back to their homes, and prepared to defend them. All joined in the erection of a new fort in a stronger location. It stood on level, rather marshy ground, but it was a far more satisfactory site than that of the old fort because the besiegers could not have a vantage point within gunshot where they could hide. Because the fort was built almost entirely of beech logs, it was called Beech fort, a name which stuck for a year or so, and then the settlers returned to the old designation of West's fort. It is supposed that the beech fort was more capacious than the old fort, and that it was a stockade of logs enclosing a much larger house of hewn logs.

Beech fort was used for other purposes than for defense. The Rev. John Mitchell, the first minister of the gospel on Hacker's creek, alternately fought Indians and shepherded a more or less wayward flock, holding services within its walls. Other preachers came later and held their services there. There is a tradition that the first school in Lewis County was held in the new fort, with the Rev. Mitchell as its teacher. The fort soon became the social center of the settlement. Primarily, however, it was for defense; and the settlers behind its strong walls, their numbers increased by new arrivals and perhaps by militia from the counties east of the mountains, had well-founded hopes of maintaining their positions against any force that the Indians were likely to send against them.

The year 1781 was a quiet one so far as the settlements on Hacker's creek were concerned. Henry Flesher left his cabin at the present corner of First street and Main avenue, Weston, and went to Buckhannon to spend the winter, returning apparently the next spring. The only military operations in the upper West Fork valley that were of any importance were those connected with the pursuit of a party of Indians who had broken up an outlying settlement on the Tygart's Valley river. Colonel Lowther and his company of scouts gloriously avenged the murder of the settlers and recovered several of the prisoners they had captured. The Indians received a lesson on the strength and unity of the settlements.

The usual reinforcement from east of the mountains failed to come to the aid of the western settlements in 1781 on account of the invasion of Virginia by Lord Cornwallis. Every nerve of the state was being strained to add new recruits to the forces of Lafayette, who was attempting to defend the state. Additional volunteers were raised wherever possible. Even Hampshire county, which had furnished the bulk of the militia for the defense of the west, sent a regiment to Yorktown which included some of the Monongahela pioneers.

The Trans-Alleghany settlers were thus left to shift for themselves, but the activities of General George Rogers Clark in the Illinois country had the effect of keeping the Indians occupied at home. In May, 1781, George Jackson, of the Buckhannon river settlements, recruited a company for service against the British and Indians. General Clark had planned an expedition against Detroit to capture that stronghold of British influence over the western Indians, that headquarters for Indian supplies, that refuge from which British agents kept continually stirring up the savages against the settlements. Clark hoped by destroying the evil at its source to end all Indian wars, and he invited settlers from all over the western territory to take part with him. William Lowther also responded to the call, and was raised to the rank of colonel for meritorious services rendered. The expedition failed to secure its expected strength, and nothing was accomplished except that the Indians were kept occupied beyond the Ohio by the threat against their villages.

Colonel Lowther gained experience while on the expedition which served him in good stead in organizing the defense of the settlements at a later date. He saw the need for improvements after his return as never before, and he took the lead from that time on, not only in pursuing Indians who had committed depredations, but in preventing the depredations.

The militia of Monongalia County in 1781 was estimated at not less than a thousand men. The number in the valley of the upper West Fork must have been in the neighborhood of 150 men between the ages of sixteen and sixty The actual population was probably six or seven hundred. Colonel Benjamin Wilson wrote to the governor at the beginning of the year 1782 stating the effective force of the West Fork at eighty men, and urging that reinforcements be sent from east of the mountains. "If the Indians pursue the war as they did last spring," he wrote, "it will cause the settlers to leave the country." In response to the appeal, seventy men of the Hampshire County militia were sent to help defend the Trans-Alleghany. They were stationed at Beverly, (now in Randolph County) St. George, (now in Tucker County) and Clarksburg.

Early in the spring a large war party invaded the Buckhannon valley, and 8 March 1782, they attacked the homes of some of the settlers before they had time to move into the fort. Some of the people were murdered without warning. Captain White, "the lion in the defense of the settlement in the absence of George Jackson," was killed within plain view of the fort, and Timothy Dorman, who had been a subaltern in Captain Jackson's company of scouts, joined the Indians. So bad was the character of Dorman, so many were the threats which he had made against the other settlers, and so well acquainted was he with the habits of the settlement and the weak points in its defense, that in despair of successfully resisting an attack, the whole body of the inhabitants left the fort and went to Clarksburg.

Dorman returned in the same year at the head of a war party of savages. A number of settlers who had come from Nutter's fort for the purpose of gathering the grain on the Buckhannon and transporting it to Clarksburg, found Bush's fort in ruins. They suspected from certain signs that the Indians were still in the neighborhood, and they therefore exercised all possible vigilance. All attempts to lure them into an ambuscade having failed, Dorman and others fired upon them while they were near the fort, and they were forced to take refuge in a cellar. Here they remained all night while George Jackson ran to Clarksburg for help.

The year 1781 saw the surrender of Cornwallis at Yorktown; and in 1783 commissioners appointed by the Continental Congress signed a treaty of peace by which Great Britain recognized the independence of the United States and admitted their right to territories reaching as far west as the Mississippi. The Revolution was fought and won on the eastern seaboard; but the humble part of the settlers on Hackers creek and the other outlying points west of the mountains kept the savage allies of the British king from harassing eastern Virginia, and allowed the state to devote practically all its energies to the defeat of the red-coated British and their German hirelings. For six long years the devoted bands of settlers had sustained the weight of the Indian assaults, suffering untold privations and hardships, but still maintaining a foothold in the region west of the

Alleghanies, as a basis for a tremendously important later development. Now that the war was over they expected that the Indian outrages would stop and that they would be allowed to pursue their accustomed employments of hunting and tilling the ground unmolested.

CHAPTER VI.

THE END OF THE INDIAN WARS

The treaty of Paris, 1783, did not bring peace with the Indians. For twelve years longer the settlements on the western border were subject to sudden attacks and raids conceived and executed with all the fiendish cruelty common in savage warfare. The Indians were, however, unable to press the attack with their former vigor on account of the fact that their supplies were not forthcoming from the British stations at Detroit and other points in the northwest. In Virginia the Indian wars ceased to be carried on for the purpose of exterminating the whites and they consisted merely of raids for the purpose of securing plunder and scalps. It was not uncommon for young Indians to come to the settlements alone to steal horses or to waylay members of the pioneer families who ventured far from home. If they returned with plunder or a scalp their reputation as warriors was assured. The young warriors were encouraged to make these raids because they resulted in broadening their experience as warriors. Alexander West once discovered a lone Indian in the field where Beech fort was afterward erected. He fired, and the Indian made off evidently wounded. West did not pursue him, fearing an ambuscade. Two weeks later, upon following the trail, it was found that the warrior had bathed his wound in Indian spring near the mouth of Life's run, and had then crawled into a rock cliff where he perished miserably.

The Trans-Alleghany settlers were disappointed in their expectations of strong reinforcements from eastern Virginia. All possibility of danger from the British had been removed and the people east of the mountains were henceforth left free from attack. They did not choose to devote much attention to the problems of the west. If the new state government of Virginia had been as energetic in the defense of the western frontier as the old royal government under Lord Dunmore, an expedition could have been sent out strong enough to break the power of the northwestern tribes. Much of the difficulty came from the fact that Virginia had ceded her lands northwest of the Ohio river to the federal government, which was then powerless to act. Virginia refused to conquer Indians who lived outside the boundaries of the state. The state was content to confine her efforts in defense of the frontier to sending a few militiamen from east of the mountains to assist in garrisoning the forts. The number of men sent was never large enough to be of much service, and appeals were made to the governor every year for more troops. Colonel Benjamin Wilson in 1784, wrote to the governor inviting attention to the fact that their fellow citizens who reside east of the mountains were enjoying themselves in peace "while neglecting to secure that privilege to the west."

An act was passed by the legislature in 1784 which aided the citizens to organize more effectively against the Indians. The number of settlers who came to the west during the closing years of the Revolution, the prospect for a larger immigration as soon as peace could be made with the Indians and the desire for a more compact political organization, caused the creation of Harrison County in 1784.

The first fruits of the creation of the new county, from the standpoint of measures for the protection of the inhabitants, was the appointment of John P. Duvall, one of the most prominent of the early landholders in what is now Lewis County, as colonel of the county militia. Colonel Lowther, upon whom the duties had previously devolved, accepted the appointment as sheriff of the new county. Colonel Duvall immediately made requisition on the governor for additional arms and ammunition for the men of militia age in the county. He reported that the effective force of the county was in the neighborhood of 215 men, for whom there were but 130 rifles in 1785. Two hundred additional rifles were requested at once. It was not to be supposed that there were nearly one hundred settlers in western Virginia in a time of more or less active Indian warfare without firearms. Each man carried a flint lock musket, but it was not rifled, and hence not so accurate and effective as the newer firearms which had been introduced into the colonies after the French and Indian war, but which had not been manufactured in sufficient quantities to supply all. Colonel Duvall reported also that ammunition was very scarce.

Colonel Duvall continued in general command of the militiamen formerly led by Colonels Benjamin Wilson and William Lowther, though the last named, as sheriff, continued to pursue Indians. Duvall went from one end of the county to the other—from the dividing ridge separating the watershed of the Cheat from that of the Potomac to the mouth of the Little Kanawha river—inspecting blockhouses, organizing for defense and giving encouragement. Despite the fact that the settlers continued to be thrown largely upon their own resources, the strength of the settlements became greater than ever before.

Beginning about the close of the Revolutionary war there was a rush of emigration to northwestern Virginia. Dwellers east of the mountains who had been despoiled of their property by the British, who feared the high taxes after the war, or who wanted to get a new start on the cheap lands of the west, braved the dangers of Indian warfare and came in a constant stream. Within a short space of time after the close of the Revolution hundreds of new settlers came into the territory drained by the headwaters of the Monongahela. Among the new comers were William Powers, afterwards one of the first justices of the peace in Lewis County and one of the early chroniclers of the county's history; Henry McWhorter, whose descendants have made their mark in county and state affairs; Patrick McCann, builder of a fort, Indian scout and hero of the border, who settled at the mouth of Edward Hughes' run, afterwards called McCann's run; the Rev. John Mitchell, who was the first preacher in the county; the Browns, who settled on White Oak Flat run, where they built the Mongue (or Mung) fort which stood a short distance from the later site of the Broad Run Baptist church; and a host of others only less prominent. John Waggoner, Joseph Glanfield, Thomas Short, Peter Swisher, Jacob Wolf, George Dobson, John Starcher, Peterman Hardman and Jacob Cozad are names worthy to be recorded. Hacker's creek was becoming rather thickly settled for a frontier community; and had it not been for the incursions of the Ohio Indians, settlement would have been far more rapid.

The first attack following the close of the Revolution took place on the spot destined in later years to be chosen as the seat of government of the county. About the middle of October, 1784, assisted by Paulser Butcher, then a mere youth, but later one of the largest landholders in the county, Henry Flesher had been engaged in hauling logs for a stable to be built near where the Baptist church now stands. Flesher went to his house to get a bell to put on his horse preparatory to turning him out to graze in woods. When he reached the ravine which came down the hill about where Bank street now is he was fired upon by an Indian lying in wait. The ball passed through his arm, and he immediately started to run to his cabin. The savage ran after him and almost succeeded in overtaking him at his own door. In attempting to kill him before he entered the house the Indian, using his gun as a club, brought it down against the logs of the house with such force that the stock was shattered. Mrs. Flesher succeeded in pulling her husband into the house, and then scared the Indian away by calling upon the other men in the house to fire. The family spent the night in the woods, fearing a renewal of the assault. There is a tradition that Mrs. Flesher carried her husband into a thicket near the house and spent the night under the widespread limbs of a sycamore which stood at the mouth of Stone Coal creek. The next morning she met John Schoolcraft, who summoned help from West's fort. Another account states that a young woman of the family reached Hacker's creek the next morning and that the remainder of the family were guided into West's fort by Edward Hughes. The Flesher family and young Butcher remained at West's fort until the near approach of winter made it unlikely that any savages were in the vicinity, when they returned to their home.

In December, 1787, occurred perhaps the most frightful of the Indian outrages perpetrated in Lewis County; and for sheer barbarity and brutality its equal is scarcely to be found in any of the border annals. Earlier in the fall the Indians had come into the valley of the West Fork above Clarksburg and had stolen some horses. Their trail was followed by Sheriff Lowther, who overtook them at the mouth of the Little Kanawha river. Three Indians were killed and the stolen property recovered. The Indians never believed the whites justified in killing them to punish plundering and they made swift reprisal—as usual directed against the innocent and the helpless. The war party was accompanied by Leonard Schoolcraft who had been taken captive some years before at Bush's fort. The settlers, believing that they were safe from attack owing to the lateness of the season, did not take the precautions usual at other times of the year.

The Indians came upon Martha Hughes, a daughter of Jesse Hughes, not far from her father's home and took her a prisoner. Proceeding farther some of them came upon Edmund West, Sr., while he was engaged in bringing in his fodder. He was caught unawares and could not make any resistance. Upon being led to the spot where Martha Hughes was being held by the Indians, he fell upon his knees and begged that they would spare his life. A stroke of the tomahawk answered the plea. The party then went to the cabin of Edmund West, Jr., where they found his bride of a few months, his 12-year-old brother and Mrs. West's sister, a daughter of John Hacker. Mrs. West and the boy were immediately tomahawked. The girl took refuge behind a door. A savage aimed a blow at her head, but she dodged and the tomahawk took effect in her neck, wounding her severely. She had presence of mind to fall to the floor and lie as if dead. The savages then sat down at the table and ate a hearty meal, the little girl silently observing them all the time. At the close of the meal they scalped Mrs. West and the boy and plundered the house, even emptying the feathers to carry off the ticking. They then dragged the Hacker girl by the hair to a fence about fifty yards from the cabin where she was scalped and thrown over it. Schoolcraft, noticing some signs of life, observed, "That is not enough;" whereupon the savage thrust a knife into her side. Fortunately the knife came into contact with a rib and did little injury.

Meanwhile old Mrs. West who was alone with her two daughters became uneasy when her husband failed to return. She feared that he had fallen into the hands of Indians, as she could not account for his continued absence in any other way. They went to Alexander West's in the hope of finding old Mr. West and to give them warning. Alexander West was then on a hunting trip with his brother Edmund. The women, now thoroughly frightened, went to the home of Jesse Hughes, who had become alarmed by that time at the failure of his daughter to return home. He determined to warn the neighbors to be on their guard. Knowing that Edmund West, Jr., was not at home he went first to the house to remove Mrs. West to his own home. The ghastly scene which met his eyes at the West home—Mrs. West and the boy weltering in their blood and not yet dead—confirmed all his fears. Hughes determined to protect his own family, and he barricaded his house and watched all through the night. As soon as it was possible to venture forth a party was collected to determine the full extent of the tragedy. Mrs. West was found dead in her home; she had probably lived but a few minutes after Hughes had left. The boy was found standing in the creek about a mile from the West cabin. His skull was fractured and the brains were oozing from his head; yet he lived in extreme suffering for three days. The Hacker girl was found in bed at the cabin of Edmund West, Sr., where she had taken refuge after a night spent in the woods. She survived, grew to maturity, married, gave birth to ten children and died from a nasal hemorrhage caused, it was believed, by the wound she had received in 1787. Martha Hughes was ransomed by her father in 1790.

It seems that for once no attempt at pursuit was made against the Indians who had taken part in the murder at West's. There is a tradition to the effect that the warrior who stabbed the Hacker girl was afterwards killed when he ventured back to the settlement. He was disemboweled, according to the traditionary account, and the body was filled with sand and sunk in Hacker's creek.

In August 1789, some Indians came to the house of John Mack on a branch of Hacker's creek. The husband and two of the little girls were away from home; but the savages killed all the other members of the family and set fire to the house.

A year later, the cabin of John Bush on Freeman's creek was besieged by the Indians. Late in the evening, 24 August 1790, Bush became alarmed at the screams of his children who had been sent to drive the cattle home, and started with his gun to learn the cause of the trouble. He was met at the door by an Indian who deftly disarmed him and shot him with his own gun. Bush fell across his threshold. The savage drew his knife to scalp him, but at that moment Mrs. Bush appeared upon the scene and sank an ax into the back of the Indian's shoulder with such force that when he fell away the ax came off the handle. She then pulled her husband into the house and shut the door. Other Indians came up, and after attempting for some time to force the door open, they began shooting through it. Eleven bullets passed through the clothing of Mrs. Bush, but fortunately she remained unhurt. One of the savages attempted to shoot through a crack in the wall at her, but with another ax she bent the barrel of his gun. The Indian is said to have exclaimed "dern you." At this juncture the Indians were frightened away. Adam Bush, who lived nearby, determined to find out what the trouble was at the home of John, and to aid him if necessary. The noise made by the dogs which accompanied him in crossing a small stream, led the Indians to believe that a large party was coming to the relief of Bush and they withdrew. A party from the neighborhood was organized for the pursuit, who came so nearly upon the Indians at the mouth of the Little Kanawha river that they were forced to abandon seven horses they had stolen from the settlement before their attack on Bush.

About the middle of May, 1792, Tecumseh led an expedition of Shawnees against the settlements on Hacker's creek. He evidently feared to make an attack on any of the houses in the more thickly settled portions of the valley, and led the men to Jesse's run where they came, late in the evening, to the clearing of John Waggoner. He was discovered sitting on a log resting, with a handspike across his knees. Tecumseh sent the other members of the band to secure those within the house while he should attend to Waggoner. The future British general was either under the impression that the handspike was a gun or he was excited at the prospect of securing a scalp. His aim was wide, though his intended victim was a large man in plain view, and the distance was not more than thirty or forty yards. Waggoner immediately sprang up, and seeing Indians at the house, ran in the opposite direction, followed at an ever increasing interval by Tecumseh, until the young chief finally gave up the chase.

Meanwhile the Shawnees who had gone to the house found a small boy in the yard and killed and scalped him, after which they took Mrs. Waggoner and her six other children prisoners. On being rejoined by Tecumseh they set off with all possible speed to place the Ohio river between them and any pursuers who might take up the trail. Finding that the smallest boy impeded their progress they beat out his brains and took his scalp before they had gone more than a mile. A short distance farther on they killed and scalped Mrs. Waggoner and two others of her children and from that time forth they made all possible speed to get out of the country. So great was their fear of retaliatory vengeance at the hands of the whites that the party did not even stop to secure food until after they had crossed the Ohio and were well within the Indian country.

Waggoner went to the cabin of Hardman, a neighbor, to secure a gun as quickly as he could, but the latter was out hunting at the time with the only gun in the possession of the family. Jesse Hughes was communicated with and he ran to West's fort, organized a pursuing party, and took up the trail. The pursuit was unsuccessful.

A local tradition states that the Indians in the party numbered but three and that they had lain in a ravine near West's fort all the day before while a religious meeting was in progress in the fort. The dogs within barked furiously at them and ran toward the ravine, trying to lead the settlers, but no attention was paid to them.

The number of successful incursions by the Indians and the utter futility of stopping their outrages by pursuing them as far as the Ohio river whenever they made their presence known, was by this time apparent. Colonel Duvall was not slow in realizing the strategical importance of the mouth of the Little Kanawha river, and before the year 1785 he had sent a party of scouts to see that a fort was built and properly garrisoned there. In the same year Captain James Neal settled on the southern side of the two rivers. From that time on Neal's station became the first line of defense for the settlements along the West Fork. From that point as a center the scouts ranged the woods on the Virginia side of the river and occasionally crossed into the Northwest territory observing the country carefully for indications of Indians, and if any were found, reporting them without delay by swift runners to the exposed settlements. In this way the military authorities were able to warn the inhabitants to go into places of safety where they could make better resistance to the attack if one were made. When Indians succeeded in getting past the scouts at Neal's station and first made their presence known by plundering and murdering in the settlements, the scouts could intercept them on their retreat. So effectual was the plan that later parties of Indians who ventured into the settlement on the West Fork, generally came by way of Middle Island creek until the mouth of that stream was also guarded.

From 1786, the Ohio line of defense proved increasingly strong. In that year Fort Harmar was built at the mouth of the Muskingum. In 1788 General Rufus Putnam's colony of New Englanders came down the Ohio and settled at Marietta. The next year a settlement was made at the mouth of the Little Miami river just above the bottom where Cincinnati was afterwards built. In 1790, the settlements had spread to the interior twenty miles above Marietta. It was not long until the national government sent several regiments of regulars into the Northwest territory to protect the settlers against the Indians. After the establishment of the Ohio settlements the people there became the main object of the savages, who were being constantly urged on to murder and plunder. Isolated attacks were, however, still being made in western Virginia by the now infuriated savages. Colonel Duvall stated in 1791 that the idea of federal troops being a protection to the settlers was "only a shadow without substance."

In 1792 the command of the militia of Harrison and Randolph counties again passed into the able hands of Colonel Lowther, after he had served Harrison County as sheriff. He reported to the governor that he had under him " one Insign, two Sergeants, two Corprils, and forty privates." He had also appointed four scouts, of whom he had stationed two at the mouth of the Little Kanawha river and the others along the West Fork. He divided his men into four detachments with one sergeant and eleven men at the mouth of the Little Kanawha and the others at Flesher's Station, now Weston, Salem and the mouth of Ten Mile creek. Adam Flesher (called a captain in the traditional account) had charge of the Weston station, and under him in the beginning were Peter Bonnett, Samuel Bonnett, Louis Bonnett, Jacob Starcher, Thomas Short, Joseph Glanfield and Peter McKensie. The Buckhannon settlement was then being garrisoned by Randolph County militia.

The men who had seen service in preceding years had not received their pay and consequently Colonel Lowther had considerable difficulty in enlisting a sufficient force. Subsequently Captain James Wood came to the west to inspect the condition of affairs and to suggest changes. His determined action infused new courage into the people. Colonel Lowther was given command of the Monongahela district including all of northwestern Virginia. The disposition which he made of his troops was changed only slightly, the force at Neal's station being a little more than doubled and the garrison on the upper West Fork being placed near the mouth of Freeman's creek instead of at Flesher's station. The last named change was not permanent.

No Indian forays were made in the year 1793 into what is now Lewis County. A settlement made by the Carpenters on the Elk river in what is now Braxton County was completely broken up. One family was murdered and the others, owing to the fact that their numbers were too small to cope with the savages, moved to the West Fork. Jesse Hughes afterwards avenged the murder of the Carpenter family by killing the two Indians concerned. He took strips of skin from their backs from which he made razor strops.

In 1794 as Joseph Cox, a trapper, was riding down Leading creek for a load of furs which he had left at the mouth of the creek the fall before, he unexpectedly came upon a small party of Indians in a defile. He immediately wheeled his horse and applied the whip, but the animal became balky and would not move. Cox was captured and taken beyond the Ohio, but he escaped the same year.

On July 24 of the same year they took prisoner the daughter of John Runyon near the mouth of Freeman's creek. Two of the savages were detailed to conduct her to the Indian villages, but after going about ten miles, they tomahawked and scalped her. The other four attacked the house of William Carder which stood just below the mouth of Lost Creek, but were frightened away.

A few days later while proceeding toward the head of Hacker's creek by the ridge on one side of it, the Indians were attracted to the swimming hole just above the mouth of Little Stone Coal creek by the shouts of four sons of Jacob Cozad who were bathing. The Indians cautiously approached the place and took all four of the boys prisoners. The youngest boy, Benny, aged six, began to cry piteously for his mother and could not be hushed. One of the warriors seized him by the heels and dashed his brains out against the roots of a beech tree. The others of the party climbed the ridge and proceeded westward. The oldest boy, Jacob, hoping to attract the attention of the settlers, gave a prolonged whoop when the party had reached the summit, but he was immediately knocked senseless by a blow from a gun barrel. When he regained consciousness he was being dragged up the hill by one foot by a squaw, according to his later statement. The party encamped that night on the West Fork near the spot where Edward Jackson's mill was afterwards built. The Indians escaped pursuit. After the peace made with the whites in 1795 the three boys were returned by their captors.

The prolonged stay of this small party in the West Fork valley and the great amount of damage done produced a panic among the settlers. In order to prevent the people from abandoning their habitations Colonel Lowther felt impelled to grant them a guard of men and two scouts. One Indian was killed, another was wounded and the scalp of the Runyon girl was recovered in an attack made later in the year by Colonel Lowther's rangers.

The next year, 1795, the last Indian outrage was perpetrated in northwestern Virginia. The trail of a party of Indians going up Leading creek was discovered and all the settlements were notified. The settlers on the Buckhannon who had not suffered from Indian raids for ten years, failed to heed the warning. As a result of their carelessness several members of the Bozarth family were killed.

Some time afterwards the last Indian killed in Lewis County is said to have been shot by Henry Flesher as he was trying to escape by climbing up the west bank of the river near the mouth of Polk creek.

The issue between the whites and the Indians was decided far away on the plains of northwestern Ohio at the battle of Fallen Timbers. There General "Mad Anthony" Wayne, at the head of an army of 2,000 regulars, went into battle with the flower of the tribes of the northwest who had chosen their positions with remarkable strategic insight. The Indians were unable to withstand the rush of the first line of the whites, and they gave way in confusion. The Shawnees sued for peace, followed by all the tribes of the northwest. By the treaty of Greenville, 1795, they agreed to give up all their lands in what is now Ohio with the exception of a strip in the northern part of the state.

The Indians remained peaceful for several years until another forward movement of the settlers induced them to take up arms again. The later wars were waged at such a distance from the West Fork valley that the inhabitants knew of them only by reports that reached them from the frontier. The settlements which had been maintained through nearly twenty years of incessant Indian warfare were at last free to expand without fear of further massacres.

CHAPTER VII.

THE BEGINNING OF LAW AND ORDER

The lawless state of the country during the first few years of the settlement of Lewis County has been alluded to briefly in other chapters. It is now proposed to show how the legal processes of England and America took the place of community remonstrances, and became the basis of united action. It was the year 1779 before the Virginia legislature was made to realize that it had not incorporated all the inhabited Trans-Alleghany territory into Trans-Alleghany counties. From an oversight due to the lack of geographical knowledge, the region now contained in Harrison and Lewis counties was still included in Augusta County, which paid little or no attention to the life and death struggle with the Indians which was being waged in its western marches. In the absence of other authority, Monongalia County exercised jurisdiction over the whole West Fork valley. Petitions for the formal inclusion of the region in that county which were presented to the General Assembly in 1779 resulted in the extension of the boundaries of the county to include all the territory drained by the Monongahela and its branches and nearly all that drained by the Little Kanawha.

The territory included in the new county was far larger than that of some of the states lying on the eastern coast. It extended from the Maryland boundary westward to the Ohio river, and from the headwaters of the Elk river almost to Pittsburgh. The seat of justice was first at Fort Redstone, afterward at Morgantown. By far the largest part of the population at first lived on that part of the Monongahela valley now included in the state of Pennsylvania. Most of the interests of the governing authorities of the county were in that section. Later it was in the district immediately surrounding the court house at Morgantown.

The southern part of the county, embracing the headwaters of the West Fork and the Tygart's Valley rivers was far from the county seat and separated from the other settlements by a comparatively unsettled region where the land was more rugged and where wide river bottoms did not exist. The enormous extent of the county resulted in considerable difficulty in the administration of justice. The settlers at West's fort and other places were at great inconvenience in attending court, and the officials of the county were at equal difficulty in collecting taxes, levying on property and arresting violators of the law.

Under the circumstances it was inevitable that before long there should be agitation for the division of the county. A strong memorial was presented to the General Assembly by residents of the upper valleys. The representatives from Monongalia County did not appear to object to the division, and in 1784, the southern part of the county was formed into the county of Harrison. The boundaries of the new counties were as follows: beginning at the point where Ford fork crosses the Maryland boundary; thence by a straight line to the headwaters of Big Sandy creek; thence down Big Sandy creek and the Tygart's Valley river to the mouth of West Fork; thence up West Fork and Bingamon creek to its source; thence with the ridges separating the waters of the Monongahela from the Ohio to the head of Middle Island creek; thence with that creek to the Ohio. On the east the county was bounded by the ridge separating the Potomac from the Monongahela drainage basin; and on the south the line extended from the point on the Alleghany Mountains where Rockingham and Botetourt counties meet, north fifty-five degrees west to the Ohio river, a distance of 108¾ miles. The area of the county was not much less than 4,000 square miles, and the population in 1784 is estimated to have been about 2,000.

The act providing for the formation of the new county specified that the justices to be named in the commission of the peace should meet at the house of George Jackson, near Bush's old fort, to take the oath of office, select a site for the court house, and transact other business. The location was probably chosen because it was midway between the settlements of the upper Tygart's Valley and those of the West Fork. In the discussion as to the permanent location of the county seat, most of the justices objected to Bush's fort. The settlers in that vicinity were not numerous, and the location probably pleased none of the justices, the majority of whom were residents of the prosperous community around Nutter's fort. This fact probably determined the location of the county seat at Clarksburg.

At the first session of court held, 20 July 1784, the justices recommended persons suitable for appointment for the offices of surveyor, heads of the militia, coroner, and justices of the peace to the Governor of the Commonwealth. They also appointed constables and viewers and overseers of the roads. A grand jury was summoned, a mill seat established, a donation of lots accepted for the court house and jail, and one civil suit was brought before the court adjourned. John Sleeth, a resident of Hacker's creek, was recommended for appointment as justice of the peace and for authorization to celebrate the rites of matrimony. John Runyon, whose cabin stood not far from the mouth of Freeman's creek, was one of the constables. The civil suit was brought by John Hacker against Elijah Stout for "detaining said Hacker out of his landed rights."

The duties of the county courts were many and varied. From the year 1623 the county courts of Virginia were supreme in the county government, in both administrative and judicial affairs.

THE BEGINNING OF LAW AND ORDER

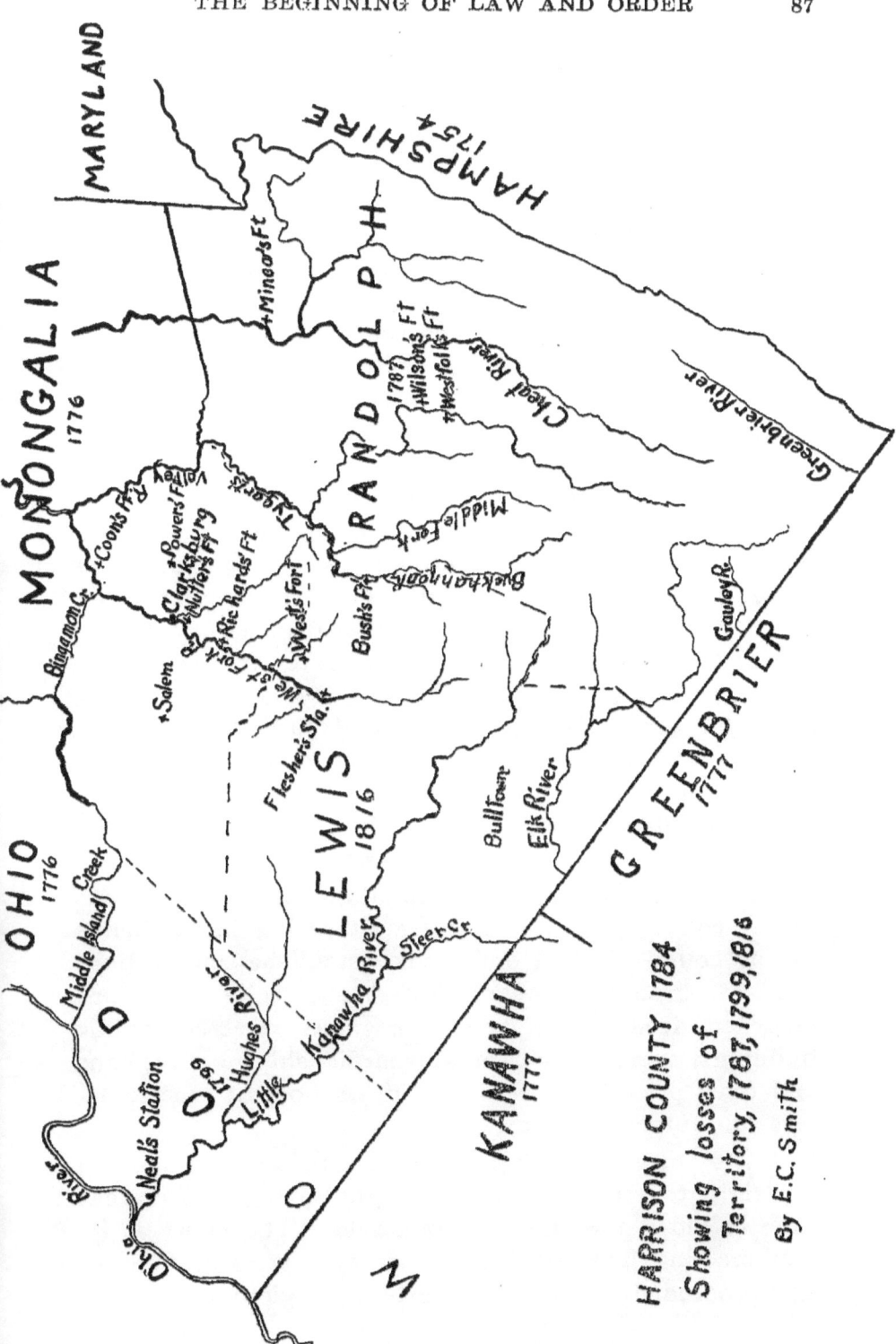

HARRISON COUNTY 1784
Showing losses of Territory, 1787, 1799, 1816
By E.C. Smith

The county court was composed of all the justices of the peace in the county, who were appointed by the governor. No new justices were appointed without the recommendation of the justices already sitting, and the body thus became self-perpetuating and all-powerful. The important office of sheriff was filled by appointment by the governor, but the justices recommended three freeholders for the office from among whom the appointment was made. It was the custom of the county court to recommend three of their own number, and the office was handed around among them according to seniority. With the system of fees then in force, one or two years incumbency in the sheriffalty was sufficient to lay the foundations for the fortune of the holder. All the other officers of the county were either recommended by the court for appointment by the Governor, or were appointed outright. The only officers elected under this democratic (?) system of local government were overseers of the poor and the delegates to the legislature.

The court also possessed real judicial functions. The county court was the only tribunal in Harrison County for fifteen years after its formation. It settled small disputes, punished breaches of the peace and established law and order throughout the county.

As might be expected the administrative functions of the county government were altogether in the hands of the court. It laid out roads, established mills, built bridges, granted licenses, levied and collected taxes, recorded deeds, wills and mortgages, erected public buildings, exercised a general guardianship over orphans and fixed prices at taverns besides a host of other matters too numerous to mention.

The authority to license establishments presupposes the right to regulate; and the right to regulate at that time included the right to fix prices. The court at its first meeting licensed one or two ordinaries or taverns, and proceeded to fix rates for liquors, victuals and forage for horses. Beer was to be sold for twelve cents a quart, and rye whiskey, cider and apple and peach brandy were the same for one-half pint. A warm breakfast cost nine pence, or eighteen cents, a warm dinner, one shilling, or twenty-four cents and a warm supper nine pence. A bed for one night with clean sheets was four pence (eight cents). The custom of fixing prices at ordinaries continued for many years after the formation of Lewis County, the schedule of rates being revised at intervals.

The assessors who had been appointed by the Harrison County court had a much easier task than the assessor has nowadays. At the June term, 1785, the court entered an order that a list of all the whites and of all the buildings should be taken by the assessors, in order that the court could proceed with the business of laying a levy. The total of the whole county, comprising, with few exceptions, only the valleys of the Tygart's Valley and the West Fork, was 318. John Sleeth, of Hacker's creek, was appointed to make a list of all those residing "from the mouth of Lost creek, upwards, including the whole of the livers in the West Fork settlement." The district included all the territory in Lewis County that was then inhabited, and also the settlements on Lost creek and above West Milford on the river. The whole list is as follows.

Alex West
Matthew Richards
Conrad Richards
Jacob Harleson
James Sleath
Thomas Doyle McCune
Elizah ————————
John Runyon
Joseph Kester
Samuel Norris
Ebenezer Haley
Samuel Bonet
Joseph Crozan
Thomas Hughes
Daniel Cane
James Campbell

John Richard
John Brown
Jacob Cozad
John Waggoner
Jacob Bush
Abraham ————————
John Huggle
Henry Flesher
Christen Harrison
Jesse Huse (Hughes)
Alex. Sleeth
George Collins
Edmund West, Constable
James Schoolcraft
Adam O'Brien
Elias Huse (Hughes)

William Hannan
David Wales Sleeth
John Sleeth
Adam Bush
Joseph ─────────
Isaac ─────────
James Tanner

John Collins
George Brush (Bush)
John Hacker
Richard Clark
Edmond West
Joel Lowther

Even before the completion of the enumeration the court directed that the sheriff should collect from "every tithable in this County 2s. 6d., being the County levy for the year 1784, and pay the same as directed by the proportions." There was no property tax collected at that period, only a poll tax on males over 21. The amount of the tax for 1784, reckoned in terms of dollars and cents, was $41\frac{1}{3}$ cents on each individual. The expenses of the county government were not large, being confined at first to the erection of the public buildings. Roads were worked by the tithables, who may on that account be said to have paid an additional poll tax in labor. The justices of the peace received no salaries, but they had considerable fees and an occasional turn at the sheriffalty.

The first care of the county court was to provide for public buildings. A court house thirty-six by twenty-six feet set eight feet above the ground, was contracted for. John Prunty undertook to build a jail for £19 15s., and Daniel Davisson was to erect the whipping post, pillory and one pair of stocks for £5 19s. 11d. All were completed by 1789.

Just how primitive the justice established in Harrison County was in the beginning may be inferred from some of the records of the court in the latter part of the eighteenth century. A female prisoner convicted of felonious taking was given ten lashes on her bare back in 1788. In the same year a man was convicted of having stolen an ax, a hat and a pair of stockings. The court ordered "that the sheriff immediately tie the prisoner to the public whipping post and give him thirty-nine lashes well laid on & deliver him to David Hughes

Constable" who should deliver him to the next constable and so on until he was conveyed out of the county. In 1791 John Jackson was given a verdict by a jury in a slander case, but the damages were fixed by the jury at only seven shillings. Jackson demanded a new trial on the ground that the sheriff had conveyed apple brandy to the jury in a tea-pot while they were engaged in considering the case, and that the jury drank it. The motion was granted, and all twelve of the jurymen were fined twelve shillings each. In John Hacker's lawsuit concerning a tract of land, a jury of twelve men was summoned to appear on the land and inquire into and settle the bounds between the claimants.

In 1795 a prisoner entered the plea of guilty to a charge of felonious assault. While the members of the court were discussing whether the prisoner should be tried by the district court, the prisoner escaped. The sheriff was ordered by the court to raise the "hue and cry" and command assistance to take him. The same year Sheriff John Prunty objected because the court called a witness without having a subpoena issued, thus cheating the sheriff out of his fee. In the old record book is to be found a full account of the proceedings that followed: "Ordered that the said John Prunty be confined in the stocks for the space of five minutes" * * * for his "damming the Court and the attorney who was there supporting the client's claim, and the whole bunch. The Court and the attorney was D——d fools and a set of d——d scoundrels." After being released he again showed disrespect and was confined for the remainder of the day. The court bound him over to keep the peace. After spending some time in jail bond for his good behavior was obtained. Attempts of the court to oust him later were unsuccessful.

In spite of the crudeness of the administration of justice the establishment of the courts was a good thing for the people of the community. The substitution of orderly government for mob rule was the beginning of real social progress on the upper reaches of the Monongahela.

Above the county court was the district court, which was organized in 1785. Judges of the General court were detailed to hold court twice a year in each of the districts into which the state was divided. The sessions for the district in which Harrison county was included were generally held at Morgantown. Circuit courts superseded the district courts in 1809, and two sessions were held each year in each county.

The new county government began at once to look after the interests of the people. Means of communication were most needed in the settlements, and many orders were passed within the first two or three years following the formation of the county providing for the location of new roads. The first order of the Harrison County court dealt with territory afterwards a part of Lewis County: "Ordered that the road from Richards' Fort be extended by Edmund West's mill to John Hacker's the nearest and best way. Nicholas Carpenter, Isaac Richards and David Sleeth be appointed to view and lay out such road and make report to the next Court to be held for this County is hereby revived." The following year a road was ordered opened from Clarksburg to the Flesher settlement at the mouth of Stone Coal creek. Other roads were opened at a later period to all the settled portions of the new county. Though they were mere dirt trails, often no more than pathways through the woods, they represented some advance in communication and a great advance in community consciousness, because they were public property, owned and operated by the public.

One of the most important offices in the county during the first four or five decades of its history was the land office. It was opened almost immediately upon the establishment of the county government. As soon as the surveyor was qualified he began issuing patents for lands and recording surveys for homesteaders or purchasers.

In direct opposition to the policy of the royal government of the colonies in attempting to restrict settlements to the fringe along the Atlantic coast, the State of Virginia did all in its power to encourage settlers to make their homes west of the mountains, both to assure her hold on the territory for future occupancy and to provide outposts for defense against the British and Indians, who, if they succeeded in crossing the Alleghanies, would be able to strike at the vitals of the commonwealth. In order to make it worth while for settlers to cross the mountains and to hold those who had already gone to the west, the General Assembly in 1777 passed an act providing free land for every settler. Every person who had secured a settlement right or a corn right was to receive 400 acres with a preemption to 1,000 acres adjoining if he chose to take it. The price fixed for the additional land was so high that few of the settlers cared to take out preemptions. They eagerly took advantage of the opportunity to secure homesteads, many of which were claimed on the basis merely of deadening a few trees and planting corn. The legislature in 1779 provided that a settler must have lived on land one year and have raised one crop of corn from it in order to be entitled to a homestead. Few large tracts west of the mountains had been patented up to that time.

By another provision of the act of 1777, it was provided that as soon as possible the land claimed as homesteads by settlers should be patented and recorded. In order to settle disputes which might arise between settlers who had built their houses close together and who claimed the same tracts of land, a temporary commission was appointed with both executive and judicial powers to determine who was rightfully entitled to the land. The commission for the district including Monongalia, Ohio and Youghiogheny counties was composed of John P. Duvall, James Neal and Will Haymond. They held sittings at many different points throughout the district in the summer of 1781, and issued certificates to settlers which entitled them to enter the tracts specified with the county surveyors.

Not all the persons who were given certificates afterwards perfected their titles. Some sold their claims and others failed altogether to pay attention to the matter, preferring to be squatters on the lands of others. Many of the lands for which certificates were issued in 1781 were surveyed in Monongalia, but in other cases the owners waited until after the formation of Harrison County. Before the close of the year 1784, the surveyor's office of the new county had returned as surveyed and entered no less than eighty tracts. In 1785, 960 surveys were made, and the next year the number was 365.

The number of surveys indicates that the country was being filled up very fast with settlers following the close of the Revolution, and such was, in fact, the case, but the tide of immigration was not nearly so great as indicated by the number of tracts surveyed. In some cases they represented the patenting of lands by wealthy capitalists in Boston, in New Jersey, or in eastern Virginia, who had purchased large tracts of land from the state and who hoped later to sell the lands to settlers at a profit. The act of 1779 had fixed the price at forty pounds per hundred acres, which proved to be beyond the ability of the hunter-trapper-farmer of the frontier to pay. In 1792 the price was reduced to the merely nominal charge of two cents per acre.

Some of the tracts sold under both acts were very large—for instance, the Pickering survey of 100,000 acres made in 1785, lying on the headwaters of the West Fork and the Little Kanawha rivers, and the Banks survey, equally large, which was located at about the same time on the watershed of the Little Kanawha river, lying partly in Lewis and partly in Gilmer counties. After the price of land was reduced in 1792 thousands of acres of land were entered, embracing practically the whole area of the state. Often a large survey would include the homesteads of settlers, or lands claimed by other large holders, and the result was a series of lawsuits which began almost with the establishment of the courts in the Trans-Alleghany region and continued until long after the formation of West Virginia.

Henry Jackson was one of the most widely known surveyors of Western Virginia during this period. He went into the forests with only one or two assistants and surveyed thousands of acres. Often the work was not done thoroughly, as in the case of the Banks survey which he completed far from the spot, after having been compelled to flee for his life from the Indians. The only data which he had secured was his beginning corner, from which it could be seen that the boundary line of the survey would cross Leading creek three times.

The political beliefs and opinions of the people of Harrison County during the eighteenth century were not difficult to determine. During the Revolution, with few exceptions, they espoused the cause of independence, and against heavy odds defended the frontiers of Virginia. After the close of the war they had some bitter experiences with the delays of the state government in the Indian wars, which caused them to favor the establishment of a national government strong enough to cope with the Indians. George Jackson, who was sent by the citizens of Harrison County to represent them in the state convention of 1788 to consider the proposed constitution of the United States, voted in favor of ratification. His experience in the Indian wars and his national patriotism caused him to disregard the claims of eastern politicians who favored a loose confederation. He truly represented the political opinion of his constituents.

Though politically coherent, Harrison County was not a geographical unit. Diverse elements came into existence almost with the formation of the county. The fixing of the county seat at Clarksburg was almost as much of an inconvenience for the people of the upper Tygart's Valley section as the former location at Morgantown. The people of that section were almost as well off before the formation of the new county. The objection early took form, and three years after the creation of Harrison, an act of the General Assembly was passed cutting off all that portion of the county east of the Tygart's Valley and Buckhannon rivers and establishing it as the county of Randolph.

Both sections were gainers by the separation. On the one hand the people of Randolph were able to transact their legal business without the inconvenience of a long journey to the county seat; on the other hand the people of the West Fork watershed were relieved from the burden of having to share the expenses of government with a section which lagged in its development as compared with the more favored valleys toward the Ohio. Henceforth the officials of Harrison County could devote their whole attention to the more and more complex problems of making the administrative machinery keep pace with the rapid course of development of the county.

The settlements near the mouth of the Little Kanawha river, which began about the time of the close of the Revolution, developed rapidly in their favored locations on the rich Ohio river bottoms in contiguity to the New Englanders who had settled around Marietta. The likelihood of a further rapid increase all along the Virginia side of the Ohio river made it clear that a separate county government would be necessary within a short time, especially since the new center of settlement was separated from the court house at Clarksburg by a wide expanse of unbroken forest. The General Assembly in 1799 formed Wood County from parts of Harrison and Kanawha. The new county was a narrow strip extending all the way from the Great Kanawha river to Middle Island creek.

After the cutting off of the Ohio river settlements, the inhabited portions of Harrison County formed a fairly homogeneous district, embracing most of the valley of the West Fork river from Buffalo creek in what is now Marion County to Bulltown. The most thickly settled portion of the county was around Clarksburg, on Elk creek, Simpson's creek, Lost creek and the country along the West Fork river. Few settlements had been made along the Little Kanawha or its tributaries, and the West Fork settlements had not extended far enough southward to make Clarksburg inconvenient as the county seat. The population of Harrison County in 1790 was 2,080.

NOTE—The author is indebted to Colonel Henry Haymond's History of Harrison County for many of the facts set forth in regard to the formation of Harrison County.

CHAPTER VIII.

ECONOMIC BEGINNINGS

We have seen how the settlers on the western frontier of Virginia maintained their position in spite of the raids and depredations of the Indian allies of Great Britain during the Revolution, and more than held their own against the raids for twelve years afterwards until the troops of the federal government defeated them and compelled them to sign a treaty of peace. The deeds of the Hugheses, the Wests, the Jacksons, and a host of other heroes in the desperate struggle with the Indians have been handed down by a grateful people who owed the peaceful possession of their lands to their efforts. We have also seen the establishment of justice and traced the beginnings of law and order in the settlements of the upper Monongahela valley. Colonel Lowther, John P. Duvall, David Sleeth and others had a great share in the movement and the records in the court house at Clarksburg show how important their work was for the future of Hackers' creek and the surrounding region.

There were other pioneers in the region whose deeds have been forgotten for want of a chronicler, and whose very names would be lost if they had not been recorded in connection with the entry of homesteads or the purchase of land, or as having been appointed to view the location of a proposed road, or summoned to give evidence before a grand jury. These obscure citizens were the ones whose humble efforts finally brought about civilized institutions in place of the primeval forest. Their collective endeavors have made Lewis County what it is.

William Powers, Indian fighter, justice of the peace and chronicler of the events of the stirring years of the Indian wars, is said to have made the statement that in his opinion the settlers west of the mountains did not intend to remain permanently, but would leave when the game became exhausted. He believed that the soil of the county would not support a white population for any length of time. Others were of the same opinion. They thought that certain fields would bring crops for a certain number of years, and that other fields would bring a greater or less number, according to the lay of the land. The possibility of raising live stock on a commercial scale did not apparently present itself as a basis for prosperity in after years. The growing of grain and fruit in large quantities for distant markets was not to be considered without means of transportation better than any known at the beginning of the eighteenth century. The presence of hidden treasures of petroleum and natural gas was unsuspected. Bituminous coal (called by the settlers stone coal to distinguish it from charcoal) was known to exist in the valley of the upper West Fork and some of its tributaries, but it was apparently not much used for fuel by the earliest comers. If any one had suggested that some day it could profitably be mined and transported to a seaboard market he would have been considered eligible for transportation to a seaboard lunatic asylum.

The principal industries of the pioneers were hunting and trapping. Agriculture was in a very elementary state—so elementary, in fact, that it can not be considered in any other light than as a means of maintaining existence. After the close of the Indian wars many of the settlers came because they had been attracted by the land and intended to make improvements, raise larger crops, breed live stock and gain wealth from the produce of their farms and from the increased value of the land which would follow the expected rush of settlement and the gradual improvement of the country.

It was the settler's first care after locating his claim and building a cabin, to clear a small tract of land where he could raise a crop of corn and some vegetables to reinforce and balance the supply of wild meat which needed only to be sought in the woods with a gun. Most of the clearings were made by grubbing the bushes and saplings and chopping and burning the smaller trees. The monarchs of the primeval forest were deadened by girdling them with an ax or by building fires at their bases. It was impracticable to clear the land in any other way, for the labor of chopping the larger trees would have been too great for the pioneer farmers. The deadened trees were sometimes allowed to stand in the clearings for several years until the danger of limbs falling upon the stock or on the corn fields became too great; they were then generally destroyed by piling logs or smaller pieces of wood at their bases and setting them on fire. Often dead trees continued to burn for several days. The smaller trees at the edges of the clearing were not burned, but were split in halves or fourths and used to make rail fences to keep out the stock. Usually the fences needed to be heavier than now. The high bottoms of the streams and the flats were cleared first because the land there was more fertile than elsewhere, and there was no danger of the crops being destroyed by floods.

When the ground had been cleared and burned over it was stirred lightly with a shovel plow, an implement made often with a forked sapling for a stock and a small piece of iron rudely fashioned, for the point. The handles were fastened to the stock with wooden pins. The horse was hitched to the plow by means of grape vines tied with thongs to hames made from stumps of large ash trees, and the hames fitted around a buckskin collar stuffed with fibers of linden wood. The corn was dropped by hand and covered with a hoe. It was cultivated by plowing with the shovel plow and then cutting the weeds around the hills of corn with a hoe—a laborious process which has survived from pioneer days in most parts of the county. The early corn fields were hoed more often than not by the women and children of the family. There were no crop failures unless wild animals or live stock broke into the enclosures and destroyed the crops. In spite of the poor quality of the seed planted the yields compared favorably with crops produced on the same fields today. The crops were gathered and hauled to the houses of the pioneers on sleds.

Corn was the staple food of the pioneers. No other grain was raised for many years. When the settlers came across the mountains without having raised a crop of corn they were obliged to subsist throughout the spring and summer without breadstuffs. Dr. Joseph Doddridge, whose father brought him to the west when he was a mere boy, wrote later of his experiences: "The Indian meal which my father brought over the mountains was expended six weeks too soon, so for that length of time we had to live without bread. The lean venison and the breast of wild turkey we were taught to call bread. The flesh of the bear was denominated meat. This artifice did not succeed very well. After living this way for some time we became sickly, the stomach seemed to be always empty and tormented with a sense of hunger.

"I remember how narrowly the children watched the growth of the potato tops, pumpkin and squash vines, hoping from day to day to get something to answer in the place of bread. How delicious was the taste of the young potatoes when we got them. What a jubilee when we were permitted to pull the young corn for roasting ears. Still more so when it acquired sufficient hardness to be made into 'Johnny cakes' by the aid of the tin grater. We then became healthy, vigorous and contented with our situation, poor as it was."

Besides the tin grater referred to, which was merely a piece of perforated tin affixed to a block of wood, the corn was also prepared for hominy and bread by a mortar and pestle. The mortar was usually a block from a beech tree with a hole burned in the center, large enough to hold a peck of grain. The pestle was a short length of a sapling. The settlers on Hacker's creek did not long have to depend upon such primitive appliances for their meal. John Hacker, on one of his trips across the mountains, is said to have brought two small buhrstones with him. Edmund West also brought a small hand mill to the fort and rigged it up very early to run by water power. It is thought that this is the mill to which Isaac Washburn had been when he was killed by the Indians while riding toward home in the vicinity of Richards' fort. Both mills were very crude, however. It is supposed that their capacity was not much more than one and one-half or two bushels of meal a day. Some of the Hacker's creek settlers may have had their grinding done at George Jackson's mill on the Buckhannon, which was in existence by 1780 or 1781. It was destroyed by the Indians in 1782, after which time the nearest large mill was at Clarksburg. S. Stratton was given permission to erect a mill on Hacker's creek by a court order made in 1785, but apparently he failed to take advantage of it.

The first large mill in the upper West Fork valley was built at West's fort in 1793 by Henry McWhorter. It was far superior to any that had thus far existed in the Trans-Alleghany settlements. McWhorter had come three years earlier from New Jersey where he had been apprenticed to a miller and had received a thorough training. His mill had a capacity of only fifteen bushels of corn a day, but it ground practically all the corn meal for the settlers in the vicinity for several years, and finally gave its name to the village which grew up around it. For many years all the settlers from the Buckhannon river valley came to McWhorter's mill with their grists. So also did the settlers of Lost creek and the upper one-third of Harrison County until the establishment of Clement's mill at West Milford in 1800. The earliest mills did not grind wheat or any other grain than corn.

After providing for sufficient corn to furnish bread and hominy for his family throughout the year, the chief agricultural interest of the pioneer was in his live stock.

None of the farmers thought in the beginning of clearing land for pasture, though most of the early comers transported their goods to the west on the backs of horses and drove cattle and hogs and sometimes a few sheep before them when they first came. The live stock were belled and turned into the open woods, where they fed upon succulent grasses, wild pea vines and the edible leaves of some of the trees. The horses and cattle were allowed free range of the woods during the day, but at night they were driven in by the children of the family when they did not come home of their own accord. The stealing of horses and the killing of cattle were the objects of many of the Indian raids against the settlements. Hundreds of horses were ridden away to the Indian villages. Cattle were never stolen from the western Virginia settlements, because they could not travel fast enough to allow the Indians to escape pursuit. Many were killed and their carcasses left to decay on the ground merely to gratify the destructive instincts of the savages and to make life on the frontier intolerable for the settlers.

Cattle were kept at first only for their milk. Their flesh was not of such good quality as the beef raised now in Lewis County, and besides there was plenty of bear meat and venison which could be had for the killing. Later, when the national government built forts along the Ohio, the live stock industry of the upper West Fork river received a great stimulus. The large garrisons maintained at the forts required a supply of meat greater than could be secured from hunting or from the farms in the immediate vicinity. Cattle were collected from different parts of the West Fork valley and driven overland from Clarksburg as early as 1790 and 1791 by way of the new road to Neal's station, which had been opened by William Haymond, Sr., soon after the establishment of Harrison County.

Until their numbers became too great for the forage, the cattle were usually fat after ranging the woods for a summer season. As the herds became larger the settlers sought to augment the amount of forage by going into the woods and cutting poplar, linden and other trees both in summer and winter. Cattle were allowed to run out all winter, subsisting on corn fodder, browse, or other forage. As a rule they were extremely poor in the spring. There was no attempt to breed the cattle scientifically; indeed only scrub stock was to be found west of the mountains in the eighteenth century. "Linebacks" were common, as shown by old sale bills, and some of them were good dairy cattle though they were not as a rule good beef cattle.

Sheep raising was a necessary industry in the new community, and it was perhaps the most discouraging of all to the settlers. Many of the pioneers brought a few sheep with them in order to raise wool for the manufacture of cloth and yarn. The small flocks were given the greatest possible care to prevent their being killed by wolves. In the thinly settled districts it was impossible for many years to allow the sheep to run in the woods, and they were therefore kept on clearings adjacent to the houses of the pioneers. The depredations of the wolves, which sometimes grew so bold as to come to the enclosures in broad daylight and throttle the sheep at the very doors of the cabins, always kept the number of sheep very low. As a substitute for wool, flax was grown on almost every farm, and the housewives of the early day were skilled in the manufacture of coarse cloth from it by means of the hackle and the spinning wheel.

Hogs were owned in large numbers by the pioneers. "Hog and hominy" had an important place on the tables of the pioneers. Pork was a welcome change from venison and bear meat, especially since it was of good quality. The hogs were always fat in the autumn from feeding on the plentiful mast, and the flavor of the meat was sometimes preferred to that of corn-fed hogs. Of all the live stock of the farmers, hogs alone were able to brave all the dangers of the forests and come out unscathed.

For many years they were allowed to run wild. Each owner had an old boar at the head of his drove which would protect it against the attacks of wild animals, and the boars, with their long tusks, were able to ward off all comers. Instances have been known of their having killed bears; and even men were sometimes compelled to climb trees when charged by one of the fierce brutes. The hogs did not seek the protection of the cabins as the other live stock did, and often they were neglected by their owners until different herds united, making property in hogs exceedingly difficult to identify. Much of the business of early county courts was in determining law suits concerning the ownership of hogs.

To obviate the difficulty of determining ownership the farmers adopted the practice of branding their live stock. "A swallowfork in the right ear," or "two notches on the lower side of the right ear," were marks of prominent stock raisers of that day. In order to prove ownership in case of a lawsuit, the mark was recorded with the clerk of the county court.

Hunting and trapping, which had begun even before settlements were made, long remained the principal industries of the country. From the time of John Simpson, adventurers penetrated into the wilderness to shoot deer, bears and buffaloes and to trap beavers, otters and smaller animals for their furs. Buffalo robes were in great demand east of the mountains, and furs were eagerly sought by the merchants of the old world. The trappers usually selected their fields of operations in the autumn and established their camps. During the winter they secured as many furs as they could and then left their exposed camps in the early spring before the Indian forays began. Their furs were hidden in a hole of water in some stream and securely tied to prevent their being washed away. There they would be preserved for many months. In the summer the trappers would return to their caches with packhorses and transport their furs to the nearest market.

Some were carried over the mountains to Winchester on packhorses; others, and perhaps the greater number, were loaded on boats and taken to Pittsburgh where they were sold to the fur dealers. In 1791 or 1792, a party of hunters came to Leading creek and other branches of the Little Kanawha river where they made an extended hunt. They carried their spoils, consisting of beaver skins, buffalo robes and bear skins and meat, by canoe down the Little Kanawha river to Neal's station and thence up the Ohio to Marietta, where they disposed of the furs to traders and the meat to the garrison at Fort Harmar.

Exports of furs by professional hunters and trappers were of little economic advantage to the country. They did not add to the wealth of the permanent residents or improve the conditions of living. On the contrary, as the supply of fur-bearing animals decreased, conditions of living on the frontier became harder. It was fortunate for the settlers that there was in the beginning a large number of fur-bearing animals in the country, for they afforded practically the only convenient article of export. Every settler was a hunter and most were trappers. The furs which they secured in the winter became the basis of their first commerce with the older settlements. It was the custom for every settler to make at least one trip to Winchester every year to procure supplies.

As a rule their wants were few and simple. Ammunition, salt and iron were the only absolute necessities that could not be secured from the forests.

The trip was made by packhorse over trails only wide enough for a horse to walk without danger of scraping off the packs against trees. There were no hotels on the way at which the pioneer could stop and procure food for himself and forage for his horses. For practically the whole distance there were no settlements. The traveler was compelled to sleep out under the stars and eat the johnny-cake which he had brought for his lunch and such game as he was able to kill on the way. The horses secured their food by foraging in the woods, for it was not customary to burden them with grain. It was considered that two bushels, or 168 pounds, of salt was all that one horse should be made to carry.

The journey was often very dangerous. The wild beasts were of course a menace to the traveler. There were also undesirable characters who lay in wait for an opportunity to waylay and kill the lonely traveler in order to secure his horses and goods. The cause of greatest fear, however, was the intense cold of the mountains in winter. It is related that John Hacker was caught one night in a terrific snowstorm somewhere high in the Alleghanies. He tried to make a fire from the flint and tinder he carried, but could not on account of the increasing numbness of his hands and arms. He would certainly have perished but for the fact that he bethought himself to lash his two horses together and lie between their backs with two deerskins over him.

Once when John Sims and Henry McWhorter were making the trip to Winchester together, Sims was overcome by the cold while walking and sat down by the side of the trail to rest. His companion, realizing the danger, cut a beech withe and began beating him with it. Sims roused and made for his tormentor. He failed to catch him and, after a short distance, again sat down. Again McWhorter vigorously plied the beech withe and again Sims became angry and attempted to lay hands on McWhorter. After enduring several beatings in this way Sims at length became warm enough to proceed.

The difficulties of carrying on commerce with Winchester were so great that the settlers could not have brought to the West Fork anything other than the barest necessities of life even if their stock of furs had been sufficient to purchase luxuries. When John Reger married Elizabeth West at West's fort in 1788, the bride wore a wonderful store gown of calico which the groom had purchased in Winchester, having walked the entire trip with a gun on his shoulder. The incident caused such a flurry of excitement in the settlement that it has been handed down in tradition to the present day.

The commerce with Pittsburgh, which later became considerable, was of slower growth. The settlers took their furs and meat down the West Fork and Monongahela rivers in canoes and flatboats and exchanged them for powder and lead. They also resorted to the village to have their guns repaired by the gunsmiths there. Salt at Pittsburgh was more expensive than at Winchester, and it was more difficult to transport up the river. The shipbuilding industry which developed around Pittsburgh, created a market for walnut logs from the upper Monongahela.

The building of forts on the Ohio river, as we have seen, furnished a market for the agricultural produce of the West Fork valley, and led afterwards to considerable trade.

Clarksburg, the county seat and the metropolis of the upper Monongahela valley, was without a store until 1788, and perhaps after that time. The records of that year show that one Joseph Anderson was licensed "to retail goods in this County as the law directs." Whether Anderson was a merchant or a peddler is not clear. There is, unfortunately, no corroborative tradition. The fact that there was a pioneer on the upper West Fork with sufficient enterprise to make a business of transporting goods from the east and exchanging them for furs and other produce was a long step in advance. It marked the beginning of trade—of an important division of labor—in the community.

The lack of roads was keenly felt by all the settlers in northwestern Virginia. Pittsburgh had taken the lead as a commercial center largely owing to the fact that a good military road had been built from Cumberland by Braddock in 1754, which had been somewhat improved and kept in repair after that time. Shortly after the close of the Revolution, when it had been definitely determined by the boundary commission that Pittsburgh was in Pennsylvania and not in Virginia, the General Assembly, desiring to cement the upper Monongahela valley to the eastern section of the state by commercial ties, opened a wagon road from Winchester via Romney to Morgantown. This was the famous State road. In 1786, the legislature appointed a commission of Harrison County citizens to lay out and open a wagon road from some point on the State road to the mouth of the Little Kanawha river. The road was first located and constructed from Clarksburg east to some point on the Cheat river, now in Preston County. It could not have been a well constructed thoroughfare until a later date. The first wagon did not reach Clarksburg until 1798, twelve years after the road was located. West of Clarksburg the road was only a blazed trail through the wilderness until the beginning of the new century.

The roads which had been established by the Harrison County court to connect different sections of the county were mere trails cut through the woods, barely wide enough to allow a packhorse to pass over them without scraping off his pack. On account of the value of every bit of cleared ground no road was ever located through a clearing. It followed the bounds of the clearing on one side. The unfavorable location of many of the roads in Lewis County at the present time is due to this fact. A traveler inquiring his way from one place to another would be told to follow the beech or other blazes. Cross roads or branch roads were marked with blazings on different kinds of trees.

In spite of the lack of good roads, there must have been some travel through Clarksburg, for there were taverns in the county seat from the beginning of Harrison County. This fact is partly explained by the fact that many citizens came from the outlying sections of the county to attend court, but there were also many emigrants with their worldly possessions on packhorses, passing through the town on their way to lands farther west.

There was no postoffice in the village until 1798. The postoffice address of citizens of Hacker's creek was "Winchester, Va." until that date.

CHAPTER IX.

LIFE OF THE PIONEERS

Conditions of living among the pioneers were simple in the extreme. There were no social castes, neither were there persons of great wealth or extreme poverty. All were the owners of four hundred acres of land which might be worth a hunting dog and a captured rifle or it might not; it depended partly upon the location but far more upon the extent of the clearings. It was impossible for a man to have a house much better than those of his neighbors; if he did, it was because he was more industrious or a better workman. If there was an aristocracy of fine houses it was not a bad sort of aristocracy. The furniture in one log house could not be far superior to that in other cabins nor could there be a much greater quantity of imported utensils, for the limited transportation facilities prevented settlers from bringing more than the barest necessities.

The settler usually walked all the way across the mountains with his goods on packhorses. Only the simplest tools could be brought. The ax was of course indispensable; so also was the mattock for grubbing, the hoe for cultivating and a small plow point for stirring the ground. The frow was necessary in splitting shingles for the roof of the house. An indispensable tool was the auger, which was used for boring holes for pins to fasten various parts of the house together in the total absence of nails of any kind. A few pots and pans and spoons and skillets and an oven made up the kitchen furniture. The spinning wheel, or such parts of it as could not easily be made in the woods, and a pair of wool-cards made the remainder of the furniture. There were also a supply of salt, some ammunition, seeds of various kinds including sometimes some flower seeds, and corn for bread in greater or less quantity, depending upon the amount of other goods brought and the number of pack horses.

Upon arriving on the land selected by the settler for his future home, he chose the best possible site for his cabin near a spring. He then began to fell trees nearby and cut them into the proper lengths for the side and end walls of his cabin. If there were neighbors, they would assist the newcomer in his house-raising, which would often be completed within a day or two. The first dwelling was extremely rude and hurriedly made. The logs composing it were untouched by the ax except near the ends where they were notched and roughly fitted together. The space between the logs was blocked up with short pieces of rails and small stones, and the wall was made tight by daubing all the crevices with mud. The chimney was built of rough stones half way up the end of the house, and for the remainder of the distance there was a crib of sticks. Both stones and sticks were cemented together with clay mortar.

After the first year the settler usually erected a more pretentious house of tulip poplar logs hewed square and notched so carefully that only a small crack was left between them.

The cabins of the pioneers reflected the conditions under which they lived. When John Hacker first came to Hacker's creek the whites and the Indians were at peace, and the first cabin he built is said to have been crudely built of logs, and with the cracks chinked with slabs and mud. The chimney stood at the end of the house on the outside. Later the houses were built of logs which had been nicely squared so that there were only small crevices to be filled up, and the chimney was placed on the **inside** of the house to prevent the Indians' tearing away the stones from the mud mortar which held them and gaining an entrance through the fireplace, which afforded a far larger opening in the log wall than the door. With the chimney on the inside of the house, the inhabitants were protected on all sides by a wall of logs which the Indians could destroy only by burning. Some of the great interior chimneys took up nearly all the space in one end of the cabin, and afforded openings for two fire places on the ground floor and one on the second floor. The third development was the fortress-like cabin which could readily stand a siege provided the defenders were numerous and active. A second floor was added, which was sometimes made to project about a foot beyond the walls of the lower rooms. From it the settlers conducted their principal defense. They were enabled to gain a wider field of fire, and at the same time shoot down upon any of the warriors who might attempt to force an entrance through the doorway or set fire to the house.

The door of the cabin was built especially strong so as to resist any attempt to force it open. It was composed of two thicknesses of heavy boards hewn out and fastened together diagonally with wooden pins. The door was hung on ponderous iron or wooden hinges that reached nearly across it. Space was sometimes left for windows, but heavy shutters were provided. The floor was made of puncheons, that is, thick boards split out of white oak trees in the same manner that shingles are made. They were afterwards smoothed with an ax or drawing knife. No nails were used in the construction of the houses except perhaps for the door. They were too scarce. The roof was held in place by timbers laid on the clapboards. Sometimes a log was placed on the roof just above the door, so fixed that it could be released from the inside upon the heads of Indians who tried to gain entrance. Secure within the walls of such houses the frontier settler could bid defiance to a small band of savages until help should arrive from the other settlers.

The early homes of the settlers were not uncomfortable. In summer the greased paper in the windows was taken out, and the air was free to circulate. In winter even with the greased paper in the windows the air was also free to circulate through the house, especially through the loft or second story where the boys of the family slept. The snow frequently sifted through the spaces between the rough shingles or was blown through the cracks in the end of the house. The deerskins under which they slept would be covered with snow in the morning after every snow storm. On the lower floor it was comfortable on the long winter evenings when the hickory logs roared in the huge fireplace. The family sat around the fire doing some simple tasks to while away the time. The hunting dog toasted his nose at the very edge of the fireplace in front of the group.

The furniture of the earliest settlers was extremely simple. Chairs were frequently only blocks of wood which had been hewn into shape. Beds consisted of poles laid upon a framework built in the corner of the house and supported by one block or post. As might be expected they were exceedingly uncomfortable. Deerskins were the coverings universally used. Bishop Francis Asbury wrote in his journal an account of a trip to Clarksburg, in 1788. After an all day's ride he came to a cabin where the settler agreed to take him in. All the beds were already occupied. "I lay along the floor on a few deerskins with the fleas," he says, and continued further, "Oh, how glad I should be for a clean plank to lie on, as preferable to most of the beds, and where the beds are in a bad state the floors are worse. This country will require much work to make it tolerable."

The tables consisted of two or three slabs with one end stuck into the crack between two logs and the other end supported on two legs in the middle of the cabin. Wooden platters and bowls were used almost to the exclusion of other ware, and the settlers drank from gourds. Pewter ware was considered unusually elegant. Most of the early blacksmith shops had copper moulds for making pewter spoons. China ware was slow in being adopted by the pioneers. It was many years before the old "ironstone china" made in England and considered elegant by the newcomers from east of the mountains found a place on the tables in the Trans-Alleghany region. It was too easily broken, and besides it dulled the hunting knives of the pioneers.

Cooking utensils were few and simple. The meat was generally prepared in a frying pan or roasted by placing a piece of meat on a sharp stick and holding it over the coals. A cooking pot for boiling vegetables and meat, a tea-kettle and a covered oven consisting of a large pan with an iron cover, completed the list of vessels found in most of the cabins. The food was nearly always well cooked. The pioneers delighted to have it said of them that they set good tables.

Corn and game were the staple articles of food for every frontier household. The venison was sometimes cured for emergency use in the winter by "jerking" it. The process consisted of cutting it into narrow strips and drying it before the fire. It was carried on every journey along with the johnny-cake, and eaten raw. Corn pone and johnny-cake were the only kinds of bread used for breakfast and dinner, and the children of the settlers who came from the centers of a higher civilization sometimes forgot the taste of wheat bread. It is related that once when John Hacker made a trip to the South Branch for salt and ammunition, he brought some biscuit on his return, and gave it to a small child. The child looked at it a moment, then evidently thinking it some strange toy, he began rolling it on the floor. It is said that the father wept to think that his children had been so long in the wilderness that they had forgotten the taste of bread. The evening meal was perhaps the simplest of all. The staple dish was mush and milk when it was possible to procure the milk. Mush was also eaten with maple syrup, bear's grease or gravy. Hog and hominy was a substantial dish. Vegetables and fruits seem to have been used only in the summer, fall and early winter, owing to the limited supply grown and the inroads made upon the stock of provisions by large families of hungry children. "Few settlers had land in cultivation more than sufficient to raise food for their own consumption," says an early resident of northwestern Virginia, writing of conditions in 1792. "Generally by spring there would be no bread in the country and people lived on greens, of spontaneous growth, which were daily gathered by women and children until they could raise vegetables. It was some time before we had tillable land enough to raise wheat. Butter we could not indulge in. with our maple sugar at six cents a pound and a few eggs was all we could market to get money to pay taxes."

Coffee and tea were unknown, and were not regarded with favor for many years. They were considered at first as slops which did not "stick to the ribs." Tea made from wintergreen or pennyroyal leaves, sassafras roots, and spicewood twigs was generally to be found on the tables. In the early spring when the sap in the maple trees was running, the settlers drank practically nothing but sugar water, which could be had within a few feet of the door of every cabin by boring a hole in a sugar maple tree, inserting a short length of sumac bush hollowed out for a spile, and setting a wooden trough under it.

Cane sugar was unknown in western Virginia for many years. The substitute was maple sugar. Many of the farmers left regular sugar groves where they built a temporary shack and made sugar during the nights of early spring. Candles were made from tallow either by dipping a string several times in melted fat or by pouring the fat in candle moulds which one settler in every community generally brought from the east. Soft soap was made from waste pieces of fat which were thrown into the "soap-grease barrel", and later reduced with the aid of crude potash leached from wood ashes. Matches were unknown anywhere, and fire was made by striking steel against flint and catching the sparks on a piece of "punk" or half-burned rag. When the housewife was in a hurry for a fire she usually sent one of the children to the nearest neighbor's to borrow a few blazing chunks. The family medicine chest was prepared from the products of the forest, and consisted of a great variety of herbs and roots. Poultices for gunshot wounds and burns were made from scraped potatoes, elm bark and the leaves of various plants. Snake bites were treated with a decoction of white plantain boiled in milk taken internally, and by applying salt and gunpowder and binding a portion of the snake to the wound.

The dress of the pioneers was extremely simple. The characteristic part was the loose hunting shirt, of linsey-woolsey, coarse linen or dressed deerskins. So universally was the hunting shirt worn by the settlers that the British called the Virginia bordermen "Shirt Men." Breeches were worn by the first comers, but the conditions of life in the woods caused a change in the costumes of the rangers not altogether to the liking of the female population. This was nothing more nor less than the adoption of the most characteristic portions of the Indian dress.

They early discarded breeches and lengthened the leggings until they reached far up the thigh and fastened to the belt by means of strings. The Indian breech clout, a piece of cloth a yard or more long and eight inches wide passed around the waist, one end passing under the belt in front, the other behind. The ends, which stuck out as flaps, were sometimes ornamented with a crude sort of embroidery. When the belt to which the clout was attached passed over the hunting shirt, the thighs and part of the hips were bare. A coonskin cap and moccasins of deerskin completed the costume. As a whole it was well adapted to life on the frontier, especially in summer. The leggings fitting closely did not impede the legs in running, and the shirt of wool or linen was as comfortable as can well be imagined. Jesse Hughes is said to have always worn a costume colored with bark of chestnut-oak. Attired in it he was as inconspicuous as he could possibly make himself against the forest background. In summer the settlers frequently appeared without their leggings, because they deemed them unnecessary. Long afterwards men working on farms wore only a very long shirt, claiming that it was the most comfortable garment that could be worn.

Shoes were very scarce, and they were a subject of comment whenever worn. Deerskin moccasins, which were universally worn by the pioneers, were perhaps the most comfortable covering ever devised for the feet in the summer. In winter they were very cold, on account of the absence of thick soles as well as the porous character of the skin. They were frequently lined with fur or dried leaves to keep the feet warm. In wet weather the pioneers claimed that the wearing of moccasins was "only a decent way of going barefooted." The spongy leather was no protection from rain or heavy dews no matter how heavily they had been greased with bear fat or mutton tallow. When the snow was melting few of the settlers cared to go outside their houses. The pioneers suffered much from rheumatism, which they believed was caused by wearing moccasins.

The dress of the women was simple and unadorned linsey-woolsey dresses with short skirts and numerous petticoats. Store dresses were practically unknown and calico could be had nowhere in the west. Very few jewels were worn for years after the first settlements, and the commonest toilet articles of milady's boudoir today were unknown to the women of a century and a half ago.

The settlers also adopted the arms of the Indian. The tomahawk and the scalping knife hung from the belt of every ranger, who understood thoroughly the use of both weapons in combat with the savages. The chief reliance of course, was on the rifle, with which every pioneer had had long practice, both in the hunt and in fighting Indians. The guns of the pioneers were principally smoothbore firelocks of rather large caliber, the bullets weighing about forty to the pound. Some, however, were of smaller caliber, like those sometimes found now among the old hunters who have become accustomed to the muzzle-loader and refuse to give it up for the breech loading rifle or shot gun. Most of the Indians were owners of guns, these having been furnished by traders, by the French at the time of the French and Indian wars, or by the English throughout the Revolution, from the time of the bloody year of the three sevens onward. The guns in the hands of the settlers were more accurate than those of the savages on account of the fact that the settlers regularly cleaned and oiled them, and the Indians only cleaned theirs by discharging them every few days. The firing arrangement of all flintlock guns was imperfect. Many on both sides met death because of the failure of their guns to discharge when the enemy was almost upon them. Sometimes the guns would "flash in the pan," and whenever there was a rain or a thick fog the priming was likely to be dampened, in which case the guns refused to work.

In carrying on warfare with the Indians the frontiersmen took scalps, just as the savages did, partly to show their prowess and partly because they knew that the red man without his scalp had no hope of entering the happy hunting-ground. They not only cut off his life but they doomed his soul. Some of the scouts also killed women and even children as well as the warriors. The old Indian fighters never forgot their early hatred for the Indian race. It is related of John Cutright, that long after the close of the Indian wars, when he was so old and infirm that he could walk only with the aid of his cane, he attempted to get his gun and shoot a friendly Indian whom he saw passing through the settlements. He had to be guarded closely by his family until after the Indian had left the vicinity.

The pioneers who braved the dangers of the forests and the Indians were men of the hardiest stamp. They were rude and ignorant for the most part, caring nothing for the finer sentiments and having little regard for anything which did not add to their physical well-being. Ability to draw a fine bead along the barrel of a gun was more highly regarded than any other accomplishment. "The people, many of them," said Francis Asbury, pioneer bishop of Methodism, "are of the boldest cast of adverturers, and with some the decencies of civilized society are scarcely regarded." They were a hard-fighting, hard-drinking, quarrelsome set for the most part.

The conditions of the wilderness did not suit the institution of negro slavery, which flourished east of the mountains. All the settlers were obliged to labor in clearing the fields, raising their crops, and making all the improvements on their farms. There was little other work the slaves could do. The settlers naturally objected to having slaves working in the fields, because their own work was the same, and they did not wish to be considered to be on the same level with them. The institution of slavery could not be profitable unless it were possible to export great quantities of agricultural produce; and this was impossible both because of the lack of adequate transportation facilities and the absence of large tracts of comparatively level land for tillage. Only a few slaves were brought with the first settlers. Colonel Lowther owned two, who worked in the fields and produced grain enough for himself and some of the neighbors. The Colonel was thus released from the necessity of working in the fields and could devote all his energies to the defense of the settlements, leading parties of rangers against the Indians and inspecting the posts throughout the frontier of northwestern Virginia. No slaves were brought to the district now included in Lewis County until later. The system of indenture was also in vogue as shown by a record of the court, 1785; "On motion of Richard Hocklin, servant of John P. Duvall, complaining against his master, in regard to wearing an iron collar its the opinion of the Court sd. collar be taken off by his master." There was a sort of system of apprenticeship from the earliest times. All the orphans were deemed to be wards of the state whom the county court ordered to be bound out by the overseers of the poor until they reached the legal age. The laws required that they should be "found" in return for the work they did, and they were usually allowed a sum of money when their term of service ended. There were many of these wards of the state among the scattered settlements of northwestern Virginia.

Unless a pioneer lived at a great distance from all other human habitations—something which occurred rarely—it cannot be said that he was lonely. There was always a community of interest in warding off Indian attacks, in helping to perform labor on different farms which could not be done by one man, and in countless other matters. The settlers of a neighborhood were continually being thrown together, and the neighborhood then included all the settled portions of what is now Lewis and Upshur counties and half of Harrison. When the dangers of an Indian attack or house-raisings did not throw the settlers together often enough, other social diversions were arranged. In the spring some popular, but lazy, farmer might hold a grubbing bee to which all the neighbors were invited for a day. Large numbers came, because they knew that the mistress of the house would have a fine dinner for the occasion and that there would be games and a dance after the day's work and play were over. In the fall there were corn huskings, which were always occasions of great gayety. Neighbors came for miles around, particularly young men and women. Preparations had previously been made for the husking by pulling off all the ears of corn from the stalks and hauling them to the appointed place where they were piled in a long row. Husking usually began just after dark by the light of the full moon and the huskers managed to make the job last until nearly morning. Sometimes a contest was arranged in which two good huskers chose sides and divided the pile in half. Then followed a good-natured race to see which side could finish first. The work was likely to be interrupted whenever a young man found a red ear, because immemorial custom of the frontier gave him the right to kiss the prettiest girl present.

There were also many informal gatherings of neighbors. Occasionally there was a traveler who wanted to stay all night. The settlers were most hospitable and gave him his food and a place to sleep in return for gossip of the frontier or of the regions east of the mountains whence all had come.

The greatest social occasions among the settlers were the weddings. There was no labor of log-rolling or house-raising or other hard work in connection with them, and they attracted universal interest. On the morning of the day set for the ceremony all the friends of the groom met at his father's house to escort him to the home of the bride's parents. They formed a procession in double file along the trail, all attired in their best and riding their best horses. Frequently their progress would be interrupted by grapevines tied across the path as a joke or through the ill will of some neighbor who had not been invited to the wedding. The time was taken up with good-natured banter and songs and yells and perhaps a race for "Black Betty," a bottle of whiskey or rum.

The marriage ceremony was performed by a preacher, if there were one in the settlement, if not, arrangements were made to call in someone who had been designated by the county court to officiate. After the ceremony the guests were seated at the table to eat the most sumptuous meal which it was possible for the housewife of the frontier to prepare. Meats and vegetables were cooked in every known way, and crowded upon the table until it would hold no more. The dearth of pewterware made no difference to the guests. They were accustomed to eat with their hunting knives.

After the dinner the festivities commenced. It was not long until dancing commenced, and the couples were soon engaged in three or four-handed reels or in square sets and jigs to the tune of "The West Fork River." The dancing continued until morning, and if any couple became tired and attempted to hide from the others they were hunted up and compelled to dance while the fiddler played "Hold on Till Tomorrow Morning." During the night the spirits of the party were kept up by the frequent passing of "Black Betty." The feasting and dancing frequently continued for several days until all concerned were too exhausted to continue further.

The earliest settlers were without schools. The children had to depend for an education upon what their parents or older brothers and sisters could teach them. There are traditions that William Powers, after his coming to the West Fork valley in 1785, taught a term of school at West's fort. The Rev. John Mitchell also gave the children instruction in the rudiments of the three R's while he was engaged in the double duty of preaching the Gospel in the wilderness and helping to keep the Indians from the gates of West's fort. Both these schools were irregular and the term was short. Teachers could not always be found nor could the settlers always be induced to subscribe enough to employ a teacher. The result was that many years later the records of Lewis County show the signatures of many of the largest landholders and most important citizens made with a cross and witnessed.

The state government early took action to light the torch of learning in the hills and dales west of the mountains. The General Assembly in 1787 chartered the Randolph academy, which should in a sense take the place of William and Mary college for the youth of the counties of Ohio, Monongalia, Harrison and Randolph. John P. Duvall, George Jackson, John Powers, Robert Maxwell and John Jackson were appointed trustees of the institution with power to select the most eligible site within the counties, to make contracts for the erection of buildings, and to employ teachers and act as the general board of management.

The General Assembly provided for the support of the academy one-sixth of the surveyor's fees of the four counties, which had formerly been paid for the support of William and Mary college in Virginia. The trustees designated Clarksburg as the most eligible location for the academy, and in 1793 they let the contract for the first building. A short time afterward the work of construction started. Many students took advantage of the opportunity to secure an education within the walls of Randolph academy, among whom were many young men who later were numbered among the most prominent citizens of Lewis County.

The religious interests of the pioneers were not overlooked. Hardly were the first settlements made until Baptist and Methodist itinerant preachers followed the trails that had been made and attempted to establish churches in the virgin soil of the new settlements. The founding of churches in some places antedated the establishment of that other influence of civilization, orderly government. Baptist preachers and Methodist circuit riders braved all the perils of the wilderness to bring their message to the benighted people on the frontier. Before the close of the Revolution the Methodists had established classes at various places in the Trans-Alleghany district. Classes were in existence by 1781 in the West Fork Valley. There was a flourishing class near Richards' fort under the leadership of Moses Ellsworth. A society was organized at John Hacker's on Hacker's creek as early as 1786, probably by Rev. John Mitchell, but no church was erected for several years afterwards. The Rev. Henry Smith, who visited the region in 1794, found a good society there. The Rev. Joseph Cheuvront, a Frenchman, took up his residence near the mouth of Hacker's creek shortly afterward and was licensed to celebrate the rites of matrimony in 1790. He was regarded as a very eloquent preacher by the people of the community, and even the circuit rider confessed that he "could preach all around him." Henry McWhorter, who came to McKinney's run in 1790, soon became one of the leading members of the Hacker's creek Methodist society. It is said that he was a member of the Methodist church for sixty years and a class leader for fifty. Under his leadership the class grew and prospered. Regular preaching services were begun early in the last decade of the eighteenth century and have been continued without serious interruption until the present time. The number of Methodist societies in the upper West Fork valley was so great that in 1788 Bishop Asbury came to Clarksburg to hold a quarterly meeting, where he preached to an audience of about seven hundred people. In the letters and journals of some of the old circuit riders are to be found interesting glimpses of the pioneer settlements. The Rev. Henry Smith came to the Clarksburg circuit in 1784 and held a meeting at the house of Joseph Bonnett. Of his congregation he says: "The people came to this meeting from four or five miles around. * * * They were all backwoods people and came to the meeting in backwoods style, all on foot, a considerable congregation. I looked around and saw an old man who had shoes on his feet. The preacher wore Indian moccasins. Every man, woman and child besides was barefooted. The old women had on what we called then short gowns, and the rest had neither short nor long gowns. This was a novel sight for me for a Sunday congregation. I soon found if there were no shoes and fine dresses in the congregation there were attentive hearers and feeling hearts. In meeting the class I heard the same humble loving religious experience that I had often heard in better dressed societies. If this scene did not make a backwoods man of me outright, it at least reconciled me to the problem and I felt happy among them." At "Brother Stortze's" not far from the West's fort, the new preacher saw "men coming to meeting with rifles on their shoulders, guarding their families, then setting their guns in a corner of the house until after the meeting, and returning in the same order." At West's fort, "before I had got to sleep the dogs raved at a terrific rate. I did not know that I was in any danger; but the Indians having but a little while before this been through the country and done mischief, and this being a frontier house, I did not feel myself secure in my exposed situation."

Not all the people of northwestern Virginia received the preachers as kindly as these earlier settlers of Hacker's creek. Bishop Asbury says that after he and a companion had ridden all day "near midnight we stopped at A's, who hissed his dogs on us."

As to the character of the people, he says: "On the one hand savage warfare teaches them to be cruel, and on the other the teaching of Antinomians poisons them with errors in doctrine. Good moralists they are not, and good Christians they can not be unless they are better taught."

The Baptists were on the field about the same time as the Methodists and their preachers likewise travelled through the wilderness and organized churches. There was a Baptist congregation at Buckhannon in 1786, and other societies were soon organized throughout the Trans-Alleghany. Bishop Asbury's quarterly conference at Clarksburg was held in "a long close room belonging to the Baptists." In 1790 a deed is recorded by which the Baptists of Hopewell meeting-house secured possession of a lot in Clarksburg for a burial ground. There was no Baptist church established in what is now Lewis County until 1805, but their preachers came frequently to the neighborhood. Jacob Cozad, who lived not far from the present site of Berlin, was licensed as a preacher of the Baptist church in 1797.

CHAPTER X.

THE EXTENSION OF SETTLEMENT
SKIN CREEK

The treaty of Greenville, 1795, removed the last barrier to the coming of settlers in large numbers. It was evident that the treaty must make the Ohio river barrier permanent. Settlers had gone into the Northwest Territory in large numbers before the close of the Indian wars, and a tremendous emigration was bound to follow the conclusion of peace. A wide barrier of settlements had been interposed between northwestern Virginia and the Indians. For a half century thereafter the current of life on the West Fork was to be as calm and unruffled as the current of that sluggish stream.

There was an almost immediate shifting of population. The old Indian hunters found the unaccustomed life of quiet too monotonous. Jesse Hughes disposed of his farm at the mouth of Jesse's run and moved far to the west, locating among the miasmatic swamps of the Wabash, so that he could maintain contact with the Indians. His health was affected by the change, and after wandering about uncertainly for some time he finally returned to the hills of western Virginia. He built his cabin in what is now Jackson County. By a strange freak of fortune he who had done so much to wrest the land from the savages and to make conditions of life endurable, found himself in his old age without an acre to call his own, the tract on which he had settled having been included in a large survey before he left Hacker's creek. John Radcliff and Elias Hughes followed close upon the footsteps of the Indians, and became the first settlers in Licking County, in central Ohio. "They lived mainly by hunting," says the his-

-torian of Licking County, "raising, however, a little corn, the cultivation of which was left, in great measure, to their wives."

The lands of the scouts and the Indian hunters were quickly filled with permanent settlers who had come to western Virginia seeking new homes. The new settlers were different in many ways from the pioneer hunter-scout-farmer. If they were less expert with the rifle, they were more skilled with the ax; if they procured less venison for their families, they furnished a greater variety of domestic meat and vegetables; and if they were less bold in trailing Indians, they were at least unafraid of the task of clearing their lands, tending their crops and caring for their live stock. Many of the new comers had been men of property in the east, who did not wish to risk their all by coming to the Trans-Alleghany country while the Indians endangered the very existence of the settlements. The stake was too great. Men with property usually waited until conditions became tranquil before moving west.

Beginning about 1797 there was a rush of settlers to the hills of the upper West Fork. Hacker's creek and Stone Coal creek received most of them, but others took up their abodes on Freeman's creek, Little Skin creek, Sand fork of the West Fork, and the valley of the river all the way from the mouth of Hacker's creek to the forks of the river. The movement was profoundly influenced by conditions across the Ohio river. There the national government owned the land, and was selling it to the settlers with a clear title and at lower cost than they could buy the lands in Virginia from speculators. The lands of Ohio were considered superior in fertility, and settlers went there. That part of the Northwest Territory now included in the state of Ohio was far more quickly settled than Virginia. The comparatively poor bottom lands on the Ohio side of the river were settled long before the more fertile lands just across the river in Virginia. Perhaps it was because many of the emigrants wanted to get away from the institution of slavery; perhaps the Ohio country was better advertised and settlers went there because others were going. Many of the best lands in western Virginia were passed by carelessly by the emigrants in their rush to gain the choice tracts in the Northwest Territory. Practically the whole of continental United States was settled before the land-hungry multitude turned their attention to the hills of West Virginia and found the country extremely well adapted for raising live stock. Lewis County should have been settled faster, and would perhaps have been settled by more progressive people if it had not been for the rush to Ohio. Some of the settlers in the West Fork valley were merely transients who had started to Ohio, but who had stopped for a season in order to make a crop.

Whatever land had escaped the speculators in the period immediately preceding the close of the Indian wars was patented, and the surveys made and recorded. Among the most important of the new surveys was one issued in 1797 for 100,000 acres on the West Fork and Little Kanawha rivers to Benjamin Haskell and William Warren. David Lockwood took out 40,000 acres lying on Sand fork of Kanawha, partly in Gilmer, partly in Lewis. The Reed and Ford survey containing 27,000 acres was also made. It began near the head of Rush run and extended southwestwardly. Upon the failure of the expected rush of immigration to materialize, the original owners allowed the title to lapse through non-payment of taxes, and it afterwards became a part of the Camden-Bailey-Camden estates, and eventually passed into the hands of Irish settlers. Most of these surveys were made by the famous surveyor, Henry Jackson.

The first section where actual settlements were made besides those maintained under the shadow of West's fort were on Stone Coal creek, the first Lewis County stream discovered and explored by white men. Several settlements had been made in that beautiful valley, which is reputed to be perhaps the best farming section of the county, but the settlers had been forced to abandon their claims during the Indian wars. The noteworthy exceptions were John Schoolcraft, who had established himself on Schoolcraft's run—now Smith's run, and Henry Flesher, at the mouth of the stream.

After the treaty of Greenville the lands filled up very fast. Abner Abbott settled near the head of the creek not far from the present Lewis-Upshur line, about the year 1798. George Sommers came immediately afterwards and settled just below him. Just above the present site of Gaston, in perhaps the most beautiful section of all the Stone Coal valley, John and Benjamin Taylor built their humble cabins about the year 1797. John Curtis settled on the site of Gaston and Henry Hardman located his claim near the forks of the creek. James Paines was also one of the earlier settlers in the upper valley of Stone Coal.

On the lower course of the stream no new settlements appear to have been made for several years. Schoolcraft's run had become so thoroughly peopled with Smiths by the year 1805 that the name was changed to Smith's run. Isaac and William Smith came in the last years of the century and took up tracts of land on the run, and perhaps purchased the claim of John Schoolcraft. In 1805 Mark Smith moved his household goods from his cabin near the mouth of Freeman's creek, where he had settled the year before, and also settled on Smith's run.

By 1808 the Stone Coal settlement had become numerous enough to justify the establishment of a mill on the upper course of the stream. George Bush secured the necessary machinery and began grinding corn on the later site of Gaston. The village which grew up around the mill was known locally as Bush's Mills for the next eighty years. Henry Curtis acquired possession of the mill in 1812 or 1813 and made many improvements. In 1814 he added to his grist mill the first sawmill on the creek. It consisted of a rude sash saw run by water power, and, needless to say, the capacity of the mill was limited. Most of the earlier sawmills could not saw large logs, and most owners objected to sawing any but soft woods like tulip poplar. A still was in existence at about the same time a little farther down the creek.

The community at first had to depend upon the schools established in the Hacker's creek valley. Several young men in turn tried their skill at teaching with rather indifferent success. In 1815 Henry Hardman taught a select school near the forks of the creek. It resulted in the training of several young men who afterwards taught school in the valley. Bush's mills became rather prominent as an educational center in the early history of the county.

The Rev. John Mitchell, first preacher in Lewis County, came to Stone Coal creek before the settlement had fairly started and held meetings in the homes of some of the pioneers. Soon services were held at regular intervals by the Rev. Mitchell and the circuit preachers. A class was formed, and a log church erected a little later by the Methodists. The Presbyterians also established a church on the creek at a later date under the leadership of the French creek pastor.

Across the ridge to the south of Stone Coal lies a fertile territory drained by Skin creek. It also attracted considerable immigration within a few years after the treaty of peace. Skin creek was first explored by John Hacker in 1769 while on his famous buffalo hunt. Later it was a famous hunting ground for parties from Hacker's creek, so that the desirability of the land was well known. Only the danger to such an isolated settlement from war parties kept the pioneers from going there. There is fairly good evidence for the statement that Alexander Hacker settled at the Ward place (now the Jewell farm) on Big Skin creek about the year 1778, but he abandoned his settlement.

On the tomahawk claim made by John Hacker at the mouth of Curtis run on Little Skin creek, his son Jonathan Hacker settled in 1796. Young Hacker soon became tired of the location and moved to another of his father's tomahawk improvements at the mouth of Crane Camp run; but learning that the land had already been surveyed as a part of a large tract, he soon abandoned his cabin and returned to Hacker's creek. His farm at the mouth of Curtis run had been purchased by the Rev. John Hardman, the mechanical genius of the new settlement. He immediately proceeded to establish a small mill, which was far superior to the tin grater—when there was water to flow over the dam. Hardman is said to have lacked patience to watch the "corn-cracker" mill, and he sold it to Rev. Anthony Spaur, who hailed from Holland. Hardman moved to a tract about two miles farther up the creek. Henry Bott settled on one of the best locations on the creek near where the road leaves the valley to pass over the low gap to Hall's run. Felix Albert, who came a little later, made his settlement near the mouth of Blacklick run. He later sold out to John Clark. William Peterson and John Helmick settled on tracts farther up the stream. All these settlements were made probably within five or six years after the close of the Indian wars. Louis Bonnett, one of the garrison at Flesher's station during the last years of the Indian wars, and a younger brother, Philip, came to Skin creek early in the century. They remained there long enough to rear their families and then left for the cheaper lands farther west. Nicholas Linger came from Germany about 1815 and made his settlement on Little Skin creek. A family of Stalnakers from Randolph County, natives of Holland, also came very early. The Bonnetts were Dutch also and never wholly mastered the English language. Before the coming of the Chidesters and the Corathers, the settlement was overwhelmingly Dutch. By the time of the formation of Lewis County in 1816, Little Skin creek was the most compact settlement between Stone Coal creek and the Great Kanawha river. It was also a settlement of progressive, intelligent pioneers. It is said that every resident of the stream could read and write. In order that the gift of learning should not die out, a school was arranged almost as soon as there were settlements. The first school of Little Skin creek was taught by Anthony Spaur, who, according to one who knew him, "was a man of Herculean strength and stentorian voice." Like all the teachers of his time he was a strict disciplinarian. Michael G. Bush, who followed "Old Father Spaur", was one of the best teachers of Lewis County, and later he became one of the most active men in establishing schools who lived in the county before the Civil war. He had had the advantages of one or more terms of school under Isaac Morrison, one of the leading educators of northwestern Virginia, and he possessed the gift of imparting his knowledge to his pupils. Two very successful teachers were graduated from Bush's school—Henry D. Hardman, who taught the first schol on Big Skin creek, and Daniel R. Helmick, who succeeded to the school on Little Skin creek. He was in turn succeeded by George R. Marsh.

As in the case of the Stone Coal settlement, the Rev. John Mitchell was early in the field preaching to the people of the district On account of the diversity of creeds represented and the number of ministers on the creek, it was impossible to organize a church until 1823. The erection of a church building came much later.

Big Skin creek, though not as thickly settled as the other fork, contained the nucleus of a future great community in the half dozen families who settled there in the first two decades of the nineteenth century. On the Ward place—abandoned homestead of the pioneer Alexander Hacker—Richard Johnson built his cabin just below the mouth of Charles run in 1797 or 1798. His son John is said to have been the first white child born on the creek. Spencer Marsh lived just above the present site of Vandalia. The first settler on the present site of the village is said to have been Peter Bonnett who, with his brothers, were members of the first garrison at Flesher's station. His cabin stood just across the creek from the site of the village church. About 1820 David Hall came to the valley and took up the land upon which most of the village was later laid out. His brother Jonathan settled on Hughes fork, near the site of the camping ground of the deer hunters who took part in the famous Skin Creek hunt. Henry Wheeler was the first settler on Wheeler's fork, which empties into the creek just above Vandalia. William Wilson, in 1802, entered a homestead on the right fork of Skin creek.

An Indian trail up Big Skin creek was at first the only means which the settlers had of gaining access to the outside world. Some time before 1813 a road was opened through the settlement in consequence of the activity at the Haymond salt works on Salt Lick creek. Over the winding trail from the valley of the Buckhannon came not only people in search of salt, but also many settlers on Big Skin creek.

Near the mouth of Skin creek few settlements were made for nearly fifty years. Brownsville had no existence for nearly eighty years after the settlements on the creek above it. Joseph Alkire is said to have settled on or near the present site of the town shortly after the close of the Indian wars. He was followed by Stephen Coburn, who lived either on the West Fork river or a short distance up Skin creek. These were the only settlements above Bendale on the river for a distance of ten or twelve miles. Others came and spent a few years on the river, but, except in the more favored locations the settlements were not permanent. The narrow bottoms which were alone fit for tillage were soon worn out, and the homesteaders moved to more congenial locations.

CHAPTER XI.

THE COLLINS SETTLEMENT

Collins Settlement, the most southern district in the county, shows the greatest diversity in topography. The valley of the West Fork from its source to where it passes out of the district is equal in fertlity to any section of the county. The bottoms are level and well adapted to cultivation. It is one of the garden spots of West Virginia. On the other hand, in the extreme southern part of the district there are deep, narrow valleys and towering mountains. The surface is not adapted for anything but stock raising except in the narrow bottoms and on the summits of the mountains, where it is possible in places to raise corn. The crop from the hilltops is largely brought to the valleys below on wires. On account of the magnificent crops produced in the upper valley, it was formerly known as "Egypt"; and from the number of famous men who are natives of the district, it has sometimes been called by the high-flown title "The Athens of West Virginia." During the Civil war it was known as "Dixie".

The excellent quality of the land was known to the Hacker's creek settlers at a very early date. John Hacker's war of revenge against the buffaloes in 1769 led him through the district from one end to the other, and he located two claims—hunter's camps—within the boundaries of Collins Settlement. One was at the mouth of Crane Camp run, now on the Davisson farm at Crawford, and the other on Hacker's Camp run in the "Shoestring". Hacker's oldest son Jonathan, to whom he gave these claims, left the one on Little Skin creek to settle on Crane Camp. His abandoned cabin, reputed to be haunted by ghosts, stood on the site for many years, and furnished shelter for numerous hunting parties. The lower course of the West Fork was thoroughly explored by 1774 by Jesse Hughes, John P. Duvall and others.

That the upper valley of the West Fork was not permanently settled following the explorations is due to the Indian wars. Among the records of land certificates granted in 1781 is one to Joseph Hall "on the east side of the west branch of the Monongahela river to include his settlement made thereon in 1777." At the same time Jacob Bush received a certificate for "400 acres on the West Fork about two miles below the main fork of said river to include his improvement made thereon in 1777." The latter tract was probably above Abram's run. No trace of the settlement has been found, nor is the nature of the "improvement" known. He evidently never returned after the Indian wars to occupy it. John Pierce Duvall, whose claims were strategically located all through Lewis and Harrison counties with a view to their later importance as town sites, bought out two early settlers in the district. One was at the Indian carrying place, now Arnold, near the lowest point in the divide between the West Fork and the Little Kanawha rivers, to include a settlement in 1776, and the other at the forks of the West Fork, to include a corn right dating back to the same year. It may well be doubted whether there were four acres cleared and planted in corn above Walkersville by 1776, which would have given the right to the 400 acres of land included in the grant. John P. Duvall was one of the three commissioners to adjust disputes and issue certificates. The land opposite Walkersville on the south side of the forks of the river was not surveyed until 1820.

By far the most important tract of land in the history of the district was that patented by Colonel George Jackson. It included five thousand acres in the valley of the West Fork lying between the two town sites of John P. Duvall. In the middle of the tract he selected a plot of ground on a high bottom near a good ford of the river where later the future town of Jacksonville was to be located. There was at that time not a single settler in the upper valley of the West Fork. Years afterward he confirmed the location of the town in a deed granted to his daughter Mrs. Prudence Arnold.

In order to bring about the settlement of this land as soon as possible and to encourage further settlements in the region round about his tracts, Colonel Jackson agreed to donate to some Irish settlers of the South Branch valley small tracts of land if they would make settlements here and stay until the settlement became permanent. They were also to mark a bridle path from their settlement to the Flesher settlement at the mouth of Stone Coal creek. The offer was accepted by several families.

John Collins and his three sons, Jacob, Cornelius and Isaac, were the first permanent settlers in the district. They brought all their worldly possessions to the upper West Fork on packhorses in the winter of 1797-98, and selected the broad bottom facing the rising sun which is now part of the George I. Davisson farm about one mile south of Jacksonville. The first cabin was located on the right side of the river and not far northeast of the sugar orchard. The Collins' were industrious and cleared a considerable portion of the land in the immediate vicinity of their homes. They remained in their original location until after the formation of Lewis County when they sought a more favorable situation in the west.

Captain James Keith and Dan T. Turvey emigrated to the same region immediately after the Collins settlement was established. Captain Keith's cabin stood on the south side of Calamus hollow a short distance above Jacksonville. He had the reputation of being by far the best hunter in all that section, averaging, it is said, fifteen or twenty deer a week during the hunting season. He was also one of the largest fruit growers in the

West Fork valley, and years afterwards his orchard was resorted to by the people of the neighborhood.

In 1799 a man named Shoulders settled at the forks of the river. The next year the Bennetts came over the old Seneca trail from the upper Potomac valley. William Bennett located on Colonel Jackson's land just below the tract selected by Shoulders. Abram Bennett located on Abram's run, which took its name from its first settler. Joseph Bennett located on the stream a little later. Jacob Bennett made his settlement farther up the Right Fork on Leatherbark run. The Bennetts were fruit growers and propagated apples from seeds which they had brought with them from the Potomac valley. Captain James Keith married a daughter of William Bennett, and doubtless received as part of her dowry the apple seeds from which grew his famous orchard. The Bennetts have continued to the present time to occupy the ancestral farm of William Bennett. He died in 1857, and his tombstone in Long Point cemetery states that "he lived 29,780 days, without guile and without reproach, progenitor of 248 descendants."

One of the most important settlements on the Jackson tract was that made by Rev. Henry Camden in 1804. His cabin stood a short distance west of Jacksonville where Camden hollow debouches into the valley of the river. Here he cleared the high bottom, reared a large family, and was a leader in the community for years. He was one of the earliest preachers on the Lewis circuit of the Methodist Episcopal church which at first embraced appointments all the way from Burnersville in Barbour County to Salt Lick creek in Braxton. The Camdens remained there for many years. The old Camden-Collins cemetery containing the graves of the pioneers of the district, unmarked save for rough flagstones, is on the hillside above the site of the Keith house.

Shortly after the Rev. Camden located in the valley, John Byrne settled on the right bank of the river about one mile below Walkersville. Robert Crawford built his cabin in the broad meadow near the mouth of Indian Cap run in 1815. The Bennetts, Crawford and the Camdens became the mainstays of one of the most important Methodist congregations in the Monongahela valley at an early date. Jesse Cunningham came about the same time as Crawford and settled on Abram's run. Elijah Arnold, who married Colonel Jackson's daughter, settled on the town site of Jacksonville in 1830. The old manor house is still standing, and is occupied as a summer home by Mrs. Mary A. Edmiston, a great-granddaughter of Colonel Jackson.

On John Pierce Duvall's town site at the Indian Carrying place, George T. Duvall settled at an early date. He is supposed to have been a son of Colonel Duvall.

On Sand fork of the West Fork, the first settlement appears to have been made by Samuel Wilson, near the mouth of Sammy's run. His cabin stood where John Rollyson formerly lived. He came from Staunton, and some of his descendants bear a marked resemblance to President Wilson. He did not continue long on Sand fork, but moved to the Right fork of West Fork. The Rev. George I. Marsh settled farther up Sand fork also at a very early date. Below the mouth of Sammy's run the McCrays had made their settlement before 1820.

For years after the Collins Settlement became permanent and prosperous, the pioneers on the upper West Fork were cut off from all the other settlements by a wall of primeval forest. Their nearest neighbors were on Salt Lick creek, at the Ward place on Skin creek, and at Weston. The valley below Arnold was not occupied for a distance of ten miles. In 1808, Abner Mitchell located about one mile below the site of the village of Roanoke. He was for years the only settler on the river from George Duvall's to the mouth of Skin creek.

The bridle path which had been blazed by the Collins' continued in use for many years without improvement. It was occasionally followed by the residents of the older settlements on their trips to Haymond's salt works· The trail from the Buckhannon river settlement to the same place entered Collins settlement from Skin creek and again plunged into the wilds. The West Fork river in its upper reaches was far too small to consider building flat boats, and the problem of transportation for the Collins settlement remained for a future generation to solve.

Reference has already been made to the Methodist society which had been organized in the Collins settlement, and which continued for years to prosper under the guidance of the Rev. Camden. Apparently no representative of other sects entered the valley of the upper Fork until later, and even at the present time the churches of other denominations are few and far between, so strong is the hold of the Methodists there.

The early progress of education in the Collins settlement is unknown. Unfortunately the early traditions have failed to hand down the location of school houses and the names of the early teachers who helped to produce coming leaders of the state—a United States senator, jurists, legislators, constitution makers, empire builders, capitalists, educators and officials of the nation and of the state. William Schoolcraft, who lived on the upper West Fork at an early date, is said to have been a "noted school teacher and hunter." Further than the one entry the record is blank.

CHAPTER XII.

FREEMAN'S CREEK DISTRICT

Freeman's Creek district is the largest in the county, the richest by far, and has the greatest population. The soil is very fertile, though, aside from the West Fork river bottoms, there is a less proportion of tillable land in the district than in any of the other districts with the exception of Court House. The farmers are prosperous, and better farming methods are employed than in most other sections. The district does not represent as homogenous a territory as most of the others, since about three-fifths of the territory is drained by Freeman's creek, Polk creek, McCann's run and the southern hollows of Kincheloe creek, all of which are tributaries of the West Fork; and the other two-fifths lies on Fink creek, Alum fork and other tributaries of Leading creek. There is an overflow of the Irish settlements from Sand Fork and its tributaries in the southwestern portion of the district.

The derivation of the name of the creek is uncertain, but it was evidently named for some early explorer. Lieutenant Edward Freeman, who served in Captain Booth's company of militia at the beginning of the Revolution, was one of the earliest comers to the upper West Fork valley, and the stream was probably named for him.

Reference has already been made to many of the homesteads which were taken out in 1781. The most important of them is the town site of John P. Duvall at the forks of the creek, and the patents on Gee Lick run. Land on Horse run was originally granted to Alexander West, the scout. By 1808, George Arnold was a large landholder, in partnership with John P. Duvall. He added to the plot owned by Duvall in the forks of the creek, and took up other tracts in various parts of the district, so that the possessions of Duvall and Arnold bear a somewhat similar relation in the later settlement of the district to those of Col. George Jackson in the Collins settlement. James Arnold was also a large landholder on Freeman's creek and Polk creek at a somewhat later date. Owing to the number and scattered locations of homesteads taken up before the close of the Revolution, unbroken tracts of thousands of acres were not numerous.

Mention has already been made of the settlements of Edward Hughes and Edmund Radcliff near the mouth of McCann's run, and of the settlement made by Patrick McCann about 1785. He was followed a little later by Daniel McCann, and these last named settlers continued to live in the community for several years. Following the close of the Indian wars Richard Hall, progenitor of one branch of the numerous Hall family in Lewis County, built his home on McCann's run. His brother-in-law Smith Gibson settled on the farm now owned by George Neely.

The first permanent settlement on Freeman's creek is supposed to have been that of John Runyon at the mouth of the stream. Adam and John Bush took up homesteads before 1790 not far above the settlement of Runyon where they successfully repulsed an Indian raid. On the future site of Freemansburg George Bush took up his residence in 1790. He industriously cleared the forest around his cabin, took up adjacent lands, purchased the rights of other homesteaders who had become discouraged, and eventually became the owner of one of the most extensive estates in the county. The next resident of the vicinity is supposed to have been Jacob Schoolcraft who settled on the Alexander West patent at the mouth of Horse run. John Smith and Robert Hitt came to Horse run soon afterwards, and they were followed in their turn by William McKinley, who settled on a branch of the stream not far from the site of Freemansburg.

Soon after the last of the Indian raids, George Woofter and Jonathan Woofter moved to the valley. The former settled on Rush run, and the latter on the Solomon White farm on the left fork of Freeman's creek. Their descendants have done much in the later development of the western part of the district. Carr Bailey moved from the Bailey settlement which later became Westfield to a tract which he purchased on Rush run. Shortly afterwards the land near the forks of Freeman's creek was settled by John and William White. Hezekiah Tharp located about a mile below their settlement very early in the nineteenth century. In later years he built a mill on his farm at which all the grinding for the settlers on the creek was done for many years. The mill was afterwards sold, and Tharp sought a home in the west. The Norrises are thought to have come to Freeman's creek about the year 1800. Richard Norris settled on the south bank of the creek about one-half mile above the lower bridge across the stream, and John Norris became the first settler on Millstone run.

One of the first settlers on Gee Lick run was Charles Fisher, whose cabin stood near the forks of the stream where Minor Lough now lives. John Waggoner located about one mile further up the creek on what is now the Lot Hall farm, also at an early date. One of his neighbors was a man named Nair. Much of the land on Gee Lick soon passed into the hands of Paulser Butcher, whose children and grandchildren occupied most of the attractive farms on the lower course of the stream.

The first religious services on Freeman's creek were held at the home of George Woofter on Rush run by Rev. John Davis, an intinerant preacher of the Baptist church. The date must have been at the very beginning of the century. After the establishment of the Broad run Baptist church, its pastors occasionally came to upper Freeman's creek to hold services. Interest grew, and the community became a regular preaching place. A church was organized in 1820—the first offspring in Lewis County of the Broad Run Baptist church—by the Rev. John J. Waldo. Among the first members were Carr Bailey and wife, George Woofter and wife, Mrs. Jennie Woofter, John White and wife, James Cox and wife, Isaac Woofter and Mrs. Rachel White. The church, under a succession of pastors of more than ordinary ability, has expanded to meet the needs of the community. The Bible school which has always been a strongly emphasized feature of the work of the church, has developed until now it is regarded as the best organized country Sunday school in the state.

The first school of which there is any tradition was taught in an abandoned log cabin on the Bush estate near Freemansburg about the year 1818.

The lands of Polk creek were not occupied so early as those on Freeman's creek on account of the well traveled Indian trail which followed the course of the stream. The name was given to it on account of the fact that an early explorer found a pokestalk growing in the forks of a sycamore tree near the mouth of the creek. The spelling was changed to its present form in the early 'thirties. After the close of the Indian wars the land on the lower course of the stream gradually came into possession of the Fleshers, whose descendants continued to occupy it for many years. Leonard Burkhammer settled on a claim about two miles from the mouth of the stream about the year 1800. Adam Hoover, who came at a somewhat later date, became the first settler on Dry Fork. On the present site of Camden, John Nicholes built his cabin early in the last century. It became an important stopping place for travelers to and from the Leading creek country in after years. The greater portion of the lands on the creek were undeveloped for many years on account of the holdings of great landowners who allowed it to lie idle. John Connelly built a small water-power mill about one mile above the mouth of the stream which was in existence by about 1816, but its owner discontinued it not long after the completion of the more modern mill at Weston.

Below the mouth of Polk creek on the West Fork river, Paulser Butcher, later an important citizen of the community, established himself about the time of the treaty of Greenville. Little is known of his parentage or family connections. He was evidently an orphan, and after the customs of the time he had been bound out to Henry Flesher, the pioneer of Weston, until he reached his majority. He early showed a marked degree of business ability. Before his indenture had expired he took out a homestead for himself in the valley below Weston, and upon reaching his majority he built his house on the opposite side of the river and a little below the mouth of Maxwell's run. He improved the land to some extent by clearing it and planting an orchard of peach and apple trees, but he soon found an easier means of increasing his wealth. He brought a thirty-gallon copper still across the mountains from the vicinity of Richmond by packhorse and set it up on his farm. Here, according to tradition, he made the first peach brandy produced west of the Alleghanies. He also made whiskey from corn and rye which were grown on his farm or bought from his neighbors. He also made liquor for the farmers for miles around on the shares, taking a reasonable toll. The demand for the product of the still was very great. The owner grew wealthy and added most of the lands in the vicinity to his farm. He was able to give a large farm to each of his sons and a respectable dowry with each of his daughters.

Just below the mouth of Freeman's creek was another landholder with estates equal to those of a feudal baron. Edward Jackson, who had attained the rank of colonel in the Virginia army, and whose deeds as an Indian fighter are only less than those of his distinguished brother Colonel George Jackson, acquired title to the lands at the mouth of Freeman's creek, and settled there after the close of the Indian wars. In 1808 he built a combined grist and sawmill just below the mouth of Freeman's creek, which has become famous from its associations with the boyhood days of Stonewall Jackson. The mill was long regarded as being one of the best in the county. The supply of raw material to keep it in operation came from the numerous farms round about and from the estate which included it. The slaves of the proprietor raised corn and wheat in the broad bottoms in the summer season and cut poplar logs in the winter.

Colonel Edward Jackson was one of the most prominent surveyors in the history of Lewis County, and his profession often took him far from his estate. Almost from the first the management of the mill was in the hands of Cummings Jackson, and within a short time he acquired possession of it. The new owner added to the family possessions until his estate included fifteen hundred acres. Though he was accused of being an unusually great violator of the laws in his time, he was extremely popular with the people round about, and was the idol of the laboring classes, because he gave employment to many persons at all times of the year, either on his farm or in getting out timber for his mill. Poplar logs were cut on the banks of Freeman's creek and floated to the mill. After the establishment of Weston, the mill was kept running day and night throughout the late fall and winter seasons. Most of the lumber used before the Civil war in building the frame houses of Weston, was sawed at the Jackson mill.

Kincheloe creek, named for its first explorer, was not very thickly settled before 1860. Most of the pioneers took up lands on the north side of the creek in Harrison county, where the bottoms were wider. Some of the Hugheses, relatives of the Indian fighters, moved from McCann's run and settled very early on Turkeypen run on the Lewis County side. The family has continued until the past few years to occupy the ancestral estate.

The western part of Freeman's Creek district which is drained by streams flowing into the Little Kanawha was settled much later than the lands on the West Fork and its tributaries. It was by no means neglected, however. The rich pasturage found in the sheltered coves of Fink creek was used for grazing purposes by the settlers on Hacker's creek following the close of the Indian wars. Fink creek and Leading creek were both famous for the products of the chase. Trappers secured some of their best furs in that region. The mouth of Fink creek was the favorite site for hunters' camps even before the close of the Indian wars. For many years the valleys of both streams continued to be clothed in the primeval forest.

The first settler on the lower course of the creek was John Hurst, who had formerly resided on the Tygart's Valley river. He came late in the spring of 1815, completed his cabin on the tenth of April and moved into it. Later in the season he cleared a corn patch from which he secured sufficient breadstuffs for his family. It was the most strenuous sort of labor. During the day he would grub out saplings, pile brush and cut down trees; at night he would chop logs by the light of the burning brush heaps. Sometimes it is said that he would continue his work of chopping all night. His Sundays were spent in killing rattlesnakes and copperheads which infested the country. In later years he continued to increase the circle of his clearings, meanwhile fighting the panthers, wildcats and wolves which threatened the destruction of his live stock.

On the upper course of Fink creek, Isaac Woofter, son of George Woofter, settled near the mouth of Isaac's fork on the present site of Churchville at about the same time as the settlement of Hurst farther down the creek. The contiguity of his farm to the Freeman's creek settlements made his task an easy one in comparison with that of Hurst.

Leading creek remained practically a wilderness until the middle of the nineteenth century. Lewis Stallman, who was one of the earliest residents along the course of the stream, made his first settlement near the present site of Troy in Gilmer County. John Moneypenny settled near the head of the creek not far from John Nicholes very early in the century and he was followed at a later date by Amos and William Woofter, sons of the pioneers of Freeman's creek. It was not until after the completion of the Staunton and Parkersburg turnpike that the valley became attractive to sett.ers.

CHAPTER XIII.

PROGRESS IN THE OLDER SETTLEMENTS

It must not be taken for granted that the other settlements on Hacker's creek were marking time during the twenty years after the peace of Greenville. While oases of settlements were being created in the primeval forests on Skin creek, the Hacker's creek settlements felt the surge of energy and the revivifying effects of the infusion of new blood. On the creek the older settlers had begun their clearings and had laid the foundations for the structure of a later society. The settlers who came after 1795 had the advantage of their toil. They lived in comparative comfort, even in backwoods opulence. There was no struggle with the savages, no uncertainty respecting the maintenance of law and order, no necessity for the head of the family to come to the land he had selected and cultivate a crop before he could bring his family. If the supply of venison was somewhat less, there was assured plenty of grain in the settlement to furnish his family with breadstuffs, and the pioneers were only too glad to dispose of the surplus in return for money which the new comers brought with them from the east. There was a mill in the settlements on which the corn could be ground without having to depend upon the slow process of grinding in hand mills or the unsatisfactory method of grating the corn on a tin grater. There was reasonable assurance that a school would be established in the neighborhood at some time during the winter, so that there was no fear that their children would grow up without the rudiments of an education. Some of the young men in fact were attracted to Hacker's creek because of the profitable employment in teaching school. Those who were religiously inclined need have no fear that their spiritual wants would remain unsatisfied or that their children would grow up in ignorance of religion, for a church had been established in the neighborhood. It was by virtue of these facts that men of property and influence in the eastern part of the state left their homes and came to the valley of Hacker's creek. The character of the later immigrants was of the highest in all respects, and their descendants have taken a part in the political, social and economic life of the western part of Virginia second only to that of the descendants of the pioneers.

The names of some of the immigrants to Hacker's creek in the last years of the eighteenth century are John Marple, John Kee, Elijah Waggoner, George Cunningham, Joseph Straley, Thomas C. Hinzman, Joseph Pumphrey, Jacob Henline and Alexander Morrison. John Life, whose parents were natives of Germany, settled on a branch of the creek which now bears the name of Life's run. Jonathan Hacker returned from his wanderings on Skin creek and the upper West Fork and settled near his father's home.

Just how fast the rush of settlements was may be inferred from a study of the statistics given for Harrison County in the decennial census reports. In 1790, the population was 2080; in 1800, 4848; in 1810, 9958; and in 1820, after the formation of Lewis County had cut off two-thirds of the territory of the county, the population was 10,932, and that of Lewis County 4,247. If the same ratio of increase applied to Hacker's creek as to the older settlements in Harrison County, then the increase of population in the valley of the creek must have been much faster than that of the outlying sections of the county where land was far lower in price.

The land on the eastern side of the West Fork river was also well settled within the two decades following the cessation of Indian hostlities. The Broad run settlement received an important addition to its numbers from a great immigration of New Jersey citizens which occurred about 1806. The Newlons, Minters and Baileys came from Fauquier or Culpepper County, Virginia, and settled on the wide bottoms of the West Fork where the town of Westfield afterwards grew up, sank into obscurity and finally altogether ceased to exist.

The increase in the population brought further improvements in the conditions of living, which is apparent from an examination of the records of the time. Puncheon floors, rough-hewn doors and split log benches ceased to exist in the better houses with the addition of a sawmill to the grist mill of Henry McWhorter on the later site of Jane Lew. The owner of a thousand acres could now sit at a level table and eat his food in greater comfort and security. If he were wealthy enough and had sufficient patience to wait a long time, he could even have the front of his house weatherboarded, and thus deceive the stranger into thinking he lived in a frame mansion. The sawmill of Henry McWhorter, like his grist mill was a crude affair. It consisted principally of a vertical sash saw attached to run by water power. There was no limit to the raw material available for the mill. A poplar log could be sawed in half the time required for a white oak log, and poplar lumber was therefore the only product of the sawmill for years to come.

Another improvement introduced after the peace of Greenville was the wagon. The first wheeled vehicle to cross the mountain roads and reach Clarksburg arrived in 1798. It is related that when it was sighted on the opposite side of Elk creek, the news spread like wildfire, and the excitement was intense. Rich and poor alike left their employments and hastened to view the hitherto unknown spectacle in the quiet valley of the West Fork. Even the judge of the circuit court adjourned the session for the day and went to the scene. The bank of Elk creek was dug down at the ford in order to make the passage of the wagon possible. His Honor Judge Jackson took hold of one of the wheels of the wagon and assisted its passage to the high bottoms on the other side. It was a great day for Clarksburg—as great a day as that which marked the coming of the first railroad train—for if one wagon could successfully accomplish the passage of the mountains and the rivers from the east, others could do the same, and there would soon be wide roads and more comforts in the settlements and perhaps—later on—a stage coach! The pioneer who dared to bring the first wagon into the county was held in such honor that most of the population of the county seat accompanied him to the tract of land he had purchased and assisted him to build his home. Other wagons were brought west in a steady stream. By 1804 the demand for repairs for the large number of wagons in the vicinity and on the state road, and for new wagons to be built for use in the county, became so great that a wagon-shop was established in Clarksburg.

The first wagon reached the Buckhannon valley in 1800. It was brought by Jacob Lorentz and others, emigrants from the South Branch. There were no roads over the mountains, and on several occasions it was necessary to take the wagon apart and carry it and its load over a particularly difficult part of the way on the backs of horses. Eventually it reached its intended destination on Saul's run.

Just when the first wagon reached Lewis County is not known. There is a tradition in the McWhorter family that when Henry McWhorter came to the Hacker's creek valley in 1790, he moved his goods by wagon, but this is believed to be a mistake. If he brought the first wagon to the county it must have been at a later date. For a long time wagons were very scarce west of the mountains, and one wagon was often used by several families.

Though stores had been established in Clarksburg before the opening of the century, the first store which really had much influence on the later development of Lewis County was that established by Jacob Lorentz just over the present boundary line in Upshur County, shortly after his arrival in the Trans-Alleghany region. For many years it continued to be the only store for miles around. It was not at first a pretentious establishment. The stock of goods was necessarily limited by the difficulties of transportation. A department store could not now exist in Weston if the stock of goods had to be brought on pack horses from Winchester. Calico was fifty cents a yard, nails were twenty-five cents a pound and other goods in proportion. Little cash was taken in by the proprietor. Most of the sales were made in exchange for the products of the pioneers' farms or the neighboring forests. Hogs, cattle, skins and the roots of medicinal plants were the principal media of exchange. It is said that at a later date the proprietor took a drove of 937 hogs over the mountains. A wagon load of corn to be fed to the hogs, accompanied the party.

The same year that marked the advent of the wagon at Clarksburg also witnessed the coming of another great convenience. The postoffice address of the pioneer residents of the upper West Fork was no longer "Winchester, Va.," but "Clarksburg, Va."

The number of long trips to the east was still further reduced by the establishment of a manufacturing industry in the valley of the West Fork. Early tradition states that Henry Flesher operated a still on Town run, which is called "Stillhouse run" in the early records. Possibly Paulser Butcher acquired his skill in making liquor from having assisted around Flesher's still. Other pioneers besides Flesher and Butcher engaged in the production of ardent spirits, which were then regarded as a necessity by most of the settlers.

The manufacture of salt also began very early in territory included for a time in Lewis County. Calder Haymond, in 1781 received a certificate for 400 acres of land on Salt Lick creek by right of residence there and raising corn before 1778. The land was regarded as of small value until about 1807 when Benjamin Conrad's cow discovered a saline spring and made a path to it. By following the path the owner of the land came upon the spring which produced an excellent quality of brine. Operations were begun there the following year. The spring, which is located not far from Bulltown, produced many hundreds of bushels of salt, operations being conducted on an especially large scale during the war of 1812. Salt works were also established on the West Fork above Clarksburg by John G. Jackson and others. Several wells were drilled, and a fairly good qualilty of brine was procured. Eventually, however, these wells failed to yield salt in paying quantities and the operations were abandoned.

Clarksburg naturally became the metropolis of the county. A newspaper was established there in 1815. At a very early date it had a boat-yard where flatboats were built to be floated down the river to Pittsburgh loaded with the products of the pioneer farms. Whisky, grain, furs, skins, lumber and country produce were the principal articles shipped down the river. Many flatboats were built at various places and sent down the river on the autumn rise with cargoes consisting of the varied produce of the country.

When the number of wagons became large enough to compel the opening of wagon roads to the east, articles, such as hides, linen, butter, honey, beeswax, ginseng and snake root were shipped over the mountains where they brought higher prices than at Pittsburgh.

As in earlier periods of the history of the upper West Fork valley, the principal export of the farmers was live stock. They could be raised easily on the succulent pasturage of upper Freeman's creek, Fink creek and other sections, and they possessed a great advantage over all other kinds of agricultural produce in that they could be driven to market.

The first improvement in the kind of stock kept by the farmers of the county followed the emigration of an isolated group of New England colonists who settled on

French creek, now in Upshur County in 1810. The cattle they drove before them were so far superior to the scrub stock which had been brought from eastern Virginia that the farmers in the surrounding region began cross-breeding their cattle with them. The result was a decided improvement in the quality of cattle kept. The upper valley of the West Fork soon became famous as a cattle raising section.

Methods of handling live stock changed little from the earlier day. They were still allowed to run out in the winter, being fed fodder and some hay. In the summer they roamed the woods, feeding mainly from the wild pea-vine. The extent of the range was increased greatly when the menace of the Indians was removed. Farmers were accustomed to brand their cattle and turn them out on the range, salting them at stated intervals, and always at the same place. Upper Freeman's creek and Fink creek were the choicest districts for pasturage; and many a Hacker's creek farmer became wealthy from the herds of fat cattle which he sold off the range every fall.

In those days wealth was estimated principally in terms of land. The value of land was determined principally by the improvements which had been made upon it. The amount of land which a farmer was able to have cleared depended mainly upon the number of sons, nearly grown, which he had in his family. All the families of that day were large, but if there was an undue proportion of daughters too much emphasis was likely to be placed upon raising corn instead of upon clearing more land. The farmers did not understand the simplest laws governing soil fertility, and they continued to till a field as long as it would produce a crop.

The growing of wheat which was made practicable by the construction of the Edward Jackson mill and the later improvements on the mill of Henry McWhorter, soon attained considerable proportions. Biscuits and salt-rising bread soon relieved the settler from the monotony of a steady diet of corn pone and johnny-cake. The growing of wheat, as practiced on the upper West Fork in the earliest period was an exceedingly primitive industry, hardly advanced at all from the methods in use five thousand years before. The grain was cut with a sickle and threshed with a flail. The equipment of the early mills was also exceedingly primitive. Instead of bolting cloths, deerskins, pierced full of holes with a red-hot needle, were in use.

The citizens of Hacker's creek had a share in the war of 1812. John McWhorter had been commissioned a captain of the Harrison County regiment of Virginia militia a year or so before the war. When the war broke out he raised a company of volunteers which was mustered on the wide bottom of Hacker's creek just below the mouth of Life's run. The company was marched to Parkersburg, where they took boat for Point Pleasant. There they were mustered into the federal service and sent to the Maumee river to join the forces of General Harrison. They remained at Fort Meigs until their terms expired, 13 April 1813, when they returned home on foot. Captain McWhorter continued in the service until the close of the war and was promoted to the rank of colonel. The war had little effect upon the upper West Fork. Aside from the number of young men withdrawn from farm work, it was hardly noticed. Development continued quietly.

About the year 1815 the beginnings of towns in the southern portion of Harrison County could be discerned. A few settlers had continued to live near West's fort after the Indian attacks ceased. McWhorter's mill later proved to be a good nucleus for a village. Daniel Harpole, who owned the land now occupied by the town at that time, is said to have started a tannery about 1815; but he soon became discouraged and sold out to Jacob Bonnett, a farmer.

Three or four miles west of McWhorter's mill and about the same distance from Colonel Edward Jackson's mill, a small settlement grew up about William Newlon's store under the name of Westfield. It seems to have been the outgrowth of the movement to form Lewis County, and the promoters doubtless expected to secure the designation of the village as the county seat. It was expected that industries, such as mills, tanyards, etc., would follow. There was a population of five or six families in 1816, the year the county was formed. An act creating the town on land belonging to the heirs of William Newland (Newlon) was passed shortly after the act for the formation of the county. John Bailey, Elijah Newland, Jacob Minter, Minter Bailey and William Powers were designated in the act as the trustees of the town, and it was provided that vacancies in the board should be filled by the other trustees. According to the act, "whenever any purchaser of a lot build a dwelling house thereon equal to twelve feet square with a brick or stone chimney, such purchaser shall enjoy the same privileges which the freeholders of other towns not incorporated hold and enjoy." A year or two later Westfield had attained to considerable importance for that time. Besides several new dwellings a school house had been erected in which at least one term of school was taught by Weeden Hoffman. The schoolmaster turned storekeeper in the town within a year or so.

Buckhannon was also established as a town by the legislature in 1816. Aspirations of the people to obtain the seat of justice of the new county were partly responsible, but there was a small settlement there which would perhaps justify the creation of a town. A ferry had been established across the Buckhannon river near the mouth of Jawbone run some years before, and a small settlement had grown up around it. Weston was then an improved farm.

The first church building erected within the present limits of Lewis County was the Harmony Methodist Episcopal church in 1800. The building was the outgrowth of the society formed in 1786 at the home of

John Hacker. It stood on a slight rise above the mouth of Jesse's run. For its day it was a pretentious structure, being constructed of hewn logs with a gallery. From this church there went out later a number of prominent ministers of the gospel like the Rev. John Mitchell and the Rev. David Smith who sowed the seeds of other organizations in outlying parts of the county and made class leaders out of mob leaders. The second church to be built on the creek was at the forks of Hacker's creek, near the present site of Berlin, under the leadership of the Rev. John Mitchell. Both became Methodist Protestant churches when that church was split off from the Methodist Episcopal church in 1829. It is said that Harmony church was the first Methodist Protestant church in existence west of the Alleghanies.

One of the most important churches ever established in the county from the standpoint of its influence over the future development of the religious life of the people of northwestern Virginia was the Broad Run Baptist church which began its existence in 1805. Elder John Carney, an itinerant Baptist preacher from the Buckhannon valley, came to Duck creek, now in Harrison county, about four miles north of Broad run, in 1804, and began a series of meetings among the New Jersey settlers who had lately emigrated there. As his monthly visits continued considerable interest was awakened in religion. Settlers who had been good Baptists in New Jersey again felt the impulses of faith. A meeting was called for the purpose of considering the wisdom of forming a Baptist church. On February 5, 1805, the people of the community met in a private home in the presence of an advisory council. The meeting is said to have been "one of great solemnity and glorified by the conscious presence of the Holy Spirit." An opportunity was offered for those who wished to become members of the Baptist church, and while the congregation sang,

"Am I a soldier of the Cross
A follower of the Lamb—"

eight persons presented themselves for membership. The charter members of the church were Walter Smith and wife, Job West and wife, Samuel Romine and wife, and Solomon Wires and wife. They were declared to be the Good Hope Baptist church. Elder Carney continued his monthly visits to the church for some years.

The Baileys and Minters and others, Baptists from Fauquier County, Virginia, who had come to Whiteoak Flat run in the latter part of the eighteenth century, also formed a congregation under the guidance of the Rev. John Carney, in 1806. The pioneer members of this church were Jacob Minter and wife, Alexander West, Edmund West, James Bailey and wife, and Elizabeth, wife of Captain James Bailey. Because of the fact that most of the members had belonged to the Broad Run Baptist church in Fauquier County, they chose the same name for the new congregation.

Meanwhile some of the New Jersey settlers moved from Duck creek to land in the West Fork valley about the mouth of Whiteoak Flat run. The church at Duck creek became divided geographically but not in a religious sense. Meetings of the Good Hope church were held in private homes both on Duck creek and on the West Fork farther south. The membership of the two Baptist congregations increased rapidly. In 1808 the congregations had outgrown the accommodations to be found in the cabins of the pioneers, and a movement was begun to erect a church building. John Brown donated a few acres of land for a church and a cemetery about two hundred yards from the location of the old Mongue fort. A building of hewn logs, twenty-four by thirty feet, was constructed in the same year, and here the united churches worshipped for many years, until the log structure became inadequate for the purpose. A frame church, "low and squatty," took its place, followed by another frame church and finally by an imposing brick edifice.

THE JACKSON HOMESTEAD AND MILL

The second pastor of the church was Elder John Goss, of Georgia, an evangelist in the employ of the Southern Board of Missions. He is described as being tall, of angular build and of quick, nervous movement. His sermons were interspersed with humorous anecdotes and quaint illustrations. Elder John J. Waldo succeeded him after some years. Benjamin Holden, one of three brothers who did much to extend the Baptist faith in Northwestern Virginia, came next, and he was followed by Elder Carr Bailey, one of the pioneers of the Freeman's creek country and the leader of the church there. Anthony Garrett, one of the earliest converts of the church, whose ministerial labors are said to have been more abundant than those of any of his co-laborers, followed Elder Bailey in the ministry.

The influence of Broad Run church in the religious development of northwestern Virginia was tremendous. From Broad run as a center Baptist preachers went forth over the whole northwest, from the mountains to the Ohio river, riding on horseback through trackless forests, preaching to small groups collected in the homes of the settlers, baptizing converts, forming new churches and carrying the seeds of a higher civilization with them all the while. The Broad Run Baptist association, which was formed as a result of their labors, embraced at its inception about half the territory now included in the state of West Virginia. The great number of Baptist churches scattered over the northern part of the state attests the success of their endeavors.

CHAPTER XIV.

THE FORMATION OF LEWIS COUNTY

The system of local government in Virginia before the Civil war demanded small counties. The judicial and administrative work was so centralized in a small body of men that it was practically impossible for the justices to look after the interests of a great number of people scattered over a wide expanse of territory. The business of the county court was usually transacted with four justices present unless there was a levy to be made or officers to be elected, when all the justices were summoned by the sheriff. The presiding justice and three others who lived near the county seat usually made up the court, and the same ones were not necessarily present on two consecutive days. Under such conditions the public business was more or less neglected, especially that in which the people who lived at a distance from the county seat were concerned. For some time prior to 1816 there had been much complaint among the people residing along the upper West Fork, the Buckhannon and the Little Kanawha rivers that their interests were being neglected by the county court, which seemed intent upon developing Clarksburg and the country round about it. It was the age-old complaint of the communities on the frontier—of western Virginia against that part of the Old Dominion east of the mountains, and later of the frontier sections of Lewis County as they began to reach their full development.

The progress of settlement in the southern part of Harrison County, though not quite so rapid as around Clarksburg, was very swift. Three or four thousand people were living on the Buckhannon, the upper West

Fork and the Little Kanawha by 1816. They demanded a new community center where they could attend court and vote at the general elections without having to travel for long distances from their homes to Clarksburg over the narrow trails which the Harrison County court called roads. The agitation came to a head in the election of 1815 for members of the General Assembly. The leaders of the movement for the division of the county determined if possible to elect members of the House of Delegates from Harrison County who would see that an act was passed creating a new county from the southern part of Harrison. They therefore requested Colonel John McWhorter, a rising young attorney of Clarksburg and a native of Hacker's creek, and Col. Edward Jackson, who had served in the preceding legislature, to be their candidates. Col. Jackson had no opposition, but some of the residents of the northern part of Harrison County, who were opposed to the proposed bill, concentrated their opposition on Colonel John McWhorter, knowing that if they were successful the county could not be divided.

The contest was a very unequal one, for all the voting was done at the county seat. It was necessary for Colonel McWhorter, if he expected to be elected, to get out the vote; and for the people of the southern part of the county to come to the polls at some time within the three days that they were open. The Colonel stumped the county, assisted by Joseph Johnson, a prominent local politician, who afterwards became governor of Virginia. The settlers in the outlying parts of the county responded in great numbers to the call. Dressed in their best homespun and carrying their rifles on their shoulders and some jerked venison and johnny cake in their hunting shirts, they made their way to Clarksburg over trails blazed through the forests.

The election was made a gala occasion by the voters. Many of them hunted on their way to the polls, and carried their game as presents to their hosts at the county seat. The candidates were expected to provide meals and sleeping quarters for the voters. The opposition had engaged all the available room in the hotels, but the headquarters of the "new-county" party were opened at the home of Dr. Williams. So great was the crowd during the three days of the election that Mrs. Williams was frequently compelled to step across the bodies of sleeping men with scarcely room to place her feet, and many could not be accommodated in the house at all. They found more commodious quarters in the nearby woods, where they built huge fires, roasted their venison and slept in the open. Each candidate had a barrel of whiskey sitting beside the polling place, and when a voter announced the name of the candidate of his choice he was entitled to help himself. The barrel provided by Colonel McWhorter was emptied first. The farmers from the southern part of the county had won.

In the following term of the General Assembly McWhorter and Jackson introduced a bill for the creation of a new county from the southern part of Harrison, to be called Lewis, in honor of Colonel Charles Lewis, who was killed at the battle of Point Pleasant. The bill was amended in the Senate, substituting the name of General Andrew Lewis, but the delegates from Harrison stood their ground and when the measure was finally passed, 18 December 1816, that part of the act providing that the county should be named for Colonel Charles Lewis was left unchanged.

The boundaries of the county as set forth in the act were as follows: "Beginning at the mouth of the Buckhannon river; thence a straight line to the head of the left hand fork of Jesse's run; thence a straight line to the mouth of Kincheloe Creek; thence up the said Creek with the meanders thereof to the dividing ridge between the Waters of the West Fork river and Middle Island Creek; thence a west course to the Wood County line, to include all the south part of Harrison down to the mouth of the Buckhannon River."

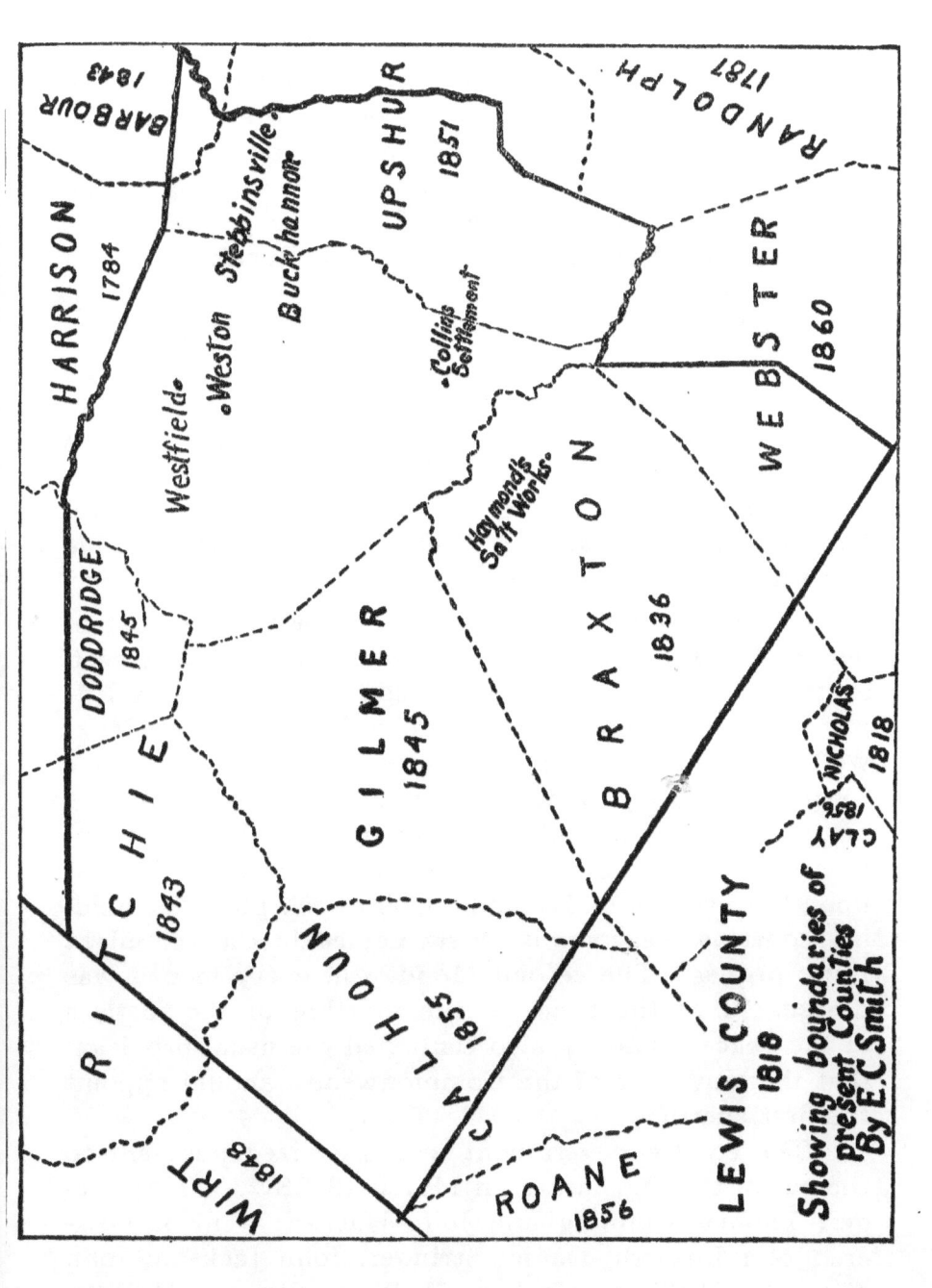

By an act passed, 4 February 1818, Lewis County received an accession of territory east of the Buckhannon river from Randolph County. The boundaries were as follows: "Beginning at the dividing ridge near the head of the Buckhannon river, thence a straight line to the head of Grand Camp River; thence a straight line to the head of the Left Hand Fork of Big Sand Run; thence with the dividing ridge between Buckhannon and Middle Fork Rivers."

Lewis County as thus constituted was bounded on the north by Harrison, on the east by Randolph, on the south by Greenbrier and Kanawha, and on the west by Wood. It had an area of 1,754 square miles. Besides the present territory of Lewis County it included nearly all of the present counties of Upshur, Gilmer and Braxton, and parts of Barbour, Webster, Doddridge, Ritchie and Calhoun.

As customary in acts providing for the creation of new counties, no town was designated as the county seat. Instead the act named a commission, to consist of Edward Jackson, Elias Lowther, John McCoy, Lewis Maxwell and Daniel Stringer, to "ascertain the proper place for holding courts, erection of public buildings, etc." The act provided further that the justices of the peace appointed for the new county should meet at Westfield upon the first court day and appoint such place for holding court as the commissioners named in the act might think proper. The second Monday in every month was designated as the time for the meeting of the justices of the peace. The act also contained the usual provision that the Governor of the Commonwealth should appoint the first sheriff.

The county government was organized pursuant to the act of the legislature on March 10, 1817. Philip Reger, Thomas Cunningham, John Hacker, William Powers, John Bozarth, Daniel Stringer, John Jackson, John Mitchell, William Hacker, William Simms, William Peterson, Abner Abbott, John Hardman, George Bozarth,

Elijah Newlon, Peyton Byrne, Jacob Lowrentz, (Lorentz), Samuel L. Jones and James Keith, all of whom had been appointed justices of the peace by Governor James P. Preston, met at the house of the Rev. Peter Davis, at Westfield, and resolved themselves into the county court of Lewis County. Philip Reger produced a commission from the governor as high sheriff of the county, and after taking the oath of office, the oath of fidelity to the Commonwealth and the anti-duelling oath, and giving bond, he entered upon the duties of the office.

The first work of the court was to fill the remainder of the county offices. Several applicants presented themselves for each of the places, and the disappointments were many when the results were announced. Daniel Stringer was appointed clerk of the court, Edwin S. Duncan, attorney for the Commonwealth, and John Mitchell commissioner of the revenue. The following named citizens of various sections of the county were appointed constables: Joseph Davis, Henry Reger, George Duvall, Adam Alkire, Isaac Collins, Jeremiah Howell, David W. Sleeth, Walter McWhorter, Walter Wilson and John Peterson. George Bush was recommended to His Excellency James P. Preston, Governor of the Commonwealth, as a suitable person to fill the office of principal surveyor of the county. On motion of Philip Reger, high sheriff, it was ordered that William Martin and Thomas S. Hacker be and are appointed deputies for the said Reger. They came into court and qualified according to law. The following named attorneys, most of whom resided at Clarksburg, were licensed to practice in the court of Lewis County: Lemuel E. Davisson, James Pindell and George I. Davisson. It will be seen from the bare enumeration of the acts placed upon the record books that the court transacted a great amount of important business on the first day of the session.

The next day, 11 March 1817, the constables who had been appointed on the preceding day came into court and gave bond in the amount of $500. The court ordered that the county should be laid off into three districts for the election of overseer of the poor. In the order passed by the court, the natural geographical divisions of the county were followed: "The settlement on the Buckhannon and its waters is to comprise one district, in which Abraham Carper is to superintend the election of overseer of the poor for the said district at the house of John Jackson; That the settlement of the West Fork, Hacker's creek and the waters thereof, do compose the second district, and that Henry McWhorter do superintend the election of overseer at his own house. That the settlement on the Little Kanawha river and its waters do compose the third district and that William Hacker be appointed to superintend the election of overseer at his own house." The overseers of the poor were the only county officers elected by the people. All the others were appointed either by the county court or by the governor upon the recommendation of the court. Samuel L. Jones acknowledged his acceptance of the appointment of coroner. On motion of Daniel Stringer, clerk of the court, it was ordered that Robert W. Collins be appointed as deputy clerk, and he qualified as the law directs. The machinery of the county was in complete running order, and after the transaction of some miscellaneous business, the court was adjourned until "court in course."

Immediately after the adjournment of the court, the commissioners named in the act creating Lewis County to select a site for the county seat, met and organized and then began inspecting the most eligible sites in the county to find the "proper place for holding courts." There were at that time two regularly established towns in the county, Buckhannon and Westfield, both of which had been established at the preceding session of the General Assembly. The people of Buckhannon had expected that in the original bill for the creation of the county some territory would be carved from Randolph, but the measure was not carried through until the next session of the legislature, and Buckhannon was left on the border between two counties with little hope of receiving the coveted designation. Westfield had a far better chance, owing to its more central location. It had also a large population—five or six families—and had been designated by the General Assembly as the place for holding the first courts. The location of the courthouse there was no doubt an accepted fact among the people of the town. But the designation of the legislature did not always mean that the final action taken would be the same, as happened in the case of Buckhannon when Harrison county was formed.

At the following term of court, which met, 11 April 1817, at the home of Mrs. William Newlon of Westfield, the commissioners reported that "the most suitable place for the purpose aforesaid is on the farm of Henry Flesher, lying and being on the West Fork of the Monongahela River, above the mouth of Stone Coal Creek, on the east side of said river, and the particular spot of the grounds on said farm agreed upon by us is on the rising ground east of said Flesher's dwelling house, near the threshing floor of said Flesher, where his stack now stands."

Just why the commissioners should have chosen the improved farm of Henry Flesher for the location of the courthouse in preference to the location farther down the river at Westfield is a matter of conjecture. It has been suggested that the location was made at the suggestion of John G. Jackson, who had formed grandiose plans to make the mouth of Stone Coal creek the head of navigation on the Monongahela. There is a possibility that the members of the commission from the western part of the county objected to a location so far from the geographical center as Westfield, and they finally acquiesced in the selection of Flesher's farm as a compromise because it was on the natural route from the Buckhannon settlements to the Little Kanawha river as well as from the upper West Fork to Clarksburg.

Upon the receipt of the report of the commissioners the county court passed an order to the effect that succeeding sessions should meet at the point recommended. For some reason, possibly on account of the fact that Flesher's cow had not completely devoured the strawstack on the site selected, or more probably because no houses suitable for the purpose had yet been constructed on the Flesher farm, the court continued for some time to meet in the Newlon home at Westfield.

After acting upon the report of the commissioners the justices next proceeded to take up matters relating to the administration of the new county. They declared that the bills and notes of certain banks in Virginia, Pennsylvania, Maryland and Tennessee were lawful currency within the county; they ordered several deeds recorded; they appointed viewers to lay out new roads· and they designated road supervisors to see that the roads of the county were kept in proper repair. Negotiations were begun with Joseph Johnson, Lewis Maxwell and John G. Stringer, the new owners of the Flesher farm, for the purchase of the real estate on which Henry Flesher's strawstack stood. After the lapse of two years the deed was recorded. The price paid for the "publick squeare" was $300.

At the June term of the court the business transacted was somewhat widened in scope, and with what had gone before, completes practically the whole round of administrative duties of the old county courts of Lewis County. The first letters of administration were granted to James Mays, administrator of the estate of Jonathan Mays, deceased. He was also appointed guardian of the infant children of Mays. The first levy of the new county was a poll tax of $1.05 on each tithable· The court also approved a list of claims amounting in all to $174.41, which were mainly for rent of a temporary courthouse, stationery and office furniture, extra services of county officers and claims of two of the commissioners appointed to locate the seat of justice of the county. The complete list of claims is as follows:

To Mrs. Newlon for use of home to hold court in	$20.00
To Jacob Minter for making one writing desk	8.50
To Clerk of this Court for extra services (four months)	8.33
To same for books for use of county	18.39
To same for paper for use of county	10.83
To Robert W. Collins, Clerk of the Superior Court for books furnished for use of County	15.37
To same for paper	4.17
To Edwin S. Duncan, Esq., Attorney for the Commonwealth in the Court for his services for four courts	16.33
To Sheriff of Lewis County, for extra services	12.50
To Lewis Maxwell, Commissioner to locate the seat of Justice for Lewis County	30.00
To John McCoy for same	30.00
	$174.31

Meanwhile the circuit court for Lewis County was being put in operation. In April, 1817, "the Honorable Daniel Smith, one of the judges of the General court present to hold a Superior Court in the Eleventh judicial district of the Commonwealth," came to the county and set up the "Superior Court of Law for Lewis County." Robert W. Collins was appointed clerk. He took the several oaths and gave bond in the amount of $10,000 John G. Jackson was appointed prosecutor for the Commonwealth. Edwin S. Duncan and Oliver Phelps were given leave to practice in the court. The first grand jury to be empanelled in the county consisted of William Hacker, foreman, William Simons, William Bennett, James Allen, Daniel Harpold, Alexander West, Samuel

Bonnett, John Bailey, Thomas Batten, David Smith, John Starcher, John Life, Jacob Bonnett, Mark Smith, George Fisher, Adam Flesher, Paulser Butcher, Jacob Bush and Robert Simpson. It returned indictments, all for assault and battery, against the following named citizens of the county: Zechariah Westfall, Samuel Hall, John Hall, Levi Nutter, Joshua Russell, Travis Walker, Adam Alkire, Jacob Bennett, Mark Hershman and Jacob Romine. A petit jury was summoned upon the indictments. In September, 1817, Judge Smith returned for the regular term of court which met every six months. In 1819, Lewis County was made a part of the Fifteenth judicial district and Judge Lewis Summers, perhaps the most distinguished jurist in northwestern Virginia before the Civil war, came to Weston to hold court.

The county court of Lewis County held a session for the transaction of judicial business in June, 1817. A grand jury composed of George Dobson, foreman, John Brown, Peter Hardman, Samuel Stalnaker, William Moneypenny, John Cline, Jacob Wolf, Samuel Oliver, Minter Bailey, Emanuel Alkire, Daniel McCann, George Stealy, David Wolf, Paulser Butcher, William Peterson, Jr,. Martin Life and Jacob Abbott, returned one indictment against Presley Hamilton for keeping a tavern and retailing liquor without a license. The usual indictments returned to a county court were for assault and battery, profane swearing, failing to observe the Sabbath day, horse-racing and against road overseers for failing to keep their roads in repair. The overseers usually laid the blame on their companies. At first indictments were also made against some of the citizens of the county for failing to work on the roads when called The overseers generally filed a plea in abatement and were allowed to "go without day". In 1819, the court found Lucy, the female slave of Thomas Batton, guilty of having murdered her infant. She was sentenced to be hanged in the courthouse yard at Fleshersville. Her value was appraised at $500, and ordered to be certified

THE FORMATION OF LEWIS COUNTY   173

to the auditor of public accounts for the reimbursement of her owner.

In 1819 the following named citizens of the county were appointed school commissioners by the county court: Joseph McCoy, John Mitchell, Asa Squires, David W. Sleeth, Edward Jackson, Lewis Maxwell and Aaron Gould.

The first term of court at the permanent seat of justice appears to have been held in 1818 in a house then being constructed for Lewis Maxwell just across the street from the public square. It is said that Judge Smith sat on a chair placed on Maxwell's workbench. The records were carried about on the person of the clerk or left at his home for the next year or two.

Work on the permanent courthouse was not begun at once, partly owing to the dissatisfaction of the people of Westfield with the site chosen for the county seat and the threatened appeal to the General Assembly, partly through the lack of funds.

In 1819, the justices were summoned by the sheriff for the purpose of taking action regarding the construction of a permanent courthouse. Two brick kilns which had been burned by James M. Camp, were tendered to the court for use in building the new structure. They were inspected by a commission appointed by the court and were reported to be "good merchantable brick." The court accepted them. Colonel Edward Jackson, Henry McWhorter and Jonathan Wamsley were appointed to contract with a superintendent for constructing the building. At the session of the court held in February, 1820, Jacob Lorentz, Joseph McCoy, R. W. Collins and John Mitchell were appointed to submit a plan for the structure. Another committee, consisting of James Allen, Henry McWhorter and R. W. Collins, were appointed on behalf of the court to let the contract which should "be advertised in some publick newspaper in the Town of Clarksburg as well as at the front door of the courthouse of this county." Only the walls, doors and windows were to be contracted for at first, and the court gave notice that only $500 would be paid to the contractor the first year.

The committee for submitting a plan for the structure made their report at the next term of court recommending the construction of a courthouse thirty-six feet long and thirty feet wide. Later an allowance was made for an addition for the clerk's office. The contract was let to James M. Camp, who, besides being a building contractor and brickmaker, was also the jailer, captain in the 133rd regiment of the Virginia militia, coal bank owner, real estate dealer, trustee of the town of Weston, tavern keeper and justice of the peace. The building was ready for occupancy some time in 1821. According to the description given by 'Squire Oliver, who saw the building as it was in 1844, it was not a model of architectural beauty. "It would make you laugh," he says, "to see such a building. It was constructed of brick, two stories high with a cupola enormously high, all out of proportion, and when the wind would blow, which it often did, it would sway the whole building. It was, after the style of most of the dwellings, only partly finished. The jury rooms were unplastered. In fact, it never was finished."

The courthouse was used for a great variety of purposes. Some of the religious societies in the making held their meetings there; new and struggling congregations listened to their circuit preachers discoursing from the rostrum; the trustees of the town of Weston shaped the policies for development of the town in the jury room; a few terms of school were taught in the building, the classes being dismissed during the glorious period when court was in session; home talent plays were staged and public meetings were called to meet in the old building which continued to be the courthouse of the county until a more imposing structure was erected in 1856-7. The courthouse yard was "pailed in" in 1832 at a cost of $64.

The county was without a permanent jail until 1824, the prisoners being kept in a building adjoining the home of Jailer James M. Camp, which was erected in 1818 of logs two feet thick. In 1823 a commission was appointed for the erection of a suitable jail. The next year, in accordance with the report of the commissioners, a jail was constructed on the public square. The walls were solidly built of sandstone, but the flues of the chimneys were so large that prisoners frequently climbed up them and escaped.

In order that prisoners for debt should not be confined too closely and also that they might have an opportunity to go about their business and raise money to pay their debts, the court directed Adam Baird to lay off prison bounds not to exceed ten acres in extent. The bounds at first practically followed the limits of the town of Weston, and also included part of the lands on the west side of the river. Within the bounds the prisoners were allowed to go at will; but they could not go outside the bounds without being in custody. A room was reserved for them in the second story of the jail where they slept at night.

Lewis County in 1820 contained a population of 4,347, of whom 125 were colored. The settlements were still confined mainly to the West Fork and Buckhannon river valleys with a few on Elk river and on the tributaries of the Little Kanawha. There was little danger that the settlers in the outlying portions of the county would be numerous enough to demand separate county governments for many years.

NOTE—The statement that Joseph Johnson was a part owner in the Flesher land on which Weston was built is based on his own declaration made late in life. The original deed conveys the land to Maxwell and Stringer, and Johnson's name was not mentioned; nevertheless his great interest in the campaign and in the building up of the town gives color to his statement of financial interest. As the craftiest politician of his section, his desire to keep the transaction secret is easily explained.

CHAPTER XV.

THE BEGINNING OF WESTON

The improved farm of Henry Flesher became a thriving village soon after its selection by the commissioners as the county seat of Lewis County. Shortly after the new county was formed Henry Flesher seems to have conveyed about one-third of his farm, embracing all that part east of the river to Joseph Johnson, Lewis Maxwell and John G. Stringer. Johnson lived near Bridgeport, and was afterwards to become famous as the only man west of the Alleghanies who ever became governor of the State of Virginia. His interest soon passed to Maxwell and Stringer who were both young men, and the former had been a member of the commission which selected the permanent county seat.

The new proprietors immediately took measures to develop the old farm as a town-site. Early in 1817, Colonel Edward Jackson was employed to lay off the town into lots and mark the streets. Later a day was set for a great lot sale, and the announcement was posted all over the new county and in Clarksburg. A great crowd was attracted, partly by the desire to secure lots in the new town, partly to partake of the refreshments, partly to meet their friends. It was an occasion long to be remembered by those who came to the old farm of Henry Flesher, which was then unoccupied, except for a house being built for Lewis Maxwell just opposite the lot designated as the public square. At the end of the day the promoters of the lot sale had no cause to be disappointed with their sales. Lots were sold to Thomas M. Batten, James M. Camp, George Conley, Edward H. Jackson, Paulser Butcher, Adam Flesher, Alex Kester,

William Moneypenny, Sarah Batton, Richard Johnson, John Sprigg, Moses and John West, Charles West and John Pritchard. The last-named purchaser selected lot No. 22 on the right side of Main street, which was the farthest out in the country of any of the lots sold.

The plan of the town as laid off by Edward Jackson is practically the same as the plan of Weston today, and shows the good sense and vision of the surveyor. His employers were not entirely satisfied with the plan, however, and ten years later they secured an act of the legislature which blocked the head of Main street where the Bland hotel was afterwards built, and extended Water street to connect with Run street. All the streets that now exist in the central part of Weston were surveyed and marked by Colonel Jackson. The lots each contained practically one-fourth acre, having seventy-two and one-half feet frontage and extending back from the street one hundred and fifty feet.

Building operations began at once on most of the lots purchased on the day of the sale, and the village soon contained ten or fifteen log houses. There was only one frame building in the town at that time. It stood opposite the court house and was occupied by Lewis Marwell for several years until he built a more imposing house a little farther down Center street. Parts of the first house built in Weston are still standing.

In January, 1818 the General Assembly passed an act establishing the town as Preston, the inhabitants to have the same rights and privileges which have been noted in the case of Westfield. The following named citizens of Lewis County were designated as trustees: Henry McWhorter, Paulser Butcher, William Peterson, James M. Camp and Robert W. Collins. The town was called Preston in honor of James P. Preston, then governor of Virginia. In the autumn of the same year a new county named Preston was formed from Monongalia, and the name became undesirable for the town; for anyone not acquainted with the geography of northwestern

Virginia would probably take it for granted that the town of Preston was the county seat of Preston County. It was very usual in those days for the county seat to bear the same name as the county. The awkward situation was seen immediately by Colonel John McWhorter and John Bozarth, who then represented Lewis County in the House of Delegates, and they introduced a bill at once changing the name of the town from Preston to Fleshersville. The new name of course was to commemorate the name of the first settler who had come to the site of the town before the Declaration of Independence was signed.

The citizens of the town, particularly the purchasers of the original farm, objected strongly to the new name. Henry Flesher, upon selling that part of his farm on the east side of the river, had moved to the other side, and had built his cabin upon what is now a part of the hospital lawn. He had consistently refused to have anything to do with the development of the town. So strong were the objections of some of the influential citizens of the town that at the next session of the legislature the delegates from Lewis County again secured a bill changing the name of the town. This time it bore the nondescript designation of Weston, which has at least the advantage that it can be borne by any town west of Eastport, Maine, without awakening jealousies or causing bitter feeling among the first families. The town has since borne the name without serious opposition.

The same year the first postoffice in Lewis County was established at Weston, under William Y. Henry as postmaster. The location of the office and the duration of his term are unknown. The mail was brought once a week from Clarksburg on horseback.

Until the opening of the Clarksburg and Weston turnpike in the late 'forties the streets of Weston were under the supervision of the county court, which appointed overseers to keep them in repair. All the citizens of

Weston between the ages of sixteen and sixty were compelled to work their own roads and streets. By an order of the county court passed in 1819, the road down the river from Run street to Maxwell's run was made a separate precinct and "all the hands of Weston (were) to work same." The precinct remained unchanged for a quarter of a century, and it was a regular spring and fall occurrence for all the lawyers, merchants and other citizens of high and low degree to take mattocks, picks and shovels and try to put the road in passable condition.

One of the first duties of the governing authorities of the town was to secure ground for a cemetery and the public buildings. The trustees of the town obtained from Stringer and Maxwell an acre of ground lying on the hillside at the head of Center street "for the purpose of a Publick Burying yard for the Burying of those who may die in the Said Town and its vicinity and for the purpose of erecting thereon a publick meeting house and School house in Such manner as may hereafter be agreed on by the freeholders and house keepers resident in the said town." This tract is known as the Arnold cemetery. For half a century after the establishment of the town it was the burial ground of most of the dead. The trustees never erected upon the lot the town hall and the schoolhouse for which purpose it had been donated by the promoters. The courthouse was used both as a meeting place for the trustees and for a schoolhouse for many years afterwards. The people of early Weston seem never to have suffered from too much government at the hands of the trustees.

The early prosperity of Weston was largely due to its position as the political center of the county. The location of the courthouse was a prime factor in inducing citizens from the surounding country to locate in Weston. The court officials of course found it convenient to live near the seat of government. Lawyers and others whose business led them often to the courthouse also located in the town. The crowds who came to the courthouse every court day—and court day came every month—led to the establishment of hotels for their entertainment. One of the first court orders after the establishment of the town gave to Thomas H. Batton the right to keep an ordinary at his house in the town of Weston. An ordinary was a place where meals were served, liquors sold, and lodgings furnished at a certain fixed price. James M. Camp, jailer, militia captain, etc., was given a similar license. Both establishments prospered. Colonel Camp, in spite of his various occupations, found time to be a very hospitable tavern keeper, and it is said that no guest ever went away dissatisfied with the treatment he had received. People who knew Colonel Camp speak feelingly of his kindliness and good breeding. He seems to have been a man of large vision in business matters, but careless of detail, and the large tracts of land which he at one time owned slipped from his grasp because he failed to have his deeds recorded.

The county court fixed the prices to be charged by the ordinary keepers. Following is the first schedule of prices in effect:

> For dieting of every meal's victuals............ .25
> For a night's lodging........................ .12½
> For Liquors for Rum per ½ pint............... .18¾
>   For Wine per do.................... .25
>   For Whiskey and Brandy
>   per do. .... .12½
> Oats and Corn per gallon..................... .12½
> For Horse to Hay 12 Hours................... .17
> For same to pasture 12 hours................. .12½

It will be noted that the prices are expressed in most cases in fractions. This is due to the fact that the English sixpense (12½ cents), ninepence (18¾ cents), and shilling (25 cents) were the principal coins in circulation.

The first homes of Henry and Adam Flesher were heated with wood, but Colonel Camp introduced the burning of "stone coal" which was dug by slaves from the bank on Stillhouse run (now Town run). This bank continued to be the principal source of fuel for some of the residents of the town until about 1826 when the road to it was discontinued.

Aside from the attraction which the town had as the county seat, Weston possessed many advantages over Westfield and most of the other sites of the county which the commissioners might have chosen. As a commercial center the location could hardly have been improved upon at that time; and the county has been so judiciously pared down in the creation of other counties that Weston remains still the commercial as well as the political center of the county. The road along the West Fork river was the natural route of travel for all the residents of Collins Settlement to reach the state road at Clarksburg. The old Indian trail through the Polk creek and Stone Coal valleys was the natural route of travel from the settlements on the Buckhannon and the upper Tygart's valley sections to the west. The site was already an important center of roads when it was chosen by the commissioners. It would probably in time have become a considerable center of trade even if the courthouse had been located at Westfield, and it might have become the leading town in the county without the residences of the court officials and the crowds on court days.

It was not long after the establishment of the town that its importance as a business center was realized. Weeden Hoffman, who had started a small store at Westfield about 1817 or 1818, moved his stock of goods to the county seat about 1823, locating about where Kaplan's store is now. The first store building was not a large one and the stock of goods was not very extensive, but it was nevertheless a great improvement for the town. People were able to secure their goods without having to go to Lorentz' or Westfield. On account of the small amount of currency in northwestern Virginia at that time most of the receipts of the merchant were in produce. Whiskey at ten dollars a barrel, ginseng, hides, butter, maple sugar, honey, beeswax and other products of forest and farm were stored in the wareroom adjoining until the wagons could go to the east.

Most of the stock in trade came from Baltimore, and was hauled over the wretched roads in monster covered wagons. Merchants went east on horseback once or twice a year to purchase their stocks, which were delivered in Weston by teamsters who made a regular business of hauling goods. The charges for transportation were about three cents a pound. The trip one way required eighteen days, though the bill of lading allowed three weeks. The price of the goods was reduced as the distance necessary to transport the goods by wagon was lessened. The Baltimore and Ohio railroad reached Harper's Ferry in 1839, Cumberland in 1842, Piedmont in 1850, Fetterman (near Grafton) 1852, and Clarksburg in July, 1856.

The second store established in Weston was that of R. P. Camden, who commenced business apparently on the corner now occupied by the National Exchange bank, about 1827. The business was continued there and elsewhere for many years. After 1834 the proprietor of the store was also the postmaster, and the mails were sorted in one corner of the building set aside for the purpose. Other early merchants were Allen Simpson and McBride and Smith.

The county seat was also recognized as an excellent location for the establishment of a mill by several citizens. Wheat and corn could be ground in 1819 at the Jackson mill below Weston, and corn at the Connelly mill a short distance out Polk creek. It was thought that Weston was a better location than either because of the number of residents in the town and also because of its being a center of travel. There was considerable rivalry among the applicants for permission to erect the mill. Joseph Johnson, who was one of the proprietors of the land on which the town was built, in order to increase the desirability of residence on his lots, applied, in April, 1817, to have a commission appointed to condemn land for a mill below the mouth of Stone Coal creek. Before his application could be acted upon he sold out his interest in the town site to the other two partners, and allowed it to lapse. A little later in the year the court granted permission to John Burnside to erect a mill dam across the West Fork river on Johnson's location. The order was contested by John West, who in the September term of the Superior Court of Lew, appealed from the judgment of the county court. The Superior Court declared the judgment of the county court erroneous, but without prejudice to any future application of Burnside. A little later in the year, Daniel Stringer obtained permission to build a mill on First street. He and John Burnside erected the first mill in the town on the site of the present mill, in 1818. West secured a *certiorari* to the action of the county court the same year. After a prolonged contest in the courts, John Wamsley, clerk of the county court, was in 1823, declared by the Superior Court guilty of unlawful gaining in issuing the permit. The mill continued to stand, and the punishment of the clerk was apparently the only satisfaction that West received. West shortly afterward secured permission from the court to construct a mill at Bendale, and from that point of vantage he was able to cut off much of the up-river trade. His mill was not a paying proposition and he abandoned it after a time.

The mill at Weston was operated by Burnside for a few years until his interest was taken over by Stringer, who sold it to Thomas Bland in 1830. The mill has since passed through many hands and experienced many vicissitudes of fire and flood and decay. Citizens of Weston have at times been obliged to have their wheat ground at the Jackson mill, the McWhorter mill at Jane Lew, the Holt mill at Bendale and even at the Waldo mill above Roanoke.

The new proprietor of the mill added a carding machine to his equipment. On account of the number of sheep then being kept in the county, the new department was well patronized from the start. The housewives of Weston found it a great convenience as compared with the laborious process of carding the wool by hand.

Many of the owners of farms near town owned stills in which they worked up their surplus grain and fruit. Since it was impracticable to transport a bulky commodity like farm produce across the mountains or down the Ohio and the Mississippi to market, and since there was a considerable demand for the product of the stills near home, it was the most profitable way in which surplus crops could be utilized, even though whiskey was worth only $10 a barrel. The Fleshers continued the manufacture of whiskey at a still on Buck Knob, which was perhaps the most important one near Weston at that time.

A gun shop was established very early in the history of the town, probably by Alexander Kester. A blacksmith shop was in operation in the late 'twenties where not only were horses shod, but butcher knives, scythes, hoes, frows, axes and other implements were made for the people of Weston and the surrounding country. Every shoe and every nail used in the operation had to be made by hand in the shop.

The first tannery established in the town was owned by Daniel Harpole who had previously operated a tannery at McWhorter's mill with indifferent success. After operating the plant for several years, he sold it to John Lorentz about 1825, who added new equipment and operated it for a number of years. The business required a capital of about $800 or $1,000 and gave employment to two boys. When it was operated by Lorentz, the plant was located at the head of Run street. Two buildings, one for the vats the other for preparing the hides, made up the establishment, which long remained one of the most important of the manufacturing plants of Weston.

In 1830 the town contained about thirty dwellings representing a population of about two hundred. The streets were in bad shape from the fact that many of the farmers insisted upon hauling logs through them in wet weather. Pigs wandered through the premises of the inhabitants or wallowed in the mud holes. The cattle grazed in the woods near town or in some of the land which had been cleared nearby and left unfenced after several crops.

The establishment of good hotels early differentiated Weston from most of the backwoods towns of northwestern Virginia. The record book of the county court for 1852 contains a notation to the effect that one Minter Bailey had applied for a license to keep an ordinary in the Weston Hotel, and "being of good appearance and likely to keep an orderly house of entertainment," he was granted the desired right by the court. Bailey had lately come across the mountains from Fauquier County and was a member of the Bailey family, which had settled on Broad run and later on Freeman's creek.

The hotel thus established has remained one of the most noteworthy institutions in Weston from the time of its establishment to the present. It never had a season of depression, never had a great boom. From the first it has remained in the hands of the proprietor or his descendants. For the first twenty years after its establishment it was located in a two-story frame building which stood on the southwest corner of Main and Second streets, opposite the present site of the hotel.

It may well be doubted whether the house has had greater popularity among travelers or greater fame throughout the surrounding country than it enjoyed in the old frame building. Major Bailey was a born host. He knew how to dissipate the fears of timid boys away from their homes for the first time. He would show them his surveyor's compass, or ask them about their parents, and so gain their confidence. Other guests were regaled with tales of his experiences. All were made to feel almost as if they were in their own homes. The atmosphere of the hotel is still largely that of the old times when the citizens of Weston and travelers sat around the spacious fireplace and discussed the relative merits of Andrew Jackson and Henry Clay, or expressed their disgust at the government of Virginia as administered by the politicians east of the mountains for the benefit of their own section. Next to the urbanity of Major Bailey, the success was due to the abilities of Mrs. Bailey as a housewife. "Any man could run a hotel with such a landlady as Mrs. Bailey," said one of the visitors. The venison always roasted to just the proper turn, the delicious wild turkey roasted or fried in its own fat, but above all the fried chicken, prepared as only Mrs. Bailey knew how, spread the fame of the establishment far and wide.

The bar at the Bailey house was the best in the town in the early 'thirties. It consisted of a small space in one corner which was enclosed by a railing like a postoffice window. The purchaser came to the window, paid for his drink, drank it and gave way for another customer. It sometimes happened that the guests became too hilarious. Then the barroom would be locked and the key would suddenly disappear. It was of no use for the guests to protest. Major Bailey was very sorry, but the key was nowhere to be found. On one occasion the crowd became too noisy to be controlled, and the proprietor went to the river bank and cut a stout limb from a sycamore tree. Using it as a club he cleared the room in a very short time.

The Weston Inn was established at the head of Main street in 1827 by Lucinda Lazell, but it never attained the popularity of the Weston Hotel and the later Bailey House under Major Bailey. Within a few years it was sold to Thomas Bland, and for a long time thereafter continued to be one of the leading hotels of the section—second to the Bailey House in Weston—but better than the hotels in the neighboring towns. It continued to block Main street at First street until it was destroyed by fire late in the century.

Following the construction of the Staunton and Parkersburg turnpike, a wagon shop was established in Weston about 1842 by W. W. Warder, a young man just graduated from Rector college at Pruntytown. Some of the best wagons of the day were made in the shop. When the lumber, stone and other material was hauled for the construction of the Weston State hospital, many of the old wagons made in Warder's shop were impressed into service. Many of the farmers who had not previously been able to own wagons, furnished material in return for the finished product.

Rapid as was the material development of the town, the educational development was very slow. There was no concerted attempt of the citizens to secure good schools, such as took place in other and smaller communities at the same time. The people were content to depend upon subscription schools established by such teachers as could secure a sufficient number of pupils.

There were no theaters in Weston until several years after the Civil war, but the citizens did not suffer from lack of theatrical entertainments. In 1838 a Thespian society was organized by some of the younger people for the purpose "of studying the masterpieces of the drama and presenting the best popular selections of the day." The use of the courthouse was granted to the society by the county court, but after the first two or three performances, the permission was withdrawn. The society did not suspend performances, but secured another hall. At intervals until the beginning of the Civil war, plays were presented at various places, and the society was even reorganized after the close of the war for a brief, but very popular existence. Some of the plays presented were worth while, but others, like "East Lynne," could hardly be justified as worthy of study. The young men of the town organized a debating society about 1840, which enjoyed a brief existence.

The religious organization of Weston was far behind that in the country districts round about. While churches were being organized on Freeman's creek, Skin creek, the Collins settlement and even at Bulltown, the citizens of the county seat had not a single church of any denomination. No church building had been erected there until 1844, twenty-seven years after the first establishment of Preston. Other towns in northwestern Virginia were in a like situation. The circuit riders considered them stony fields, not easily susceptible to cultivation. It may be that the county preachers, with their backwoods manners, were made fun of when they attempted to preach in the towns, and their sermons, delivered in language more forceful than grammatical, were probably laughed at. Many religious meetings were held at the courthouse by different denominations, but there does not seem to have been any tangible result until about the year 1830. The Rev. John Talbott, a preacher of the Methodist Episcopal church, became a permanent resident of Weston. He gathered all the Methodists of the town together into a small class which met at first in the home of Elias Fisher. Later, when the number of members had outgrown the accommodations, he secured permission to use the courthouse for regular preaching services every two weeks. In 1831 the class at Weston was added to the Lewis circuit, of which Jonathan Holt was then assistant pastor. Later pastors were Thomas Williams, B. F. Sedwick, Thomas Baker, Joseph Ray and David Cross.

The class grew and prospered during the ten years following its organization. In 1840 the quarterly conference of the Lewis circuit appointed a committee consisting of Elijah Flesher, Daniel Turney and Matthew Holt to secure funds, draw up plans and supervise the construction of a church building in Weston. The result was that late in 1844 the Methodists were established in their own church, a small brick structure located on the site of the present church. Though it was not a large structure and though it was lacking in the facilities which are found in even the country churches of today, being lighted with lard lamps, it was sufficient for the needs of the congregation until 1874, when a more commodious church was erected.

The new church was a community enterprise. All denominations were given the right to use it for their meetings, and they no longer had to depend upon the court room. The Rev. Daniel Helmick of the Methodist Protestant church would preach at stated intervals. There were then two families of Episcopalians in the town, who had to depend upon occasional services of visiting rectors. The Baptists, Presbyterians and Methodist Protestants did not have a very great following in 1844. The Methodist church received a wonderful impetus from its having the first building in the town, but it was soon much weakened by a division within its ranks. The general conference of the church in 1844 split over the question of slavery, and the Methodist Episcopal Church, South was formed with a membership embracing most of the classes south of the Mason and Dixon line. Largely through the influence of the Holts the church at Weston determined to remain in the northern branch of the church, though most of the Methodist churches in the southern part of the county voted to join the southern branch. A number of the Weston Methodists withdrew from the church and formed a separate organization. About 1847 they erected a church building on Center street on the lot now occupied by Linn Brannon. The southern church never was strong, and it finally died out about 1880. The Sunday school of the Methodist church was in full operation in 1846, when it was reported that its membership was fifty scholars. The West Virginia conference of the Methodist Episco-

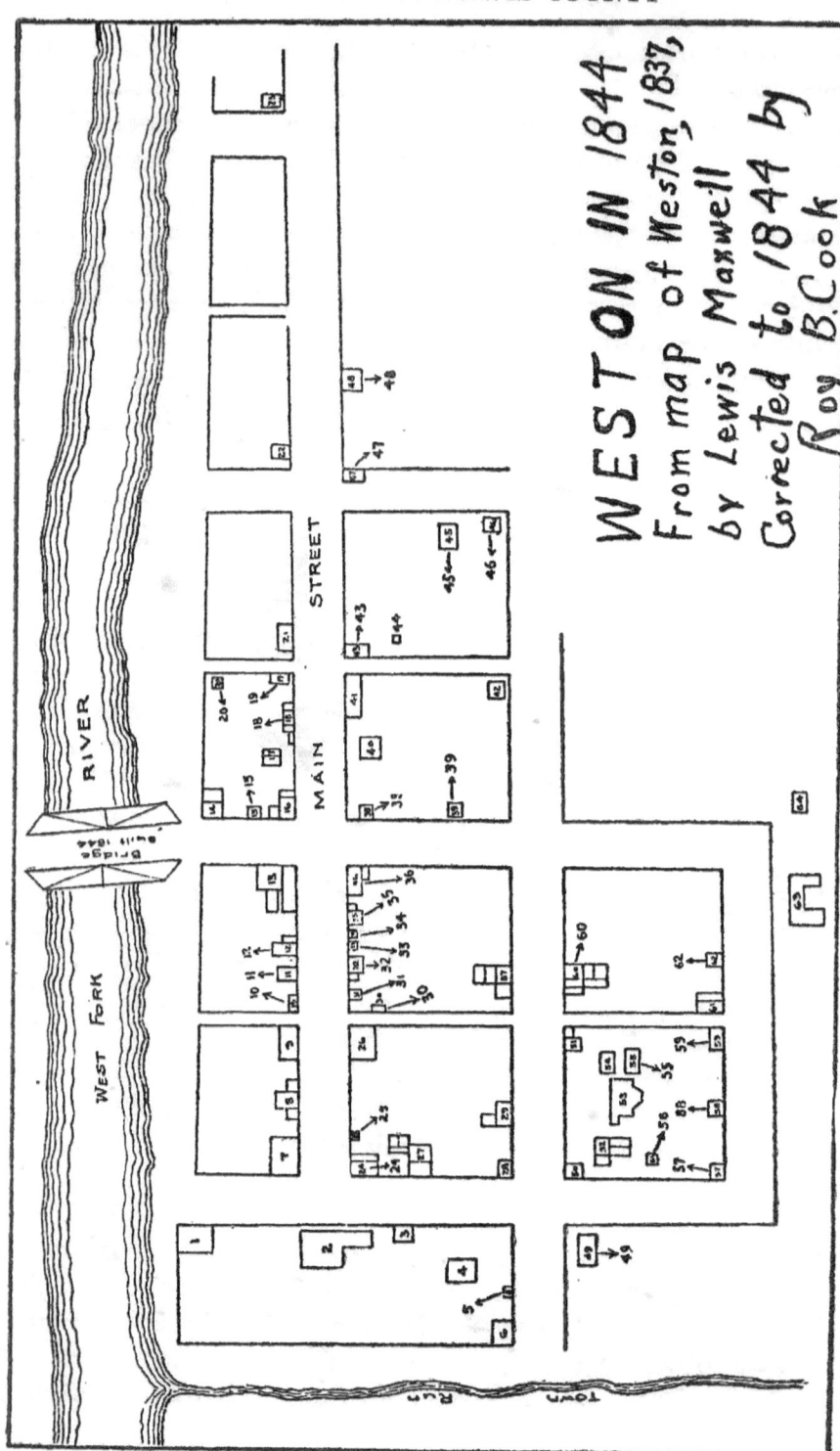

pal church, which was held in Weston in 1851, was an occasion long remembered by the people. Pastors who followed the Rev. Cross before the Civil war were W. D. F. Lauck, Caleb Foster, Moses Tichnell, Gideon Martin, W. C. P. Hamilton, Franklin DeHass, James L. Clark, J. S. Patterson, S. R. Dawson, Samuel Steele, T. H. Monroe, A. J. Lyda, J. Hare, H. C. Sandford, J. W. W. Bolton and A. B. Rohrbough. A parsonage was constructed in 1866.

'Squire George H. Oliver came to Weston in the early part of 1844 when he was a young man. The appearance of the town and its people made a vivid impression on his mind, and later he wrote a description of the town at that time. Most of the buildings of the town were then on upper Main street and on First and Second streets nearby. Lower Main street was then out in the country, and the Moore house, which had been erected by the Rev. John Talbott some years before, was considered a country mansion. The new home of John Brannon on First street, according to popular opinion, was much too fine a house to be located so far from town.

Log houses were in the great majority. The best houses in the town were a story and a half in height, built of poplar logs hewn to shape, over which weatherboarding had been nailed. The aristocrats among the houses had brick chimneys. Few of the buildings had ever come in contact with a paint brush, and the result was a dilapidated and woebegone appearance. In the majority of the houses the interior had not been finished. Some of them had only a single room furnished in which the family cooked, ate, slept and received their guests. Others had two rooms finished, and the remainder postponed to some future date. There was only one brick building, the residence of M. W. Harrison, on the west side of Main street. On the corner now occupied by the National Exchange bank, stood an old rambling one-story frame structure owned by Hoffman and Camden, which was then unoccupied. The south side of First street was vacant from the Bland hotel at the head of Main street to the corner of Center street; from that point eastward was a cornfield. One hewn log house stood on the opposite side of First street. Center avenue had three houses on each side, not including the courthouse and jail. On the east side of the street the house farthest down was the two-story brick residence of Lewis Maxwell on the lot now occupied by W. W. Brannon. All the land north of the Maxwell home and east of Center avenue was included in Maxwell's meadow. It was enclosed, of course, in order that the cows which ran loose in the town could not get in. The stake and rider fence along Center avenue was at that time one of the most modern fences in the county. The old-fashioned worm fence could not always be depended upon to turn the Weston cows, trained as they were through years of experience in getting their food from forbidden pastures. There were three buildings on each side of Court avenue occupied as residences by the elite of the town. In all there were about fifty dwellings.

It is hardly correct to call the principal thoroughfares of the town streets. Main street had never been graded. It was still under the control of the county and was worked by the people of the town under the supervision of Cabell Tavenner, the leading member of the Weston bar, who had probably been chosen for the position because he was of slender build and could not wield a pick as successfully as some of the others. There were neither horses nor plows; every bit of dirt had to be moved with pick and shovel. There were no sidewalks. "In some places there were some slabs—two laid side by side and spiked to cross pieces laid along for the purpose." At the corner of Main and Bank streets there was a very low place which became almost impassable in the fall and winter. Four-horse teams frequently became mired there, and had to be pulled out. As a temporary sidewalk across the alley, which had all the advantages of a drawbridge, the people built a trestle work with slabs laid on top of it. In winter it was a not uncommon occurrence for the citizens of Weston to lose their footing on the icy slabs and fall into the almost unfathomable mud below. A board sidewalk would have been a novelty.

There were in Weston five stores owned respectively by Weeden Hoffman, R. P. Camden, Alexander Scott Withers, McBride and Smith and Addison McLaughlin; three saddle and harness shops, owned by Thomas Fisher, John Morrow and George A. Jackson; three tailors' shops owned by David Bare, John Flesher and James Ferguson; and two clock peddlers selling brass wheel clocks which were just then superseding wooden-wheel clocks in the mountains of northwestern Virginia. Conrad Kester then owned the gunsmith shop and W. W. Warder the wagon shop. Benjamin Pritchard and Preston Dawson were the two blacksmiths in the town, and there was also a shop about a mile out the Polk creek road operated by Elijah Flesher. Pritchard was considered especially good on edged tools, and most of the butcher knives used in Weston at that date came from his shop; Flesher specialized in hoes, frows, and axes; and Dawson devoted his time principally to making horseshoes and shoeing horses. Allen Simpson and George W. Sleeth were the two cobblers, and both were overworked. They made all the shoes and boots worn in the town and in the surrounding country with the exception of ladies' fine shoes which were brought from the east and sold by some of the merchants. John Lorentz still owned the tannery. Isaac P. McBride and Jesse Woofter were cabinet makers, and Thomas W. Morris, John R. Beall, Joseph Minter, and William Beard were house carpenters and joiners. There was no meat market in the town, and none was needed, for all the citizens raised their own hogs. When butchering time came, most of the people employed Joseph Minter, whose skill in securing just the right scald, and whose knowledge of how to cut up the carcasses were unexcelled.

There were then two physicians in Weston—Dr. William J. Bland and Dr. N. B. Barnes. Dr. Bland is the first one who came to Weston. 'Squire Oliver says of him that "he traveled through this county where there were no roads, through the woods and over the hills. . . . . The night was never too dark or the weather too stormy to deter the doctor when there was a call. He did not stop to inquire if the party were able to pay the bill" but saddled his horse and was away as soon as the call came. His practice extended over all of Lewis, Upshur and Gilmer and parts of Harrison and Braxton. Dr. Barnes was also an able physician, and he also regarded his profession as a means of prolonging life rather than of making money. His health would not permit him to expose himself to the elements as Dr. Bland did, and his practice therefore included only Weston and the country in the immediate vicinity.

The Weston bar in 1844 was a brilliant one. It was composed of eight lawyers, all of whom made their mark in the development of northwestern Virginia. The oldest in point of service was Colonel John McWhorter, who had been instrumental in the formation of Lewis County. He was an able lawyer, but given to lapses of memory. Cabell Tavenner, son-in-law of Alexander Scott Withers, was the recognized leader of the bar. He is described as a "slender, rather delicately featured man who combined logic with fluent speech and graceful delivery." Matthew Edmiston, later destined to make his mark in the judiciary, was then a new comer from Pocahontas County. Another very young lawyer was Jonathan M. Bennett, whose early education had been gained in the country schools of the Collins settlement, who had studied one year in Weston, served as deputy sheriff, and had been admitted to the bar in 1842. 'Squire Oliver says that he was better as thinker than as a speaker. Addison McLaughlin had lately come from

Nicholas County where he was so popular that he was elected to the legislature before he was twenty-one years of age. He later moved to Braxton and championed the creation of Webster, whose county seat was named Addison in his honor. Others were Jonathan Holt, Lewis Maxwell and Dexter Williams. Politically they were divided. McWhorter, Holt, McLaughlin and Maxwell were Whigs and Tavenner, Edmiston, Bennett and Williams were Democrats.

The postoffice in 1844 was conducted by George A. Jackson. The mail arrived once a week by horseback from Clarksburg. On Sunday afternoons toward the hour of four the citizens could be seen wending their way to the postoffice where they collected in a group and talked over questions of the day until a blast from the post boy's horn announced his coming. The mail was quickly sorted, and the return mail prepared and handed to the postboy for his return trip usually within twenty minutes. About twenty-five newspapers were regularly received by the citizens of the town. The Whigs divided their allegiance between the Richmond **Whig,** the Louisville **Courier** and the **National Intelligencer,** published at Washington. The Democrats subscribed for the Richmond **Enquirer,** then under the able editorship of Thomas Ritchie. A few subscribed for the Pittsburgh **Christian Advocate.** Several copies of the Philadelphia **Dollar Newspaper,** and the **Saturday Evening Post** furnished all the current literature which came to the county. The Clarksburg **Scion of Democracy** was the only newspaper published in northwestern Virginia which had any circulation in Weston.

The circulating medium in use, aside from the products of farm and forest, were Spanish silver dollars; French five franc pieces with the head of Napoleon I; English threepence, sixpence and ninepence; a few dimes, quarters and half dollars struck by the Philadelphia mint; and the banknotes of banks at Baltimore, Knoxville, Richmond, Philadelphia and Wheeling.

Two schools were in operation in Weston during the late fall and winter of 1844-45. Mrs. Mary Wilson and daughters, Anne and Fronie, had a school for young ladies and small boys in their house, and a Mr. Foster, a Yankee direct from Vermont, taught a school attended by the larger boys. The latter school had sixteen pupils, of whom eight were taught the higher branches for $1 per month, and eight were classified as primary students at seventy-five cents per month. Some little difficulty was experienced by the pupils in solving the problems in Pike's Arithmetic, which counted in pounds, shillings and pence instead of in dollars and cents.

The Weston housewife in 1844 had practically the same equipment as the housewife of pioneer days. There were but two stoves in Weston, one in each of the hotels. The baking was done in Dutch ovens buried in embers at the capacious fireplace. Wild turkeys were dressed and hung up by the legs above the fire. A platter on the hearth caught the drippings which were poured over the fowl from time to time until it was done. The older inhabitants say that the old-fashioned roasts were better than those prepared today with the modern utensils of the ultra-modern housewife.

The first piano in Weston was brought over the Staunton and Parkersburg turnpike from Parkersburg in the summer of 1844. It was purchased by Mrs. Wilson, whose daughters had attended a school in Canonsburg, Pennsylvania, where music was one of the accomplishments taught.

Weston in 1844 was without any manufacturing industries except for the wagon shop, the tan yard and the combined grist and carding mill, which was still run by water power. There was not a single steam engine in the town and only one in the county at that time.

CHAPTER XVI.

PROGRESS UNDER THE NEW REGIME

Aside from the development of Weston and the country about the town, the creation of Lewis County apparently made little difference in the establishment of new settlements, and the extension of the older communities. From the standpoint of government there was a decided improvement, for the inconveniences of going to Clarksburg for the transaction of legal business were obviated and more attention was paid to the details of administration in the county.

The founding of Weston had considerable influence in the development of the surrounding lands, because of the fact that most of the inhabitants of the town bought small farms in the vicinity, where they obtained their firewood, cut lumber and raised their breadstuffs. Some of them bought farms and then let the land lie idle to increase in value with the development of the town. Part of the land on the river above Weston was cleared very early by the slaves of the owners, and large crops were cultivated by them. Stillhouse run (now Town run) was developed in the same way far earlier than it would have been without the close proximity to the town. Some of the citizens of Weston busied themselves in locating lands in the surrounding country which had not been taken up, or if taken up, had been abandoned. Several tracts were located on Murphy's creek, on Middle run, on Rush run or on the river above Weston.

The Lewis County surveyor's books for 1817 show that most of the new surveys of lands were being made on Steer creek, Cedar creek, Hughes river and the lower course of the Little Kanawha. But tracts of land were also being surveyed in what is now Lewis County in numbers and location which were surprising. Five thousand acres in a single tract on Freeman's creek; twelve hundred acres on Cap run; and smaller tracts on Sand fork of West Fork, Skin creek, Polk creek, Leading creek, Gee Lick run, Saul's run and Ward's run were surveyed. Smaller tracts continued to be patented from year to year, sometimes in surprising locations. There was much confusion, and it was difficult to determine just what land had been surveyed, especially since the boundaries of tracts were fixed by the purchasers, and they usually located only three sides and noted that on the fourth side the tract "extended for quantity." The man who occupied the post of county surveyor had a good opportunity to find out whether or not land was claimed by any private owner, and many of the early incumbents of that office became wealthy by keeping the secret of the location of vacant lands until their terms had expired and then securing a patent for them. Other surveyors had also a rare opportunity. The profession was recommended for the young man who wanted to get ahead in the world.

In 1836, land that had never before been patented, was surveyed on Clover fork, Murphy's creek, Oil creek, Skin creek, Gee Lick run and on Laurel Lick not far from the original settlement of John Hacker, made sixty-seven years before. Six years later small tracts were being surveyed on the upper reaches of Hacker's creek and on the tributaries of Sand fork of West Fork.

The amount of land which could be had by taking out warrants for it was so great that for years, land values were extremely low. One hundred acres on Stone Coal creek, adjoining lands of Henry Flesher, was sold in 1817 for $300, and the price was considered high. The usual price for a farm was from one to three dollars per acre, depending upon the amount of the land that had been cleared. The large unwieldy tracts which had been surveyed in the last years of the Indian wars were not settled except by squatters, owing to the fact that the owners were non-residents, and the tracts did not fall into the hands of citizens of the county until the titles were forfeited through non-payment of taxes. The more enterprising of the new owners subdivided their lands and sold them in small tracts to settlers.

When the county was established the citizens lived in islands of settlement in a sea of forest without means of ingress or egress. The development of communication between different settlements and the extension of their boundaries until they touched each other and included all the lands in the county was the problem which faced the leaders of the new county after its creation— a problem which was not wholly solved until after the development of the lumbering industry caused the timber to be cut and made easier the clearing of land.

The population of Lewis County increased but slowly in comparison with the expansion of the settlements of Indiana and Illinois during the same period, but the growth was equal to that of most of the counties of northwestern Virginia. In the first ten years of the existence of the county the number of inhabitants increased about forty-five per cent. The same ratio of increase continued until the Civil war, though the statistics of the census seem to indicate a less rapid growth in later years. This apparent slowing up is readily explained by the formation of new counties out of the original territory of Lewis.

The county government was expanded to meet the needs of the large population. An act passed in 1824 provided that the county court of Lewis County should appoint two commissioners of the revenue (assessors) "in lieu of the one appointed heretofore." On account of the growth of communities at a distance from the county seat and the difficulties of attending the polls at the courthouse, it was provided in 1827 that separate elections should be held at the house of Daniel Farnsworth on the Buckhannon river, at the home of Benjamin Coonrod on the Little Kanawha river, and at the home of Benjamin Riddle at the mouth of Leading creek, in addition to the one at the courthouse. A new regiment of militia, the 133rd, was formed in 1829 out of the 125th regiment, which had previously been created for Lewis County.

The consolidation of the old settlements is shown best perhaps by the example of Hacker's creek, which in 1840 had about reached maturity as a community. The first pioneers and their descendants had been reinforced by newer comers until the population of the valley was soon almost as great as it is at the present time. The third postoffice in the county was established at Mc-Whorter's Mills with Fields McWhorter as postmaster, in 1829. The number of residents in the vicinity and the natural importance of the site as a center for the Hacker's creek community led Lewis Maxwell, one of the founders of Weston, to purchase the Jacob Bonnett farm and divide it into town lots, in 1835. The town thus laid out was named Jane Lew in honor of Jane Lewis, mother of Lewis Maxwell. There were several purchasers of lots, and within a few months a half dozen or more dwellings were in process of construction. A store was established in the village in 1837 by S. P. Jackson, which was operated by Blackwell Jackson until 1844, when he established a store of his own. The first ordinary was established about 1840 by S. P. Jackson. In 1844 he started a tannery, which was soon sold to Isaac Jackson. To S. P. Jackson far more than to Lewis Maxwell is due the development of the town. In 1844 a traveler in Jane Lew saw six or eight dwellings, a frame hotel, a livery stable, a store, a blacksmith shop, a tannery and a large flag pole nearly one hundred feet high bearing the names of Polk and Dallas, Democratic candidates for President and Vice-President respectively.

The community had a house painter in the person of John P. Peterson, who lived not far from the mouth of Life's run. He later came to Jane Lew and bought the tannery. Ezekial Boilan and Albert Jewell, a school teacher from Maine, who lived at the head of Life's run, were prominent new citizens in 1845. Nicholas Alkire was reputed to be the second richest man in the county, his wealth having grown with the increase of the herds which he pastured during the summer in the rich coves of Fink creek.

Westfield had maintained a precarious existence following the failure of the town to secure the courthouse, but its citizens did not wholly give up the struggle. In 1833 one lot brought $50. The establishment of Jane Lew in 1835 and the building of Lightburn's mill farther down the river led to the abandonment of the site. By the early 'forties it was an improved farm occupied by Minter J. Bailey. One large log house in which the Lewis County court is said to have held its first session —a melancholy memorial of disappointment and blasted hopes—marked the site until after the close of the Civil war.

The populous and prosperous Broad run community continued to expand, as did also the McCann's run district. Benjamin Lightburn's mill, which was established near the mouth of Broad run some time before 1840, formed the nucleus of the present village of Lightburn.

The settlements on Freeman's creek expanded during this period perhaps faster than at any other time in their history. The farmers cleared their lands and placed them in cultivation or in bluegrass pasture, which more than doubled the capacity of the land to fatten cattle, and still left a great acreage of pea-vine pasturage. The Hacker's creek ranchmen were obliged to depend more and more on the land farther west in the rich coves of Fink. About 1840 there was a considerable immigration of great importance to the later history of the community. Several families, including Jesse Coler, Solomon

White, David Simmons and the Rexroads and Haltermans, migrated from Highland County. Some of the new immigrants were members of the United Brethren church, and one of their first acts upon coming to the Freeman's creek valley was to commence holding their religious meetings. The first services of the United Brethren church in Lewis County were held in the home of David Simmons about 1841 or the year following. A church was soon organized, and largely through the generosity of Mr. Simmons, a house of worship was erected on the Simmons farms above the site of Freemansburg. From the parent church a number of others have sprung, including Valley Chapel, the Polk Creek church, the congregation at Churchville, and the Broad street church at Weston.

Daniel Harpole is said to have been the first settler on Murphy's creek about the beginning of the century. He was followed by the progenitor of the Jarvis family in Lewis County at a period so remote that his name has been lost. George Fisher settled on the creek at a somewhat later date. About 1840 the Bankheads, Spears, and Henrys, who had come from Scotland, settled on Limestone, a tributary of Murphy's creek. They were coal miners, and took up the business of supplying Weston with coal after the abandonment of the bank owned by James M. Camp. A Baptist church, the third in the county, was organized on the creek in 1844.

Middle run and Rush run were settled at a later date than Murphy's creek, and for a long time they remained practically in the wilderness. By 1844 each of the valleys of the streams had a population of four families. The Rush run settlements and those above its mouth on the river, induced the building of a mill by Jonathan Holt in 1840. It subsequently passed into the hands of John Detamore, who continued it in operation until late in the century, when it was destroyed by fire. Dr N. B. Barnes organized a Sunday school in 1855 in an old building which stood near the mouth of Middle run.

In the valley of the West Fork below Roanoke, new settlements began to be made around the homestead of Abner Mitchell. The Heavners settled at first on the Rhodes place where they lived until the coming of Rhodes, shortly before the Civil war. Samuel Bond came from near Lost creek about 1825, and settled not far from the later site of the Seventh Day Baptist church. The first services of that denomination were held in the home of one of the Heavners shortly after the close of the Civil war. Before 1820 the pioneer Abner Mitchell applied for permission to construct a dam in the river, to furnish motor power for a small mill which he proposed to establish. The mill was constructed, but the venture was not a success owing to the small number of settlers near him and the later competition of other mills in the neighborhood.

The town of Roanoke at the mouth of Sand fork and near the mouth of Canoe run occupies a strategic location which was not appreciated for a long time after the first settlement had been made in the vicinity. John and William Godfrey, brothers, are credited with having been the first to occupy the site. They were lumbermen in addition to being farmers, and with every rise in the river they floated hundreds of logs to Weston and points beyond, where they were formed into rafts and sent down the Monongahela. Michael G. Bush, a former school teacher, millwright and farmer, moved from Skin creek to the mouth of Sand Fork about 1835. About the time that Mitchell's mill suspended operations he is thought to have established a mill which had a brief existence, almost forgotten by the sons of pioneers in that section. The mill gave the name to the postoffice of Bush's Mills, which was in existence just below Roanoke in 1851 with William Rohrbough as postmaster Isaac Waldo came from Harrison County about 1840 and established a mill in the bend of the river about one-half mile above the mouth of Sand fork. It continued in operation for many years until it was burned to the water's edge in the 'seventies.

The progress made in the Collins settlement was largely in the nature of the extension of clearings. New farms were settled by the descendants of the first comers, and the area of improvements was gradually extended to include both forks of the river. A postoffice, the second in the county, was established under the name of Collins Settlement with Joseph H. Camden as postmaster in 1821, when there were no roads connecting the section with Weston. At the forks of the river, William Bennett established a mill prior to 1820 which became the nucleus of the present village of Walkersville. A postoffice was established there under the name of Bennett's Mills about 1835, and a polling place was established at his home in 1838. The Right fork was settled first, as indicated by road orders of the county court which found it necessary to establish a road only to the mouth of Crane Camp on the left fork in 1820, but which a little later caused a road to be viewed up Right fork to the mouth of Glady. Andrew Wilson settled near the present site of the village of Ireland, James and John Anderson built their homes about half way between Ireland and Bennett's mill, some of the younger Bennetts took up land near their fathers, and Isaac Bouse settled near the present village of Ireland where he became the first postmaster about 1845. The place was called Ireland in honor of Andrew Wilson, a son of Erin, who voted for James K. Polk for president in 1844 at the age of 113. Abram's run was rather thickly settled by 1845. Sand fork had more than a dozen families by the same date. Henry Gilson, Robert Irvine, James Brady, Henry McCauley and others lived on the stream, but they left on account of the conflict of land titles and went farther west.

One of the first settlers of Clover fork and Oil creek was Alexander Skinner, who lived in the forks of the creek where Orlando is now located. John Riffle was also on lower Oil creek by 1827. He established the first mill in that section some time prior to 1853, and he also had the honor in that year to kill the last panther seen in Lewis County. The Poseys were also pioneers on lower Oil creek; James Posey lived just above Orlando. Clover fork was settled about the same time, and had grown so swiftly through the colonizations of G. J. Arnold and others that there were sufficient settlers to justify the establishment of a store a few miles above the mouth of the stream by a man named Townsend in 1853. A blacksmith shop was also in operation. Near the head of the stream the first settler was William B. Holbert, who came before 1836. The Cunninghams and Traylors were there a little later.

Skin creek district as a whole reached maturity perhaps earlier than any of the other districts of the county with the exception of Hacker's creek. Big Skin creek was a fairly compact territory by 1840. In addition to the earlier settlers the Petersons had established themselves at the head of the creek, and there were several families of Hardmans living between David Hall's and the mouth of Charles' run. George Harris lived just below the present Jewell farm, and William Warner had settled on Glady fork. Philip Linger established a mill about 1830 on the farm just adjoining the land on which Vandalia was afterwards built. A church building was erected nearby about 1838, which served for many years both as a place for worship and as a schoolhouse.

Little Skin creek, about the year 1850 was probably as thickly settled as it is today. Colonel John Corouthers, who was of Irish descent if not a native of Ireland, and whose residence on the creek dates from about 1825, was regarded as the richest man in the county in 1844. He was a prominent cattle dealer, as well as a farmer whose methods were superior to those of other farmers of the vicinity. The Rev. Phemeno Chidester, W. M. McNemar, David Whetsel and Jacob Hudson were other new residents in the valley. A separate polling place was established there about 1848.

Stone Coal creek, which is now regarded as being one of the best agricultural sections in the county, had a population in the 'forties of intelligent and enterprising farmers. To them is partly due the present fertility of the soil, for they never cropped their fields until the land became worn out. The Rev. Henry Hardman, Peter Smith, Mark Hersman, John Yoke, James Wilson, Jacob Whetsel, Thomas Hawkins and Levi Maxwell were some of the more noteworthy residents of the valley. In 1844 there were no villages along the whole course of the stream. The Lorentz store near the head of the creek and the various establishments of Weston furnished sufficient stocks of goods from which the people might select. The Curtis mill was supplanted in 1836 by the Shoulders mill. Shortly after the Methodist congregation on the creek voted to cast their lot with the Methodist Protestant church, Henry D. Hardman, at his own expense, erected a church for the few members who decided to remain with the older organization. There were then three churches on the creek. The community was then too weak to support all of them, and the Presbyterian congregation, which had maintained a precarious existence for some time, ceased to exist by 1840. Following the construction of the Staunton and Parkersburg turnpike the village of Gaston began to take form.

In what is now Court House district settlements were slow in being founded. Jim Ditcher, a freedman, was the first settler on Goosepen run, or for that matter on any of the streams which are tributary to Sand fork. He located there in the early 'thirties. Tom Boilen settled at the mouth of Rock Camp run a little later. Until the coming of the Irish, these were the only settlements in the whole region.

Those communities which had not reached a sufficient stage of development to have stores, were served after a fashion by peddlers, who with a greater or less quantity of trinkets on their backs or of store goods in their wagons, made their way from one settlement to another. A peddler's license fee was $25 per year, except for clock peddlers, who paid $100. William T. Knotts and William M. Grimes were two of the first peddlers in the county who sold at retail "goods of foreign growth and manufacture." The old peddler was a picturesque figure as he made his way over the trails in his light wagon filled with his stock of groceries, notions and dry goods which he exchanged for the products of the farm. His wagon always was full, even at the end of the trip; for the goods which he took in trade were heavier and more bulky in most cases than those he sold. The peddler was always welcomed, for his wagon was the only source from which store goods could be procured by the families who lived in the valleys remote from the older communities, and he retailed not only goods but gossip of the whole region through which he traveled.

The first show to come to Lewis County was owned by Miller, Mead and Olmstead, who gave performances in 1853 in many of the more populous communities. At intervals thereafter shady individuals gave performances in the old field schoolhouses for the edification of the natives. Most of the amusements of the people consisted, as at an earlier date, of corn huskings, grubbing frolics, quilting bees and hoe-downs.

Very few of the farmers owned slaves, because they could not afford to keep them throughout the year for the small amount of agricultural produce which resulted from their labor. The lack of a good market made the institution unprofitable; the fact that all the farmers of the county worked their own land made it unpopular. Only the nabobs at the county seat and the very rich farmers could afford to keep slaves, and they were used for a great variety of domestic service as well as for grubbing in winter and tending crops in summer.

The influence of religion upon the pioneers often led to a combination of the wild and uncouth with the pure and noble. The great revivals of that day when the unlettered preacher spoke forcefully before an even more unlettered audience were calculated to instill the fear of God into the hearts of the people and to frighten them into the fold. Perhaps it was the only effectual means of accomplishing the end for which the frontier church existed.

The influence of the church was always directed toward a higher plane of civilization. Many a community was "cleaned up" by a vigorous revival meeting and sometimes the results were fairly permanent. The regular meetings of congregations were always worth while, even aside from their spiritual importance.

The Methodists and Baptists were the leading denominations in the county until a later date. Members of other churches who settled in the county usually affiliated with one or the other of them. The Lewis circuit of the Methodist church in 1827 included ten churches, of which one was located in Harrison county, one in what is now Barbour, two in Upshur, one in Gilmer, one on Salt Lick creek, now in Braxton County, and four churches in communities now included in Lewis. Two of the classes were located on Hacker's creek, one on Stone Coal and one on Skin creek. There were but three church buildings on the circuit, and Harmony church on Hacker's creek was the only one of these now in Lewis County. Two preachers were assigned to the circuit. In 1829 occurred the schism in the Methodist church over the question of the admission of laymen to a share in the government of the church· The two congregations on Hacker's creek went over to the Methodist Protestant church, as did most of the members on Skin creek and Stone Coal.

Among the pioneer preachers of the Methodist Episcopal church whose influence helped to mould the character of the community were Forest W. Peterson,

Asa Shinn, George Brown, John Strange, and at a later date, Edmund Leehon and James G. Samson. The two last-named have perhaps never been excelled in this country as pulpit orators. Among all those of the Methodist Protestant church none ever was more widely known or more influential than the Rev. Samuel Clawson, who first came to Lewis County in 1839. He was a man of tireless energy, who rode from one section of the county to the other preaching the gospel of redemption from hell fire in the few churches of his denomination, in schoolhouses and in private homes, forming congregations and building churches. "Put that fire out," he said before a service to some members of his congregation who had gathered about a huge fireplace, "I'll soon make it hot enough for you in here." He did, according to the testimony of disinterested spectators. Among the Baptist ministers in the county there was none more successful than the Rev. Anthony J. Garrett. Though uneducated, in fact almost illiterate, he was gifted with fluent speech. He traversed all of northwestern Virginia, living a great part of the time on horseback, preaching wherever the opportunity presented itself, and always with remarkable results·

The Presbyterian church which had been established by the New Englanders soon after their coming to French creek was not in Lewis County, but it exercised a great influence over the people of the upper West Fork valley, particularly those on the Left fork. The Seventh Day Baptist church near Roanoke was not yet in existence; its greatest period of usefulness to the community came at a later date. The same may be said of the nascent United Brethren churches on Freeman's creek. The Christian church, which was established by Alexander Campbell of Brooke County early in the nineteenth century, never obtained a foothold in Lewis County; but one of its ministers, the Rev. James Shurtleff, spent some time preaching in the county.

The chronicles of the stirring times of the Indian

wars in northwestern Virginia were published in 1831 under the title of "Chronicles of Border Warfare." The author, Alexander Scott Withers, came to Harrison County in 1827, and engaged in the collection of historical materials for the work. He was greatly assisted by Judge Edwin S. Duncan, first commonwealth's attorney for Lewis County, and by William Hacker and William Powers, both residents of the district around West's fort. The work was read with avidity by old and young of the county. It has been recognized by critics as one of the best chronicles of Indian wars ever written. The author moved to Weston some time before 1837, taught school, kept a store and became a justice of the peace.

The exploitation of the natural resources of the county began about 1840 when the cutting of timber which lined the banks of the larger streams was begun for commercial purposes. Part of the lumber was sold in the home markets, but a vastly greater quantity of timber, particularly poplar and walnut logs, was floated down the West Fork and its tributaries to the mouth of the river where rafts were formed to be taken to Pittsburgh. Where clearings were made on the smaller tributaries the large trees were deadened and burned as before.

Conditions in agriculture improved somewhat. In all but the extreme southern and western portions of the territory at present embraced in the county, the farmers were raising wheat in sufficient quantities for home consumption. The establishment of new mills made this form of agriculture general, and the improvement in the equipment of all the mills made it exceedingly popular. Soda biscuits and salt-rising bread supplanted the humble corn pone at some of the meals. The methods of raising wheat were still very crude. It was cut with a sickle or cradle, and threshed with a flail or by spreading it on the threshing floor and running horses over it. The straw was afterwards thrown off with a fork, and the grain separated from the chaff by means of a crude fanning machine. Flailing wheat was a hard task, and there were many men who went from one farm to another flailing grain for a fixed price per bushel.

In preparing the seedbed the crudest kind of appliances were in use. Wooden mouldboard plows were in common use among the more progressive farmers where the land had been cleared sufficiently long to be free from roots. Crude iron plows were used on more freshly cleared lands. The "coulter" was a small bar of iron or steel which was fitted into the plow stock to cut roots; the "bulltongue" a very narrow, strong plow was run next; lastly, a shovel plow was used to tear up the soil and put it into proper shape. The harrows in use were usually equipped with wooden teeth.

The principal source of wealth continued to be cattle, though the prices were low. An appraisement bill of an estate in 1828 shows the following prices:

1 pide cow	$7.00
1 red cow	8.00
1 brindle pide Heifer	5.00
1 2 year old stear	8.00
1 red heifer with white back	3.00
1 small black bull	1.75

The cattle were driven east to Baltimore or to the terminus of the Baltimore and Ohio railroad. Helpers were given twenty-five cents a day. They traveled on foot. On their return they received one cent a mile with which to purchase food. In order to eliminate profiteering, the prices for the keeping of live stock were fixed by the county court in 1821:

For Horses per day	.8 cents
For Slaves per do	20 cents
For cattle per do	.6 cents
For sheep and hogs per do	.4 cents

A very important event in the history of Lewis County was the introduction, about 1840, of pure bred shorthorn Durham cattle. The more progressive farmers began improving their herds. Many farmers, disliking innovation or ignorant of breeding principles, continued to keep scrub stock.

Sheep raising could not reach its highest development so long as wolves continued to exist in the county. The county court very early made efforts to rid the county of them. Wolf bounties were paid to citizens of Weston in 1820. By an act passed in 1824 the county court of Lewis County was authorized to place a bounty of not to exceed $8 for an old wolf and $4 for a young one, in order to encourage the killing off of the beasts more quickly. In a few cases the effect was just the opposite of the intention of the bill. The increased reward led certain worthless individuals to take up wolf farming. When the den of a she wolf was discovered it was left unmolested until the young wolves were just ready to leave it. They were then killed, but the wolf was left in the hope that she would escape from the other hunters to return to the same place and rear her young another year. In 1832 the court paid bounties on the scalps of nineteen old wolves and fifty-five young ones. The last wolf on Hacker's creek was seen about 1854. On account of the large number of wolves in the county the value of sheep in 1828 was much greater than at a later date. By 1850 the number of sheep had increased until it was 13,393.

The administration of the county continued to be under the supervision of the justices of the peace. The court consisted of twelve justices whose remuneration consisted of the office of sheriff, which went to each justice in turn; but by the time a justice became entitled to the office he was too old for its strenuous duties. He therefore sold it to some younger man. The sheriffs rode over all the county from east of the Buckhannon river to the present Wirt County line, collecting taxes, making arrests, serving subpoenas and levying on the property of citizens to satisfy judgments. The law required that all the property of the debtor was subject to levy; but the sheriff was prevented by law from lifting a latch or raising a window. If a man could bring his property into his house before the sheriff came he could save it. That the administration of justice was somewhat crude may be inferred from the number of returns of the sheriffs which read:

"Saw the defendant, but he ran and could not be arrested."

In the absence of newspapers one of the principal sources of information was the militia organization which was formed under Camp immediately after the formation of the county. The great musters which were attended by all the citizens of the county of military age were occasions for old friends to get together and pass around the gossip of the neighborhood, for candidates to make themselves known to their prospective constituents, and for the discussion of political, moral, economic, social and religious questions of the day. The militiamen had no guns and were not drilled in the manual of arms. As a military organization they were of no value.

Lewis County had a one-man share in the Mexican war. Under the direction of Lieutenant Thomas J. Jackson, then on a furlough after having just graduated from West Point, a company was formed by Dr. Bland, who offered their services to the government. As the term of enlistment was only six months the offer was refused by the government. Lieutenant Jackson joined his regiment and acquitted himself with credit in the most difficult part of the campaign.

By the year 1845 Lewis County was just beginning to take on the air of a finished settlement. The United States government extended the postal service to reach most parts of the county at that time. The United States postal guide for 1851 gives the names of the postoffices and postmasters of Lewis County as follows:

Bennett's Mills	W. M. Bennett, Jr.
Big Skin Creek	Daniel Hall
Bush's Mills	William Rohrbough
Collins Settlement	John G. Arnold
Ireland	Isaac W. Bowse
Jane Lew	Isaac Jackson
Leading Creek	Henry W. Sleeth
Little Skin Creek	W. B. Peterson
Weston	James A. Hall

CHAPTER XVII.

EARLY TRANSPORTATION

One of the causes of the agitation which resulted in the formation of Lewis County was the neglect of the Harrison County court to furnish means of transportation for the people of the southern part of the county. There is no doubt that the people of that section had a grievance. Almost immediately following the organization of the county court that body began the work of creating a network of roads to bring all the settled portions of the county into easy communication with one another. Within two years an immense volume of road orders had been passed. Viewers were appointed to locate new roads in practically the whole expanse of the territory of the county. Especially was there an effort to develop the natural route east and west from Weston which had not been given much attention by the county court of Harrison County.

The first road order passed by the Lewis County justices appointed viewers to mark a way for a road from near Bulltown to the Elk river above Sutton. Other important roads opened within the first two years of the existence of the county were from the ford of the West Fork river at Weston to Harpold's on Murphy's creek; from Abner Mitchell's mill below the present site of Roanoke to the ford of the river below Henry Camden's (now Jacksonville); from the head of Rush run to First street in Weston; from the forks of the West fork river to the mouth of Crane's Nest Camp; up Dry Fork of Polk creek to intersect the road from the mouth of Freeman's creek to the mouth of Rush run; from Freeman's creek to the Harrison County line at Middle Island creek; from the forks of West Fork to the Haymond salt works. Every road mentioned afterward became an important highway, and practically every one at its establishment gave an outlet for a flourishing settlement. Like most of the other roads in northwestern Virginia at that period, these roads were hardly more than trails through the woods. None of them was metaled. In most cases they led through the primeval forest where the action of the sun in drying up the ground was not often of much effect. There were no culverts, and as a result the roads were generally muddy. They were not ditched properly, if at all. Yet they were roads, common property of the people of the county, which had been secured at little or no expense, and which held possibilities of being later important arteries of commerce.

The roads were not kept in good condition at all. Sometimes they were not even worked by the people who had been designated in the order creating the road. Road overseers were frequently in trouble with the courts for "failing to keep the road in repair." At a single session of the county court held in 1821, indictments were returned against George Fisher, John Waggoner, Henry Flesher and John Sleeth, all of whom were in charge of important roads through rather populous communities. Two of the roads which were not in repair were approaches to Weston, one by the river from the north, the other from Polk creek.

The hopes of the early residents of Weston for the rapid growth of the town were not so much in the building of roads, as in the development of slackwater navigation on the West Fork river. One of the reasons for the choice of the site as the county seat was the belief that the mouth of Stone Coal creek was the head of navigation of the Monongahela. In 1817 a company was in process of formation to canalize the river, which, if it had succeeded, would have made Weston a great commercial center.

The launching of the enterprise was not a sudden spurt, but followed a long period of agitation accompanied by some development. In 1793 the General Assembly passed its first act for the improvement of the Monongahela and West Fork rivers, making them navigable for passage by canoes and flatboats. In 1800 it declared the Monongahela a public highway. As we have seen, it was much used by the settlers along its course. Almost from the beginning it was the surest and best highway by which the produce of the upper valley could be taken to market.

The prospects for a great increase in the amount of the agricultural produce in the upper valley of the West Fork, if adequate means of transportation could be secured, led to the incorporation of the Monongahela Navigation Company in 1818. The prime mover in the enterprise was the indefatigable John G. Jackson, who was the business genius of the early northwest. He associated himself in the enterprise with the leading men of the section. The charter conferred upon the company authority to make the Monongahela and West Fork rivers navigable for rafts, flatboats and lumber by building dams throughout the course of the stream and by diverting the flow of the Buckhannon river into the West Fork by way of Stone Coal creek. The capital stock of the company was fixed at $150,000, of which two-fifths was to be subscribed by the state as soon as the remainder was subscribed by private parties.

The company began work of construction at once. Several dams were constructed, mostly on the lower course of the West Fork in Harrison County. The company did not build any dams in Lewis County, nor did it attempt to divert the waters of the Buckhannon to the West Fork. It was soon discovered that more water already coursed down the channel of the West Fork than the dams could hold back, for during the exceptionally great floods of 1819, most of the improvements were washed out or were completely ruined.

Twenty-one thousand dollars had been sunk in the enterprise without apparent result, and the stockholders determined to abandon the project. In 1820 the Board of Public Works ordered a survey from the courthouse of Lewis County to the Pennsylvania line to determine the advisability of taking up the work further. Ten years later proceedings were begun in the courts to have the franchises of the Monongahela Navigation Company declared void and to vest them in the Board of Public Works of the state. The opportunity was never taken advantage of by the state. Before long the dams of the company which had withstood the flood were declared public nuisances and ordered to be removed by the courts. Thus ended the only serious attempt to improve the navigation of the West Fork river. The people of northwestern Virginia were never able again to secure the aid of the state in a project for making the river navigable.

If the roseate dreams of John G. Jackson and other promoters of the enterprise had been fulfilled, Weston, at the head of navigation of the West Fork river would have been the metropolis of central West Virginia. If the project was to fail, it is as well that the work was abandoned before the added volume of the water from the Buckhannon river spread over the rich bottoms of Stone Coal.

The trade with Pittsburgh and other points down the river grew in volume notwithstanding the failure of the Monongahela Navigation Company. Flatboats continued to be built and canoes continued to be floated down the river filled with the produce of the settlers. The owners generally returned in canoes, bringing the necessities of life or cash which they had received for their produce. The river was also used for the transportation of poplar and walnut logs which were floated to Clarksburg, and there formed into rafts to be floated to the shipyards above Pittsburgh.

The principal interior routes of transportation continued to be the roads which had been constructed through the forests or along the edges of clearings. New roads were located every year, and those in existence were improved. The worst places were corduroyed with poles. Gradually bridges were being provided to enable the traveler to cross the streams at all times. In 1820 a small bridge was thrown across Maxwell's run by the supervisors of three nearby precincts on the order of the county court, but it was an insignificant structure, the work of thirty men for two days. Most of the smaller bridges of the county were similarly constructed by the combining of "companies" of different overseers. A special act was passed by the Assembly in 1826 which enabled the county courts of Lewis and Tyler counties to lay an additional levy of 33½ cents to build bridges, repair roads and locate new roads. The act bore immediate fruit in Lewis County. The same year the first bridge of any considerable size in the county was constructed across Stone Coal creek near its mouth by Jasper Butcher. It was a rather sorry structure which required considerable repairs in 1832 and was replaced by another bridge after ten years' service.

The next bridge to be built by the county was one across the West Fork river at Weston. In July, 1829, the county court appointed Levi Maxwell and John Lorentz commissioners to build a frame bridge across the West Fork river at the western extremity of Second street, to be placed on stone pillars "if in their Opinion it will be best." The bridge was completed the next year "on stone pillars." It remained in use until replaced by the state bridge in 1847-48. In 1832 the court ordered the erection of a large and expensive bridge across the Buckhannon river at the mouth of Jaw-bone run, which stood for many years. The same year bridges were built across Hacker's creek just below McWhorter's Mills, and across Freeman's creek about a mile above its mouth. The latter continued to do service until the present century, though it was often in poor repair. The efforts of the court for the next few years were confined to meeting the assessments for the construction of the Staunton and Parkersburg turnpike. In 1839, the building of bridges was resumed when Abner Mitchell was designated to construct a wooden bridge to span Canoe run near its mouth. From that time forward many of the most important crossings of the county were bridged with more or less permanent structures, some of which have continued in use until almost the present day.

A last attempt to clear the West Fork and the Little Kanawha rivers and render them navigable was made by the court in 1836. A resolution was passed ordering the sheriff to summon the justices to meet at the October term to determine the advisability of letting a contract to clear the rivers of stones, trees and rubbish. A copy of the resolutions was ordered forwarded to the courts of Monongalia, Harrison and Wood counties, but no answers were received, and there is no record of any further action having been taken by the court of Lewis.

Prosperity was to come to Weston from the improvement of the old Indian trail through the Polk creek and Stone Coal valleys, which by 1847 was a part of a main highway extending half way across the state. As early as 1823 the General Assembly directed the Board of Public Works to inquire into the expediency of a survey by the principal engineer of the state to fix the location of a road from Staunton to the mouth of the Little Kanawha river. The board reported promptly, affirming the desirability of such a survey. In March, 1824, the General Assembly passed an act providing for the opening of the road "to promote the improvement of that part of the State," and "to reduce the amount of the mileage of the public officers going to and returning from the State Capital." The sum of $1,600 was appropriated each year out of the revenues derived by the state from Pendleton, Pocahontas, Randolph, Lewis and

Wood counties to open the road, provided, that the counties named would raise an equal amount.

The share apportioned to Lewis County was $400, but the county court seems not to have taken any action toward laying a levy for the construction of the road. Private citizens resolved not to allow the opportunity to pass for want of sufficient funds from Lewis County. They organized a campaign and raised the amount by subscription by the latter part of 1825.

Most of the funds raised at this time were expended in making improvements in roads already in existence. The Randolph County court in 1814 had provided that a packhorse road should be laid out from Buckhannon to Beverly; Harrison County had established a ferry across the Buckhannon river and provided for laying out a road from Buckhannon to Henry Flesher's (Weston); Lewis County had established a road from the ford of the West Fork at Weston to the ford of Polk creek above Henry Flesher's, and later (1821) from Lewis Stallman's on Leading creek to the Wood county line on Hughes river. The Staunton and Parkersburg turnpike followed practically the route of these old trails, which may be said to have been the beginning of the through route from Richmond to the Ohio river at Parkersburg.

The location of the turnpike was not finally fixed for several years. By the end of 1826 it had been surveyed only to the mouth of Riffle's run in Randolph County. In order to hasten the work, the General Assembly directed that the county courts of Lewis, Randolph and Wood counties should each appoint one commissioner to lay off the remainder of the road by way of Beverly and Weston to Parkersburg. In 1828 the principal engineer was directed to examine the location of the road from Weston to Parkersburg with power to change the location already fixed by the commissioners. The work of surveying the route was finished the same year.

An act of the general Assembly, passed in 1830, provided for the raising of $50,000 by a lottery, the proceeds of which were to be divided among the counties of Pendleton, Pocahontas, Randolph, Lewis and Wood according to a stated proportion. The act also directed the county court of each of the above-mentioned counties to appoint a superintendent of construction. Two years later the amount appropriated for the construction of the road by the General Assembly was further increased, provided the county courts of the four counties through which the road passed should raise an equal amount.

The work of construction of the road to Weston was vigorously pushed. With the completion by the Lewis County court of the bridges across the Buckhannon and the West Fork rivers, the turnpike was a fairly good dirt road from Staunton to a point beyond Weston by 1835. The effects of the construction of the turnpike were already being seen in that year in the great number of new settlers who bought lands on Stone Coal and Polk creeks, and in the increased patronage of the Weston Inn and the Weston Hotel. The crowds were made up mostly of emigrants who came as far as Weston and then went either to the Northwestern turnpike at Clarksburg or followed the trails which led westward from Weston. By 1836 the business of keeping emigrants had become so profitable that Martin Smith, of Stone Coal creek and William J. Rice, of DeKalb, on the Little Kanawha river, applied for licenses to keep houses of public entertainment.

The work of completing the road west of Weston was delayed by the slowness of Wood County in raising the amount apportioned by acts of the General Assembly. In 1837 it was reported that the road was uncompleted through Wood and the western part of Lewis. The principal engineer of the Board of Public Works made an examination of the country the following year with a view to eliminating the difficulties with the Wood

County court, which seemed satisfied with the Northwestern turnpike then connecting Parkersburg with the east. In his report he recommended several alternative routes west of Weston which would have made it join the Northwestern turnpike east of the boundaries of indifferent Wood County. The change in the location was not carried out, as the General Assembly had determined to construct the road by the most direct route without regard to the aid received from the county courts. A long step forward was taken in 1838 when the legislature authorized the Board of Public Works to borrow $150,000 for the construction of the road from Staunton westward.

Work was begun in earnest in 1838. Large forces of men were engaged at both ends of the line but little progress was made in the eastern section for some time. The Board of Public Works experienced considerable difficulty in securing laborers due to the higher wages paid in the east and to the competition of such works as the Valley turnpike and the James River canal. The difficulties were gradually overcome and the construction of the road hastened somewhat by the large grants of money from the state legislature. No longer compelled to rely upon support from the backwoods counties through which the road passed, the promoters had reason to expect that it would soon be completed according to the best principles of highway construction then known.

In 1841 parts of the road were formally placed in operation. The Board of Public Works was given authority to establish toll gates and levy tolls on users of the turnpike, subject to certain restrictions as to maximum tolls.

An act of the General Assembly appointed a commissioner to sell out short stretches of the road along the Hughes river in the extreme western section of Lewis County. Beverly was made a point on the road in 1842, by the machinations of the delegate from Randolph County, although the route was thereby made more roundabout and the construction more difficult. An act of the legislature in 1845 appropriated $30,000 for the completion of the road between Beverly and Weston. By an act passed in 1847, bridges were provided for over the Tygart's Valley river at Huttonsville, over Hughes river, over Stone Coal creek and over the West Fork river at Weston to replace the dilapidated structure which had been completed in 1830. The next year funds were provided for additional bridges, among which, in Lewis County the more important ones were across Polk creek, and across Alum fork near its mouth.

The new bridges were solid, substantial structures without the faults of those hurriedly erected at an earlier date by the county courts. Many of them have continued in use until the present time. The Stone Coal, Polk creek, and West Fork river bridges were built by Lemuel Chenoweth, of Philippi, who had received the contract under rather interesting circumstances. He took a model of the bridges he proposed to erect to Richmond and entered it in competition with the plans and models submitted by bridge builders from all parts of the country. Few persons paid any attention to his rude unpainted model until he placed the ends on two chairs and then stood in the middle of the bridge. He dared his competitors to do the same, but none of them ventured to try it. The finished structures have proved themselves as strong as the model, as shown by the fact that the bridges across Stone Coal and Polk creeks are still in use after seventy years of constant service, and they are apparently good for another seventy years.

In order to make the turnpike fit for a considerable winter travel, an act was passed in 1849 appropriating $60,000 for macadamizing parts of it. The next year the General Assembly authorized the Board of Public Works to borrow $150,000 on the credit of the state to complete the road through the wild lands, and to macadamize the sections of the road where there was greatest need for repairs. It was provided by the same act that the maximum grade might be four and one-half per cent "at difficult points where it was unavoidable," because a great deal of trouble had been experienced in securing a suitable location in crossing Rich mountain and other high hills. Some of the bridges having been destroyed by floods in 1852 an appropriation was immediately passed to provide for rebuilding them. The amount named in the act was $100,000, which was to be used for planking and macadamizing in addition to the replacement of bridges. Heavy rains following the melting of snow which had laid on the ground through most of the winter of 1852, caused a great deal of damage to the road, apart from the washing away of bridges. According to the report of Superintendent John Brannon, of Weston, the road was in very bad condition, owing to the number of serious washouts. The tolls were reported to be wholly inadequate for the proper upkeep of the road. The legislature made no new appropriations of importance except to repair damages resulting from floods and hard usage in some sections. In 1860 the turnpike was divided into two sections with a superintendent in charge of each, their jurisdictions being divided by Cheat mountain.

The road was an ambitious attempt of the state of Virginia to establish a route for commerce between the eastern and western parts of the state. It was the only turnpike of importance entirely owned by the state, and for which the state took all responsibility, north of the Kanawha valley. Its total cost within the present limits of West Virginia was $264,043.07. Of this amount $146,403.47 had been borrowed on the credit of the state, and formed part of the Virginia debt in 1863. That the investment of Virginia in constructing the turnpike was not a profitable one is shown by the fact that only $17,080.71 was collected as tolls upon travelers. It was not expected that it would be a financial success for many years, otherwise the Board of Public Works would not have had the burden of constructing it. Private capital could easily have been secured for the task. The state took charge of the construction largely to tap the resources of a hitherto undeveloped section, and to make it commercially dependent upon the business men of the region around Richmond.

The results of the building of the road were far-reaching. While it was in course of construction work was provided for many citizens of Lewis County, for which they received payment in cash. It had been facetiously said that the mileage of members of the legislature and the income from digging ginseng had furnished the only sources of ready money in the backwoods counties. Henceforth Lewis County was out of the backwoods. Its citizens had to depend no longer for their income from agricultural produce sold in distant markets, but had markets at home. The labor required to finish the road was even greater than the local supply, and many Irish immigrants, who had just arrived in America, were attracted to the work. The great amount of unoccupied lands along the route and the easy terms of purchase offered by the proprietors, led many of them to settle permanently in Lewis County. Their wages were used for the purchase of the necessities of life or were devoted to making payments on land, and the prosperity of the county was thereby increased. The construction camps were a ready market for agricultural products. For the first time in the history of the county the people had an important local market. After the completion of the road the market still existed. The steady stream of emigrants gave great prosperity to the keepers of hotels. Ordinaries sprang up at the foot of Buckhannon mountain, at the present site of Camden, at Steinbeck's (below Alum Bridge) and at the important road junction at Linn. Minter Bailey erected on the northwest corner of Second and Main streets a three-story brick hotel building which was perhaps the largest in central West Virginia at the time of the formation of the state. A regular line of stagecoaches was established to run between Weston and Staunton. The hauling of manufactured goods over the mountains from Baltimore was largely given up on account of the fact that they could be shipped to Parkersburg and then hauled to Weston much more cheaply. The establishment of the road thus for a short time changed the course of commerce in the county.

The Staunton and Parkersburg turnpike was one of the principal causes of one of the greatest eras of business prosperity ever experienced in the county. Lateral roads were constructed almost immediately following the completion of the road, which connected the county seat with points north and south of the turnpike. The most important of these were the Weston and Charleston, the Clarksburg and Weston, the Weston and Gauley Bridge, the Weston and Lewisport, the Weston and Fairmont, the Buckhannon and Little Kanawha, and the Weston and West Union turnpikes.

The first of these roads to be established was the Weston and Charleston turnpike, which was authorized by the General Assembly in 1836. The road was to be constructed by a joint stock company in accordance with the policy of the state at that time. The capital stock was $10,000, three-fifths of which was to be appropriated by the legislature and the remainder to be raised by levy, donations and subscriptions in the counties of Lewis and Kanawha. Braxton county had no part in the construction of the road, which did not pass through the territory of that county. In 1837 Lewis County raised $1,000, of which $300 was raised by levy and the remainder from a subscription among the people. Kanawha County furnished its quota by 1842, when a commissioner was appointed to supervise the location and construction of the road.

The route as finally determined upon followed the Staunton and Parkersburg turnpike to the present site of Linn, where it crossed to Stewart creek by way of

State Road run. It passed through the present villages of Glenville, Lettergap, Normantown, Stumptown and Millstone, and reached the Elk river at Clendenin. The act of the legislature apparently did not contemplate a real connecting link betwen the northern and southern parts of the state. The appropriation was entirely inadequate for the construction of other than a dirt road. It was well graded, however, and furnished a far better means of communication than any that had previously existed in that section.

The immediate effects of the Weston and Charleston turnpike upon the development of the extreme western part of Lewis County was out of all proportion to the cost of the road. It has continued to exercise great influence over the development of Gilmer, Calhoun and Roane counties. By 1842 the town of Hartford was established at the point where the road reached the Little Kanawha river. When Gilmer County was formed, this town became the county seat. The whole district drained by the West Fork of the Little Kanawha river and by Steer creek was opened up to settlement. So great was the rush to these lands, and so brilliant the future apparent for that region that the citizens began a movement for the formation of Gilmer and Roane counties shortly after the opening of the road. It was the principal route from the West Fork to the Great Kanawha river until the construction of the Weston and Gauley Bridge turnpike nearly twenty years later.

The other roads constructed following the completion of the Staunton and Parkersburg turnpike will be treated in another chapter. They exercised a tremendous influence over the history of the county, but not perhaps as great an influence as they would have had but for the advent of the Baltimore and Ohio railroad into northwestern Virginia at this time. The new and more powerful agency of transportation had come to take the place of the slow moving wagon on the dirt road even before the completion of the Staunton and Parkersburg turnpike.

While Virginia was attempting to construct a canal from the James river to the Kanawha valley which would capture the trade of the entire west for Richmond and Norfolk, a group of Baltimore capitalists was engaged in constructing the Baltimore and Ohio railroad to the west. The locomotive reached Harper's Ferry in 1833 and Cumberland in 1842. The effect was immediately felt in the quiet dales of the West Fork. Merchants who had previously hauled all their goods from Baltimore now hauled them from the nearest railroad stop. They were thus enabled to sell them cheaper, and the citizens of the county were enabled to buy greater quantities of manufactured goods. It was no longer necessary to drive cattle all the way to Baltimore to market. They could be shipped part of the way, and they brought more per head at home because part of the expense of marketing them at home had been eliminated.

The railroad was pushed farther westward until it was opened as far as Fetterman in 1852. In 1856-7 the Northwestern Virginia railroad was completed from Grafton to Parkersburg. The final completion of this last link enabled the business men of Lewis County to have their goods hauled all the way by rail with the exception of the distance from Clarksburg.

CHAPTER XVIII.

THE IRISH AND GERMAN IMMIGRATION

The last of the five districts of the county to be settled was Court House. By 1840 every other considerable territory in the county had a number of families, and the beginnings of institutions could be discerned. Sand fork and its tributaries, Butcher's fork, Cove creek, Indian fork, and other smaller streams, together with a considerable territory on Leading creek remained unsettled except for Tom Boilen, who had settled at the mouth of Rock Camp run, and Jim Ditcher, colored, who lived on Goosepen. Everywhere else was dense wilderness. The primeval forest covered the slopes of the hills and dales. The creatures of the wild, then rapidly being exterminated before the advance of the white man found their last refuge in Lewis County on its western borders. Sand Fork in the thirties was a paradise for hunters. Deer, bears and all the other animals of the western Virginia forests remained in the valley and furnished good hunting though they had been made wary by the number of hunters who invaded their haunts.

The greater portion of this land had, of course, been patented even while the Indian wars were in progress, and some surveys had been made by the intrepid Henry Jackson and others. The Pickering survey of 100,000 acres on the headwaters of the West Fork and Little Kanawha rivers, which included part of the Sand fork lands, was made in 1785. The Ford grant made in 1797 for 27,000 acres, extended southwest from a corner near the head of Rush run. Many smaller tracts had been patented and surveyed by speculators. In almost every case the large surveys had been made with the view of inducing immigrants to make settlements; but the abundance of more desirable lands, both in western Virginia and beyond the Ohio, and the small number of immigrants who stopped in this section, caused the investments to be unprofitable. In the first quarter of the nineteenth century, most of the surveys had either been sold or had been reported delinquent.

Tracts of 100,000 acres were sometimes mortgaged for small sums and the mortgage left unpaid until it was foreclosed. Large estates changed hands for a few cents per acre. Colonel James M. Camp bought up many of the tracts on Sand fork in early years, and stored the deeds for them in his trunk without having them recorded. Unfortunately for him and for his heirs the confusion of land titles in that region was so great that other claims to the same land, almost equally good, were admitted to record by the courts. Several younger citizens of the county, believing that the Sand fork section had a future, bought up small tracts as they came on the market.

The process was hastened by a change in the policy of the state with respect to delinquent lands. The laws of Virginia respecting these lands had always been very reasonable. Under them the owners always had a long period of grace for the payment of taxes. By acts passed in 1831 and 1835, however, the titles of lands published as delinquent and not redeemed were declared forfeited. Under an act passed in 1837, a commissioner of delinquent and forfeited lands was to be appointed in every county of the northwest. His duties were to survey the tracts declared delinquent, to make adjustments for the payment of taxes if possible, and if not to sell the lands for what they would bring.

One of the first holders of the office in Lewis County was Minter Bailey, proprietor of the Weston Hotel, who had achieved some local fame as a surveyor and land speculator. Among other land dealers in the county, none were more prominent than Gideon D.

Camden and Richard P. Camden. Just what the relations were between Bailey and the two Camdens before his appointment as commissioner of forfeited lands is not clear. By 1841 a partnership between them is evident. In that year Bailey, as commissioner, "after advertising in one of the Clarksburg papers, and at the front door of the courthouse", sold a large tract to G. D. Camden for about ten cents per acre. He reconveyed one-third of it to R. P. Camden and one-third to Minter Bailey at the same price per acre he had paid for it. The greater part of the Reed and Ford surveys and part of the Pickering survey also came into the possession of the firm within a few years.

In addition to the land sold for taxes there were to be found on Sand fork isolated small tracts which had never been patented, or if patented had never been surveyed. Many of them were taken up by one of the partners and added to the common stock of Camden, Bailey and Camden. A tract of 2,172 acres lying in Gilmer and Lewis counties, but mostly in Lewis, was patented by R. P. Camden in 1846, and smaller tracts were afterwards purchased through the land office. The largest tract—one which had been overlooked, and the existence of which had probably been discovered by Minter Bailey when he was county surveyor—was taken out in 1856, a great quadrangle extending from Leading creek across Cove lick, Left fork of Sand fork, Butcher's fork and Indian fork, and containing 20,000 acres. It was unbroken except where one homeseeker had located a farm which included forty-seven acres on the eastern boundary.

It should be explained that there is no evidence of unfairness or of sharp practices in the possession of the Sand fork lands by Camden, Bailey and Camden. The old deeds show that the sales of forfeited lands at the courthouse were always well advertised according to law. Minter Bailey did only what most other county surveyors and commissioners of forfeited lands have done both before and after his time. As commissioner, he knew the legal status and the quality of all the forfeited lands, and as county surveyor he had unusual opportunities to know the location of a great deal of unpatented land. The other two members of the partnership were far sighted business men. Gideon D. Camden was a capitalist of Clarksburg, who probably financed the operations. R. P. Camden was a business man of Weston who seems to have devoted a great deal of his time to the business, and probably did most of the detailed work. It was a well-balanced partnership.

Other great landholders in the Sand fork watershed were James Bennett, Jonathan M. Bennett, George J. Arnold and William E. Arnold. Their lands were located in various parts of the region. They did not exercise as great influence in the settlement of the country as Camden, Bailey and Camden. The lands in the Sand fork watershed were seen to be desirable on account of the fact that the Staunton and Parkersburg turnpike was nearing completion. It was confidently expected that settlers who came west over the road in search of homes would be attracted to the lands, now that means of transportation were assured.

They were not disappointed in their hopes of forming a colony. Many of the laborers engaged in the construction of the Staunton and Parkersburg turnpike were recent immigrants from Ireland and Germany. They had been engaged in construction work on many of the public works then building in all parts of the United States. The effects of the panic of 1837 in decreasing the amount of construction work everywhere continued to be felt for many years thereafter. The Staunton and Parkersburg turnpike, being under construction by the state, did not feel the effects of the panic as did enterprises of private concerns. When it was practically completed the laborers seemed to be out of employment, for all the other construction projects had all the laborers they could use. They were glad of any opportunity to make a living until conditions should improve. The advantages of settling on the lands owned by Camden, Bailey and Camden were early brought to their attention. In order to provide farms within range of their means the large tracts were divided into smaller tracts of from fifty to one hundred acres. Few of the Irish laborers had sufficient funds to purchase their lands outright, but the matter was waived by the owners who arranged that they should pay for them as soon as they were able. Meanwhile the Irish were to build their homes on the land, clear as much as they wished and raise their crops.

The first Irish to take advantage of the opportunity were John Hayden, Thomas White, John and Michael McLaughlin, Michael and Patrick Copely, Patrick Hare, James and Thomas Mullady, Thomas and Anthony Hart and William Murphy. Minter Bailey needed a varied supply of provisions for the Bailey House, including venison, chickens, potatoes, corn, wheat and pork. The need was partly met by the residents on the lands of the firm, who received credit on their accounts; but by far the greater amount was paid in cash.

The clearing of the land was done by the men during the winter when the demand for labor was not very great. As soon as spring came, the Irish put out their crops and then went in search of work to do either on the farms of other citizens or on public works. The cultivation of the crops was left in the hands of the wives and children. Sometimes the men went away from home in the spring and did not return to their farms until the beginning of the following winter—but they always returned. Soon by the united efforts of husbands and wives they accumulated sufficient ready money to buy their way to landed independence.

One of the first deeds recorded from Camden, Bailey and Camden in the county clerk's office in Lewis County transfers title to land on Sand fork to Thomas and James Malady, 1845. From that time on a great number of these deeds were recorded every year. The price paid for the land was from $2.75 to $3.00 per acre.

The proprietors could afford to allow the Irish and Germans to settle on their lands without requiring the payment of rental of any kind because of the fact that every small tract improved enhanced the value of all the lands in the vicinity. Every acre grubbed and put under cultivation or seeded to grass meant an increase in the value, not only of that parcel of ground, but of all other lands in the vicinity. The proprietors would have lost nothing if an occasional settler had become discouraged and left his farm without making any payment at all.

As a matter of fact few of the thrifty immigrants were ever long in arrears in making payment for their land. 'Squire Oliver says that not a single Irishman abandoned his farm or allowed it to slip from his grasp. They had stopped working on construction jobs in order to settle on Sand fork and they meant to stay there no matter what happened.

By 1848 the Irish colony on Sand fork was so large its permanence so evident and its prospects for a further great development so bright that steps were taken by their leaders to secure a church of their faith. The next year Camden, Bailey and Camden conveyed to Bishop Francis V. Whelan of the diocese of Wheeling, thirty acres of land on Loveberry run and Rock run for the purpose of building a church and laying out a cemetery. This tract was afterwards utilized as the site of the first Catholic church on Sand fork.

Other owners of lands on Sand fork also became interested in the possibility of developing them by settling a colony of Irish and Germans upon them. George J. Arnold and William E. Arnold, owners of an extensive block of land, busied themselves in competition with Camden, Bailey and Camden, and succeeded in forming what is known as the "Murray Settlement" on the upper tributaries of Indian fork. It grew and prospered with only less rapidity than the Sand fork settlement.

The potato famine in Ireland, 1846, drove a large

proportion of the population to the United States. Many of them found employment in the construction of the Baltimore and Ohio railroad which was then being pushed westward from Cumberland to Wheeling. Practically all the excavation for the roadbed was done by the new immigrants. Some of those who had been in America for some time held positions as foremen. Some of these immigrants were also attracted, before the completion of the railroad, to the route of the Staunton and Parkersburg turnpike which was then being macadamized. From either of these improvements it was only a step to the magnificent domain of Camden, Bailey and Camden, and many of the laborers settled among the earlier comers. It is related that R. P. Camden went to the camps along the Baltimore and Ohio railroad and explained the advantages of the land on Sand fork, and that the Arnolds also made special efforts to bring the Irish to the lands. It is also reported that Bishop Whelan, who had gone among the immigrants establishing missions from the time they came to western Virginia, also recommended that they buy land on Sand fork and settle there. After the movement had begun, the best advertisement for the lands was the sight of the farms which had been established on Sand fork. The completion of the railroad left many of the laborers out of work temporarily, and more of them sought jobs along the turnpike or purchased lands from Camden, Bailey and Camden and others along Sand fork and its tributaries.

Michael Collins, James Dempsey, Thomas Kenstry Thomas Mulvaney, Peter Doonan, Edward Doonan, Michael Carroll, Thomas Timms, Thomas Lynch, Patrick Hoar and others were all on Sand fork or its tributaries by the end of 1852. Among the Germans who came about the same time were Lorentz Schuhtretler, John Finster, Bernard Krouse, Johannes Martin, Anthony Stark, George Scherer and Joseph Stark, all attracted to the western part of Lewis County by the prospect of securing cheap lands. The center of the first

German immigration seems to have been on tributaries of Leading creek, though they were also scattered among the hollows of Sand fork.

Not all the Irish in Lewis County settled on Sand fork. According to a census of the town of Weston by a boy in 1845, there were then living in the town "one Irishman and five children." There were doubtless others in the vicinity. Bishop Whelan in that year established a Catholic mission at Weston, and held services in the Bailey House for the benefit of all members of the Catholic faith in Lewis County. Most of the Irish citizens of Weston made their living at first by working at odd jobs or helping contractors at various work. Later they established themselves in business.

The first comers to Sand fork and Leading creek were frugal and enterprising. Though their lands were so rough and so little desired for settlement that they had been left in the wilderness for over sixty years after the more desirable lands in the valley of the West Fork were occupied, yet the immigrants, by careful clearing, close cultivation and constant care have developed them into excellent farms of bluegrass pastures. The example of the Irish had a good influence over other farmers in the community who copied their methods of raising potatoes with profit. There was little inclination on the part of the citizens of the county to associate with the immigrants for several years, and the feeling was reciprocated to some extent. Yet the Irish and Germans, by attending strictly to business, got along well. They became good citizens, all of them. The records of the courts for 1857-8 are filled with notations of applications for citizenship or for first papers. Martin Kinney, John Finster, later the millwright of Sleepcamp run, Simon Finster, John McCally, John Mellett, John Collinan, John Bergin, Elick Burk, Thomas Conroy, John Tully, Lawrence Dunagan, Patrick Downey, Patrick Hoar and Michael McLaughlin are names of some of the applicants. The new settlers had traveled over all the United

States in laboring on public works, and they were perhaps more national than the citizens of the county who had lived all their lives here. They hated slavery; they knew nothing and cared nothing for state's rights; they knew only that their prosperity and independence were due to America. During the war they were staunch Union men, regarding their oaths to their new country before their allegiance to their state. A great portion of Company "B", 15th Virginia Infantry, was made up of Irish and Germans who served under an Irish captain.

After the war the development of the Sand fork watershed continued. Many roads were caused to be viewed by the county court and many schoolhouses were erected in a district which twenty-five years before had been a wilderness. There were many other signs of increased prosperity.

In 1866 occurred the death of Minter Bailey, and the firm of Camden, Bailey and Camden was broken up. Their lands were divided. The third portion assigned to the estate of Minter Bailey was cut up into small tracts to be sold at auction by a commissioner. The terms of sale were as liberal as any arrangement that had so far been made, purchasers being given an extended time in which to make payments. Sixty-three tracts were sold in 1870 alone, and the sales continued for some time thereafter, it being the policy of the commissioner to sell to actual settlers as far as possible. Many of the farmers took advantage of the opportunity to add to their farms, especially since the large number of sales caused the price of the lands to be reduced from their pre-war figures. The Camdens continued to sell small tracts from their holdings at intervals almost to the present time. They are still charged on the Lewis County assessor's books with many hundred acres of land.

CHAPTER XIX.

LOSSES OF TERRITORY

It was unavoidable that when the outlying portions of Lewis County were settled they would break the slender bonds which held them within the county and form new local political divisions. The establishment of the seat of justice at Weston, less than ten miles from the Harrison County line, rendered it very inconvenient for the citizen who lived on Steer creek or on the Elk river to attend court. There were few settlements or none at all in these valleys in 1817, and the county seat was then located where it would best serve the majority of the people. By 1840 it was no longer convenient for half the people of the county.

The first sign of approaching dismemberment is indicated in the formation of Nicholas County from Greenbrier in 1818. It included settlements which had been made on the Gauley and its tributaries and some on the lower Elk river. There were many other settlers in the valley of the Elk who had been attracted there by the prospects of good hunting and also by the fertile soil and the broad valleys of some of the streams. Even before the close of the Indian wars there was a respectable settlement in the vicinity of Sutton. These settlers were in close proximity to the principal settlement which had been made by that time on the Little Kanawha river and its tributaries. Salt Lick creek was the most compact of these settlements. In 1773 more homesteads were located on the creek than on Hacker's creek. The establishment of Haymond's salt works in 1808 had attracted many settlers who made a living from the produce of their farms and even sold supplies to other settlers who had come to buy salt. The upper valley of the Little Kanawha around the present site of Burnsville had also attracted immigrants far more than the lands on the small eastern tributaries of that river. Here was a considerable community cut off from the county seat by the unbroken wilderness of Oil creek, Leading creek, Sand fork and other streams. The people were dissatisfied almost from the first with their position on the edge of the two counties, and at a distance from the county seat of either. In 1836 the settlements on the Elk and the upper course of the Little Kanawha were detached from Lewis, Nicholas and Kanawha counties and formed into the new county of Braxton. It extended in a broad semicircle between Lewis and Nicholas from Webster Springs to the present site of Clay Court House. From its peculiar shape, it was called for years "the jug handle county."

A part of the northeastern corner of Lewis County was next detached to form a part of Barbour. The community on the lower Tygart's Valley river had grown rapidly with the advance of settlement in northwestern Virginia. It was one of the first regions settled, and by 1843 there were five or six thousand people living within the present limits of the county. The natural center of the community was at Philippi on the edge of Harrison and Randolph. In order to secure a sufficient radius of territory around it, a portion of Lewis, including about eighty square miles, with a population of about five hundred, was attached to the new county.

The progress of construction on the Northwestern and the Staunton and Parkersburg turnpikes was instrumental the same year in causing the formation of another county out of the princely domain of Lewis. Opened in 1838, the Northwestern turnpike brought life to the sleepy settlements on the North fork of Hughes river and caused the acceleration of immigration to the region, where lands were cheap and very desirable as compared to the other vacant lands in northwestern

Virginia. The simultaneous construction of the Staunton and Parkersburg turnpike brought a corresponding development to the South fork of Hughes river. Both valleys had an outlet to the Ohio river, and to the eastern markets for their produce. In 1842 the legislature established the town of Smithville in Lewis on the South fork of the river, which became a center of commerce between Weston and Parkersburg, just as Pennsboro and Ellenboro were centers on the Northwestern turnpike. Nearly three thousand people were living in the Hughes river valley remote from their courthouses at Weston and Clarksburg when a bill was introduced in the legislature, 1843, providing for the formation of the county of Ritchie. No objection to the measure was made by delegates from Lewis and Harrison, and the bill became a law. Ritchie included part of Wood and a part of what is now Doddridge.

Lewis County was then left with the valleys of the upper West Fork, the Buckhannon and the Little Kanawha from Braxton to the present Wirt-Calhoun line. The last named region was undeveloped except for three sections—along the Little Kanawha river, on the route of the Staunton and Parkersburg turnpike, and in the territory south of the Little Kanawha river which had been opened to settlement by the construction of the Weston and Charleston road. The whole region was isolated. The settlements in the Sand fork and Leading creek valleys were then in their infancy. The settlers of the Little Kanawha had different economic interests from those of the remainder of the county. Their trade was down the river toward Parkersburg, where they sold their rafts of logs cut at the water's edge, and brought back merchandise. The establishment of Hartford on or near the present site of Glenville in 1842 gave the settlers of that section a common center for trade and a nucleus for a county town· The two thousand people living in the district now known as Gilmer and Calhoun counties started a movement for independence at the same time as the people in the Hughes river valley, but the persuasions of the people of the county seat caused the movement to be prosecuted half-heartedly, until the success of the Hughes river residents caused them to redouble their efforts. Some objections from the eastern part of the county were still to be overcome, but in 1845, they secured the election of the delegate to the legislature to champion their cause. The result was that the citizens of the western part of Lewis and the northern part of Kanawha were formed into the county of Gilmer. The selection of Glenville as the county seat of the county was very unsatisfactory to the people living in the western portion of the county, who split off in 1855 to form Calhoun.

The year 1845 was also memorable for the creation of another county in the Virginia northwest which took part of the territory of Lewis. The formation of Ritchie in 1843 had included in its eastern part settlers who had been accustomed to making their business as well as their political center at Clarksburg, and the change was unsatisfactory to them. The dwellers of the valley of Middle Island creek, who still belonged to Lewis County, found that their interests were mainly along the Northwestern turnpike, rather than across the divide on the upper West Fork. Many of the settlers who had been left with Harrison County joined with the others, with the result that Doddridge was formed.

With the possible exception of the northeastern part of the county which was cut away to form a part of Barbour, the division up to 1850, of the territory of Lewis into other bailiwicks was a distinct advantage to the remainder of the people of the county. The center of wealth and commerce was around Weston and Buckhannon. The western part of the county, which had long been neglected, was just beginning to demand attention from the county court, and new improvements were demanded which would require large expenditures from the county treasury—improvements like the Weston and Charleston turnpike, which, though valuable to the region through which it passed, were of little use to the citizens of the county who paid the greater portion of the taxes, and who preferred that the proceeds should be spent nearer home. The needs of the western part of the county were perhaps being neglected to some extent by the selfish county court. Such a state of affairs was to have been expected. The upper West Fork valley had suffered from like treatment at the hands of the Harrison County court before 1816. Western Virginia was at this time suffering intensely from the treatment of the eastern politicians who insisted upon taxing the citizens of the west unjustly and spending among them less than the amount paid in. The remedy for the discontent—the only remedy that would be fair to all sections—was dismemberment.

After the loss of the western section of the county, Lewis was fairly homogeneous. A little further reduction of territory drained by the tributaries of the Little Kanawha would have made the county more of a geographical unit, and it would not have affected the interests of the inhabitants, because there were none. Collins Settlement was loyal to Lewis County. Many of the prominent leaders of the county had been born there. There was no danger of a movement being begun to form the southern end of the county, with parts of Braxton and Randolph, into a new county. The eastern part of the county alone desired an independent political organization. Three years after the formation of Gilmer and Doddridge, the people of the Buckhannon valley began to agitate for the creation of a new county.

Various reasons have been assigned for the discontent. In the first place the county seat was at Weston, and the town derived all the honor and emoluments which belonged to that important spot in every Virginia county. Weston merchants were able to keep better goods than those of Buckhannon, though they had a tough competitor in Jacob Lorentz. The schools were better at Weston than elsewhere in the county. The Weston mill had better patronage. Buckhannon business men thought that all the inequalities would be abolished by the establishment of a county seat east of the Buckhannon mountain. A second reason is to be found in the different political views held by the people of the two sections. Those in the Buckhannon valley were largely Whigs of the Henry Clay type; but those of the West Fork valley were almost solidly Democrats.

In 1848 the citizens of the Buckhannon valley demanded that a vote be taken on the question of the division of the county. It carried almost unanimously in the precincts now embraced within Upshur County, only thirty-seven votes being cast in opposition to the measure. James Bennett, who was then the delegate from Lewis, Gilmer and Braxton counties in the General Assembly, paid no attention to the vote of separation. A petition asking that a bill be introduced in the legislature for the formation of a new county was prepared by citizens of the Buckhannon valley and handed to him in December, 1849, just after the General Assembly went into session; but no bill was introduced. A second petition was given to him early in January; a third, on January 8; a fourth on January 24. Against these petitions, which might have made the position of Delegate Bennett rather uncomfortable without a counter-movement, the citizens of the West Fork valley, principally of Weston, prepared a memorial remonstrating against the formation of the new county.

At the next election, 1850, the division of the county was the principal issue. Samuel L. Hays of Gilmer was nominated for House of Delegates by the Whigs. Being from Gilmer, he of course cared little for the territorial integrity of Lewis; and early in the campaign he announced his intention of supporting the movement to form a new county. He was elected through the almost unanimous vote of the Buckhannon valley. Immediately upon the opening of the legislative session in the fall of

1850 he introduced a bill into the house for the creation of the new county. The citizens of Buckhannon sent a lobbyist to Richmond to work for the measure both in the House of Delegates and in the Senate. In spite of the opposition offered by the residents of the West Fork valley, the measure became a law, and in 1851, Upshur County began its separate existence. Besides the eastern part of Lewis, the new county included part of Randolph and a small portion of the strip ceded by Lewis to Barbour in 1843.

Lewis County was thus reduced to its present boundaries. It has remained a geographical unit from 1851 to the present time, without any serious attempts being made to form new counties from parts of its territory.

CHAPTER XX.

THE GREAT BUSINESS BOOM, 1845-60

The period from 1845 to 1860 may rightly be called the era of commercial awakening in Weston and Lewis County. Beginning about 1845 there was a tremendous burst of energy among the people; internal improvements had broken down the barriers which had heretofore circumscribed the interests of Lewis County and the people found themselves in a world bigger than any they had ever dreamed of. Industry was stimulated; living conditions improved; and before the period was half over Weston was a center of the business life of northwestern Virginia, and Lewis County was regarded as one of the most prosperous agricultural communities in the state.

There were several reasons why Weston took the lead during this period. The completion of the Staunton and Parkersburg turnpike brought immigration, stimulated business prosperity and established a home market; but it alone could not have produced the result. The effect of the great panic of 1837 which had stopped investment of capital and temporarily checked the wheels of industry, had practically disappeared; but the return of prosperity would only have meant a consolidation of the results already accomplished and a further growth along the old lines for a number of years.

A community is rarely singled out by fortune to be the recipient of a very great development. The real explanation is believed to be in the great number of men of large vision and of untiring energy who formed a part of the population of the county—men like Jonathan M. Bennett, R. P. Camden, Minter Bailey, C. J. Moore,

David S. Peterson, George W. Jackson, A. A. Lewis, George J. Arnold, William E. Arnold, R. J. McCandlish and others of like stamp. The efforts of the Camdens, the Arnolds and Minter Bailey to settle the wild Sand Fork country have been noticed already; Jonathan M. Bennett, one of the greatest of the luminaries, a young man who had only just begun to come to the front in 1844, deserves special mention. He was born in Collins Settlement, the son of William Bennett, 4 October 1816. His early education was obtained in the schools of the neighborhood, and in the school taught by Matthew Holt in Weston. In 1844 he was a young lawyer of diffident manners. He soon became a leader in the councils of the Democratic party in the northwest, and one of the leading capitalists of the county through his attention to business and his careful investments. David S. Peterson was a farmer who lived about a mile out Polk creek, and was regarded as one of the wealthiest men in the county. A. A. Lewis was a new comer in the county, as was R. J. McCandlish, first cashier of the Exchange bank, who came from Norfolk.

One of the signs of the new era was the formal incorporation of Weston as a town. The government by trustees was superseded by a government with a mayor, sergeant (chief of police), recorder, and five aldermen. The limits of the town as fixed in the act of incoporation were about the same as those before the coming in of the McGary addition, North Weston and the other late accretions. Jonathan M. Bennett was the first mayor of Weston. The aldermen were Addison McLaughlin, lawyer; John Lorentz, tan-house owner; Conrad Kester, gunsmith; Elias Fisher, and M. Lazell. So far as improvements were concerned there appears to have been little difference between the new government and the old. There was a police protection of a sort, and added dignity and importance.

The Staunton and Parkersburg turnpike had scarcely been completed when Weston made efforts to secure a railroad. The Baltimore and Ohio railroad, which had reached Cumberland in 1839, was anxious to extend its lines to the Ohio river. The logical route was by way of Wills creek and the Youghiogheny—the old Braddock road, and the route used later in part by the National road; but Pennsylvania also had a road in process of construction to Pittsburgh and the route through the state was refused. The company applied to the legislature of Virginia for permission to build the lines across the northwestern part of the state and to make its terminus at Parkersburg or Point Pleasant. The matter was under consideration in 1846. Virginia capitalists in the Tidewater section did not wish to see the trade of the northwest diverted to Baltimore but wanted Richmond and Norfolk to secure it. They therefore proposed an all-Virginia railroad which would start at Alexandria, and run by way of Moorefield, in Hardy County, and Weston to Parkersburg. In the summer of 1846 a monster convention of 1400 delegates from all the counties in the Parkersburg district assembled at Weston in the interest of the proposed railroad. Strong resolutions were adopted in favor of it—resolutions which called the attention of the assembly in no uncertain terms to the magnificent improvements which had already been constructed in the eastern part of the state, while the people of the west had not a single railroad or canal.

The people did not secure their railroad. By a compromise the Baltimore capitalists were allowed to construct the Baltimore and Ohio railroad through Virginia, but it was confined to the northern limits of the state, with its terminus at Wheeling. Other means of transportation were taken up by the people of Weston and other points with the result that before many years, Weston became a center of improved roads which radiated, like the spokes of a wheel, in every direction.

The first of these turnpikes, which were really lateral feeders of the Staunton and Parkersburg turnpike, was constructed in 1847. The inconvenience of having to depend upon the narrow, muddy road connecting Weston with points north in the Monongahela valley led to the incorporation of the Clarksburg and Weston turnpike in 1847. The capital stock was fixed at $12,000 in shares of $100 each. Lewis Maxwell, Minter Bailey and J. M. Bennett, at Weston; Stephen P. Jackson and Walter McWhorter, at Jane Lew; and three citizens of Clarksburg were authorized to open books and receive subscriptions of stock for the new road. It was also provided that the county courts of Lewis and Harrison might make subscriptions. It was the favorite method of road improvement at that time for private citizens to form companies to construct roads. Tolls were charged to meet the expenses of upkeep and to provide dividends for the stockholders. The road was opened via Jane Lew and Lost Creek the same year. Like the Weston and Charleston road its surface was clay, and it was not of much use in winter. The route was further improved two years later.

In 1849 the Weston and Fairmont turnpike was incorporated with a capital stock of $16,000 in shares of $25 and the Board of Public Works was authorized to subscribe $9,600. The company opened the road along the route located through Jane Lew. The road was hampered by lack of funds, and in spite of the fact that the Board of Public Works borrowed $4,000 for the road in 1848 it remained little better than it was before the company relieved the citizens along the route of the task of keeping the road in repair. The road was designated as the route for mail from Clarksburg, in 1850, and a regular mail stage was established the next year.

In 1858 Mail Contractor John D. Sinnett, filed notice that he would apply to a justice of the peace to have a jury summoned to examine the section of the road near the county line to determine whether the tolls should be discontinued on account of the damaged condition of the road. The section was repaired by the company.

It was upon this turnpike after the completion of

the Northwestern Railroad from Grafton to Parkersburg that a regular stage line was put in operation which brought better mail service in addition to greater convenience in traveling. The coach was driven by Peter Dargan for many years, who, following the custom of the drivers of the old stages, would let his horses go at the regular speed until he came to the bridge across Stone Coal and then drive furiously to the corner of Second street.

In 1847 a company was incorporated with a capital stock of $25,000 to build a turnpike between Weston and Lewisport, in Doddridge, a few miles east of West Union. The county courts of Lewis and Doddridge were also given permission to make subscriptions. The route for the road was disputed among various communities, special objection coming from West Union; the capital stock was too large for two-fifths of it to be raised in order to secure the subscription of $15,000 authorized by the legislature from the board of Public Works; and other impediments caused the abandonment of the scheme. It was taken up again in 1851 when the Weston and West Union Turnpike Company was incorporated with a capital stock of $14,000, the road to be built on a route surveyed by Joseph McCally, engineer of the Board of Public Works. The state's subscription was to be $8,400. The road followed a direct route via Dry fork, Left fork of Freeman's creek, Fink creek and Indian fork of Middle Island creek. It made use of the Staunton and Parkersburg turnpike to the mouth of Dry fork, but owing to the fact that part of the route was new, the opening of the road as a public highway was delayed until 1862. It later accomplished much for the development of the northwestern part of Lewis County.

The Buckhannon and Little Kanawha turnpike (sometimes called the Buckhannon and Bulltown road) was incorporated in 1849 to run by way of French creek to some point on the Weston and Gauley Bridge turnpike south of Weston. The capital stock was fixed at $12,000, of which the state was to take the customary three-fifths provided that the other two-fifths should be raised by private subscription. The road was opened about 1855. It entered the present county of Lewis by way of the Left fork of the river and followed that stream to Bennett's mill where it crossed and proceeded up the Right fork for a short distance. It then crossed to Abram's run, and thence to the present Lewis-Braxton line. Not well constructed in the beginning, it is still the rockiest road in the county. The important bridge at Bennett's mill was its chief contribution to the development of Lewis County.

By far the most important of all the lateral feeders of the Staunton and Parkersburg turnpike was the Weston and Gauley Bridge turnpike, incorporated in 1851. The necessity for a north and south road connecting the Great Kanawha and Monongahela valleys had been felt almost from the establishment of Lewis County. As early as 1827 the surveyor of the Board of Public Works was ordered to survey and locate a road from Gauley Bridge to Nicholas Court House (Summersville), thence to Haymond's salt works (Bulltown), thence to Lewis Court House and thence to Salem. If the survey was made nothing came of it at once. The next attempt to unite the two sections resulted in the construction of the Weston and Charleston turnpike in the late 'thirties. Though it followed a roundabout route, it was the only connecting link between the Monongahela and Great Kanawha valleys other than the narrow trails hacked out through the laurel thickets of the back counties and utterly unfit to be used for wagons.

The plan to build the road from Weston to Gauley Bridge met with great favor among the people because it was seen that the completion of the road would make the whole district tributary to Weston. The opening of the books for subscriptions was so successful that the entire amount was quickly subscribed, and the work of construction began the same year.

In general the route decided upon followed the old roads marked by commissioners, appointed by the Lewis County court thirty years before, except where a change was necessary by reason of the legislative proviso making the maximum grade five per cent. In 1820 commissioners had been appointed to locate a road from First street in Weston to the head of Rush run, and the next year from the head of Rush run to the head of Granney's creek at the Nicholas County line. The last named road was declared a public highway in 1832. Both together formed what was known for many years as the "Salt works road."

The Weston and Gauley Bridge turnpike was surveyed and located by Minter Bailey and others. It ascends high mountains, like Powell's mountain in Nicholas County, by easy grades, rarely reaching the maximum of five per cent. It winds round ridges, descends into valleys for a space and then climbs to the ridges again. From its location on the benches along the divide between the West Fork and the Little Kanawha river systems can be seen the hills and valleys for miles around, making it perhaps the most picturesque road in the county. The turnpike was constructed thirty feet wide throughout. In a few places it was macadamized or corduroyed but for the most part it was simply a well constructed, well drained, dirt road, its high location making a metaled surface less important than in the case of other West Virginia roads. The initial capital stock of $30,000 was increased by $15,000 in 1857. Thirty thousand dollars was added the same year for the purpose of building bridges over the Little Kanawha and West Fork rivers and Salt Lick creek and for graveling the roadbed. It was following this act that the Bendale bridge was constructed.

The importance of the road in the development of Collins Settlement can hardly be estimated. From almost the opening of the turnpike there was a great volume of travel. A blacksmith shop was built at the foot of the hill on the Carrion run side as soon as the road was opened. The community at the mouth of Sand fork and Canoe run, which had grown up around Waldo's mill, was augmented by a store and ordinary operated by Joseph Hall, and the postoffice of Bush's Mills was established before the outbreak of the Civil war with one of the Rohrboughs as postmaster. The office was kept in a log house which still stands by the side of the road between the mouth of Canoe run and Roanoke. Jacksonville became probably the most important place in the county next to Weston. It had the advantage of a location at the junction of the turnpike and the road coming down the West Fork valley, and the citizens were enterprising enough to take advantage of their opportunities. And all the goods sold in the stores, all the imported commodities in use by the people of not only the upper West Fork valley but of practically all of Braxton County as well, were hauled over the Weston and Gauley Bridge turnpike until the construction of the Baltimore and Ohio railroad into Braxton County in the early nineties.

The possession of the road was of the utmost strategic importance in the Civil war. It was the chief line of communication between the armies of the Monongahela valley and those operating in the Kanawha and New river valleys. Rosecrans advanced over it to conquer the Kanawha valley. Confederate raiders used it in retreating from the West Fork. Weston became an important stratigic center and Clarksburg an important depot of supplies, all on account of the road.

Other important turnpikes constructed during the period were the Weston and West Milford, which followed the right bank of the river, and the West Union and New Salem road which passed up Hacker's creek and Buckhannon run in Lewis County. The outbreak of the Civil war interrupted further progress in building roads. The military campaigns cut to pieces the existing highways; the state government which followed the government of Virginia was unable to furnish aid in turnpike construction; and public sentiment in the county was not sufficiently educated to appreciate the value of good roads. Interest has only recently been awakened by the advent of the automobile.

The good effects of the construction of the turnpike system centering at Weston were not confined wholly to the country districts, but had their influence as well upon the town. New people came who constructed dwellings far more commodious than those already there. The older residents made improvements in their properties so that within a few years the whole aspect of the town was completely changed. It was no longer a collection of houses of which the log buildings were the best.

A. A. Lewis established a store in 1849 which was a center of trade under his guidance for half a century, and other stores followed. Minter Bailey built a brick building across the street from his old stand and moved his "Weston Hotel" into it. Henceforth it was called the Bailey House. He also established a still in what is now West Weston where he manufactured most of the beverages partaken of by the customers of the half dozen ordinaries in Weston. An effort was made to improve the schools of Weston through the short-lived Lewis County Seminary, incorporated in 1847. The system of private schools was, however, too deeply engrafted into the life of the town to be changed.

The first newspaper was established in 1847 by Benjamin Owen, formerly a foreman in the office of the New York Tribune under Horace Greely. The Weston Sentinel, as it was called, was a four-page, six-column journal published in the interests of the Democratic party, which was then in the ascendency in Lewis County in spite of the tremendous Whig sentiment in the Buckhannon river settlements. The paper was liberally supported from the first, both in subscriptions and in advertising. Many of the merchants of Clarksburg advertised in it.

Owen continued to publish the weekly until the office was burned down in 1853. He apparently did not care longer to continue in the newspaper business, and the paper was revived under the editorship of W. D. Tapp, who sold it to F. D. Alfred in 1856. The name of the paper was then changed to "The Weston Herald." It continued in existence, always an apologist for slavery and states' rights, until the Union troops came to Weston.

Two new churches were established in Weston shortly before the middle of the century. The first services of the Episcopal church in Weston were held by the Rev. Ovid A. Kinsolving, of Christ Church, Clarksburg. A church was organized by the Rev. Samuel D. Tompkins, of Parkersburg, at a meeting held in 1847 in the new Southern Methodist church presided over by Major Thomas Bland. The church began its existence with two members. Thomas Bland, Joseph Darlinton and Samuel Tompkins were appointed trustees, to purchase ground and erect a church building. They bought the lot where the Baptist church now stands from Lewis Maxwell for $130, and there erected a frame church, which was consecrated by Bishop Meade in 1850. The Rev. Tompkins continued to serve the church at Weston for several years, being followed by R. A. Castleman, James Page and T. H. Smythe, under whose ministry the rectory was built.

The foundation of the Catholic church in Weston was due largely to the construction of the Parkersburg and Weston turnpike and the Irish immigration to Lewis County which followed. In 1845, when there was "one Irishman and five children" in Weston, the Rev. Francis Vincent Whelan, Bishop of Wheeling, celebrated the first mass in an upstairs room of the Bailey House in the presence of a group of Irish workingmen and their families, some of whom had walked all the way from Sand fork. The visits of Bishop Whelan continued for some time. In 1848 a permanent pastor was appointed in the person of Father A. F. Crogan, who began the erection of a small brick church on the hillside where Robert L. Bland now lives. He was followed by the Rev. B. Stack, under whose ministry the church was completed.

All sects in the town had contributed generously to the construction of the church, and it became an important educational center in the community almost from the first. The priests were all men who had good classical educations, and their schools in the basement of the church on the hill were attended by boys who afterward became prominent in the life of Weston and Lewis County. Father L. C. L. Brennan, who succeeded Father Stack in 1855, is thought to have established the school, and it was continued by Fathers James V. Cunningham, L. O'Conner and John McGill.

The little brick church on the hillside had great influence over the further growth of the Catholic faith in Lewis County and northwestern Virginia. It was the fourth church of the denomination in what is now West Virginia. There were no other churches in this section with the exception of a small church at West Union which had been established for the spiritual welfare of the workmen on the Baltimore and Ohio railroad who had moved to Doddridge county and taken up lands. Churches which have since been built at Clarksburg and other towns, as well as the Sand Fork churches, are offshoots from the Weston church.

Connection with the outside world by means of the stage line to Staunton was not deemed sufficient by the people. Following the completion of the Baltimore and Ohio railroad to Wheeling, a Virginia corporation which, however, was financed by the Baltimore and Ohio company, received a charter to construct a railroad from Grafton to Parkersburg in 1852. Some of the members of the legislature fondly hoped that this home company would compete with the Baltimore and Ohio, and having the southern route, would soon acquire the ascendency in the trade. In the same year that the charter was granted influential politicians of Weston secured the passage of a bill authorizing the construction of a branch of the Northwestern railroad from Clarksburg to Weston. The corporation of Weston was allowed to borrow $20,000 to be subscribed to the stock of the company if the measure was approved by the qualified voters of the town. Apparently the promoters of the Northwestern railroad had enough to do in the construction work from Grafton to Parkersburg, for they paid no attention to the proposed branch to Weston.

In 1852 a branch of the Exchange Bank of Virginia was established at Weston, with Jonathan M. Bennett as president and R. J. McCandlish as cashier. The capital stock of the branch was fixed at $150,000, but an act of the legislature passed in 1853, provided that the capital might be increased to not more than $300,000. The bank building was located at first on the site now occupied by the store of T. N. Barnes, and was later moved to the Bennett property. The branch at Weston was at the time of its establishment the only banking institution between Staunton and Chillicothe, and between the branch at Lewisburg and the Northwestern bank at Wheeling. It served an immense territory. Business men came all the way from Parkersburg, Fairmont, Beverly, Summersville and intermediate points in order to secure loans or transact other business with the bank. The only day on which loans were made was Wednesday; and so great was the crowd on that day that extra beds were always required at the Bailey House. Banking methods were extremely crude at the time of the establishment of the bank. It was impossible, for instance, to renew a note. The borrower was obliged to come to the bank, pay off the note in cash, and then if he wished, he might borrow the money again, always of course with approved security. R. J. McCandlish was an exemplary banker. Everything he did was just right, and the banker of the present day who follows in his footsteps can not go far wrong. His services were so satisfactory that after a few months the directors of the bank gave him an unsolicited increase in salary of $500 per year and a testimonial letter.

Most of the money required for the construction of the Northwestern railroad passed through the hands of the branch at Weston. When the "Trans-Alleghany Lunatic Asylum" was located at Weston the bank furnished to the commissioners the funds with which to purchase the site. All the funds appropriated by the legislature of Virginia for the construction of the buildings was deposited in the bank, and after the division of the state it was the depository of West Virginia funds appropriated for the same purpose. Though accused of being disloyal to the cause of the North, it was one of the most loyal of the banking institutions of the country, investing its funds in United States bonds in times of the country's greatest emergency.

A charter was also granted to the Lewis County Mining and Manufacturing Company in 1853. David S. Peterson, Minter Bailey, Albert A. Lewis, George Jackson and others were the incorporators and the capital stock was fixed at $10,000, with the privilege of increasing it to $500,000 by vote of the stockholders. The purpose of the company was "to mine iron, salt, goods, lumber, and such other mineral substances as the company may determine to mine for." Lumbering seems to have been the principal activity of the company, which suspended operations almost immediately. The Lewis County Woolen and Cotton Manufacturing Company, incorporated by Richard P. Camden, David S. Peterson, Blackwell Jackson, Noah Life, Henry Butcher and others with a capital stock of $5,000 to $200,000, was another company created upon a magnificent plan, but failing in execution.

The old court house had long been considered inadequate for the busines to be transacted and not befitting a great county like Lewis, and in 1855 the county court made provisions to supplant it by another. John Brannon, Wiliam E. Arnold and Jonathan M. Bennett were appointed commissioners to contract for the construction of the work. Joseph Darlinton was the superintendent of the building. The structure was complete 16 November 1857. It was a more commodious and comfortable building than the one now occupied by the county officers, and in addition it was an imposing edifice worthy of Lewis County. The courtroom, passageway and stairs were carpeted, and the walls of the interior were elaborately decorated. The next year after its completion the court provided for the construction of an iron fence with cut rock foundations around the square.

The Weston College was incorporated in 1857 but it apparently never exercised much influence on the educational development of the town.

George C. Danser established the first foundry in Weston in 1857.

By far the greatest single event in the history of Weston was the location of the Trans-Alleghany Lunatic Asylum in the town in 1859. The growth of population west of the Alleghanies and the inadequacy of the existing asylums, one at Williamsburg and the other at Staunton, caused the General Assembly to establish the new institution. The legislature designated for the site one of three towns west of the mountains: Fayetteville in Fayette County, Sutton in Braxton, and as usual when there was a pudding to be opened, Weston in Lewis. The final selection was left to a board of three commissioners to be appointed by the Governor. Thomas Wallace, of Petersburg City; Dr. Clement R. Harris, of Culpeper, and Samuel T. Walker, of Rockingham County, were designated by Governor Wise to visit the three towns, inspect the locations offered and fix the site.

The other proposed locations were inspected first. When Jonathan M. Bennett, then serving as First Auditor of Virginia, was informed that the commissioners were coming to Weston, he is said to have hastened home from Richmond and organized a campaign to secure the location of the building in Weston. Lobbying in the halls of the legislature has secured the designation of Weston as one of the places to be inspected; but lobbying could go no further; it was necessary for the citizens of the town to impress the commissioners with its desirability for the location. The people without exception followed the directions of their distinguished townsman. Missing palings were nailed on the fences; the whitewash brush was applied to all the houses that needed it; the rubbish lying on the river bank and on the lots both vacant and tenanted, was burned or hauled away; the holes in the streets were filled up; and the whole town was made to present an outward appearance of snug prosperity and a high order of citizenship. An entertainment committee was selected from among the leading citizens, and on the day that the commissioners arrived they were shown not one but several available sites for the proposed building. They were wined and feasted. Every form of entertainment which the ingenuity of the citizens could devise was held in their honor; and at every point the advantages of Weston were presented with such force that the commissioners would almost have seemed derelict in their duty to the Commonwealth if they had made any other choice than Weston. Their unanimous opinion was that Weston possessed such advantages over the other sites offered that the institution should be located there.

Of the legislative appropriation, the purchase of land, the beginning of building operations, the interruptions by the war, the opening of the institution to patients, the successful completion of the plant and further progress, more will be said in another chapter. It is desirable to mention, however, the immediate effect of the location of the institution in Weston. Many families moved to the town, attracted either by the prospect of obtaining work, or in order to take part in the commercial activity which was evidently to follow. The farm on the west bank of the river below the grounds selected for the institution was divided into town lots and platted as Hale's addition. P. M. Hale erected a store near the site of the passenger station, which did a thriving busines before the war. The beginning of the hotel business on the site of the Monticello was a boarding house established about 1860 for the accommodation of laborers on the building. On the south side of the site purchased for the asylum, P. M. Hale purchased the land then occupied by a single dwelling and the still of Minter Bailey, and divided it into lots. The plat of Butcher's addition, as this section was called, was filed in the clerk's office in February, 1860. The population of Weston, which had been about 200 in 1844, 400 in 1855, and 820 in 1860, had increased to a thousand at the outbreak of the Civil war.

The new stores of Bailey and Tunstill, Brown and Windle, Darlinton and Wood and I. G. Waldo, which were in evidence in 1857, catered to an increasing trade, and new stores were opened to compete with them. Where there were two or three ordinaries in Weston in 1844, there were six or more in 1860, kept by C. S. Hurley, Patrick Tierney, Joseph E. Wilkinson, Francis Batten, Minter Bailey and Thomas Faulkner. Patrick Tierney was granted license to keep a "booling saloon"—the first in Weston—13 April 1857.

The prosperity of Weston was shared by the whole county. The proprietors of the Weston mill found that notwithstanding the competition of the Jackson mill and the Holt mill at the mouth of Rush run, it could not grind fast enough by water power to supply the needs of the increasing business, and a steam engine was installed a few years prior to the Civil war. It was the first in Weston, and great difficulty was experienced in making it run.

The Jane Lew mill was rebuilt and equipped with steam power by Edward J. Jackson in 1858. In the same year, or the year following, J. P. Potter and John T. Hacker established the potters' shop and kiln which has been one of the distinctive industries of Jane Lew from that time to the present. The village in 1858 had two ordinaries kept by Maxwell W. Ball and Bolivar Hawks, and had entered upon a period of prosperity which seemed to promise much for the future.

The rapid development of Jacksonville following the completion of the turnpike was one of the surprises of the period. The store of John G. Arnold had passed into the hands of Porter M. Arnold, and with it the postoffice, the name of which was changed from Collins Settlement to Jacksonville in honor of the founder of the village and promoter of the settlements of the upper West Fork. The town came into being full-fledged—blacksmith shop, carpenter shop, shoe shop, and two ordinaries, conducted by Samuel B. Hogsit and William Brake, and soon afterwards the town had physicians, church and school. At the beginning of the Civil war, it was a rival of Jane Lew for the honor of being the second town in the county.

Farther up the river, the little settlement which had grown up around William Bennett's mill as a nucleus, and which had a store and postoffice in 1851, had taken on added importance. B. J. Mills established an ordinary there in 1857. The name of the village was changed from Bennett's Mills to Walkersville in honor of Walker the filibuster whose ill-fated attempts to conquer Nicaragua and add it to the United States caused a great feeling of admiration and sympathy for him which extended from one end of North America to the other. Judge G. D. Camden pointed out that the name had no local significance: "If it had been called Crawfordsville, Bennettburg, Cunninghamton, Barnettstown, or McCraysboro, the name would have meant something."

The beginning of the present village of Georgetown may be traced to the same period. In 1851 the postoffice of Little Skin creek was conducted in the store of W. B. Peterson. Several families comprised the population of the village in 1857 when an ordinary, kept by William B. Roach was added to the town.

Improvements were made in several other sections of the county. The Freeman's creek settlers whose center up to the 'forties had been Hezekiah Tharp's mill, formed a new community center around the old Baptist church. Some time in the early 'fifties Fortunatus and Marcellus White started a store there which was the only establishment of the kind between Weston and Troy. At about the same time Reuben Kemper established a blacksmith shop in which the work was mainly done by a slave named Tobe. In his honor the place was called Tobetown, which name it bore for many years until the establishment of a postoffice long after the Civil war, when the more euphonious but less appropriate name of Freemansburg was bestowed upon it. Mail was brought from Weston by any resident of the neighborhood who happened to go to the county seat and left with the merchants who thus became, as it were, unofficial postmasters. In later years the store was operated by Hall and Gaston.

On the right fork of Freeman's creek the community had become strong enough by 1846 to have a separate church, and the Mt. Zion Baptist church was therefore organized and a meeting-house erected. The principal support for the church in its earlier years came from Jacob Straley and Alexander (Buck) Moffett.

Every section of the county showed greater religious improvement than at any other period of its previous history. The Mt. Hebron church at Jane Lew was organized from among members of the Methodist Episcopal church who did not follow the majority into the Methodist Protestant denomination. The Methodists also organized a society on Gee Lick run before the war, meeting at first in the houses of the members and later in an old log house which was donated by Mrs. Lydia Fisher, a staunch Baptist.

Farm methods changed for the better, through the introduction of improved machinery. The first threshing machine in the county was introduced about 1845. It was evidently a small four-horse "chaff-piler", which threshed the grain fairly clean but did not separate it from the chaff. The grain and chaff together were delivered by the machine into a rail pen, and later the grain was cleaned by means of an old-fashioned windmill which was hauled from farm to farm. The large eight-horse separator was not introduced until a few years before the opening of the Civil war. It is possible that there were a few mowers in the county then, but the real introduction of these machines did not take place until after the Civil war. Even then their use was regarded as being in a more or less experimental stage. The "Mitchell Bull" and the "patent lever" plows came into use among the better class of farmers about 1845; but it was ten years later before the hillside plow was introduced.

Wagons were more or less scarce, and farmers owned them "on shares" or loaned them to one another in the neighborhood. The first buggy, a crude affair without any top, was introduced about 1845. Not every citizen possessed his own saddle. It was not uncommon for a man to be seen riding in public on a pack-saddle with a sheepskin thrown across it for comfort.

The growing of livestock continued to be the chief industry of the people. Cattle predominated until about 1860, when the interest of the farmers turned largely to sheep raising. The prices of cattle had increased since 1828, a good cow bringing, by 1860, $15 or $20. The increase was partly due to the good home market after the completion of the Staunton and Parkersburg turnpike, partly to a general rise in prices. The price of sheep declined as the number of wolves became less. The general average of prices was about seventy-five cents per head for common stock, but more for an animal of better quality. The sheep were kept wholly for their wool. It was impossible to market lambs and many of the farmers preferred to make up their herds of wethers. A better breed of long-wooled sheep was introduced about 1855 or 1860, and a great deal more attention was paid to the breeding of sheep than at a later period.

The tobacco industry, first introduced by Tandy Sprouse on Rush run in 1840, had assumed large proportions in 1860, and many other farmers had taken it up following the completion of the Staunton and Parkersburg turnpike, which made the Richmond market readily accessible to Lewis County farmers. The production was in the neighborhood of 50,000 pounds per year by 1860. One of the most prominent growers of the plant was Henry H. Rittenhouse, on his farm at the mouth of Abram's run.

The first improved potatoes, the "early rose" appear to have been introduced about 1855 or 1860. Previous to that time the people had to depend for their early supply upon the "cowhorn" variety which grew about the size of a man's thumb and which reached maturity about July 4. The late potatoes were of course larger, but the quality was poor.

Sorghum was introduced as an experiment in 1856. The first crop was raised from seed brought from Georgia and it was so successful that all the seed was saved and planted, until within a few years most of the farmers had a cane patch.

The first sewing machine in the county was brought over the Fairmont and Weston turnpike in 1855.

Introduction of the process of canning fruit to take the place of dried fruit for the winter occurred about 1860. Tin cans were used, the lids being sealed with solder.

The government of the county also changed for the better during the period. Instead of a dozen or more justices forming a close corporation and filling any vacancies which occurred in their body, sometimes with politicians who were unfit for the place, there was introduced a real representative local government. Under the new constitution, adopted in 1852, the people chose their own justices of the peace, who, however, continued to exercise both judicial and executive functions, largely to the detriment of the administration of the county. The sheriffalty, instead of going to the decrepit old man who had managed to survive until his turn came, was made an elective office. The term of office was two years. If he were not an honest collector and a vigorous enforcer of the law, it was because the people had not been sufficiently trained in local affairs to protect their interests. Once having an opportunity to exercise the suffrage, they were quick in learning.

The later minor subdivisions of the county also began to take shape. After the defection of the Buckhannon river settlements resulting the formation of Upshur, the two assessors' districts were separated by a line following the Staunton and Parkersburg turnpike from east to west. The genesis of the present magisterial districts is also to be found in the division of the county into election districts in order to prevent plural voting which was likely to occur when there were several precincts in the county without any definite division line. The boundaries of the first district were identical with the present Collins Settlement; the second district included the territory now in Skin creek and Court House, except that east of Weston the line was the Staunton and Parkersburg turnpike; the third district was the present Hacker's creek with the addition of Gee Lick and Polk creek; and the fourth district included the remainder of the county, with the valleys of Freeman's creek and those of Leading creek, Fink and their branches. The election districts as thus constituted made a more even division of the county than was made later, with the exception that the Hacker's creek precinct had more than one third of the population. The voting places were in 1852: First district, J. M. Bennett's store (forks of river) and Joseph Hall's store (near the mouth of Sand Fork); second precinct, Court House and Peterson's store on Little Skin creek; third precinct, Jane Lew and Weston; fourth precinct, House of Henry Steinbeck on Leading creek and a house just below the forks of Freeman's creek.

Country life in Lewis County before the war is thus described by Captain Michael Egan in his book, "The Flying Gray-haired Yank": "Rural life in the wilds of Virginia * * * might well be envied by even the nabobs and the lords of creation. In such places, above all others, are happiness and godliness sure to be found; person and property were alike safe in the keeping of those kind-hearted, industrious and religious people. They were like one happy family in their daily intercourse, cheering and helping each other along the steep, stony path of life. * * *

"During the summer months it was customary for the young people of both sexes to attend camp-meetings, revivals, geography singing schools, and other religious or instructive gatherings. In winter the male portion of the population engaged in the exciting pleasures of the chase, hunting deer, bear and smaller game."

CHAPTER XXI.

THE DEVELOPMENT OF EDUCATION

Education in Lewis County began while yet the savages hovered around the Hacker's creek settlements. West's fort served not only as a refuge for the people in time of danger but also as an agency in the dissemination of knowledge. The fort was practically deserted during the winter months, when the danger of Indian raids had ceased, and the house within the stockade made as good a school house as there was anywhere in northwestern Virginia· When the danger from Indian raids had ceased, the old fort was still used for both educational and religious purposes until it was torn down. Recourse was then had to abandoned cabins, or if there were none, then schoolhouses were erected in abandoned fields which could no longer profitably be cropped. As each later settlement was made, the pioneers attempted to secure teachers and to establish schools. The few settlers on Little Skin creek had a school before the settlement was a half dozen years old, and schools in that community continued to be taught annually from that time forth. The pioneers of Collins Settlement, Freeman's creek, Big Skin creek and other sections were equally prompt in lighting the torch of education.

The children of isolated settlers like Tom Boilen on Sand fork, Lewis Stallman on Leading creek, or John Hurst on Fink, were likely to grow up illiterate. The poor man, who had purchased land and who faced utter ruin unless he were able to pay for it within a few years could not afford to pay the tuition and was too proud to apply for pittance provided by the great state of Virginia, "Mother of Presidents"—and of illiterates—and sometimes allowed his children to grow up in ignorance.

The educational policy of Virginia before the war was based upon the theory that education was the business of the parent or, at most, of the community. The people of the eastern part of the state had a fairly good system of private or parochial schools to which they might send their children. The man who did not send his children to school was looked down upon by his neighbors. If he could not afford the expense of an education for his children, then the state, upon his making the humiliating confession of indigence, furnished a pitiful sum from a fund created, not for the establishment of schools for poor children, but for paying their tuition in schools which happened to be in existence. The people of the west had no permanent schools, with the exception of Randolph Academy. They had no assurance of a school unless the parents of a community banded together, and employed the services of such teachers as were available. The school term was sure to be short, the instruction was likely to be indifferent, and conditions were unsatisfactory all around.

The people west of the Alleghanies were like the Puritans of New England in their belief in education as a factor in the development of democratic institutions. In general they were an intelligent and enterprising class of people, many of whom could read and write. Most of them were passionately devoted to education, and they made tremendous sacrifices in order that the gift of learning which they had received should be passed on to their children.

The schools which they established can not be compared for one moment to the rural schools of the present time, but they were far better than none at all. The "old field" schoolhouse with its old fashioned schoolteacher versed only in the three R's was a factor of greatest importance in the development of Lewis County. The subscription school has long since passed away, but it has left its indelible impression upon the character of the people.

A description of one of the old buildings erected on Skin creek, which is typical of all those of the period is quoted from John Strange Hall, formerly county superintendent of free schools:

"The house was 16x18 ft.; built of round logs, slightly scutched down on the inside. The door, loft and roof were made of boards—the latter weighted down with poles. The cracks were chinked and daubed except one at the end and one at the side next the door, which was near the corner. These were enlarged for windows. There was also a small window on the opposite side near the fire. Instead of glass for filling the windows, one of the patrons furnished a few copies of the Pittsburgh **Christian Advocate** for the purpose. These were cut into strips of suitable width and supported by upright slats, were pasted in the windows and greased to let in the light. My teacher told me it was to let the dark out. Broad poplar slabs were leveled with a broadax and closely jointed for a floor and others dressed more carefully were put up in front of the windows for writing desks. Chestnut saplings split, leveled and shaved, and supported by legs of suitable length, served for seats. Every pupil carried his own back, for the benches had none. Blackboards did not adorn the schoolhouses of that age. * * *

"The chief glory of the edifice was its chimney. It was no half wooden concern liable to take fire whenever an armful of dry wood was thrown on. One-half the north end was cut out, and a rough, though substantial, stone chimney with a capacity to absorb a respectable log heap and roast an ox on the hearth completed the schoolhouse."

All the schools were made up by subscription. Specific articles of agreement between the patrons,—including the school commissioners for the indigent children—and the teachers were drawn up showing what was to be taught. All included spelling, writing, reading, with usually a part or the whole of Pike's arithmetic. The tuition charged by the teacher in the rural districts of the county was usually a dollar and a half per term for the simpler branches, and two dollars per term when geography and grammar were included in the program. The school term was for three months or sixty-five days.

School began promptly at eight o'clock and closed at five. There was seldom a case of tardiness, though some of the children walked a distance of three or four miles from their homes· When not reciting, the pupils were kept constantly at their books, and no idleness was permitted. Pike's arithmetic, a speller and a Testament were the only textbooks in use. Discipline was maintained, not with the classic birch of the north, but with a tough hickory switch from three to five feet in length. "This in our school,' says Mr. Hall, "was used as an emblem of authority rather than as an instrument of torture; but it was convertible."

Spelling was the favorite accomplishment of the pupils, and there was no higher honor than to get the greatest number of head-marks or to stand up longest in the spelling match.

Teaching was not regarded as a profession in pioneer days. With one exception every one of the teachers made it a stepping stone to some other position. The careless and good-for-nothing teachers, of whom there were a few, sank into obscurity; the efficient passed into positions of public trust; but, as Mr. Hall says, there was none who attained to greater eminence, or who rendered a greater service to his community in his chosen field than he did in his humble position of schoolmaster. The teacher was generally the young man in the community who had stood at the head of his classes at the local school, or had attended another school or college and secured a better education than it was possible to obtain at home. Clad in their flowing hunting shirts and buckskin moccasins they were picturesque figures as they pointed the way for their youthful charges over the stony paths of learning.

Summer schools were taught in some communities which had become educational centers by virtue of the labors of a long line of especially distinguished teachers. These were attended largely by the young women of the community, for few of the boys who were old enough to guide a shovel plow between the corn rows or wield a hoe were able to take advantage of them. Sometimes teachers managed to spend a term at a school outside of their districts, where they paid their board by cutting wood, feeding the stock, grubbing, and making themselves generally useful. It was considered a far better way to secure an education than to take advantage of the provisions of the Literary fund of the state. Occasionally school teachers from New England would come into Virginia, teach two or three years and then either settle here on a farm or return home.

There was no supervision of the schools by the state—no teachers' examinations, no correlation of the work of different schools. All was left to the discretion of the citizens of the community who banded together to secure a teacher. There was a slender incentive to good schools in the fact that school commissioners might refuse to disburse any of the money furnished by the state for the education of indigent children unless the teacher met with their approval.

The Literary fund of the state was not sufficient at any time to influence greatly the schools of the county. It consisted of forfeitures and fines and proceeds of the sale of property which has reverted to the state through failure of heirs. By an act passed in 1818 it was provided that from five to fifteen school commissioners should be appointed in each county for the purpose of disbursing the pro rata share of the proceeds of the Literary fund allotted to the county. The county court of Lewis appointed on the board Joseph McCoy, John Mitchell, Asa Squire, David W. Sleeth, Edward Jackson, Lewis Maxwell and Aaron Gould, nearly all of whom had served an apprenticeship as teachers. Varying

amounts were to be disbursed, at first not more than
$200, then rising to $500, until in 1844 the General Assembly, in lieu of the annual appropriation, gave the
lump sum of $469.21. This was to abolish illiteracy in
Lewis County—a jurisdiction then extending from the
divide east of the Buckhannon river to the present line
between Wirt and Calhoun counties. Efforts had been
made at various times to increase the amount. In the
convention of 1829-30 it was proposed by a western delegate that a poll tax of twenty-five cents per year, together with an equal amount set aside by the state
should form a fund, the interest of which was to be used
for elementary education. It was shown in the convention that at that time Virginia made provision for the
indifferent education of only one-eighth as many children as were provided annually with adequate education
by the little state of Connecticut. The convention utterly ignored the plea of the people of the west for a
better system of education.

The Auditor's report for 1833 gives an interesting
glimpse into the activities of the school commissioners
for Lewis County. There were then thirty-four schools in
the county attended by poor children, and two hundred
and thirty-four poor children out of a total of five hundred applicants received the benefit of the fund. The
amount at the disposal of the commisioners that year
was $304.99, and the wonder is that they succeeded in
getting instruction for as many children as they did.
It must not be forgotten also that there were many children not in school because their parents would not apply for the benefits of the fund.

Among the indefatigable workers for better schools
in Lewis County there was none more active than
Thomas Bland who served as school commissioner for
many years, and whose efforts in organizing schools in
various parts of the county met with great success. He
was ably seconded in his efforts by Michael G. Bush in
the upper valley of the West Fork, who had been one of

the most successful teachers in the county, and by Elias Lowther and Colonel John McWhorter. The legislature was being continually reminded of the need of greater appropriations for the county. Citizens were urged to keep their schools going. Everything possible was done to increase the interest in education and to promote progress in the instruction of the youth of the county.

The need for a better system became more and more apparent. Advocates of education in other counties experienced the same difficulties. The people determined to take united action to bring pressure to bear on the legislature. In 1841 a convention met in the old Presbyterian church in Clarksburg, with 140 delegates in attendance, among whom were John McWhorter, Thomas Bland, R. W. Lowther, A. G. Reger and Cabell Tavenner from Lewis County. The convention declared in favor of better schools, and drafted strong resolutions recommending changes in the existing system.

No immediate results were apparent. In 1845, however, the legislature passed an act providing for the districting of the counties apparently with the view of securing better supervision of the schools already established. One school commissioner was to be appointed from each of the districts and the board should choose a superintendent who should keep an accurate roll of the children of the county, account for the income received from the Literary fund, and render a report on the effects of its expenditure. It was also provided by an act passed a little later that the county court might establish a school in each of the districts if two-thirds of the voters of the county were in favor of the measure. Trustees were to be selected for such schools, two by the voters of the districts and one by the school commissioners.

The county court finished the task of dividing Lewis county into eighteen districts the next year. The districts as defined were as follows:

(1) corporation of Weston; (2) Polk creek and Mur-

phy's creek and their tributaries; (3) Leading creek; (4) Sand fork; (5) West Fork river above the mouth of Sand fork, and also Oil creek; (6) Tributaries flowing into the West Fork from the west below the mouth of Polk creek; (7) Sand fork and Big Skin creek; (8) Canoe run, Carrion run, Rush run, and Middle run; (9) Little Skin creek; (10) Stone Coal creek; (11-16) districts now in Upshur; (17) tributaries from the east side of the West Fork river from the mouth of Stone Coal to the Harrison County line and the valley of Hacker's creek as far up as the mouth of Jesse's run; (18) remainder of Hacker's creek. The districts were far too large for the purpose for which they were created:—namely, to be centers each for a school. An election for the establishment of a school within one of the districts would be favored by all the people residing near the center of a district where it was proposed to establish a public school; and opposed by all who lived on the edge of the school district, for they would have to provide for the education of their children in subscription schools as before. The results was that not a single public school was created in Lewis County prior to the formation of West Virginia. The creation of the office of superintendent of schools served in a measure to increase the efficiency of the teachers. During the administration of John Morrow especially, 1857-59, much was accomplished.

In the constitutional convention of 1850 the delegates from the western counties made a determined effort to establish a system of education under which schools should be established by the state, where rich and poor children alike would be able to secure an education. The resolutions providing for a clause in the constitution on the subject of free schools were voted down. The people of the east feared that they would be taxed for the support of schools in the west—a condition that would have been no worse, however, than the long continued policy of disproportionate taxation of the people of the west for the purpose of creating internal improvements for the east.

Gradually there grew up educational centers where the schools were better than at other places, due either to the superior attainments of some teacher, or to a keen interest in educational affairs among the citizens of a community. Weston of course had good schools very early in its history, where the teachers were better than any of the country districts could afford; but there were other places like Jane Lew, Big Skin creek, Jacksonville, Freeman's crek and, at a later date, Canoe run, where there was a lively interest in education and where the schools were sometimes better than they are now.

At Weston the schools were sometimes taught by young men who had lately come into the community purposing to enter business or one of the professions. The struggling lawyer waiting for practice often turned to school teaching in his own house to earn the wherewithal to provide victuals. The young man who intended to start in business might establish a school while he was forming acquaintances among the people. Also there were a number of New Englanders, anxious to see the world, and to make a little money while on their way, who came to Weston to teach school. It was one of the first cares of the trustees of the town in 1818 to secure a lot for a cemetery on which a school house might be built; but no public building was erected for school purposes until after the Civil war. Many of the schools were taught in private houses; some teachers used the courthouse for their classes; and after the erection of churches in Weston they were favorite places for schools. The location of the dwelling which housed the first school and the first teacher in Weston has apparently been forgotten, but it is confidently asserted that Weston had a school as early as 1819, for obituaries of old men who spent their boyhood in Weston speak of their attending schools in the town.

In 1832 a school was established in Weston by

Matthew Holt, which apparently was better than most of the others, for it attracted young Jonathan M. Bennett from the forks of the river to complete his education. The Holt school was for big boys and young men who could not afford to go away to college. Schools for little boys and young ladies were maintained separately from the beginning. The most prominent of the teachers of the latter type of school was Mrs. Mary A. Wilson, who came to Weston in 1833 and opened a school the same year. This work was continued for many years by Mrs. Wilson and her daughters who were people of more than ordinary culture and refinement. Alexander Scott Withers, author of "Border Warfare," yielded to the solicitations of the people of the town and taught one or more terms of school in the old courthouse; but the work was distasteful to him and he did not continue it longer than a year or two. His daughter, Miss Janet Withers, also taught one term in the old courthouse in 1839, and taught small classes almost every winter from 1849 to 1854 and from 1856 to 1860. Other teachers were Miss Rowe, of Parkersburg, Miss Hannah Bruin of Clarksburg, Miss Maria Wheeler, the Rev. James Page, and Charles Lewis of Clarksburg, afterwards judge of the circuit court.

One of the most successful of the schools was that taught by a Vermont Yankee named Foster who came in the fall of 1844, and taught a select school for boys which was so successful that it led to the establishment of the Weston Academy by the legislature. The incorporators were John Lorentz, William J. Bland, Cabell Tavenner, Jonathan M. Bennett, John Talbott, Allen Simpson and Lewis Maxwell, who were given the right to hold property up to $25,000, and to appoint a president and tutors and a treasurer. Nothing came of the movement, as the rates proposed to be charged for teaching in the academy were higher than those which had been paid for instruction in the subscription schools. In order to popularize higher education the Lewis County

Seminary was created in 1847 with a capital stock of $10,000 in shares of five dollars. As soon as $1,000 was subscribed a meeting of organization was to be advertised, and the name of the institution might be changed to the Weston College. Aid for the new institution was promised from the proceeds of the sales of forfeited lands in the county.

The seminary never was a success. If it ever opened its doors, there is apparently no tradition to that effect among the people now living in the town. The census report of 1850 does not show a single seminary in Lewis County. A series of successful schools was taught in the basement of the Catholic church by Prof. John Kierans, James O'Hara, Prof. Seaman, Adelaide Bailey, George Duvall, Father Burke, Father O'Connor, and Prof. John Murray. A rival school was begun under the guidance of the Episcopal rector, the Rev. T. H. Smythe in his own home. Both primary and advanced work was given in the latter school, which graduated many students who later became prominent in affairs in Lewis County and West Virginia.

The Lewis County Seminary at last got under way in 1855 under the leadership of Prof. John Kierans who erected a small brick building on the property now occupied by the high school, but it collapsed a year or two later. In 1857 the legislature changed the name of the seminary to that of Weston College, the subscription of $1,000 having evidently been secured. Nothing further was done until the establishment of the free school system under the new state of West Virginia.

Some of the country districts showed much greater interest in education than the town. Michael G. Bush, who had studied under Isaac Morrison in Harrison County, taught on Little Skin creek in the early years of the century and left behind him a succession of excellent teachers which has continued to our own day. Among them are Henry D. Hardman, who taught the first school of Big Skin creek in 1811, Daniel R. Helmick, George L.

Marsh, H. M. Peterson, Aaron D. Peterson, Augustus Sexton, Job McMorrow and Robert Fox. The last named was one of the few professional teachers under the Virginia regime. If there was no opportunity to teach in his own community, he went out into some other district and started a school. Penmanship was his forte. He knew nothing of scientific teaching but he could write as few of his successors have been able to do. His specimen copies were to be seen in most of the schoolrooms of the county.

At Jacksonville, George J. Arnold taught a school in an old log house which stood near where the road from Clover fork joins the turnpike, and he was followed in the same community by his brother, William E. Arnold, one of the most distinguished teachers of grammar in the early history of the county. He had had the advantage of one or more terms in Rector College at Pruntytown.

Jane Lew had also a series of successful schools, which resulted in the creation of the Jane Lew Academy in 1850. Many of the prominent citizens of the Hacker's creek country at a later date received their training there.

One of the most remarkable teachers in the county about the time of the Civil war was Miss Phoebe Mitchell who taught the children of the Freeman's creek community for several years. The school building was poor, the equipment was that of most frontier log houses, but the school mistress was a born teacher. From the humble log schoolhouse there went forth a group of young men who attended higher schools and colleges, and have since made their mark as lawyers, physicians, and business and professional men throughout the length and breadth of West Virginia.

It remained for the government of the new state of West Virginia, starting its existence amid the chaos of war, without a statehouse, without educational, penal or charitable institutions, but with the spirit of educational progress released from its long imprisonment under Virginia, to establish a system of free schools which promises in time to equal the best of those of other states.

CHAPTER XXII.

THE SECESSION FROM VIRGINIA

Prior to the Civil War interest in politics in Lewis County was confined almost exclusively to questions of State and National concern. The campaigns of candidates for county offices attracted little attention even after the adoption of the constitution of 1852 had added important offices to the elective list. There was much interest, however, concerning such questions as the tariff, the United States bank, internal improvements, the extension of slavery into the western territories, and most important of all, the agitation for the extension of manhood suffrage, a white basis of representation for the senatorial and delegate districts, and equalization of taxation so as to make the burdens of supporting the government fall upon the planters of the east to the same extent as upon the poor farmers of the western part of the state.

It was generally felt in the west that the eastern slaveholders had far too much influence in the councils of the state. Each of them had a vote wherever he owned a plot of ground, but the small farmer of the west had no vote unless he owned a considerable plot of ground. Though manhood suffrage was granted by the constitution of 1852, there still remained the old basis of representation in which the slave population was counted. A few plantation owners sent as many representatives to the General Assembly as several thousand western farmers. The powerful eastern magnates were exempted from paying their full proportion of taxes. Their slaves under twelve years of age were not assessed for taxes at all, and slaves over that age were assessed at only $300, though many of them sold in the open market at $1200. On the other hand every pig, every calf, every chicken, every hunting rifle, in short every bit of property owned by the small farmer was assessed at its full value. Some relief from the system had been gained in 1830 and in 1852; but the burdens of the Virginia government were still indefensible, and the successes of the westerners in the earlier conventions only whetted their desire for more reforms.

The key to the dissatisfaction of the people of the west was the institution of slavery, which had received special treatment by the state to the detriment of almost all the other interests of the people. Slavery never existed in the county to any great extent. It could not exist here because the rugged nature of the surface and the difficulties of transportation made great plantations impossible. Very few of the citizens of the county owned slaves. Jacob Lorentz owned the largest number. Alexander Scott Withers owned more than anyone else in Weston, yet he never held more than a dozen at any one time. Minter Bailey at one time owned ten, Weeden Hoffman seven, and a few other citizens a lesser number. The slaves were used to work the fields in the vicinity of Weston, often under the direct supervision of their masters. All the slaves were well treated. There was a feeling of affection between the families of the masters and their servants which precluded cruelty before the emancipation of the slaves, and which continued long after the bonds were broken Negroes were never reared in the county for the purpose of selling them in the southern market. There was none of the cruelty which existed on the great plantations of the South. The people, being used to a paternalistic sort of slavery, thought the abolitionists of the North meddlers and worse.

Objection to slavery rested on economic and political grounds. In the Virginia legislature of 1831 the delegate from Lewis voted in favor of a resolution declaring it expedient to legislate to abolish the institution of negro slavery in the state. The people continued to believe that they would be better off without slavery, and agitation for emancipation continued until the growth of abolitionist agitation in the North compelled the people of Virginia to stand together in defense of their peculiar institution.

Among the New Englanders who had come to French creek in 1810 and had since maintained a connection with the thought of New England, there was a decided aversion to slavery. When the Republican party was formed in 1856 many of the people there allied themselves with it. At the election that fall, nine citizens of the community dared to vote their sentiments. The act caused much excitement and universal disapprobation among their neighbors. The names of the voters were known, for the voting was done under the old viva voce system. They were held up to public scorn. The Weston Herald, 1 December 1856, commented on the occurrence in part as follows: "Such flagrant anti-slavery action here in Virginia was unexpected. * * * That they should come out thus boldly and avow their adherence to principles and men so odious to public sentiment, and so inimical to our interests is a matter of astonishment and exhibits a social and political depravity which must arouse the indignation of our people and visit them with the burning rebuke of public sentiment. * * * The fact of their being citizens of our state by birth is no palliation." Lynch law is more than hinted at in the course of the editorial, which continues at length in the same tone, and at the end gives the names of the electors so that all citizens of the vicinity might know and recognize the arch traitors to the domestic happiness of the state.

The editorial brought forth a reply from the pen of the Rev. Amos Brooks, one of the "nine immortals." He pointed out the fact that the Republican platform opposed only the extension of slavery into the territories and did not attempt to interfere with the institution in any of the states where it existed. He made an appeal to the people for freedom of speech, of the press and of the ballot box, and said if these were denied, democratic institutions in Virginia were at an end. If the editors would not publish the contribution, he asked that they take it out and read it two or three times a week, and also read it to the officers of the bank, who were known to be strongly in favor of slavery. It is hardly necessary to state that the reply was never published by the Herald.

The tense state of public feeling in Lewis County was increased a thousand fold by the sudden news of the attack on Harper's Ferry by John Brown. If one irresponsible abolitionist could come to a Virginia town and incite the slaves to rise against their masters, why could not another of the same character come to Weston or any other town in northwestern Virginia? Who knew but that there might be a slave insurrection the next time with all the horrors which usually attend servile wars? Every colored man in the county was closely watched to see that there were no secret meetings, and that no designing white man was trying to gain influence over them.

Interest in the approaching presidential election of 1860 became intense. The final disposition of the slavery question seemed to rest on the decision of the people at that time. The times were regarded as critical. Almost everywhere except in western Virginia party ties were thrown to the winds. The peculiar outcome of the election in Lewis County is due to causes which reached back a full generation.

In the beginning the people of northwestern Virginia were in favor of a strong national government, and they were generally opposed to the doctrines of Jefferson and the early democratic Republicans. They favored the building of roads and canals by the national government. In the election of 1828, Lewis County voted for Adams against Jackson, choosing the conservative rather than the radical wing of the Democratic party. In 1824, Joseph Johnson, representing the district in Congress, was the only Virginian who voted in favor of the high tariff. By the close of Jackson's administration the rugged western personality of that leader had won over the people of the northwest. When the Whig party was formed the majority of the people in the Kanawha valley joined it and the majority in the Monongahela valley remained with the Democrats. Lewis County was on the border line between the sections, sometimes being in the Monongahela and sometimes in the Kanawha congressional district. Strenuous efforts were made by both parties to secure control of the county.

The Democrats had the advantage from the start, their majority being about 100 in a total vote of 700. The Whig strength was generally in the valleys of the Elk and the Buckhannon. After the formation of Braxton, and especially after the formation of Upshur, Lewis County was a Democratic stronghold on the frontier of the enemy's country.

The location of Lewis County gave its leaders in the General Assembly and in the party councils an influence far out of proportion to the importance of the territory they represented. Every measure concerning the west was referred to the delegates from Lewis, and they were courted by the Democratic party. They were able to secure special favors for their constituents far above those of other delegates. By crossing the river below the mouth of Stone Coal creek, the Staunton and Parkersburg turnpike would not have required bridges across Stone Coal and Polk creeks. The Lewis County delegate contrived to have inserted in the appropriation bill a clause directing that the road should pass through Weston. The location of the Weston branch of the Exchange Bank of Virginia was doubtless fixed because of the central location of the town from a business standpoint; but the loyalty of the town to the Democratic party was also a potent factor. The designation of Weston as one of three places to be visited by the commissioners to choose the site of the Trans-Alleghany Lunatic Asylum may have been on account of the geographical location of the town, or it may have been because certain Democratic politicians from Lewis County insisted upon it. Jonathan M. Bennett, one of the Democratic leaders of the county, was appointed First Auditor of Virginia by Governor Henry A. Wise partly, doubtless, as a recognition of the Democratic organization in Lewis County.

It was not surprising that the people were kindly disposed toward the Democratic party in 1860. The election was complicated by new events and new turns in the political wheel. The Whig party had been broken up. The Democrats were split into a northern and a southern branch, each with a ticket in the field. The new Republican party which had shown great strength in 1856, was believed to be sure of the electoral vote of several of the northern states. The only party which made a truly national appeal was composed of the remnant of the old Whigs with the addition of some who recognized that the sectional division of the country was a critical state of affairs, and who hoped to throw the election into the House of Representatives where the President could be elected by a deliberative body. Its nominee was John Bell, of Tennessee; its platform was purposely vague—"The Union, the Constitution and the enforcement of the laws." It was only by ignoring the question of slavery that a national party could be brought into existence.

The new party made a special appeal to the people of the border states who felt neither the economic necessities of slavery as did those of the South, nor the terrible nature of the institution as did the abolitionists of the North. A compromise which would delay the settlement of the question a little longer seemed to promise to them more than bringing the question to a final settlement in the heat of sectional passion which followed the Dred Scott decision and John Brown's raid. A vigorous campaign was waged in the interests of the new party. The anti-slavery men supported Douglas, the candidate of the northern wing of the Democratic party, first, because his election seemed to promise a definite check to the further extension of slavery, and secondly, because there was a very real danger of their being lynched if they voted for Lincoln.

The final returns gave Breckenridge, the candidate of the southern wing of the Democratic party, 604; Bell, 332; and Douglas, 247. Lincoln received not a single vote. The Breckenridge victory was not an approval of the states' rights sentiments in the platform, not a sign of devotion to the slaveocracy, but the result of the thoroughness of the Democratic organization in Lewis County. The people voted for the Democratic party because it was the party of Jackson.

Then came the startling news that Abraham Lincoln had been elected through the division of the vote among his opponents. Before the year was out South Carolina had left the Union, followed by six other southern states. Rumors of war were in the air. As one of the citizens of the county wrote, (quoted in Roy B. Cook's Pioneer History) "On every hand you heard hushed voices, almost in whispers, discussing the oncoming horror. * * The very air seemed full of distant mutterings of an angry, surging, restless people, divided, yet most intimately associated; opposite in views, but of the same family. Where once there had been friendship and love, there came bitterness beyond belief." The question in the minds of the people was, "What would Virginia do?" A convention of the state was called early in 1861 to consider the course to be taken.

The action of Governor Letcher and the other officials of the state added to the general fear of impending war. During the winter of 1860-61 there was a great military stir throughout Virginia, and every effort was made to put the slender militia of the state on a war footing. In the midst of the flurry and excitement in the west, there came orders for the 125th and 192nd regiments of state militia to proceed to muster near Weston, about the middle of February, 1861.

About two weeks before the day appointed for the muster, the officers of the two regiments met informally to discuss plans for the ceremony. One of the questions which came to their attention was the propriety, under the conditions then existing in the community, of carrying regimental flags and the Stars and Stripes when the regiments passed in review before General Conrad. The almost unanimous decision of the meeting was that such a course would lead to bloodshed, and it was therefore decided that the colors should not be carried. Michael Egan, who afterwards organized Company "B", Fifteenth West Virginia Volunteer Infantry, alone dissented from the opinion of the council of officers, his oath of allegiance to the government of the United States being, as he said, yet too fresh in his mind to permit it to be secondary to his allegiance to any state. The majority of the people approved the action taken by the council; but Major Egan made a trip over the county, addressing the citizens wherever he could secure an audience, urging them to stand by the flag of the United States. In this way he secured pledges from about fifty men to assist him in upholding the flag at the coming muster. Gasper Butcher, of Butcher's fork, went to Weston and procured red, white and blue cloth from which a flag was made by Misses Julia and Cecelia Flesher of Polk creek.

On the day appointed the brigade formed on the farm of Henry Butcher (now the Riverside stock farm) about two miles north of Weston. Hundreds of people, the wives and mothers and sisters and sweethearts of the men in line, had gathered to witness the ceremonies. Everything bore an outward appearance of gayety; but there was an undercurrent of dark forebodings of impending trouble. Orderlies rode hither and thither over the field. Officers were busy finishing the final alignment of their men. Suddenly interest is centered in a new fig-

PRESLEY M. HALE

ure who rides upon the field at full gallop until he arrives opposite the center of his regiment. There he stops and unfurls the flag of the United States to the breeze. It was Major Michael Egan.

The action of the dashing Irishman was noticed by the whole assemblage. A few greeted the flag with cheers, but the majority gave vent to loud protests and angry mutterings. Major Egan handed the standard to John Newman, who had previously volunteered to carry it. At that moment Colonel Hanson M. Peterson rode up and requested that the flag be removed. Major Egan refused. He ordered Major Egan to the post of honor at the head of the column. The latter declined, preferring to remain with the flag. The place at the head of the column was taken by Colonel Caleb Boggess, and the review proceeded with no further incident.

At the close of the ceremonies a mass meeting was held at Weston, which was addressed by several of the officers, all of whom expressed strong Southern sentiments. Colonel Peterson, who was soon to lay down his life for Virginia, appealed to all in the approaching conflict to stand by their state, pointing out the subordinate position occupied by the federal government in any conflict as to the constitutional rights of states and nation. The Union men said nothing. As Michael Egan has well said, "They had scored their victory in deeds rather than in talk."

Meanwhile the political leaders of the county attempted to stampede the people into the ranks of the secessionists. The Weston **Herald**, which had been a Constitutional Union organ during the campaign of 1860, with the motto, "Civil and religious liberty, the Constitution and the Union," now came out boldly under the caption, "Southern Rights and Southern Independence." Mass meetings, addressed by leading citizens, were held in all parts of the county.

The convention of the people of Virginia to decide whether or not the state should remain in the Union was still in session. There were days of tense anxiety for the quiet settlements on the West Fork. The people began to reflect upon the issues at stake, and upon the probable results of a hasty decision to leave the Union, and as day after day passed with no decision, they began to take courage, and believe that after all Virginia would remain in the Union, or at least would take a neutral stand. They were disappointed. It became increasingly evident that the national government intended to use force to bring back the seceded states, and upon the President's first call for volunteers, the convention was stampeded by ex-Governor Wise and other pro-slavery politicians into the submission of the Ordinance of Secession to the people. Delegate Caleb Boggess, of Lewis, voted against the ordinance and escaped with some difficulty from Richmond.

Tremendous confusion followed the submission of the secession ordinance. Eastern Virginia leaders seized all federal property in the state and prepared for war as if the ordinance had already been ratified by the people. In Lewis County it was reported that the house of Caleb Boggess had been burned to the ground by the secessionists in revenge for his vote against the ordinance. Charges of conspiracy and treason against the state were in the air, and no man whose avowed sympathies were with the Union felt quite safe.

The majority of the people of the county believed to some extent in states' rights, but they were not in favor of dismembering the nation. Caleb Boggess had rightly represented his constituents. The attempts of the eastern politicians to coerce the people brought to their minds all the long train of grievances they had against the east—the restrictions of suffrage in the west, the unfairness in taxation, the denial of facilities of education, and the creation of an enormous debt for the benefit, principally, of that part of Virginia east of the Alleghanies. Many of the citizens of the western part of the state made up their minds not to follow the east any longer. Union men met quietly and secretly to devise measures to counteract those being taken by the former leaders in the politics of the county. Some of these meetings in Weston were held in the Hale-Vandervort store, some at the Hale shoe shop, some at Chalfant's drug store and others at various private houses, all under the cover of night and their secret closely guarded. Confederate sentiment in Weston was also very strong.

A mass convention at Clarksburg April 22, at which many Lewis County men were present, adopted resolutions calling a convention of the loyal citizens of the state to meet at Wheeling on May 13, and recommending that each county send at least five delegates. The response in Lewis County was immediate. At a meeting said to have been held in the Hale store near the western end of the covered bridge across the West Fork, the Union men chose as delegates F. M. Chalfant, Alexander Scott Withers, J. W. Hudson, P. M. Hale, Jesse Woofter, W. L. Grant, J. Amen and J. A. J. Lightburn. All attended the convention.

The purpose of the convention, which met before the vote on the secession ordinance, was to agree upon concerted action to be taken in case the Ordinance was ratified. Mr. Withers was appointed a member of the committee on state and federal relations, and in this committee the first discussion of the question of the formation of a new state came up. Some of the more advanced Union men wanted a new state immediately, the Wood County delegation, for instance, displaying a banner with the words, "New Virginia—Now or Never." While the convention discussed constitutional objections, Francis H. Pierpont evolved a plan afterwards followed by which western Virginia could be constitutionally separated from the old state. As a first step he proposed that the convention should wait until the popular vote on the ordinance had decided finally whether Virginia should remain in the Union or not. It was necessary, in order to secure a semblance of legality, that action looking toward the formation of a new state should be taken by a body duly called and whose members had been duly elected by the people. He therefore proposed that an election should be held on June 4, to select delegates for a second convention which should devise such measures as the welfare of the people of northwestern Virginia seemed to demand. His motion was adopted, and consideration of the formation of the new state was delayed.

The ordinance of secession was carried at the special election by a large majority of the state at large, but the people of western Virginia opposed it by a vote of ten to one. Lewis County was almost unanimously opposed save for the polling precincts at Walkersville, Hall's store, Little Skin creek and part of the vote at Weston.

The election of delegates from Lewis County to the second Wheeling convention resulted in the choice of P. M. Hale, a rising young business man of Weston, and J. A. J. Lightburn, a Baptist minister of the Broad run community, who was soon to lay aside the staff of the shepherd and take up the sword in order that he might make the triumph of righteousness more certain. The division which arose in the convention between Carlile, who desired to form a new state immediately, and Pierpont, who wished to reorganize the government of Virginia, led to a deadlock which was broken, so a traditional account goes, by a short speech by P. M. Hale, which won over the other delegates to the plan of Pierpont. The convention adopted the plan which provided that new officers should be elected to take the places of those who had followed the state in seceding from the Union, and that a new government should be established at Wheeling. The convention also passed an ordinance submitting to the people the question of whether they wished to form a new state out of that part of Virginia lying west of the Alleghanies.

P. M. Hale and J. A. J. Lightburn sat in the House

of Delegates and Blackwell Jackson in the Senate when the legislature declared the offices of the state vacant, by reason of the fact that the holders had renounced their allegiance to the United States, and elected loyal men to fill them.

Not all the people of Lewis County took advantage of the opportunity to vote on the ordinance to create a new state. By the time of the election, Union troops had entered the county, and the Confederate sympathizers feared to vote their sentiments. Only 455 votes were cast. The ordinance was ratified with but twelve dissenting votes in the county. Judge Robert Ervine was elected to represent the county in the constitutional convention which framed the first constitution of the state of West Virginia. The remainder of the history of the formation of West Virginia is state history rather than county history, and it is therefore passed over. One point is not to be forgotten, however, and that is that P. M. Hale, the delegate from Lewis in the first legislature of West Virginia, served on the committee on education and was largely instrumental in framing the first free school law of the new state.

During the Civil war the majority of the people of Lewis County took sides with the Union. Out of a total of perhaps 1300 voters in 1861, it is estimated that 1000 sided with the federal government or were lukewarm in their adherence to the Confederacy, and the others actively supported the Southern cause. All of Freeman's creek with the exception of the later comers like the Simmons and Rexroads were unanimously for the North; few southern soldiers enlisted from there. The same may be said of Hacker's creek, where the Confederates had high hopes that Blackwell Jackson, a cousin of "Stonewall", would be able to bring the people to their side. Unfortunately for them, he himself was one of the most loyal Union men. Stone Coal creek was almost solidly for the North, as were Murphy's creek, Rush run and Canoe run. All the Irish and Germans who had settled in the Sand fork and Leading creek sections espoused the cause of the United States because they knew nothing and cared nothing for the rights of states. They knew merely that they owed their enjoyment of liberty to the national government and that they had just sworn to support it.

The Confederate sections of the county were principally in the southern end. The citizens of Skin creek under the leadership of Colonel Peterson and others believed that the rights of Virginia were being put in jeopardy by the citizens of the northern states, and they prepared to defend the state from invasion. The Collins Settlement, which was peopled mainly by emigrants from the Shenandoah valley and other parts of Virginia, under the vigorous leadership of the Bennetts, Regers, Watsons and others presented such a united front in favor of the Confederacy that it was called "Dixie" by those of Union sympathies.

Weston was badly divided in sentiment. The representatives of some of the old families—men like Dr. Bland, Captain Boykin, A. A. Lewis, Jonathan M. Bennett and many others—sided with the Confederacy. The later comers who had been atttracted to the town by reason of the advance of industy in the 'fifties and especially through the location of the asylum in the town, generally cast their lot with the Union. The Union men were probably in a majority.

The neighboring counties were almost as much divided as Lewis. Harrison, though strongly Union for the most part, had a strong Southern group on Duck creek, just north of the Lewis County line. Upshur was almost solidly for the North, with the exception of a settlement in the extreme southern part of the county, corresponding to the Collins Settlement in Lewis; though the French creek settlement exercised a great influence in holding the region around it, both in Upshur and on the Left fork of West Fork in Lewis, for the Union. Webster, Braxton, Gilmer, Clay and most of the other so-called "back counties" sent more soldiers into the Confederate than into the Union forces. The Webster County court protested against paying taxes to West Virginia, declaring that county still a part of Virginia. Some Union men pointed out the fact that the territory of Webster was separated from the remainder of Virginia by a part of West Virginia; and if they did not want to be in the new state the only course would be to form an independent state. It has been called the "Independent State" ever since.

The state militia which had been organized with such lack of care by Virginia did not all respond to her call. Out of the two regiments which paraded on Henry Butcher's meadow, only about twenty-five men marched away to join the forces of the state. They were assigned to Company "I", 31st Virginia Regiment, C. S. A., under Captain Jackson, and experienced some of the bitterest fighting of the whole war. The bodies of many of them lie buried on the battlefields of northern Virginia. Besides the men who left with the militia for the rendezvous of the Confederates, many later joined other organizations. Thomas J. Jackson, who had been a second lieutenant in 1845, and whose later life had been spent in the army or in the classrooms of the Virginia Military Institute, joined his fortunes to those of his state, and was recognized as perhaps the greatest military genius of the war.

Four companies were raised in Lewis County for the service of the United States—companies "C" and "D" of the 10th Virginia Infantry and companies "B" and "D" of the 15th West Virginia Infantry. Company "B", 15th West Virginia Infantry was organized and commanded by Captain Michael Egan, whose bold stand for the United States on the occasion of the last muster had made him generally known throughout the county. Thomas D. Murrin was captain of Company "D", 10th Virginia Infantry; William J. Nicholes, of Company "C" of the same regiment; and Jasper Peterson of Company

"D" of the 15th West Virginia Infantry. In addition to the four companies there were numerous Lewis County citizens who joined other organizations. The most distinguished of these was J. A. J. Lightburn, who had organized the 4th Virginia regiment, commanded for a time the district of the Kanawha, conducted a masterly retreat from Charleston in the face of a superior enemy force, was wounded at the gates of Atlanta, and was promoted to the rank of brigadier-general for gallantry in action.

CHAPTER XXIII.

MILITARY OPERATIONS

Three strategic factors determined that trans-montane Virginia should be the theatre of contending armies very early in the struggle. In the first place, the Virginia frontier was the Ohio river and the Mason and Dixon line, and Virginia wished to preserve her territory from invasion. Secondly the Baltimore and Ohio railroad was the most southern line across the mountains by which Washington was connected with the rich and populous states of the middle west, by which the capital received troops and supplies and by which armies could easily be transferred from the eastern field of operations to the theatre of the Mississippi valley. It was an imperative necessity for the North to hold the railroad. With the road in their possession they could hold Washington and keep up communication between the eastern and western forces; without it they would have had to depend on roundabout routes likely to be overworked in hauling foodstuffs to the people of the seaboard cities. The Confederates wished, of course, to prevent its falling into the hands of the North. The third factor was the anti-secession sentiment in northwestern Virginia which the officials at Washington knew through their agents. If the north acted quickly, the Union men in northwestern Virginia could be encouraged. The number of Union sympathizers could be increased if the faint-hearted could be shown that it was safe for them to take their stand by the old flag.

These factors were of course not overlooked by the government of Virginia. On April 30th, 1861, General Lee ordered Major Boykin of Weston to issue a call for volunteers, proceed to Grafton and assume command of the forces raised. Two companies joined his command, one from Fairmont and one made up of the remnant of the Virginia militia in Lewis County which responded to the call of the state, armed only with flint-lock muskets, in bad order, and without ammunition. The result of the call must have been disappointing to the Confederate leaders. They doubtless expected that the people of the northwest would be able to hold the frontier until help should come, and, in accordance with their usual policy in dealing with the west, the officials concentrated most of their troops for the defense of the eastern part of the state.

On May 16, Colonel Porterfield, who had assumed command at Grafton, reported that there was much diversity of feeling and that his troops lacked arms.

The greatest efforts were made to secure volunteers. On May 30, Governor Letcher issued a flamboyant proclamation calling upon the people to rally to arms. "The heart that will not beat in unison with Virginia is a traitor's heart; the arm that will not strike for home in her cause is palsied with a coward fear." The soil of Virginia had been invaded!

Federal troops under McClellan crossed the Ohio river at Wheeling and Parkersburg, and with an energy which McClellan scarcely showed in any later campaign, penetrated at once to the heart of the northwest at Grafton, stampeded the sleeping Confederates at Philippi, and practically cleared the Monongahela valley almost without loss of life. The Confederates raised some forces from the Valley of Virginia which under the command of General Garnett attempted to drive off McClellan; but after the sharp skirmishes at Rich mountain and Laurel hill he sought safety in flight, only to be overtaken and killed at Corrick's ford on the Cheat river.

Up to the last week in June McClellan's troops had confined their attention to following up the Confederate forces and preparing to meet them when they turned with reinforcements. No troops had been sent to aid the Union men at Weston. It was important that troops should be sent quickly. In 1860 the General Assembly of Virginia had appropriated $125,000 for the construction of the lunatic asylum, and $30,000 of this amount had been deposited in the Exchange bank at Weston. It was to be expected that the Secession government of Virginia would recall the funds. The Union men feared they would be delivered to Richmond by the bank officials if such a call were made. The loyalty of the bank to the Restored government of Virginia and to the United States was seriously questioned by Weston people.

Union citizens of Weston determined, if possible, to secure the funds for the use of the newly organized government at Wheeling. On June 26 (and very late that night according to the story of Captain Wilkinson), a meeting was held in the back room of A. C. Hale's shoe shop, to take concerted action with a view to having troops brought to Weston. Those in attendance were: Captain J. C. Wilkinson, George C. Danser, William J. Daugherty, J. G. Vandervort, A. C. Hale, E. M. Tunstill, Robert Irvine, J. F. Osborn and Major Charles E. Anderson, and except for them the meeting was secret. It was decided that Captain Wilkinson should go at once to Wheeling and inform Governor Pierpont of the matter. He set out at once to walk to Clarksburg, caught an early train, and reached Wheeling late in the afternoon of the next day. He secured an audience with the new governor immediately, and within two hours thereafter orders had been issued for the Seventh Ohio regiment to proceed from Camp Dennison, Ohio, to Weston. P. M. Hale, then a member of the Legislature, also had an important part in having the troops sent to Weston. He had gone to Grafton at about the same time that Captain Wilkinson had started from Weston and had an audience with General McClellan in which he requested that the Seventh Ohio be sent to Weston because its commander, Colonel E. B. Tyler, having previously been a fur buyer, "knew every hog-path in Lewis County."

The Seventh Ohio left Camp Dennison and came by way of Wheeling and Grafton to Clarksburg where the regiment arrived at 4 p. m. on June 28. The march to Weston was taken up on the evening of the next day. The troops reached Jane Lew about midnight, where they received a royal welcome from the inhabitants. At 5 a. m. Weston was in sight. The approaches were seized, and the regiment entered the town by Main street with a fife and drum corps playing.

James Jackson and six other secessionists were immediately arrested and sent to Grafton. Other prominent men of the town, who were also arrested, were released after an examination. R. J. McCandlish, the cashier of the Exchange bank branch was arrested and forced to hand over $28,000 of its funds. Governor Pierpont, upon being notified of the action, sent John List to Weston to take possession of the money "on behalf of its rightful owners, the true and lawful government of Virginia."

The money was taken to Wheeling and deposited in banks there to the credit of the state. It was used in paying the salaries of officers, and other expenses incident to setting the Restored government in operation. A much greater amount was, however, appropriated by the Legislature of the Restored government and used later in the construction of the institution. Contrary to the general belief among the people of the town the Weston branch of the Exchange bank was loyal to the United States, and the confiscation of its funds was unwarranted. Cashier McCandlish immediately went to Wheeling, saw Governor Pierpont and, aided by the intercession of Major Anderson, secured credit for the money from the Wheeling banks in which it had been deposited.

The people of Weston received the troops with

emotions ranging all the way from fear and hatred to unbounded joy. Nothing was too great for the regiment to ask. Mrs. Osborn prepared breakfast for sixty-four hungry soldiers on the morning of their arrival and Mrs. Dinsmore satisfied the hunger of dozens of others. Camp Tyler, so-called from the name of the commanding officer of the regiment, was established on the west side of the river on what is now a part of the hospital lawn. A large flag pole was brought from the country, from which the Stars and Stripes was soon proudly waving to the breeze. The office of the Weston Herald, which had been hastily vacated by its editor and proprietor, F. J. Alfred, was seized by the young officers of the regiment, and within a few days "**The Ohio Seventh**" made its appearance. Its motto was, "We come to protect, not to invade." In his salutatory the editor says: "The **Ohio Seventh** will be published as often as circumstances will permit, and of such material as may be found in secession offices where we may chance to stop long enough to raise our flag and issue a paper. Confederate States' bonds and other 'secesh' paper not received for either subscriptions or advertising."

Though the troops had been brought to Weston primarily for the purpose of securing the Virginia funds in the Exchange bank, there was no disposition among the higher command of the Union forces to order their withdrawal. Weston was an important strategic center, the possession of which by the Union forces gave them a certain security and a point of vantage for further movements into the Confederate territory of the northwest. It was an important outpost for the protection of the Baltimore and Ohio railroad because of its location on the Staunton and Parkersburg turnpike by which Confederate raiding parties aiming at the Northwestern railroad west of Clarksburg were likely to approach. Most important of all, it was the junction of the Weston and Gauley Bridge turnpike with the state road, and was the gate to the northern approach to the Kanawha valley, and the center from which the secession territory to the south and west could be most easily commanded. Other troop movements soon showed that the Union leaders did not intend easily to relinquish the advantage gained.

On July 4, a company was dispatched to Walkersville to break up a Confederate recruiting station and bring in prisoners. At about the same time, reinforcements arrived from Clarksburg, among which was a detachment of the gallant First Virginia cavalry, which was billeted in the Bland hotel, the Bailey house and other public and private buildings. Colonel Stanley Matthews, afterwards an associate justice of the United States Supreme Court, led his regiment across the Ohio river and swept up the Little Kanawha to Glenville and then to Weston. It was not long until a detachment of the quartermaster's department was stationed in the town, which became a sort of sub-station for the main office at Clarksburg. A two-story frame building was erected out the Parkersburg pike in which goods were stored until required to be issued to the men. George Ross, who later became prominent in the affairs of the county, was one of the clerks of the quartermaster's department who came to Weston at this time. Upon the department devolved part of the responsibility of maintaining communication between the advanced posts and the main body, and the units in Weston were placed in connection with Clarksburg first by courier, and later by the erection of the first telegraph line in Lewis County.

The federal occupation of Weston was not a hardship to the people, and after the novelty of the situation wore off, they would hardly have known they were living in a military post. The proclamation of General McClellan had stated that the Union troops were "enemies to none but armed rebels and those voluntarily giving them aid," and troops which came to Weston usually refrained from molesting the persons and property of those who were known to be in sympathy with the Southern states. The troops were raw levies, however, the officers were as new as the troops, and there was unfortunately some pilfering at first. Within a few days the offenders were stopped by the heroic measures taken by the commanding officers of the Union forces. Captain Shuman, of the First Virginia cavalry punished several of his men by fastening nose bags over their heads and then tying them to the pillars of the Bland hotel, both as an example to other evildoers and to show the residents that thieves were to be punished. Drunkenness was punished by bucking and gagging a man in public.

Some of the soldiers stationed in Weston performed distinct public services, like the publishers of the **Ohio Seventh.** Practically all the soldiers were young men, who behaved themselves as gentlemen and gave little cause for complaint. They mingled freely with the families of the Union sympathizers, and after the war several of them located permanently in Weston.

The citizens of the town were subjected to some of the restrictions imposed upon the residents of every town occupied as a military post. Strong guards were placed on all the principal approaches to the town, including the two bridges across Stone Coal, the narrows above Shadybrook, the Polk creek bridge, and the narrows above the electric light plant. At the Bendale bridge there was a picket, consisting of from two squads to a company, depending upon the danger from the Confederates. All through the months of July and August, 1861, the Bendale bridge was the southernmost post in the Union lines; beyond it was Confederate territory. One of the commanders of the picket at Bendale bridge at a later date was William McKinley, afterwards President.

By the end of July the Confederates had been driven from the Monongahela valley, and all that region saved for the Union. The war department wished similarly to gain possession of the Kanawha valley. A double movement was planned. General J. D. Cox crossed the Ohio river near Point Pleasant and advanced up the valley against Generals Wise and Floyd, who had been placed in command by the Confederate government. A flanking movement was also planned over the Weston and Gauley Bridge turnpike from the north.

In the latter part of August, 1861, Colonel Tyler left Weston with the Seventh Ohio and took up his line of March to Gauley Bridge, one hundred eleven miles distant. The campaign was without incident until after the troops had passed the bounds of the county into Braxton. A man by the name of Clinebell had swept through Gilmer and Braxton counties, like another Paul Revere, spreading the warning that the Yankees were coming. The Northern sympathizers in the county made their way out to the Ohio Seventh by devious paths. Every blacksnake rifle in the county was pressed into service and some of the natives even armed themselves with butcher-knives. Trouble was experienced at Powell's mountain in Nicholas county, where bushwhackers were put to flight and one of them killed. Beyond the mountain at Cross Lanes the Union troops met General Floyd with a large body of Confederates, and fought a drawn battle. Tyler retreated to Summersville. General Rosecrans having come up with reinforcements, the Confederates withdrew to Carnifax Ferry on the Gauley. There they were severely defeated. In November the final battle of the campaign was fought at Gauley Bridge, and the Kanawha valley was cleared of Confederates.

Immediately upon the commencement of the expedition under Rosecrans it became necessary to establish a military courier line to keep up communications. The couriers were subjected to dangers from the bushwhackers who infested the road practically all the way from Weston to Gauley Bridge. James Flesher, of Polk creek, was killed by them while on the perilous service. The stretch of the turnpike along Carrion run is said to have been one of the most dangerous places on the whole route.

Bushwhackers in Lewis County were far too numerous. As a class they were worthless, taking up arms not so much because of their love for a cause as to gratify their revenge on their neighbors and to secure plunder. They would not enlist in the regular forces, but contented themselves with remaining at home and creating a reign of terror in their communities. Captain Leib, of the quartermaster department, in his book, "The Chances for Making a Million," says: "The bushwhackers are composed of a class of men who are noted for their ignorance, indolence, duplicity and dishonesty; whose vices and passions peculiarly fit them for the warfare in which they are engaged, and upon which the civilized world looks with horror. Imagine a stolid, vicious-looking countenance, an ungainly figure and an awkward, if not ungraceful, spinal curve in the dorsal region, acquired by laziness and indifference to maintaining an erect posture; a garb of the coarsest texture of home-spun kubeb, or 'linsey woolsey' tattered and torn, and so covered with dirt as not to enable one to guess its original color; a dilapidated, rimless hat, or cap of some wild animal's skin covering his head, the hair on which has not been combed for months; his feet covered with moccasins, and a rifle by his side, a powder-horn and shot-pouch slung around his neck and you have the beau ideal of the West Virginia bushwhackers.

"Thus equipped he sallies forth with the stealth of a panther, and lies in wait for the straggling soldier, courier, or loyal citizen, to whom the only warning given of his presence is the sharp click of his deadly rifle. He kills for the sake of killing and plunders for the sake of gain. Parties of these ferocious beasts, under cover of darkness, frequently steal into a neighborhood, burn the residences of loyal citizens, rob stores, tanyards and farmhouses of everything they can put to use, especially arms, ammunition, leather, clothing, bedding and salt."

In Lewis County, Ben Haymond and Perry Hays are said to have been notorious as leaders of partisan bands on the Southern side, and there were several others who infested the county. Two Connelly brothers living in the county, who took opposite sides in the war, each raised a band of partisans. At different times their adherents had fierce encounters, until finally the bands met near Sutton. The conflict soon became hand to hand. The two brothers finally confronted each other, and after a sharp struggle the leader of the Union band killed his brother. One night a band of guerillas took a young man named Mulvey from his bed and shot him in cold blood for no other reason than that he was an avowed Union man.

Not all the bushwhackers were Southern, however. One of the most notorious of all was William G. Pierson, who espoused the cause of the Union very early in the war, though two of his sons honorably took sides with the South by joining its armies. Pierson lived out the Gauley Bridge turnpike about two miles south of Jacksonville. At the very beginning of the war in western Virginia he gathered a few kindred spirits about him in an organization called Pierson's Rangers. From headquarters at Hogsett's tavern at Jacksonville they caused a reign of terror throughout Collins Settlement. Pierson was feared and hated by men of both parties. Porter M. Arnold, justice of the peace and prominent citizen of the county, asked the regular forces of the Confederates to break up his band. "If you will kill Bill Pierson," he once is reported to have said to Captain Imboden, "I'll give you two hundred acres of land." "If I see Pierson," was the reply, "I'll kill him, and you don't need to give me any land for it."

Late in October, 1861, Pierson entered Jacksonville in the night and compelled Arnold, William Brake, William Francis and a man named Blair to get out of their beds and accompany him. When the party had gone about a mile up the river with the captives a short distance in front of the party the rangers opened fire without warning. At the first volley Francis fell feigning death, and Arnold, Brake and Blair were killed or mortally wounded. The rangers proceeded on their way without further ado, and Francis ran to Weston to secure medical attention and aid. The act so incensed the people of the community, both those of Union and those of Confederate sympathies, and so increased the public detestation which his previous acts had evoked that Pierson was compelled to leave the community and go into hiding. Later in the course of the war he scouted for the Federals from his home in Jane Lew. In the autumn of 1864 he was shot by an unknown hand while standing on the porch of his home.

In order to put a stop to the outrages committed by both Confederate and Union bushwhackers and partisan leaders, as well as to render aid to the regular forces in case of invasion by armed troops, Governor Pierpont early in his administration directed the formation of home guards all over the state. J. C. Wilkinson, of Weston, was commissioned to raise a company in Lewis County. He succeeded in securing the enlistment of about forty men, and with them he did excellent work in restoring order, and scouting in the face of the Confederate raiders, though the force was too weak to oppose a large force.

The Union forces were not long left in peaceful possession of Western Virginia. For the Confederates to have sat supinely by and allowed the Federals free hand west of the Alleghanies would have been to disregard a magnificent strategic opportunity. The conquest of the territory would have been impracticable for the Confederates at any time after the defeat of Garnett and Lee, because the movements of the Federals around Washington and in the Mississippi valley kept the Confederates busy, and no large forces could be spared. With very small bodies of men, however, it was possible to do immense damage to the Union forces and to gain advantages greatly out of proportion to the number of troops employed. They could sometimes reach the main line of the Baltimore and Ohio railroad and, by burning bridges and tearing up tracks, interrupt communications and delay the arrival of reinforcements and supplies for the Federals. In order to guard against the attack of a thousand men or less the Federals were compelled to keep several thousand on duty guarding the road and scouting in various parts of northwestern Virginia. Another advantage was that the raiders also secured important additions to their diminishing supplies when horses and cattle were driven over the mountains to be used as mounts for the cavalry in the one case or food for the people in the other.

Another object of their earlier raids was to secure recruits. By some strange fatuity the officials at Richmond seemed to think that once the way was open for men to get through the Federal lines, thousands of volunteers would flock to their standards from northwestern Virginia.

Most of the raids were directed toward the stretch of railroad between Piedmont and Harper's Ferry; but several parties crossed the Alleghanies, and at least three reached Weston. The first raider to reach Weston was General A. G. Jenkins, who, on August 12, 1862, left Lewisburg in Greenbrier County with 550 men, leisurely proceeded up the Greenbrier river, crossed Valley mountain intending to attack Beverly but, finding the place strongly garrisoned, passed to the left of the town, and on the evening of August 30th entered Buckhannon after a short skirmish with the Federal garrison and home guards. The company garrisoning Weston fell back on Clarksburg the same day, taking with them all the stores that could be moved, and destroying others. Jenkins' presence west of the mountains was now known to the Federals, and troops were being concentrated to intercept him. It was imperative that he move rapidly. Early on the morning following the Buckhannon skirmish Jenkins entered Weston firing promiscuously to spread terror among the inhabitants. He was unopposed. A force of home guards which Judge Robert

Irvine had collected to prevent disorder after the retreat of the Federal troops to Clarksburg, and which was stationed on the west side of the river, dispersed upon the entry of the Confederate troops into the town.

Promptly the Confederates proceeded to the execution of the purpose for which they came. All the citizens who were on the streets were lined up as prisoners of war and compelled to take the parole not to fight against the Confederate States. Small parties were detached in different directions to clear the town of Union soldiers, if any remained. On the west side of the river a single Federal was found who refused to obey the command to halt and was shot in the leg. Small parties proceeded to the nearby country districts to round up horses. Others broke into the principal stores of the town, including that of A. A. Lewis, a Confederate sympathizer, and forced the merchants to accept payment for goods in Confederate money. They did not secure any funds from the Exchange bank because Cashier McCandlish had taken all the money from the vaults and left with the Federal troops the preceding day. After destroying such stores as could be found Jenkins left late in the evening, picking up small parties of his men who had been in the country districts at different points on the Staunton and Parkersburg turnpike west of the town. After proceeding through enemy territory for more than 500 miles, destroying thousands of dollars worth of stores, securing much property and doing great damage, the command got safely back.

The lessons of the raid were not lost to the Confederates, and they planned the next spring a more extensive raid with the double object of putting the Baltimore and Ohio railroad out of commission and gaining recruits and supplies. The railroad, according to the declaration of Governor Letcher, had been "a nuisance to the state of Virginia ever since its construction," and the next raid was an ambitious attempt to abate the nuisance. A double invasion was planned. General

Jones was to destroy the bridges and viaducts on the difficult crossing of the Alleghanies, thence go to Morgantown and Fairmont, at which place he was to destroy the bridge across the Monongahela and from there take up his march to Clarksburg. General John D. Imboden was to come from the Shenandoah Valley via Beverly and Philippi to the rendezvous at Clarksburg.

The Federal forces in northwestern Virginia, consisting of a brigade, were under the command of Brigadier General B. S. Roberts, with headquarters at Clarksburg. At the time of the coming of the Confederates his forces were distributed in several places, one regiment being at Beverly. When Imboden attacked that post, Roberts set out for its relief and had gone as far as Buckhannon when he learned that the garrison at Beverly had been forced to retreat toward Philippi. He frantically called upon Washington for reinforcements and ordered all his troops on the Weston and Gauley Bridge turnpike to concentrate at Clarksburg. Learning that Jones' cavalry was approaching Grafton, that Imboden was pursuing the Beverly garrison toward Philippi, and that in the general panic the stores at Weston had been destroyed contrary to his orders, he began to race with the two bodies of Confederates for the possession of Clarksburg. By forced marches Roberts arrived at Clarksburg first and put his troops in position to defend the town.

His cavalry under Captain Bowen fell upon a part of Jones' force below Clarksburg and drove them in a panic to the main body which had moved toward Buckhannon to join Imboden. The Confederates moved around Clarksburg and concentrated at Weston where the advance guard arrived about April 28th.

Cavalry scouts sent out by Jones reported no immediate danger of an attack from the Federals at Clarksburg who now outnumbered the combined Confederate commands, and it was determined to continue the raid. Jones with his more mobile force was to destroy the

Northwestern railroad between Salem and Parkersburg, and Imboden was to proceed south over the Weston and Gauley Bridge turnpike to raid the valley of the Great Kanawha. Jones moved out first toward West Union, but was prevented from entering that town by the presence of Federals in force, and he proceeded to destroy bridges east and west of the town, and to set fire to one of the tunnels. He went down the little Kanawha valley as far as 'the oil wells at Burning Springs in Wirt County where he set fire to 150,000 barrels of oil and practically ruined the oil industry of the place until the close of the war. He then returned to Glenville and proceeded to Summersville over the Weston and Charleston turnpike.

Imboden remained at Weston a few days after the departure of Jones in order to threaten the flank and rear of the Federals if they attempted to fall upon Jones. He improved his time in trying to secure recruits and in collecting provisions. Detachments were sent out into the Freeman's creek and Hacker's creek sections to scout, to invite enlistments and to 'trade' horses with the farmers, but they were disappointed. Most of the people were Union in sentiment, and most of the horses had been driven to the woods. In Weston he took measures to prevent looting and offenses against those of Union sympathies who had not escaped with the Federal garrison. Guards were stationed at all the stores. No soldiers were allowed to take any goods without paying for them; but as the payments were made in depreciated Confederate currency, the losses of the merchants were considerable. Attempts of the soldiers to secure a United States flag which had been hidden in the home of Postmaster George V. Strickler were frustrated by the prompt action of General Imboden in stationing sentries around the house. The Confederate soldiers under Imboden were under strict discipline and generally deported themselves as gentlemen. They gave the people to understand that they were friends returned to a friendly district, and they invited the co-operation of the civilian population.

The residents of Weston whose sympathies were with the South received Imboden's men with open arms. Many of them were Lewis County boys; Imboden himself was a son of a resident of Skin creek. The women of the town made a Confederate flag and presented it to the soldiers. Seeing the condition of the clothing of some of the men, they busied themselves with their needles and made shirts and other wearing apparel for them. Cautious business men whose sympathies with the Confederate cause had been carefully disguised during the Union occupation openly tendered them aid in various ways.

Meanwhile Roberts remained in Clarksburg and allowed Jones time to cut the railroad and Imboden time to recuperate, only sending one regiment against the former, and reconnoitering parties against the latter. On May 5th, however, he sent a strong party under Captain Bowen to reconnoiter in force in the vicinity of Jane Lew. They almost succeeded in surrounding and capturing Captain John Sprigg who held Jane Lew and inflicted considerable losses upon him. He fled to Weston. Imboden, thinking the scouting party to be the advance guard of Roberts' command hastily formed part of his men for a delaying action below Weston while the wagon trains were prepared for a hasty retreat southward. The Federal party did not pursue Sprigg, and the Confederates, still under the impression that it was the advance guard of Roberts' army, retreated in all haste, taking routes to the left of the Weston and Gauley Bridge turnpike which had been badly cut up by the wagon trains of the Federals retreating from Bulltown and points south. They were able to travel only a few miles a day. One of their encampments was at Walkersville, whence they went over the Buckhannon and Little Kanawha turnpike to the Braxton-Lewis line.

Shortly after the Confederates left, Roberts entered

STONEWALL JACKSON

Weston. He did not attempt to pursue Imboden, merely advising the War Department that troops should be sent to Staunton to cut off the retreat of the column. He himself confined his attention to the Confederates in Weston. He made wholesale arrests of the leading citizens of the town. Sixty-three women and children, the wives and children and mothers and sisters of soldiers in the Southern army were sent through the lines, where they would help to consume the rapidly diminishing food supply of the Confederate states. About an equal number of prominent citizens was sent to Camp Chase to be interned until the close of the war. The inefficient Roberts was soon relieved by General Averill, an able commander who reorganized the forces under him as cavalry and not only repulsed many of the Confederate raids, but even led an important raid against the railroad in southwestern Virginia.

Weston was not again visited by Confederate troops until the fall of 1864 when a party of cavalry under Colonel V. A. Witcher, who had been with General Jones on his western raid, suddenly appeared from the direction of Bulltown. There was no force sufficient to oppose him, and he took possession. The stores were rifled and some good horses were taken from the farms in exchange for sorry mounts, but the greatest damage done was to rob the Exchange bank of all its funds, amounting to $5,287.85. A receipt for this amount, signed by Brigadier-General John Echols, is still in possession of the bank. Jane Lew was occupied by a small party of cavalry, but the threatened pursuit of Averill's cavalry caused Witcher to curtail his visit. After appropriating the blankets in use by the patients in the newly opened hospital for the insane, he retreated with all speed to the Shenandoah valley.

The damage done by raiders in western Virginia is not to be compared to that done by the partisan bands, as witness the condition of Braxton and Fayette counties at the end of the war, with their county seats practically destroyed and many of the residences abandoned. The Braxton County records were early in the war removed for safe keeping to Weston. Lewis County was fortunate in having comparatively few partisan bands and an active and efficient company of home guards.

In general there was little confusion in the county compared with most of the surrounding counties. People of opposite views got along with each other by refraining from the discussion of politics. Farmers went about their duties as usual. Business was not wholly destroyed. Work on the hospital for the insane was continued throughout most of the war, and the institution was actually opened for patients in 1864.

There was a great undercurrent of feeling all during the war. When F. J. Alfred returned to Weston in 1862 to resume his journalistic operations under the title of "The Stars and Stripes," the Unionists remembered his former advocacy of "Southern Rights and Southern Independence," and he was soon forced to suspend publication for want of patronage.

The public business of the county suffered as a result of the military operations and the political confusion of the period. There was considerable difficulty in securing a quorum of the justices in the early days of the war; and only the public business of immediate importance was given attention. Few bridge orders, road orders and notations as to the granting of poor claims are found in the record books of the period. One of the officials of the county refused to recognize the existence of the new state of West Virginia and paid to the Virginia government at Richmond the sum of $3,575.30, being the judgments of commissioners of delinquent taxes and forfeited lands.

The Restored government infused new strength into the county court, and it seemed for a time to regain all its old time vigor as an administrative body. It could not, however, repair the roads as fast as the troops cut them to pieces. The business of being a sheriff in the early days of the war was not the safest or most pleasant occupation in the world. There were the usual taxes to collect and the accounts to be kept; and in addition the duties of the sheriff as a peace officer were vastly augmented. At one time early in the war it was impossible to find a man so foolhardy as to accept the office. The presence of Union troops made the position much safer.

The most important duties of the county officers after the formation of West Virginia were in connection with furnishing soldiers for the Union army and giving aid to the dependent families of those who had volunteered. So far as the greatly diminished revenues of the county would admit, assistance was given in all deserving cases. When President Lincoln issued his call for 500,000 men in 1864, the board of supervisors of the county, following the custom in other states, offered a bounty of $300 to every soldier who enlisted in the service. In order that those who had volunteered at an earlier date should not be discriminated against on account of their patriotism it was ordered at the same time that all who had volunteered previously in the companies of Michael Egan and Jasper Peterson should be paid $40, but that the amounts already paid for the relief of the families of the soldiers should be deducted from the bonus. The apportionment of the county was fifty-three men, and all were raised within a surprisingly short time. Early in 1865, upon the call for 300,000 volunteers by the President, the board offered a bounty of $400 each to secure twenty-one men. There being then no funds in the county treasury, and no provision having been made in the levy for the year, it was found expedient to issue notes on the county for $8,400, the amount required to pay the bounties.

CHAPTER XXIV.

THE POLITICAL RECONSTRUCTION

The outcome of the war determined that the United States was a nation, that the western part of Virginia should henceforth form a separate state, and that the former slaves should be citizens of both. The surrender of Lee at Appomattox did not solve all the problems of government of either nation or state, but brought many new problems of only less difficulty in its train. Though reconstruction was primarily a national and state problem, yet in Lewis County it caused such a tremendous upheaval in politics that it has influenced the whole later history of the county. The marks of the period are yet visible on our political and social life.

The constitution adopted by the state of West Virginia abolished the unsatisfactory system of county courts with both judicial and administrative functions, and in its place substituted a new and complex system of local government. The township system, borrowed from New York and the New England states, partly superseded the county as a unit. Each county was to be divided into from three to ten townships, each with its own officers and each transacting business in township meetings. The officers were a supervisor, a clerk, surveyors of roads, and an overseer of the poor, elected annually; one or more constables, elected biennially; and one or more justices elected quadrennially. There were also a treasurer, three school commissioners and two inspectors of elections. In place of the county court as an administrative body was the board of supervisors, consisting of the supervisors of all the townships in the county, meeting regularly at the county seat. The judicial business of the county was for the most part divorced from the administrative. The county officers were a sheriff, a recorder, a prosecuting attorney, a surveyor of lands and, in Lewis County, two assessors.

The county court of Lewis County, in preparation for the change in government, appointed Jesse Woofter, Esais Fetty, John S. Anderson and Mansfield McWhorter as commissioners to lay off the county into townships. The board met at Weston and, with the aid of the surveyor of lands, fixed the boundaries of the townships. The southern part of the county which had been the first election district under the constitution of 1852, now Collins Settlement, formed one township and was called Battelle, in honor of Gordon Battelle, a Methodist preacher and head of the Northwestern Academy, who had done much to counteract the influence of the eastern politicians in trying to lead the west into secession. The second election district formed the township of Weston. It included practically the territory in the present districts of Skin Creek and Court House, the only difference being that east of Weston the northern boundary was the Staunton and Parkersburg turnpike. The territory north of the turnpike and east of the West Fork river formed the third township under the name of Jane Lew. The territory drained by Polk creek, Freeman's creek and Leading creek formed the township of Willey, named in honor of Waitman T. Willey, one of the first United States senators from West Virginia.

The first board of supervisors consisted of Robert Crawford, of Battelle; George I. Marsh, of Weston; (township); Noah Life, of Jane Lew (township); and Richard B. Hall, of Willey. Henry Brannon was the first clerk of the board and Francis M. Chalfant, the first treasurer.

The transaction of business by the board of supervisors was frequently delayed in the beginning by the number of deadlocks, due to the even number of supervisors. Within a few months after the plan went into operation, a new township under the name of Georgetown was created out of the township of Weston with the addition of a strip of territory from Jane Lew. It embraced the territory now included in Skin creek district. The name was changed to Lincoln after the President had been re-elected in 1864. In June, 1865, the name of Weston township was changed to Sheridan, partly because General Philip H. Sheridan had driven the Confederates out of the Shenandoah valley and defeated them at Five Forks, partly because he was an Irishman.

The difficulties of setting a new and unfamiliar government in operation were not decreased by the fact that it had to be inaugurated in time of war often in the presence of contending troops. Civil government could hardly be effective under any system when conditions were as they existed in 1863.

The township system was unpopular almost from the start. There were too many officials, for in addition to all the usual county officers there were added as many officials for each township, and the amount expended for salaries for all seemed out of proportion to the services which they rendered. Then too, the former county officers failed for two or more years to deliver their books to the new justices of the peace. The county was at great additional expense on account of the payment of bounties for enlistment, for relief of the families of soldiers and for many other extraordinary expenditures made necessary by the war. In order that the people should have means of communication, it was necessary for the county to take over the turnpikes and operate them at great additional expense because the turnpike companies were unable to keep them in repair after they had been cut to pieces in winter movements of troops and supplies. Bridges were destroyed or badly damaged, and had to be replaced after the war.

In order to meet the increased expenditures it was necessary for the board of supervisors to increase the taxes. Such an action was sure to lead to complaint against the board, no matter how economically it administered the affairs of the county. The assessment of real estate in 1866, as provided by state law, raised a storm of protest from all sides. Assessors John P. Peterson and William A. Watson increased the average valuation on lands from $3.18, as it was in 1861, to $6.11 per acre, exclusive of town lots in both cases. The board of supervisors immediately passed a resolution declaring it to be their judgment that the assessment was too high. On account of the fact, they said, that the county was much of the time occupied by contending armies which depleted the numbers of the live stock and the means of subsistence, the lands had been neglected and were actually worth less than before the war. After the high values of Peterson and Watson had been further increased twenty-one per cent by a state board, the supervisors again protested, declaring: "Recuperation cannot follow exhausting taxation aggravated by fictitious enormous values." It is possible that the purpose of the supervisors in passing the resolution was political. The increase in values could have been balanced by a decrease in the rate.

Though the rate of levy was slightly reduced the taxes of the citizens steadily increased. The township system was blamed; the officers were blamed; the new state was blamed; and the radical Republicans were blamed. There was much discontent. At this juncture many of the ex-Confederates returned to West Virginia and in some counties attempted to take the reins of government in their own hands. The problem of establishing a satisfactory local government in the face of their criticism became more difficult.

Soon after the surrender of Lee, when it was seen that most of the Lewis County soldiers in the Southern army would return to their homes, a mass meeting of citizens was held at the courthouse to take measures to prevent others from returning and to drive out those who had already come home. Strong resolutions were drafted by a committee, said to have been composed partly of men who had first come to Weston with Union troops, and these resolutions were adopted by the convention.

There is good reason to believe that the mass meeting did not represent the real sentiment of the majority of Lewis County. The general belief seemed to be that the ex-Confederates had accepted the results of the war, and the Lewis County people were willing to forget the part they had played during the conflict. Even during the struggle there was an absence of bitterness rather remarkable considering the tension under which the people were laboring. When an act of the West Virginia Legislature was passed in 1863 declaring forfeited the property of citizens of the state who were then serving the states in rebellion against the United States, the Lewis County board of supervisors refused to take action against the property of any former resident. Even Jonathan M. Bennett, who had continued to serve as First Auditor of the Virginia government at Richmond all through the war, found all his property intact upon his return to Weston. The board of supervisors heard a complaint made by him, shortly after his return, that he was assessed with property which he did not own, and the books were ordered corrected.

The ex-Confederates, upon their return home, were confronted with laws which prevented their exercising the right of suffrage. A voter's test act, passed in 1865, required each voter to take an oath that he had "neither voluntarily borne arms against the United States nor aided those who had engaged in armed hostillity against the United States." Fearing that the registration laws were unconstitutional, a decitizenizing amendment was submitted to the people by the legislature. Under the operation of the registration law, the amendment was passed in Lewis County by a majority of 99. It is estimated that three hundred white men were disfranchised in the county as a result of its ratification.

A contest was at once begun by the ex-Confederates to secure the right of suffrage for all white men—the same rights which the radical Republicans in West Virginia seemed willing to accord to the negroes. In the November elections of 1866, less than six months after the passage of the amendment, the board of supervisors found it expedient to throw out the returns from six precincts because a number of persons had voted there whose names were not on the books. The Republicans lost the assessorship in the first district on account of the fact that their candidate was not a citizen of the county at the time of the election, and great was the rejoicing in the Democratic ranks.

The ex-Confederates were aided by the Democrats, who made common cause with them as a party of opposition, in their attempts to secure control of the county government. Their efforts to secure the suffrage met with determined opposition on the part of those who had espoused the Union cause. A bitter struggle marked all the elections from this time forth for a number of years. The political struggle soon became so desperate that the feeling soon extended beyond political matters. In 1869, one of the ex-Confederates declared that the Republicans "had become partial and political even in their business dealings." He advocated a boycott on the business of all the Republicans if they maintained their attitude.

The Republicans were again successful in the election of 1867, but it was apparent that the election the next year would be fiercely contested. Governor Boreman had appointed as the board of registration for Lewis County, James Corley and James Conrad of Battelle and Richard B. Hall of Willey. It was their difficult duty to register all the citizens of the county who were entitled to vote and to refuse to register all those who came under the provisions of the "decitizenizing amendment."

The board summoned forty-two voters, whose names had previously appeared on the books, to show cause why they should not be denied the right of suffrage. After a hearing at the county seat twenty-eight names were struck off the books, seventeen without the introduction of any testimony whatever but simply because they failed to appear in answer to the summons. The action was denounced as high-handed and arbitrary by the Democra's. Accusations were made that the registrars were actuated by ulterior motives, in view of the fact that all but three of the persons summoned lived in Battelle township, the home of two members of the board. The action aroused great resentment, with the result that in the election which followed many voters turned to the party of opposition. The campaign was also complicated by the introduction of the question of taxation. Promises were made by the Democratic candidates for supervisor that if they were successful they would reduce the expenses of the county government. The result of the election was that in spite of the disfranchisement of every citizen who could be disfranchised under the law the entire local ticket of the Democrats was elected in every township except Willey.

In accordance with their promises to their constituents the new board of supervisors began to make wholesale reductions in salaries. The salary of the clerk, which had been $200, was cut in half; the prosecuting attorney had to content himself with $200 instead of $400; and the county superintendent of schools was to receive $125 instead of $200. The expenditures for other purposes were also curtailed.

There was never a day within the next two years that the political situation in the county was forgotten. The ratification of the 15th amendment in 1870, which granted full suffrage to the negroes, caused still more liberal Republicans to turn from their party. The invitation extended by the Methodist Episcopal church in Weston for negroes to attend services on one occasion was held up before the public as evidence of the depraved character of the whole race of radical Republicans. When two of them later attended the services at the colored church the Democrats held up their hands in horror. The mother-in-law of one of the township officers of Braxton County froze to death on her way to visit relatives; the next week the Democratic organ told a story of the horrible cruelty of a radical Republican official, who had turned a defenceless woman, 98 years old, out in the cold to perish, and her body to be eaten by hogs! Even the Ku Klux Klan, an organization formed farther south for the purpose of frightening negroes away from the polls, made its appearance in Lewis County. Alfred Smith, of Weston, was attacked while out Stone Coal, but he escaped. A woman was reported tarred on Big Skin creek. Some of the Republicans were badly frightened. The organization in Lewis County was probably the work of irresponsible boys, and it was denied that it had any political significance. Republicans made political capital out of the occurrence, however.

In the election of 1870 the issues before the people were the same as at preceding elections—the disfranchisement of the white men and the high cost of government. Many of the more liberal Republicans temporarily joined the opposition party in attempting to restore the right to vote to the intelligent white men who had followed the cause of the old state during the war, and had demonstrated beyond a doubt an equal willingness to follow the fortunes of the new state. Most liberal-minded men, including the Republican governor, J. J. Jacob, were willing to let the old issues die and substitute for them live issues connected with the internal development of the state.

The Democrats, encouraged by the prospect of a large reinforcement, redoubled their efforts to carry the election They formed one of the most thorough organizations of their party that the county has ever known. A committee was appointed in every school district in the county to see that every voter was registered and that he went to the polls. Intimidation of the registrars was resorted to in some instances. The Democratic county central committee caused the arrest of several of the registrars for failing to register citizens entitled to the suffrage. The radical Republicans also waged a vigorous campaign. Both parties turned to the Irish vote in order to carry the election. Two of the candidates for county offices on the Democratic ticket and one on the Republican ticket were Irishmen who had lately been naturalized. A campaign of abuse was directed by the Democrats against "Waldo Goff's Boy" (General Nathan Goff), who had been nominated for Congress by the Republicans, and his military record was held up to public scorn.

On the eve of election there were 560 voters not registered, distributed among the townships as follows: Jane Lew, 85; Willey, 112; Battelle, 179; Sheridan, 78; and Lincoln, 106. So great was the discontent among the liberal Republicans and so thorough the Democratic campaign that, in spite of their great handicap, the county went Democratic by a majority of 145. The movement was state wide. The next week the Weston **Democrat** came out with streamer headlines—"VICTORY PRAISE GOD! THE WHITE MAN FREE AT LAST!" Immediately below it was the Democratic hymn of thanksgiving:

> "Sound the loud timbrel
> O'er Egypt's dark sea.
> Jehovah hath triumphed;
> The **White Man** is free."

The Flick amendement to restore the privilege of voting to those who had been disfranchised in 1866, was referred to the people by the Legislature in 1871. At a special election the result in Lewis County was: for ratification, 740; for rejection, 86. Though there was only a light vote, the result of the election showed the almost unanimous desire of the people of the county to have the matter settled in favor of votes for white men.

The more radical Democrats, having gained control of the Legislature, wished to go farther and destroy all traces of Republican rule in the state by the adoption of a new constitution. It was freely charged by the Republicans that the leaders of the Democratic party wished to return as far as possible to the system in vogue in Virginia before the formation of West Virginia, and thus destroy all progress that had been made. Lewis County voted against the calling of the convention by a majority of 130, and voted against the constitution, as submitted, by a majority of 332. The new constitution was ratified by the state at large. Though the people of Lewis County favored votes for white men they were not yet ready to go the full length of supporting all the measures of the Democratic party. Grant carried Lewis County again in 1872, but as usual Democratic township officers were elected in all the townships of the county except Willey.

The new constitution provided that the minor civil divisions of the county should be called districts and that a county court should take the place of the board of supervisors. One of the first acts of the county court after the adoption of the new constitution was to provide for the reorganization of the township government. The county court left the boundaries as they were, but took advantage of the opportunity to erase the names given in honor of statesmen on the Union side and to substitute for them the geographical names given to the communities. Battelle township became Collins Settlement district; Lincoln became Skin Creek; Jane Lew became Hacker's Creek; and Willey became Freeman's Creek. Even the name Sheridan ceased to designate the

Irish stronghold, which henceforth was known by the very inappropriate name of Court House.

The trend toward the Democratic party which had begun in 1870 continued after the enfranchisement of the ex-Confederates by the Flick amendment. Beginning with the election of 1874, the Democrats carried the county at every election for twenty years. Few Republican candidates for any of the county offices were successful at the polls.

CHAPTER XXV.

THE WESTON STATE HOSPITAL

Almost immediately after the report of the committee that Weston was the most available site for the proposed Trans-Alleghany Lunatic Asylum, the state authorities at Richmond began preparations for the purchase of land and the erection of buildings. In accordance with the terms of the act of the General Assembly creating the institution Governor Wise appointed nine directors "living as near the location as possible," as follows: Minter Bailey, Johnson N. Camden, John Brannon, R. J. McCandlish, George J. Arnold, James T. Jackson, William E. Arnold, Caleb Boggess and Joseph C. Spalding. The board organized immediately with Minter Bailey as president and Johnson N. Camden as clerk.

Arrangements were made at once for the purchase of the site selected by the board. A tract of seventy acres lying partly in the town of Weston was purchased from Minter Bailey for $1,500, a rate per acre cheaper than the less desirable hilly land west of the buildings was obtained from the other owners. In all 269 acres of land was purchased for $9,809.12, leaving from the appropriation a balance of $15,000 to be applied on the buildings.

It was provided in the act of 1858 that the plan of the building should be chosen by the board of directors, but that any plan adopted must be approved by two physicians who had been connected with similar institutions. The directors appointed William E. Arnold and John Brannon a committee to draw up plans for the buildings. The two men, accompanied by Dr. William J. Bland, visited the best institutions of a similar kind in the United States, including those of some of the New England states which were regarded as models by nearly every people in the world. They investigated the plans submitted by the leading architects of the United States and finally selected those of K. S. Andrews of Baltimore. The board then designated the site where the foundations for the new building should be placed.

In 1860, the General Assembly appropriated $50,000 with which to begin the work of construction, and a similar sum the following year. Work was begun at once on the main building and prosecuted diligently until in June 1861, when the Virginia authorities ordered that all work should stop, and that the funds not expended should be returned to the treasury for the defense of the state in the war. The funds were seized by Colonel Tyler two days after the passage of the resolution, and were removed to Wheeling, where in strict accordance with the resolution they were used for the defense of the state, but against a different enemy from that which the Richmond government had contemplated.

In June, 1861, the hospital buildings were far from being completed, despite the fact that $98,000 had been expended. Much of the amount had been used in preliminary work and in hauling fine stone from a quarry at Mount Clare. The main building was not completed for ten years.

The Restored government of Virginia appropriated $40,000 for the completion of the buildings in addition to placing at the disposal of the directors the $27,000 which had been appropriated by Virginia in 1861, and the work of construction was resumed the next year. When the new state was formed, the Restored government transferred to it all the property of Virginia lying within its boundaries, including of course the Trans-Alleghany Lunatic Asylum.

The new state had then no statehouse, no penitentiary, no university, no state institutions except the half-completed lunatic asylum. The Legislature, in order to

THE WESTON STATE HOSPITAL

Courtesy of Mrs. C. E. White.

secure precise information concerning the needs of the institution, sent a committee of inspection consisting of Senator D. D. Farnsworth and Delegates Lewis Ballard and L. E. Davidson to report progress. The committee came to Weston about the first of September, 1863, and reported that the plan of the buildings had rarely been excelled, and that for quality of materials and execution, the work already done was entirely satisfactory. They recommended that an appropriation of $100,000 to complete the work should be made without delay.

Governor Boreman appointed as directors for the hospital Minter Bailey, Elias Fisher, H. Daugherty, John P. Peterson and E. M. Tunstill.

One of the first acts of the state legislature of West Virginia was to change the name of the institution to the West Virginia Hospital for the Insane. On account of the military needs of the state it was impossible at once to appropriate the amount recommended, but a sufficient sum was set aside to make the building fit for occupancy. Dr. James A. Hall was appointed superintendent in October 1863. His duties were principally in connection with supervising the construction of the buildings. It was impossible to make much progress on account of the disturbed conditions then existing, and Dr. Hall was not ready to admit patients to the institution. He was superseded in October, 1864, by Dr. R. Hills, formerly of the hospital at Columbus, Ohio. The new superintendent immediately opened the institution for the reception of patients, nine being admitted from the jails of nearby counties on the day designated.

The capacity of the institution was not more than twenty until after the close of the war; and the needs of the state for the creation of other institutions and for the extraordinary expenses of reconstruction were so great that the capacity could not be increased much beyond forty until 1868. The insane people of the state were meanwhile confined in jails at state expense until the main building could be finished. Even in Lewis

County the court directed in 1866 that the the jailer fit up a comfortable room in the jail for the retention of a lunatic until a place could be found in the hospital. The unfortunates from the western counties who had been committed to the asylums at Williamsburg and Staunton before the war were retained there until 1866, when, in response to appeals from the officials of Virginia, Governor Boreman sent an agent to investigate the number and condition of the patients, and to superintend their removal to Weston. The state paid Virginia $23,700 for maintenance of these patients from June 20, 1863, to January 1, 1866. They of course had the preference in being admitted to the institution over those confined in jails.

Besides the appropriations for maintenance, the Legislature of West Virginia appropriated for the completion of the buildings $228,000 before the close of 1868. In that year 162 patients were admitted bringing the population to nearly 200 as compared with forty-five the year before. In September, 1869, it was reported that there were still seventy-five insane persons in jails of different counties and there was loud complaint that the money appropriated for the buildings was being used for walks and fish ponds and that no progress was being made toward the completion of the structures.

The Legislature in 1870 appropriated $110,000 for buildings, and a new board appointed by Governor Stevenson began work with great energy in the spring of that year. Over fifty men were employed in the construction of the central building. Instead of hauling stone at great expense from quarries ranging in distance from one-half mile to a mile from the buildings, a new quarry was opened in the river bank immediately in front of the main building. A tramway was constructed from the quarry past the cutting shop and the brick kiln to the main building, which reduced the labor of hauling to the minimum. The power house was so connected that the saw mill, the brick machine, the planing mill and the lath mill were all run from the same source. O. H. P. Washburn was in charge of the stone quarry; W. J. Kitson supervised the stone cutting; Thomas Bradbury, the brick laying, and Weeden Smith, the carpenter work. The result of the reorganization was that the central building and the east wing were finished in the fall of 1871. The formal opening of the main building was celebrated by a visit from the governor of West Virginia and the directors of the institution. There was a banquet and later a grand ball in the spacious ballroom.

The main building was constructed for two hundred and fifty persons besides the chapel and the offices of administration. At the time of its completion it was regarded as one of the best buildings of its kind in the United States. It was now possible, for the first time in the history of the state, for the jails to be cleared of insane persons.

In consequence of the election of Governor Jacob in 1872, Dr. Hills was forced to tender his resignation after serving as superintendent from the opening of the institution in 1864. His time had been occupied for practically the whole of his term in attending to the details of administration and in supervising the construction of new buildings. His assistant, at first Dr. N. B. Barnes and later Dr. A. H. Kunst, cared for the inmates of the institution, visiting every ward every day and administering medical attention. In addition to these duties, the first assistant physician was also his own druggist. A second assistant physician was not added to the staff until 1880.

The work of making additions and improvements to the plant was continued under Dr. T. B. Camden, who succeeded Dr. Hills. In 1872 the waterworks were completed, and the hospital cemetery laid off. The construction of new buildings by convict labor was urged by Governor Jacob in his first message to the Legislature, but the suggestion was not acted upon. Work continued with paid labor. In 1873 a new brick building was constructed, and room was soon thereafter provided for colored patients.

The new buildings were sufficient for the needs of the state for only a few years. By 1879, it was seen that the jails would soon again have to be used as a place of detention for insane persons. In that year a contract was let for the construction of the west wing, which was completed two years later. In 1887, another new building was completed, and messengers were sent out from the hospital to bring to the institution all insane persons who were then confined in jails. When all the unfortunates had been admitted the capacity of the building was taxed. In 1890 work of construction was begun on the Spencer hospital. At that time the capacity of the Weston institution was about seven hundred. It has been increased by later additions to about twelve hundred.

The effects of the hospital at Weston upon the later development of Weston and Lewis County have been tremendous—too great to be estimated more than approximately. The great boom in building on the west side of the river just before the Civil war was due largely to the demand for houses by the workmen engaged in constructing the insane asylum. A great deal of the prosperity of the town in the same period came from the fact that there were thousands of dollars in cash being distributed among the people every month. After the war Lewis County recovered more quickly from the depression caused by the war than surrounding counties. The re-establishment of normal business conditions in the county was almost a matter of weeks, instead of months and years.

The construction of the buildings furnished work for a great number of persons for several years. Young men who would otherwise have gone West found jobs at Weston. A large number of new citizens, most of whom were skilled artisans—the best possible addition to the population—were attracted to the town, and practically all of them have chosen to stay. The infant industry of manufacturing lumber, which had just begun before the war, received a tremendous stimulus from the ready market afforded by the construction of the buildings. Thousands of feet of oak and poplar boards were sold to the state. Farmers were no longer dependent upon ginseng for cash with which to pay their taxes. Instead it was only necessary to cut logs which would have been burned otherwise, hitch an ox team to them and haul them to Weston to be sold to the state. Thousands of feet of lumber were sawed by the mill on the hospital grounds.

The large payroll of the hospital and the payments to business men for supplies caused a large amount of money to be placed in circulation. The National Exchange bank benefited from the growth of trade. Business men followed the laborers to Weston and set up stores in order to share in the prosperity. Lawyers came in order to represent the business men when they brought suit for non-payment of debt. New doctors came to help treat the laborers and the merchants and the lawyers when they were ill; and every one was prosperous.

The institution furnished employment for many persons as administrative officers, attendants and others after it was opened. New inhabitants—and again a most desirable class of people—were attracted to Weston. The large payroll has made it posible to bring other industries to Weston and thus to increase the volume of business. The added prosperity had caused better churches and better schools to be built in the town.

The results for the country districts have not been less important than those for the town. The hospital farm, sometimes under the care of a competent farmer, has been somewhat a source from which farmers of the county secured pure bred stock, and better agricultural methods have been introduced as a result. But the farm has never produced all the grain, vegetables and dairy products necessary for the inmates of the institution. A home market has been furnished for the cattle raised in Lewis County. Before the railroad came to Weston, when the hauling of flour from Clarksburg by wagon was unprofitable, the raising of wheat on the hillside farms of Lewis County was stimulated. Corn and vegetables were also required as well as dairy and poultry products, and farmers and farmers' wives who had never thought of any sources of income other than the live stock and grain raised in their fields, the timber cut from the forests, the wild herbs found in the woods, or the skins of wild beasts, now found a profitable side line in making butter, in picking berries, and in growing garden truck. Many farmers of the better sort have been attracted from other counties by the opportunities presented by the hospital market, and their methods have been copied by the native farmers of the neighborhood. One of the old settlers in the early seventies remarked to a new comer: "So-and-so said that you are selling ten pounds of butter a week to the asylum, but I said if you are, you don't eat much yourself." The new comer replied, "You were misinformed. I'm selling twenty-five pounds a week and have plenty to eat besides." The native was selling a large amount of butter soon afterwards.

CHAPTER XXVI.

ECONOMIC DEVELOPMENT AFTER THE WAR

The position of Lws County remote from the theater of active campaigns of the war, and the small number and weak condition of the partisan bands operating within the county resulted in little damage being done. The problem of restoring conditions as they existed immediately before the opening of hostilities was an easy one. It was necessary only to replace goods stolen from the stores, and horses and cattle which had been taken from the farms, maul out rails to repair the fences which had fallen down and clear the briars and sprouts from the neglected fields. So far as the fortunes of private individuals were concerned the scars of the war would then be effaced. Few residents of the county were ruined, and few became discouraged and moved to the west as was the case with thousands of citizens in other counties of the new state. The emigration from Lewis County was confined for the most part to young men who had been in the armies, and who craved new excitement and further experiences. In the decade from 1860 to 1870 the population of the county rose from 7,999 to 10,175—an increase of 27.2 per cent as compared with an increase of 17.3 per cent in the state at large. The restoration of normal business conditions, the building of the state hospital and the comparative freedom from ruinous taxation—for after all the taxes levied by the reconstruction board of supervisors of Lewis did not compare with those of adjoining counties—are largely responsible for the increase.

The means of transportation with the outside world which had ushered in the period of prosperity from 1845 to 1860 were greatly interrupted after the close of hostilities. The heavy hauling of supplies at unfavorable seasons and other military uses to which the roads were put resulted in their becoming almost impassable.

The turnpike companies, unable to keep up the roads with the lessened receipts and the destructive traffic, soon ceased to function, and the board of supervisors was compelled to take over the turnpikes and operate them, leaving the lesser roads to the tender mercies of the township authorities. The tollgates which had been destroyed were replaced and keepers were appointed to collect the tolls. In order to place the turnpikes in operation as soon as possible without waiting for the tolls to pay for the cost of repairs, a loan of $1,200 was authorized in 1866. The amount of tolls was fixed by legislative enactment. Believing that private individuals would be able to secure labor at a smaller price per day, the board of supervisors, in 1870, adopted the scheme of leasing out some of the turnpikes for three year periods. The new plan, though it relieved the board of much detail work, was not altogether for the best interests of the people, for most contractors operated the roads in order to obtain a profit for themselves rather than for the public good, and often failed to make necessary improvements. The tollgates were defended on the ground that only the people who used the roads were required to support them; but the additional expense of collecting the tolls, together with the impossibility of securing an accounting with the collectors, the nuisance to the public and other features led gradually to dismantling the gates. Tollgates were, however, maintained on some of the roads until the early nineties.

Several of the bridges of the county had been destroyed in the course of the war, or were so badly damaged that it was necessary for the court to go to great expense in rebuilding them. The bridge at Jacksonville had been completely destroyed, and there was only a temporary structure there in 1865. The Walkersville bridge

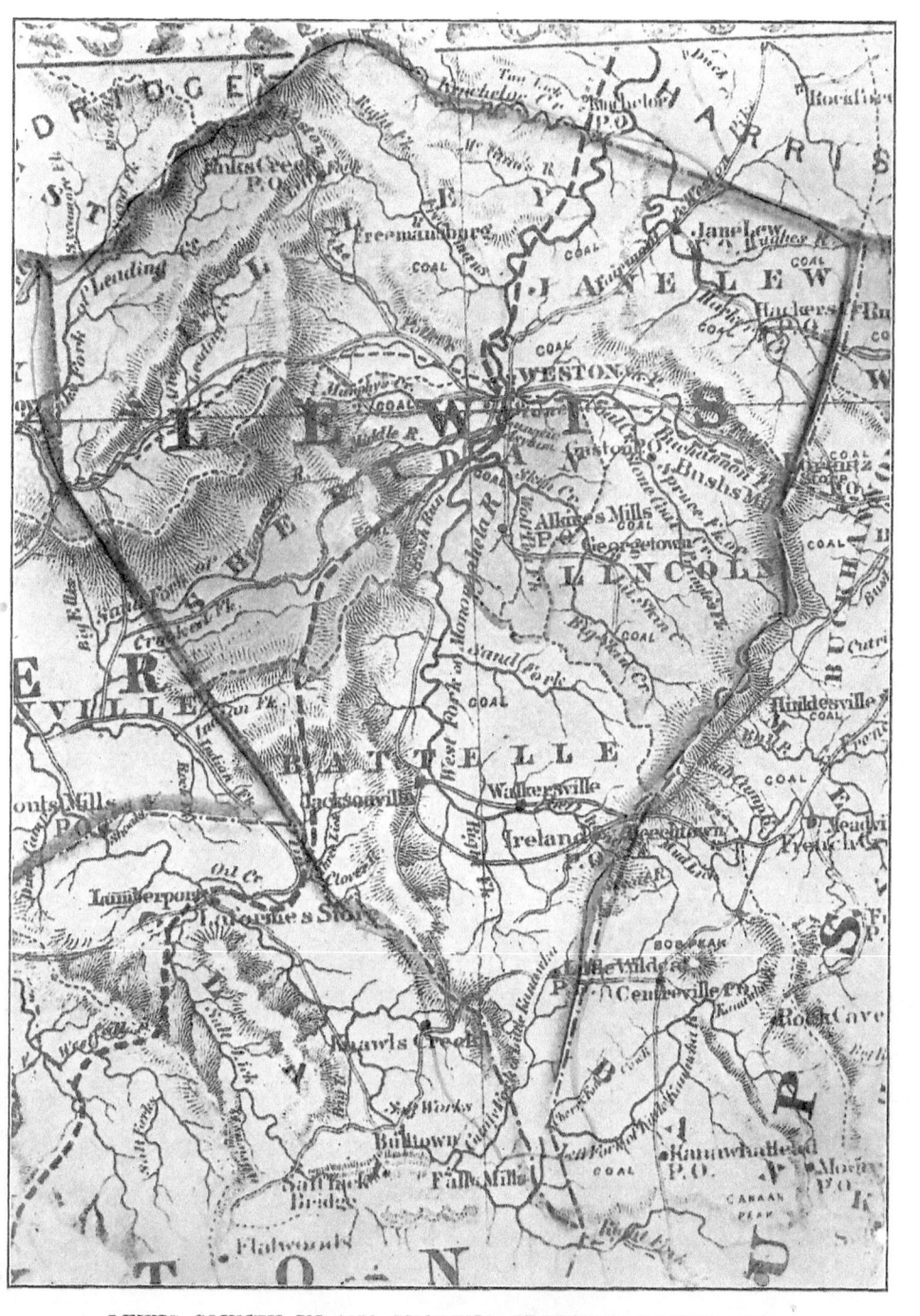

LEWIS COUNTY IN 1872 SHOWING PROPOSED RAILROADS
(From Mitchell's Geography, Edition of 1873)

was in such shape that extensive repairs were necessary. The bridge across the river at Weston was in a very unsafe condition in 1868 due to constant use both in the war and in hauling materials for the hospital. The sidewalks were torn up, and the planks and sills of that part of the bridge used for vehicles were decayed. Repairs were made which extended the period of usefulness of the bridge for another twenty years. The demands of the people for better outlets for their farms led to the establishment of many new roads. The false economy forced upon the board of supervisors and, at a later period, the county court by the campaign arguments of the reconstruction period resulted in the adoption of a hand to mouth system in the construction and repairs of roads and bridges. The building of permanent roads which had received a tremendous impetus in the decade before the outbreak of the Civil war was postponed from year to year and not taken up in earnest until 1916.

As before the Civil war, agriculture continued to be the principal industry of the county. The tendency towards sheep raising, which has been noted in a preceding chapter, was greatly increased by the habit of Confederate raiding parties of running off all the cattle they could find. The raiders could not drive sheep across the mountains, and partly for that reason, farmers whose herds of cattle had been bought with Confederate currency restocked their farms with them. The demand for woolen clothing for the armies also caused an increase in the price of wool and many found it more profitable to raise sheep than cattle. The merino was the first improved breed introduced. A great deal of attention was paid to breeding up flocks of sheep, with the result that Lewis County soon acquired a reputation for the production of fine wool. In 1870 there were nearly 11,000 sheep in Lewis County, which ranked thirteenth in the state in number of sheep and tenth in the production of wool. The introduction of the mutton breeds of sheep came years later after the creation of a market for lambs. The West Virginia Sheep Herders' association was organized in 1879 with many members from Lewis County.

Improvements began to be made on farms as a result of the cutting of timber. Beginning in 1870 when only three-tenths of the total area of the county was improved, the clearings were rapidly extended. The production of the farms was increased also by the rapid introduction of improved machinery. Hillside plows which turned the sod took the place of shovel plows which merely tore it up. Mowing machines were introduced almost immediately following the civil war. The first machine to be introduced was the Champion. In 1869 Wood's mower and reaper entered the field, and its local agents set out to disprove the assertion that the machines were useless on the hilly farms of Lewis County. The Champion machine was challenged to a contest on the farm of J. G. Vandervort with the result that Mr. Vandervort, R. P. Camden and Noah Flesher purchased Wood machines. They then cost $125.

Wheat growing continued to rank as one of the principal industries of the county, the production in 1870 being more than 50,000 bushels. The restoration of the market at Richmond after the war stimulated the growing of tobacco, in which industry Lewis County ranked tenth in the state, according to the census report.

As a means of stimulating agricultural production in the county, the Lewis County Agricultural Society was formed by Weston people, who subscribed $4,000 toward a fair. A. W. Woodford was elected president; F. M. Chalfant, vice president; and J. W. Woffendin, recording secretary of the association, which succeeded in interesting a sufficient number of people from the country to hold the first fair in 1871. The Lewis County fair continued to be an annual event for many years until the fair ground on the Minnich place was divided into lots and sold.

Interest in cattle increased during the 'seventies.

Many progressive farmers believed that there was a future for cattle raising and continued breeding up their stock. Herefords, which were introduced into the county about 1875, have gradually proved their suitability to natural conditions until they are now the predominant breed.

Horses gradually displaced oxen as beasts of burden on the farms, but no efforts were made to introduce pure-bred animals. In 1882 the significant announcement appeared in one of the county papers: "The Percheron Norman stallion, Quazzola, (owned by Clarksburg people) will be in Weston early in March."

The movement for the organization of granges struck the county about 1875, and interest in the new farmers' organization rapidly increased. Organizations were formed in several of the more progressive communities.

Lumbering became an important industry after the war on account of the excellent transportation facilities furnished by the Baltimore and Ohio railroad through Clarksburg. Thousands of logs were cut in the valley of the West Fork and its larger tributaries and floated down the river. The principal operators were the Lowndes and Steele interests of Clarksburg. Within the next twenty years most of the virgin forests of the county had been cut over. Weston citizens in 1870 organized the West Fork Manufacturing and Booming Company for the purpose of cutting timber and marketing it either in logs or in lumber. The charter granted by the Legislature conferred authority upon the incorporators to erect booms in the river from the mouth of Rush run to the mouth of the West Fork. The company was popularly supposed to have been organized for the purpose of gaining control of the market at the hospital and in Weston to the exclusion of citizens who lived farther up the river.

The manufacturing of lumber in 1870 was still in its infancy. There were a number of sawmills dotting the valleys of the small streams in the vicinity of Weston, but none of them were capable of sawing large logs with the exception of N. B. Barnes' sawmill located about two miles up the river from Weston. There was a sawmill and planing mill on the Hospital grounds which were capable of manufacturing the largest logs. In 1874, George A. Jackson erected a steam planing mill in Weston, which bore the same relation to many of the older houses now standing as Cummins Jackson's mill bore to the earlier generation of Weston homes. A handle factory employing ten or twelve men was established in Weston in 1881. A new tanyard was erected after the war on West Second street by a Mr. Burbridge of Philippi. He later sold it to Leonidas Smith. Kitsonville was partly laid out and named in 1870.

The development of agriculture and lumbering was reflected in the growth of the county seat. The business activity occasioned by the construction of the hospital was further stimulated by expected improvements which did not materialize. It was thought that the town would be a point on two transcontinental railroads and thereby become the railroad center of the state, and also the seat of government. Notwithstanding the fact that the town was already the seat of the most important of the state institutions the citizens were hardly content. In 1869, (the year the capitol was moved to Charleston), Weston citizens offered $50,000 in money, ten acres of land fronting on the West Fork river and material enough to put up the necessary buildings if the permanent seat of government should be brought there. The town council enacted that all the streets should be paved on a regular grade, and they immediately proceeded to establish the grade but not the paving. Weston was out of debt in 1869 for the first time in its existence.

The superior grade of wool grown in Lewis County led to the establishment in Weston of a woolen mill in 1871 by the Cliftons. They had formerly been in business at Beaver Falls, Pa., but had determined to seek a better location near a good source of raw wool. The exceptionally long staple produced in Lewis County was decided to be exactly the kind of raw material they desired and they moved their woolen mill to West Weston. For the next fourteen years it was the most important manufacturing industry in the town. The factory was located in a building 32 by 80 feet and two and one-half stories high. The most modern machinery was installed, consisting of 240 spindles, one picker, one steam dresser, several power looms, etc. The management advertised their ability to manufacture all kinds of fabrics, but stated that special attention was given to custom work. Goods were also exchanged for wool. The principal output of the factory was yarn, blankets and jeans cloth used by the farmers. A hat factory was established in Weston by P. M. Hale, which gave employment to several persons.

The press in Weston, which had languished during the war, started up immediately upon the cessation of hostilities. In 1865 Frederick Alfred began the publication of the Weston Expositor. He soon sold it to R. Huckles, who disposed of it in 1868 to J. G. Woffinden and George Cozad. They changed the name to the Weston Democrat. In 1871 Woffinden purchased the half interest of Cozad and continued the paper until 1876, when it was sold to Thomas A. Edwards. In January, 1869, James J. Peerson started the Weston Republican, which continued under his direction until 1881, when it was sold to Dr. M. S. Holt and Joseph Neff.

There was no dentists in Weston in 1868. All dental work was done by traveling dentists who spent a month or more at a time in Weston. The number of doctors and lawyers and hotel keepers was great enough for the size of the town. In 1871 a correspondent of the Wheeling Register stated that "the Town of Weston contains a population of about 1,200 inhabitants, and is the seat of an unusual degree of culture." A library association had just been organized by the ladies of the town, and a debating society by the young men. There was also a Young Men's Christian Association. One of the best "cornet bands" in the state was established shortly after the war. It had the honor of entertaining the state convention of brass bands in 1873. A business directory was talked of among the business men of the town in 1873, but appears never to have been published. The number of new citizens who desired to own their own homes, led to the organization of a building and loan society in the early 'seventies. Street lights were first installed in Weston in 1870 at a cost of about $125 including the posts. Kerosene was used.

The large number of destructive fires which took place in 1871 led the leading citizens to devise means of protection. A meeting was called for the organization of a fire company. Most of the younger men of the town enrolled in the organization, the equipment of which was donated by the business men. A proposition was submitted by council for a bond issue to purchase a chemical engine for the town, but it was voted down by a large majority, because an investigation made by the council after the submission of the measure cast doubt upon the efficiency of the engine which it was proposed to purchase. The fire department of Weston has made little improvement in organization since 1871. The corporate limits of Weston were reduced by the legislature to nearly their legitimate size in this period, causing much difficulty in later years when the population was extended beyond the boundary line through natural growth.

With all these improvements in Weston the streets remained in a terrible condition. The Weston Democrat advertised, 18 January 1869, for the return of a two-horse team which had been lost in the alley leading from Lewis' store to Center street. "The wagon was loaded at the time with the blank stock receipts of the Main Street Navigation Company which hoped by the aid of locks and dams (especially dams) to make it possible for ships of the largest tonnage to effect a landing at

George Fisher's store." An ordinance had been passed preventing citizens from riding on the sidewalks, so that it was necessary for them to take the street. The perils of the pedestrian were sufficiently great as it was. The crossing of Bank street was then effected by a single narrow board on saw-horses, which frequently precipitated the citizen into the ooze below. The condition of the streets was remedied somewhat by the passage of an ordinance prohibiting the hauling of sawlogs through the streets unless they were carried on wheeled vehicles, and the employment of a large force to drain the streets. Macadam was later applied with some success, but twenty years passed before any of the streets were paved with brick.

The agency for the elimination of garbage and other wastes was furnished free of charge by private individuals. It consisted of a herd of hogs, which followed squealing after every wagon loaded with grain which passed through the streets, and rendered the task of going to mill extremely arduous for the farmers' boys. This department exercised far more influence on town politics in the 'seventies than any other. Candidates for city offices feverishly canvassed the electorate on the platform of "hog in or hog out", and this question, according to the Weston Democrat, was used too often as a test of fitness for a municipal office.

There was no theater in the town as yet. The principal form of amusement in the late 'sixties consisted of a tournament which was participated in by all the leading citizens of the younger generation. Mounted on horseback in imitation of gallant knights of ten centuries before, they proceeded to a field out Stone Coal and engaged in a contest followed by the crowning of the queen of love and beauty. The proceedings caused so much interest among the small boys that two juvenile tournaments were held later in the same year. A baseball game with eight on a side furnished thrills for a Saturday afternoon crowd at the same period. A magician gave a performance at the courthouse to "a large and appreciative audience." Perhaps the most thrilling of all the entertainments of the time was a fight between a dog and a raccoon on Main street. When the time dragged heavily on their hands, the young men organized a "court of Tuckage to fool fellows from the country and from the eastern cities." The scheme was for an accusation to be brought against the intended victim, and then one of the group, professing friendship, offered to lead him out of town. When sufficiently far from the town, a pistol shot rang out, the "friend" fell, and the victim of the joke usually took to flight.

Considerable prohibition sentiment existed in Weston after the close of the war, and a prohibition ticket was elected to fill all the municipal offices in 1869.

In the late 'sixties two new churches were added to the number already in Weston. In accordance with the instructions of the Presbytery of West Virginia, the Presbyterian church was organized at the home of W. L. Dunnington, 1 April 1867, by the Rev. S. C. Faris. Captain R. C. Arbuckle was appointed ruling elder and Mrs. Mary Wood, Miss Blanche McGee, Mrs. Mary Dunnington and William L. Dunnington were the charter members. Later meetings were held in the Dunnington home. In 1868 the Rev. Mr. Young of Upshur came to Weston and held a series of meetings. Later on permission was secured to use the old Southern Methodist church, the membership of which had gradually declined on account of the fact that most of the Methodists in Weston returned to the M. E. church. The first building was not erected until 1888.

The year 1868 marked the advent of the Baptists into Weston. The church was the outgrowth of the Broad Run Baptist church. It was a struggling society for some time, but finally secured possession of the old Episcopal church building in which to hold services.

In 1876 the Catholics built a new church at the head

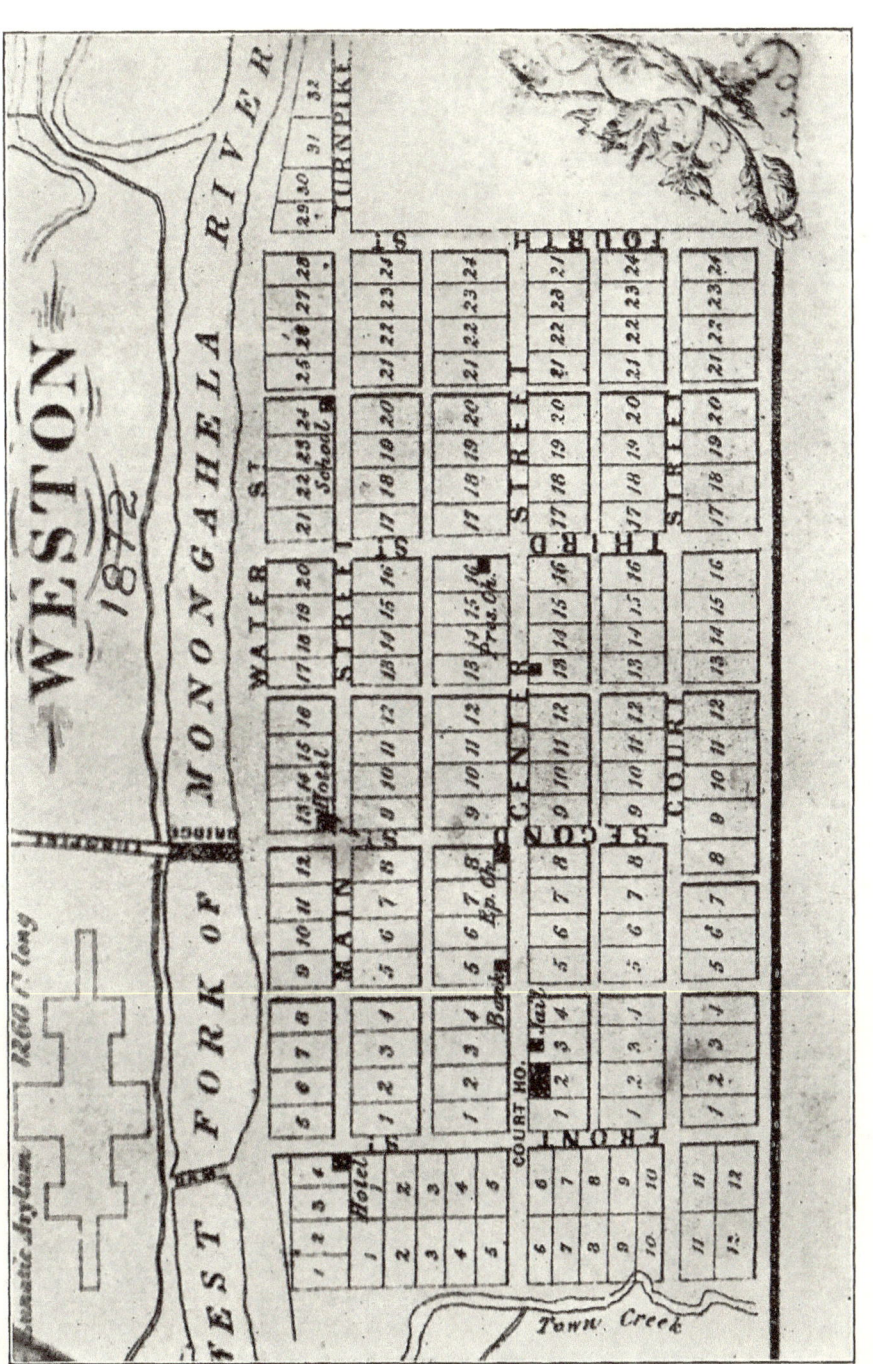

FROM MITCHELL'S GEOGRAPHY EDITION OF 1873

of Second street which they occupied until 1915, when the present magnificent structure was completed.

The next denomination to be represented in Weston was the Methodist Protestants. Members of the church had for a long time been trying to awaken enough interest in the county seat to have a church regularly organized. Ministers from the Lewis corcuit occasionally preached in the town, but all efforts were in vain until 1880 when the society seems to have been organized. A resolution of the Lewis circuit in that year directed a committee to purchase the property of the M. E. Church South, but the court refused to confirm the sale. The use of the building was secured for services alternately with the Presbyterians in 1882. The Weston mission was established by the conference in 1881 and the Rev. A. T. Cralle sent as pastor. The Rev. I. A. Barnes became pastor the next year and arrangements were begun to erect a building on the lot purchased at the corner of Third and Center. The corner stone was laid in 1883, and the building was completed and ready for services by the first of the year 1887.

Jane Lew experienced a rapid development following the Civil war, owing largely to the rich agricultural district around it. Marble works were established in 1872. In 1877 a census of the town showed two stores, two drug stores, a tannery, a saddler's shop, a wagon shop, a pottery, a tailor shop, a flouring mill, a good school and a church. All this in spite of the fact that the village of Berlin had come into existence with a postoffice, a store and a place to sell liquors.

A number of small towns received their first impetus immediately following the close of the war due to the energy and foresight of George J. Arnold in establishing a line of hotels at strategic locations. The first of these was on the Gauley Bridge turnpike near the foot of the hill on the Rush run side in 1866. Rushville, as it was called, never consisted of more than two houses, but within a year or two a postoffice had been established there. Another hotel was the famous Valley House, about a half mile below the present Arnold Station. He established the Indian Farm Hotel at Arnold Station, 1890.

Partly as a result of the settlement of the Irish on Sand fork a postoffice was established at Beall's Mills in the early 'seventies. Freeman's Creek district continued to be without a postoffice with the exception of the one at Leading creek, until about 1872. A store was established at the mouth of Isaac's fork of Fink in the 'seventies, at which Fink Creek postoffice was established and which formed the nucleus of the later village in the early 'seventies. Freeman's Creek district con- of Churchville. Lower Fink creek continued to be undeveloped for the most part, though the exceptional fertility of the soil was recognized.

The lumbering industry is responsible for the present town of Vandalia. A large sawmill was located there about 1876, which soon brought two stores, a blacksmith shop, a shoe shop, a cabinet mill and a planing mill. The name Austin was given to the town in honor of one of the residents, and when the name was changed to Vandalia in honor of the wife of a postmaster, there was almost a neighborhood row.

The village of Roanoke appeared with startling suddenness in the year of 1871 under the general management of William A. Watson, who performed the functions of mayor, chief of police and town council. Lumbering operations, a mill, and a store owned by Charles A. Horner are largely responsible for bringing the town into existence, and its excellent location has made its position secure. The name was given it by the editor of the Weston Democrat in honor of John Randolph of Roanoke. "The musty old village of Jacksonville" continued to maintain its position as the political and commercial center of Battelle district. About 1868 Captain George I. Davisson established a store in the village with a stock of goods superior to that found in most of the stores of Weston. The store building which he erected was by far the largest in the country. In the capacious wareroom he stored all his goods which were hauled from Clarksburg in the summer when the roads were good. Into the wareroom also went the produce of the richest farms in a district which was called "Egypt" because of its productivity. People came all the way from Beverly in Randolph County to buy corn at the store during a period of scarcity there. At one time three thousand bushels of wheat were taken in trade, to be hauled to Clarksburg and from there shipped to Baltimore. Although the village had not yet voted dry it boasted that it was more advanced than the county seat because no hogs were allowed to roam the streets.

Walkersville in 1869 reported that over two hundred acres of land had lately been cleared on two farms adjoining the village, forcing the squirrels to the hilltops and depriving the foxes of brush thickets in which to hide. There were then seven residences, a store, a hotel, conducted by Schuyler Moon, a blacksmith shop, a tannery, a shoe shop, a cabinet shop and a school in the village. Walkersville was a sort of center for the temperance movement in the district, the people having sent a petition to the county court asking that no license be granted. On the left fork of the river about a mile and one-fourth above Walkersville, a mill was established by one Bunten which was to form the nucleus for a later rival of Walkersville.

Settlers had penetrated to the extreme southern limits of the county by the beginning of the war, and by 1880 they were in "Shoestring" in sufficient numbers to justify the establishment of two postoffices, one at Davis, (now Wildcat), and the other at Little Wild Cat. Lower Oil creek and Clover fork began to feel the pulse of progress after the war, partly as a result of an awakening of the people to the richness of their lands, partly on account of the lumber development at Burnsville. Judge Gideon D. Camden in 1869 divided his Oil creek lands into hundred-acre tracts which he sold to his former tenants. A Frenchman named Laforme established a store on Oil creek below the present site of Orlando in anticipation of a rush of business which would follow the proposed development of the oil on Oil creek.

Though Weston by this time had daily mails, other towns in the interior of the state were forced to depend upon weekly or semi-weekly mails at the best. In 1870 Porter M. Camp left Weston on Monday morning with mail that had come by stage from Clarksburg. He stopped at Bush's Mills (now Roanoke), Jacksonville, Knawl, Bulltown, Flatwoods and Sutton the first day. The next day he went to Summersville in Nicholas County. Wednesday he started on the return trip to Weston, reaching the town on Thursday evening. On Friday morning he went to Sutton, returning Saturday on the "short trip."

An important organization which was formed in 1870 was the Lewis County Medical association which did much to discourage quacks and to improve sanitary conditions.

At about the same time the board of supervisors of the county completely revolutionized the methods of caring for the poor. Up to and including 1869 it was the practice to bind out paupers in lots to suit anyone who might be in need of additional help. Under such a system supervision of the poor was impossible and adequate care depended largely on the party to whom a pauper was bound out. The county purchased a farm on Stone Coal creek, erected the necessary buildings to house all the poor of the county, and collected them there under the care of a contractor. He has not always been chosen for the position because he was the lowest bidder, but unfortunately he was generally so. The paupers were provided with work to do on the farm, which was healthful and invigorating when they could be induced to do it. The new scheme proved to be much better in every way than the old.

One of the tasks set for the local officials of the new

state of West Virginia was to put in operation the free school system which had been provided for in the state constitution and in statutes passed at succeeding sessions of the Legislature. Tobias Musser of Broad run who had been a rather prominent teacher before the war was elected first county superintendent of Lewis County. He began his work in 1865 with five inexperienced boards of education in the townships to deal with. Only two buildings out of all the old-field schools were taken over by the county; few teachers with experience could be secured; and the boards of education had supplied no furniture. The new superintendent advised with the township boards as to the best manner of appropriating their first year's levy. Owing to the fact that the building funds were insufficient to erect all the proper buildings needed the first year, especially in view of the high prices then prevailing for lumber it was determined to resort to log houses for the emergency. Six log school houses were completed the first year, fourteen others were under construction and the remainder of the buildings were ready for occupancy by the fall of 1867. The new superintendent and some members of the boards of education insisted upon blackboards, which were a novelty in the old subscription schools and which were usually of pale color under the free schools for many years. In the remainder of the school districts where it was impossible to erect new buildings, old houses were either rented or donated by their owners for the purpose, so that about fifty schools were in session the first winter. The superintendent visited most of the schools the first session, gave advice to the teachers, and sometimes "where he thought it expedient addressed the school on the importance of education, and the happy results of the benefits of a Free School system."

Seven years after the inauguration of the free school system in the county, there were nine frame and two log schools in Willey township. The log structures were not inviting, and they were replaced as soon as possible. In Sheridan township, though the settlement was newer, commendable progress had been made in education, and three frame and nine log buildings had been constructed. In Battelle township nineteen schools were in existence, but they were in session only two months on account of the failure of the board of education to levy for school purposes. In Lincoln and Jane Lew townships greater progress had been made, practically all the log buildings having been replaced. Interest in schools in the country districts was at such a high level that in 1873 a high school was proposed for the county.

The town of Weston was much slower in organizing its free school system than the country districts. There were many opponents of free schools among the citizens of the town, and a long controversy between proponents of parochial and free public schools resulted in delaying the establishment of free schools. The school which had for several years been taught in the basement of the Catholic church opened as usual, and continued until 1869, if not later. A young ladies' seminary was conducted by Miss Brown on Center street during the reconstruction period. The first free school, partly supported by private individuals, was opened under Prof. George W. Crook in a frame building opposite the Episcopal church. He was assisted by Miss Ella Hall, Miss Mary Hamilton and Miss Etta Barnes.

In 1869 the board of education purchased a lot on Main street from George Ross, and the school was conducted in a residence there the next year. The small size of the lot and the unsuitability of the old residence for school purposes led the new board of education to sell it in 1871 and to purchase the property at the corner of Court and Third, which had once been used for a school. Plans were drawn up for an eight-room building, 70 by 45 feet. The contract for its construction was let to P. M. Hale in the fall of 1871, and the building was completed the following year. So well was the work done that it has continued to be used for school purposes to the present time.

The controversy concerning the relative merits of private schools and free schools came to an end in the fall of 1869 when the trustees of the Peabody fund offered to the board of education the sum of $300 if they would keep one hundred white children in school, or $600 if they would keep two hundred white children. In their eagerness to secure the proffered aid the people of the town forgot their differences and sent all their children to the school, except for a few young men who attended school under Prof. Donegan in the basement of the old Catholic church. At the time of the completion of the new building in 1872, the board of education in Weston had an income of $3,600 including $600 from the Peabody fund. The following named educators have been at the head of the free schools of Weston: C. B. Whitman, Samuel Steele, Loyal Young, Edwin S. B'and, Louis Bennett, James J. Peterson, Prof. Crippen, H. H. Clark, J. E. Connelly, H. C. Lawson, Meigs Bland, T. W. Hale, Dr. George Edmiston, J. W. Bonner, J. E. Galford, F. L. Burdette, Buchanan White, E. H. Knabenshue and Frank R. Yoke.

CHAPTER XXVII.

THE COMING OF THE RAILROAD

Progressive citizens of Lewis County were not slow in realizing the benefits to be derived from improved means of transportation. They bent their efforts constantly toward bringing a railroad to Weston almost from the beginning of the construction of lines in West Virginia. It will be remembered that when the extension of the Baltimore and Ohio west of Cumberland was debated in the Virginia legislature a counter proposal was made for an all-Virginia line to run from Alexandria to Parkersburg via Weston. The citizens of Weston in 1846 entertained the convention of the people of Western Virginia which met to devise means of securing the construction of the proposed line. When the measure had been defeated Weston did not lose hope. The proposition to build the Northwestern railroad from Grafton to Parkersburg led to a movement to have the new road run by way of Weston. When the route was definitely decided upon, a special act was secured in the Virginia Assembly through the influence of Weston citizens, authorizing the new road to build a branch line to Weston. After the war, when the West Virginia legislature gave its consent for the directors of the Baltimore and Ohio road to take over the lines of the Northwestern railroad, they were also given the right to extend their lines to Weston.

The Civil war caused a new policy of internal improvements to be adopted by the federal government. Land grants were given for the construction of a road across the continent. Advocates of internal improvements wished the government to take up the work of railroad building not only in the west but also in other parts of the country. The Airline railroad was projected from Washington to Cincinnati via Winchester, Moorefield, Buckhannon, Weston, Glenville and Point Pleasant, to connect Washington with the west and obviate the necessity for going around by Baltimore in order to reach the Ohio river from the national capital. Surveys were made over the proposed route and it was found to be nearly fifty miles shorter than the Baltimore and Ohio and to have a maximum grade of fifty feet to the mile, whereas the maximum grade of the Baltimore and Ohio was 106 feet to the mile. Congress refused to take affirmative action on the proposed bills, and private interests incorporated the Washington and Ohio Railroad Company to build its lines over the proposed route of the Airline railroad. Surveys made by surveyors of the new company confirmed their opinion of its great superiority over the line of the Baltimore and Ohio, and the construction of the road seemed assured. The officials of the road requested a subscription of $250,000 from the board of supervisors of Lewis County, who submitted to the voters the proposal to bond the county for $200,000 in 1872. They rejected the proposition. While efforts were being made to hold another election the panic of 1873 occurred, and the project was abandoned by its promoters.

In 1870 Weston had ambitions to be the railroad center of the state. In addition to an east and west line, another railroad was proposed by West Virginia promoters to extend the entire length of the Monongahela valley, cross to the Little Kanawha and Elk river valleys to Charleston, and thence run to Kenova in Wayne County. A monster railroad meeting was held at the Lewis County courthouse, 16 February 1870, to nominate delegates to a convention at Clarksburg. One hundred delegates were selected. The outcome of the Clarksburg meeting was the organization of the Northern and Southern West Virginia railroad which planned an eastern connection with the Pennsylvania lines and a western connection with the lines of Collis P. Huntington (the Southern Pacific) making it a part of an important transcontinental system. The right of way for the line was donated by most of the farmers along the route, and Lewis County voted in 1871 to subscribe $125,000 of the stock of the railroad. Like the Washington and Ohio railroad, the Northern and Southern West Virginia was lost in the financial cataclysm of 1873.

Impatient at the delay in the construction of the two railroads the citizens of Lewis County determined to build their own railroad to connect with the Baltimore and Ohio. The Weston and Clarksburg Railroad Company was incorporated in 1871 to form a part of the Northern and Southern West Virginia. In 1873 the county court submitted to the people the proposition to transfer their subscription of $125,000 from the Northern and Southern West Virginia to the Weston and Clarksburg company, but the proposition was defeated. "It is within the power of the people of Lewis County to build their own railroad," said the Weston Democrat, in 1873, "if not a broad gauge road, then a narrow gauge; if not a narrow gauge, then a wooden tramway." The wagon bills of Weston were then estimated to be $30,000 annually. Much opposition to the proposed line to Clarksburg developed in the legislature on account of the Northern and Southern West Virginia, and it was proposed to run the line from Grafton to Weston via Philippi and Buckhannon. This proposal was also rejected, and nothing could be done until after the directors of the nearly defunct Northern and Southern West Virginia line had given up the struggle.

In 1875 the Weston and West Fork railroad was incorporated by Thomas A. Edwards, A. A. Lewis, G. C. Danser, W. H. Aspinall, F. M. Chalfant George Ross, W. G. Bennett, Henry Brannon and E. Ralston. The capital stock was $10,000, with the privilege of increasing the amount to $250,000. The court submitted the proposition to subscribe $50,000 to the capital stock of the road and the bond issue carried almost unanimously. The town of Weston also subscribed $6,000. It was estimated that it would take $200,000 to build the narrow gauge line and subscriptions to the stock of the road, "payable in cross ties and bridge timber" as well as in money, were solicited from all the citizens of the county.

Surveying parties went over the two available routes by the turnpike and down the West Fork river. It was reported that the turnpike route was shorter, but that the river route had a better grade. The directors announced that the final choice of a route depended upon the willingness of the citizens along the route to cede the right of way. No trouble whatever was experienced among the farmers along either route, the right of way to the gates of Clarksburg being donated. Clarksburg citizens, however, did not wish the road to run through their town lots, and demanded a price for the right of way that seemed extortionate. Bridgeport, five miles east of Clarksburg, made an attractive offer of free right of way and a subscription to the stock of the road if it were made the terminus. This offer of Bridgeport, following the demands of the Clarksburg citizens, determined the selection of the turnpike route. It was at first decided to construct the line to Lost Creek, and to make the final decision as to the northern terminus later. The action of the board of directors was plainly a threat at Clarksburg, whose inhabitants seemed to have been under the impression that the new road must necessarily have its terminus there. An agreement was shortly afterwards reached between the directors of the railroad and the people of Clarksburg by which the latter agreed to subscribe $10,000 to the stock of the company. An alternate route within the town limits which would cost far less than the other, was determined upon, and condemnation proceedings were resorted to.

On 3 October 1876, the contract for the grading of the roadbed including the trestling was let to James

March for $42,500. Work was started immediately thereafter. Fifty laborers were engaged in grading the roadbed during the winter, spring and early summer following, and much of the work was done when the contractor failed, 1 August 1877. Those were dark days for the people of Weston. Private subscriptions to the stock of the company could not be secured. The telegraph service had been discontinued to the town because it did not pay, and the people felt the need of a resumption of service which the railroad would bring. They had been disappointed so many times already concerning their railroad that its abandonment was seriously proposed. An appeal to the voters for an additional subscription of $100,000 failed to secure the necessary three-fifths majority in favor of the issue of the bonds. The county court, which was the largest stockholder, came to the rescue of the railroad by agreeing that the directors might mortgage the road for $100,000, and waiving the rights of the county to dividends. Work was resumed early in 1878 with 130 laborers employed, and it was confidently expected that the railroad would be completed to Weston within a few months.

There were other difficulties to be solved before the long-looked-for locomotive reached Weston. Financial troubles beset the directors again when practically all the grading had been done and it only remained to lay the steel. Additional subscriptions to the stock of the company could not be secured, and no more bonds could be issued.

At this juncture a financial genius appeared on the scene. Johnson N. Camden, a native of Lewis County, whose business career had commenced in 1853 with a clerkship paying $500 a year, in the branch of the Exchange bank at Weston, saved the new railroad from destruction. He did this by organizing a holding company, the Clarksburg, Weston and Glenville Railroad and Transportation Company, which secured a lease of the Weston and West Fork railroad, and made sufficient advance payments to enable the directors of the latter railroad to complete the work of construction. The Clarksburg, Weston and Glenville company was incorporated, 14 August 1878. Five days later the lease of the Weston and West Fork road was completed. Senator Camden's company had no seal with which to complete the contract, but Henry Brannon had a makeshift seal chiseled out at Coon's marble shop. The impression on the contract made by the marble seal was blurred and imperfect, but it is doubtful if the impression of any other seal, either before or after that time was ever received with such a feeling of thanksgiving by the entire population of the town and county.

The small amount of grading remaining unfinished was soon done, the trestle work was completed and part of the track was laid in the first half of 1879. On 9 August 1879, the first passenger train arrived at Jane Lew from Clarksburg amid the cheers of a large crowd of citizens who had gathered from far and near to celebrate its coming. Many of the promoters of the road with their wives, who had come from Weston in buggies for the celebration, were passengers on the train when it returned to Clarksburg. The one passenger coach was described by a newspaper man who was present as being "a perfect model of convenience, and as far as style and general appearance compares most favorably with any car we have ever seen. It is divided into two compartments, the front part being used for a baggage and express room." The rear compartment for passengers was heated by a stove set in one corner. The car continued for many years to do service on the road.

A stage line was established on the road between Weston and Jane Lew to connect with the new railroad until September 1st, when it was expected that it would be possible to run trains to the temporary station which was being erected near where the entrance to Machpelah cemetery now is. The expectation was fulfilled. Agent J. H. McClellan moved into the temporary depot about the last of August, and on September 1, the first train arrived amid the rejoicings of a large crowd of citizens of Weston and the vicinity. On November 1st, the railroad began to carry mails for the government. Finally on 12 November 1879, Jonathan M. Bennett drove the last spike of the road which had its terminus at the permanent depot where the freight station now stands. Henceforth two trains daily ran into Weston.

The officials of the new Clarksburg, Weston and Glenville Railroad and Transportation Company were Johnson N. Camden, president; Henry Brannon, vice-president; W. G. Bennett, secretary; and M. W. Harrison, treasurer. The road was operated by an executive committee headed by President Camden until 1881, when Dr. A. H. Kunst took active charge of the line as general manager. Though he had had no experience with railroad operation, he soon mastered the details of the position, and for the next ten years he guided the destinies of the line. He was passenger traffic manager, yardmaster, general superintendent, train dispatcher and, in emergencies, ticket agent. It was one of his cardinal principles of railway management that no trains should be run on Sundays except during the excursion season, when the financial condition of the road made such a course necessary.

Agent McClellan had been employed by the Baltimore and Ohio railroad in a similar capacity at Parkersburg before coming to Weston, and was a practical railroad man. He was assisted by George Smith as telegrapher. Isaac Jackson was the first agent of the company at Jane Lew. The conductor of the first train to arrive at Weston was John Smith, who had been a driver on the road from Fetterman and then had had charge of the stage line from Clarksburg to Weston. He permanently forsook stage lines favor of railroads upon the completion of the Weston and Clarksburg railroad, and continued in the service for many years.

The effects of the building of the railroad to Weston were immediately apparent in the lowering of prices of goods purchased from outside of the county, and in the introduction of many articles in the stores which had never had a place in the life of the town. Haleville was laid off in lots in 1883, principally because the coming of the railroad had created a great demand for cheap building lots. The railroad gave employment to several persons. The beginnings of manufacturing to supply the demand for a larger market than Weston and Lewis County became apparent.

In addition to the improvements in the town which are directly due to the railroad, there were many changes indirectly traceable to it. There was a gradual, almost imperceptible improvement in the manners and customs of the people. Being no longer dependent almost wholly upon the products of the farms about Weston, they were able to secure more varied food for their tables and more and better furniture for their homes. Better mail service placed the people in closer contact with the world. The hindrances to travel were removed to some extent, and the way to the outside world was opened. More people took advantage of the opportunity than had ever done before. Weston was much nearer the center of things.

The railroad had an equally important influence over the development of the country districts. Better transportation made possible the manufacturing of lumber, and completely changed the character of timber exploitation in the county. Before the year 1879 logs were floated down the West Fork river to market; afterwards they were sawed and the lumber shipped over the railroad. The primeval forest, which had covered the greater portion of the county in 1879, rapidly disappeared. The hum of the circular saw began to be heard in the remote hollows of the county. Sleepy old settlements awoke and took on new life in consequence.

The railroad fully met the expectations of the farmers in furnishing cheap transportation for the products of the farms. In the fall of 1879, following the completion of the railroad, thousands of bushels of wheat, the surplus production of Lewis, Gilmer, Braxton and Upshur counties, were brought to Weston and shipped to the eastern markets. It was expected that the growing of wheat and corn and the mining of coal would be greatly stimulated.

The people of the county had apparently failed to take into consideration the fact that freight rates from Clarksburg to Weston would be as cheap over the railroad as the rates from Weston to Clarksburg. They seemed greatly surprised to find that wheat grown on the prairie farms of the west could be shipped to Weston and sold at prices actually lower than the cost of production in Lewis County. Instead of furnishing a market for the surplus wheat and corn of the farmers, the railroad actually took away the local market which they had hitherto supplied. It is true that wheat was exported from the county before the building of the railroad; but it was hauled to Clarksburg at slight expense because it was the "empty trip" for the wagons. It is true that the surplus production was shipped out by railroad after 1879; but the surplus became less and less because the farmers received so much lower prices in the local market that there was no profit in raising wheat. The result was that within a comparatively short time they ceased to raise wheat at all except to supply the needs of their own families and as a nurse crop for grass. The mills which had formed the center of every community with an importance in the development of the county much greater than we are apt to think, suffered the same fate as the wheat fields. The flour manufactured in the west was sold at prices which local millers could not meet. The result was the abandonment of all except the mills in favored locations.

The raising of oats, buckwheat and potatoes which had been supplied by the farmers in sufficient quantities to satisfy the demand in the county, was likewise given up except for use on the farms. The livery stables of

Weston were soon supplied with grain which had been shipped from the west, and oats and buckwheat were rarely seen after 1885 on Lewis County farms. The growing of corn was also somewhat curtailed, and might have been affected far more had it not been for two factors: the rapid clearing of the forest land of the county and the greatly increased production of live stock which demanded some winter feeding. The agricultural interests of the county were soon completely changed. The hill land was cleared and put in pasture and the raising of cattle and sheep occupied most of the attention of the farmers. Within a few years Lewis County became recognized as one of the three or four leading grazing counties in the state.

Upon the completion of the railroad to Weston a stage line was established to Buckhannon, which continued for two or three years, until the people of that town decided that it was to their interest to have a railroad. Many efforts were made by them to secure the extension of the road by the Clarksburg, Weston and Glenville company. Finally a proposition was submitted to a committee of citizens by the officials of the road, that if the county of Upshur would subscribe $65,000 in bonds or $60,000 in cash the proposed extension to Buckhannon would be constructed. A mass meeting of the citizens of Buckhannon and Upshur County was held at the Upshur courthouse, 27 February 1882, to devise plans for securing better transportation. The citizens voted unanimously to accept the offer of the railroad company.

The outcome of the meeting was the organization of the Buckhannon and West Fork Railroad Company in April, 1882. The work of grading was commenced immediately thereafter. The narrow gauge road was completed to Buckhannon the following year. As in the case of the Weston and West Fork railroad, the track was then leased by the Weston and Centerville Railroad Company which had also been incorporated in 1882.

Subsequently the Weston and Centerville railroad also leased the tracks and equipment of the Weston and West Fork railroad, and the name of the former company was changed to the Weston and Buckhannon Railroad Company. A. H. Kunst was at one time president, general manager and agent of the new road. It continued in operation for several years until the time was ripe for the building of a standard gauge railroad. The effects of the extension of the narrow gauge railroad to Buckhannon were quickly felt in the more rapid development of upper Stone Coal creek. The location of the Curtis mill three-quarters of a century before, which had gradually drawn about it an ordinary, a blacksmith shop, a store, and secured a postoffice, was made a stop on the new railroad. About a mile farther up the creek, a flag station was established on lands of Seymour Horner for the accommodation of the residents of the Right fork. The station was called at first Seymour, in honor of the distinguished owner of the land. When the postoffice was established, it was named Horner, also in his honor. Stores were established at both villages by Matheny and Bush which attracted a large trade that had previously centered at Weston or Lorentz.

Following the successful completion of the railroad to Buckhannon, the people of Gilmer County determined if possible to tap the magnificent resources of that county in lumber and minerals. Presumably in response to a suggestion made by some officials of the Clarksburg, Weston and Glenville Railroad and Transportation Company, the county court of Gilmer in 1883 submitted to the people the proposition to bond the county to the amount of $50,000 to aid in the construction of a railroad from Weston to Glenville. The bond issue carried; but the amount was insufficient alone for the work of construction. The interest of Senator Camden was then being directed to the coal lands along the West Fork river below Clarksburg and not to the undeveloped resources of Gilmer County. No other capital could be

THE COMING OF THE RAILROAD 363

enlisted and the people of that county were disappointed.

In 1887, attention was again directed toward the north and south route between the West Fork and the Great Kanawha valleys. The Pennsylvania railroad sent a corps of surveyors over the proposed route of the Northern and Southern railroad from Greensburg, Pennsylvania, to Charleston. The survey was completed through Weston in 1887, but nothing was heard of the construction work of the proposed extension.

As in the case of the earlier railroad from Clarksburg to Weston, the extension south from Weston was left to be made by the capitalists of Lewis County. After considerable discussion the project finally took definite form with the incorporation of the Weston and Elk River Railroad Company with John Brannon as president, and N. B. Newlon as secretary-treasurer. The object was to build a railroad to the county seat of Braxton, provide an outlet for the products of the county, and especially to develop the timber resources of that county which was covered with virgin forests from Flatwoods southwest. The route was surveyed from Weston to the mouth of Oil creek by May, and the line definitely located. The county court of Braxton County submitted a bond issue to the people to aid in the construction of the road, which was passed overwhelmingly.

Before the survey was completed the plans of the promoters of the road were suddenly changed by the entrance into the field of Senator Johnson N. Camden. whose aid, given at a critical moment, had made the construction of the Weston and Clarksburg railroad possible, and who now proposed to build a great railroad system in northern West Virginia. He had secured control of great tracts of coal between Clarksburg and Fairmont, including practically all the best acreage of the valley, and he was preparing to construct a standard gauge railroad from Clarksburg to Fairmont in order to develop it. He also had secured control of thousands of acres of timber lands in Upshur and Randolph counties around

Pickens, and in Braxton, Webster, Nicholas and Pocahontas counties. In order to develop these properties to the maximum advantage, Senator Camden determined to build a broad-gauge railroad from Fairmont to Camden-on-Gauley, with a branch road from Weston to Pickens.

On 10 April 1889 the Weston and West Fork and the Clarksburg, Weston and Glenville railroads were merged into the Clarksburg, Weston and Midland railroad, which allowed stockholders five per cent of the stock held in either of the companies. The announcement went forth from the offices of the new company that the merger was only preliminary to the changing of the narrow gauge railroad from Weston to Clarksburg into a standard gauge. The newly organized Weston and Elk River railroad was merged in the Clarksburg, Weston and Midland company a little later, on the same terms as had been given to the stockholders of the other roads. On 20 July 1889 the Buckhannon River railroad was incorporated to run from Buckhannon to Pickens and thence to Lane's Bottom in Webster County. In September following, the Buckhannon and West Fork and the Weston and Centerville railroads were merged into the Clarksburg, Weston and Midland, and on 6 February 1890, the Buckhannon River railroad was also included. Senator Camden's proposed system was complete—on paper. It comprised the companies controlling the narrow gauge line from Clarksburg to Buckhannon and those which planned to construct extensions south from Buckhannon and from Weston. The name of the Clarksburg, Weston and Midland was changed to the West Virginia and Pittsburgh railroad following the inclusion of the last of the smaller lines. Johnson N. Camden was elected president of the system and Dr. A. H. Kunst, vice-president and general manager.

The work of widening the gauge from Clarksburg to Buckhannon was begun in the summer of 1889, and was completed within less than a year. The grades were reduced somewhat where the railroads crossed the hills, and some of the shortest curves were straightened to some extent, though for practically the whole distance, the old route decided upon in the 'seventies was still followed.

At the same time the work on the proposed extensions to Sutton and Pickens was prosecuted vigorously. Hundreds of men were employed in preparing the roadbed, and it was announced in the early spring of 1890 that the railroad would be completed to Sutton and to the three forks of the Buckhannon by early fall. The rapidity of the work was partly due to the easy grades, and the fact that but little earth was moved in preparing the roadbed.

The work of construction was engineered throughout by officials of the Baltimore and Ohio railroad. Most of the financial backing of the company came from the same source. Early in 1890 the property of the West Virginia and Pittsburgh Railroad company was mortgaged to the Mercantile Trust and Deposit Company of Baltimore, as security for a bond issue of $4,000,000 sold to complete the construction of the railroad. All the outstanding debts of the company, which had previously taken over the debts of the companies merged to form it, were paid off from the proceeds of the loan. The same year a contract was entered into by which the new road was leased to the Baltimore and Ohio railroad for a period of 999 years, the lease to be effective upon the completion of the road as a standard gauge.

The railroad was completed to Sutton early in 1891, and the first train entered the station, a half mile from town, on 5 May 1891. Senator Camden, who, with other officials, was a passenger on the train, was given a monster reception by the citizens of Braxton County. The crowd was estimated at four hundred to five hundred persons, which was about double the population of the Braxton County seat at that time. The first train to reach Sutton on a regular schedule ran 15 July 1891.

One train made the trip every day—provided no wreck occurred. The inconveniences of travel were not so great as they seem; for fishing was good in the Braxton County streams in those days, and the passengers, in case of a wreck, amused themselves in this way until the train crew succeeded in placing the train back on the track.

The results of the construction of the railroad to somnolent Braxton were immediately seen. A big lumber boom was constructed just below Sutton and thousands of logs were sawed there and the lumber shipped out over the railroad. The future lumber center of West Virginia was then considered to be Lane's Bottom on the Gauley river, toward which a branch of the West Virginia and Pittsburgh railroad was then being constructed. Even before the completion of the railroad to Sutton, construction had been commenced on a branch from Flatwoods, which crossed the Elk river six miles above Sutton, passed through Centralia, and thence crossed to the Gauley by way of Laurel creek. Its terminus was at the mouth of Williams river. The route from Lane's bottom to Marlinton had been located, and the site of Marlinton had been surveyed in preparation for a lot sale. The Gauley river branch was constructed to develop a tract of 140,000 acres of timber land owned jointly by Johnson N. Camden and C. K. Lord, one of the officers of the Baltimore and Ohio railroad. A band sawmill was hauled from the Chesapeake and Ohio railroad, a distance of forty miles, and set up so as to be ready for operation when the railroad was completed. Camden-on-Gauley was established in 1892. The timber manufactured on the Gauley river and at Pickens, which was reached by the Buckhannon river branch in 1892, created a great freight carrying business for the new railroad which assured its success from the start. Millions of feet of lumber have been hauled from the backwoods counties on the serpentine curves of the branch lines and over the hills to the main line of the Baltimore and Ohio.

Weston became the center of the new railroad system. The principal offices and shops of the company were established there to the great improvement and benefit of the town. The railroad company determined to erect at Weston a station befitting the importance of the town selected for its principal offices, and a contract was let the same year to William Lockhart and Jacob and Singleton Atcheson for the construction of a stone passenger station costing nearly $10,000. A tremendous development of Weston and all of Lewis County followed the completion of the standard gauge.

CHAPTER XXVIII.

TWENTY YEARS' PROGRESS, 1880-1900

The history of the development of Lewis County during the period from 1880 to 1900 is largely a survey if the improvements resulting from the building of railroads. So far as the country districts are concerned, there was a greater development than during any period of similar length in the history of the county. The effect upon the county seat was equally as great. The railroad made it possible for Weston to be a manufacturing center and thus laid the foundations for an extensive growth. How rapid this growth was in the half dozen years following the completion of the narrow gauge may be inferred from the fact that in 1885, the Weston post-office was one of seven presidential offices in West Virginia.

The construction of the state hospital was no longer the most extensive industry of Weston. From the crude beginning of the manufacture of grain, lumber and woolen goods for home consumption the industry was gradually extended until in 1900 it had attained respectable proportions. A handle factory was established in 1882, and a planing mill the next year. The Jackson planing mill passed into the hands of Atchison Brothers within a few years. Lewellen's carriage factory did a thriving business from the date of its establishment, and it later shared the field with William McGann, whose factory was opened in the 'eighties. Some of the wagons still in use in the county were made at the McGann shop.

In 1888 the factory of the Horseshoe Bedspring Company was located in Weston. It supplied a market in Lewis and adjoining counties. The Herb Medicine Company, manufacturers of Lightning hot drops, liniments and other patent medicines invented by John Morrow, began business in Weston. The stock was owned by Morrow, John Ruhl, and John and Jacob Koblegard. The business was moved to Springfield, Ohio, in 1892. Its place in the patent medicine field at Weston was taken by the Dupont Medicine Company which had a brief existence.

Shortly after the completion of the railroad to the permanent depot on Second street, John Ruhl and the Koblegard brothers established a wholesale grocery business under the name of Ruhl, Koblegard and Co., which usurped the place formerly held by Clarksburg establishments in distributing groceries to the stores of Lewis and adjoining counties.

In 1885, new machinery was installed in the woolen mills in West Weston in preparation for an increased trade. The factory had hardly resumed operations when it was totally destroyed by fire. The loss was estimated at $20,000 and the proprietors were unable to secure sufficient capital to rebuild the plant. They purchased the old Jackson mill property, intending to fit out the old mill as a combined grist and woolen mill, but abandoned the idea, presumably on account of the difficulty in establishing adequate means of transportation to and from Weston.

In this period Weston experienced one of the greatest building booms in the history of the town. Gradually the old frame buildings were removed from the Main street and their places were taken by substantial brick structures. The greater number of business blocks now standing on Main avenue were erected in the ten years following the widening of the gauge of the railroad. A building ordinance was adopted in 1889, which forbade the erection of wooden buildings within certain limits. The R. P. Camden Hotel, which at the time of its construction was one of the most modern and convenient hotels in the state, was opened to the public in 1896.

In 1892 the population of Weston was more than 2,000. A survey of the business of the town in 1893 showed that Weston had nine dry goods stores, seven grocery stores, three drug stores, two jewelry stores, three saddle and harness shops, seven milliners, one tailfour meat markets, four hotels, four restaurants, eight saloons, three livery stables, two furniture stores, five barber shops, three tinners, four blacksmith shops, two opera houses, two banks, three newspapers, a wholesale house, seven or eight manufacturing establishments, railroad shops and main offices, and the principal office of the Clarksburg, Weston and Buckhannon Express Company.

The first permanent improvements on the streets of Weston were made in 1891 when a short stretch of Main street above Second was paved with brick. The paving was paid for out of the proceeds of an increased levy and a larger tax on saloons. The council earlier in the year had submitted to the people the proposition to issue bonds to the amount of $25,000 for the paving of streets and the installation of a sewerage system but it failed to receive the requisite three-fifths vote. The paving has been gradually extended, a short stretch being improved each year, until now practically all the important streets of Weston have been paved with brick. The work has been carefully done throughout; so that the streets are far better than those of a majority of the cities and towns of the state.

In 1890 a company was organized by local capitalists to construct an electric light plant and thus relieve the people of their dependence on kerosene lamps both for street lights and for lighting their dwellings. The plant was built in its present location later in the same year, the machinery was installed, the houses were wired, and on 1 April 1891, the current was turned on. The plant was destroyed by fire in 1893, but was immediately rebuilt. It has since continued to give efficient service to the people of the town.

The electric light company also constructed and operated the waterworks of Weston. For years the subject had been agitated on account of the great amount of sickness due to the use of wells and cisterns in the heart of the town as well as the inconvenience of the old methods of obtaining water. Shortly after the organization of the electric light company, it was pointed out that the operation of the waterworks could logically be carried on by the new company by reason of the fact that the machinery of the plant would run only at night. During the day it could be used in pumping water. The construction of a reservoir on the hill and the laying of the mains would be the only new items of expense for the company, and its expensive machinery could be made to serve the public for twenty-four hours instead of for twelve. Some difficulty was experienced in securing a franchise. A bond issue to construct waterworks by the municipality was authorized by the voters in 1893, but the election was declared invalid by reason of a technicality. In 1895 it was proposed that a public supply should be obtained from wells drilled to a sufficient depth to insure a good flow of water. Finally a supply was secured through the electric light plant. The source was the West Fork river, from which the supply of the state hospital was also drawn. Many contests took place between the workmen of the hospital and those of the electric light plant to secure the scanty amount which flowed in the channel of the West Fork in midsummer. At times there was less water than was required by the people. The condition was so unsatisfactory to the officials of the state hospital that they asked the Legislature to abandon the West Fork supply and appropriate funds for the drilling of artesian wells. The city plant was thus left alone in possession of the river. They have made the supply more certain at all seasons of the year by the construction of a dam at Bendale which impounds more than a million gallons of water to be used when the flow of the river is greatly diminished.

There has at times been much complaint against the waterworks on account of the impurities found in the city water. The watershed of the West Fork river above Weston is rather densely populated, with the natural result that much organic waste finds its way into the river. A few years ago, a filtration system, similar to some which had done excellent service in other towns, was installed, but it has not been equal to the tremendous task of removing the suspended matter in the turbid West Fork. At times within the past year it has failed to function properly.

The installation of the waterworks was followed almost immediately by the establishment of a sewerage system. For years the project had been agitated in the press and at public meetings. In the special election of 1890, in which it was proposed to bond the town for the construction of a sewerage system, the measure failed. Again in 1896 the proposition was before the people, but again it failed. A survey of the entire town was ordered to be made in 1897 in preparation for the submission of a new ordinance. Sewers were laid soon afterwards. Unfortunately the work has been prosecuted without plan and without method. No account was taken of the future needs of the town. The ditches were dug for the sewers, the tile was laid and then covered, and no map or indication of the location of the sewers was left, except the memory of the inhabitants. The difficulty of making repairs has been greatly increased as a result. Practically all the sewers were made to discharge into the West Fork river within the city limits instead of carrying the wastes farther down stream. The growth of the communities below Weston has now rendered impracticable the construction of a main sewer which would discharge into the river some distance down the river. The West Fork is too small a stream to accomplish the anaerobic decomposition of the sewage of a town the size of Weston, and the stench arising from the channel in the summer is a nuisance to the residents of the valley below the town. The division of the sewerage system into two sections, one for storm sewage and the other for sanitary sewage, and the construction of a plant for the disposal of the latter class is one of the immediate needs of the city.

The Westonite of the early 'nineties did not have to depend upon electric light, for he might use natural gas instead. Coal for domestic use was largely superseded by gas in 1893 when a line was run from the Big Isaac well, twelve miles away, by the Weston Gas Company. The service was satisfactory, but after a few years, the high rates charged caused much complaint, especially about 1898 when the owners published notice of an increase. Relief was secured from the establishment of a competing business. Rates were so reduced in the brief contest which followed that Weston enjoyed cheaper rates than any other town in the state—twenty-five cents per fire per month, regardless of the amount of gas consumed. The rates were too low to allow a reasonable profit. An agreement was reached, and the two companies published simultaneously a notice of increase. A few years ago meters were installed and patrons were charged with what they consumed instead of the old flat rate. The innovation was strenuously objected to.

Telephones were introduced into Lewis County at the very beginning of the period, and lines had been extended to all parts of the county by the opening of the new century. The first telephones in the county were not at the county seat. John Beeghley, in the early 'eighties, was the owner of a chain of stores in northern Lewis and southern Harrison counties. The delay in communication between stores was very annoying and even costly at times. Soon after the telephone was placed on the market, he built a line connecting the stores, one of which was at Lightburn. His neighbors were quick to realize the advantages of the telephone and they requested permission to connect with the Beeghley line. The merchant determined to take up the telephone business on a commercial basis. He extended his lines in all directions until within a surprisingly short time connection was established with all parts of the county.

Meanwhile the people of Weston had been trying to work out some scheme by which they might secure telephone service. In 1885 the Ceneral Telephone Company was organized with Jacob Koblegard as president and James B. Finster as secretary. This company was later reorganized as the Weston Central Telephone Company in 1888. Several telephones were installed in different places of business in Weston, and a line was run to Glenville by the company. By 1895 John Beeghley's system had grown to such an extent that he found it expedient to establish connection in Weston. He therefore leased for five years the plant of the Weston Central company, and before his lease had expired, arranged to consolidate the two companies into the United Telephone system. At the time of the merger there were eighty telephones on the Beeghley lines and about thirty in the Weston system. The formation of the new company caused a great improvement in the service and greatly extended the use of the telephone not only in business houses, but also to private residences. Practically all property-holders in Weston soon leased telephones. The service was further improved by arrangements made for switchboard connections with systems in adjoining counties.

The Bell system entered the field at the beginning of the century, and established a long distance service far superior to that of the United system Its local service was never comparable to that of the Beeghley lines on account of the larger number of subscribers of the latter company in Weston. In 1903 the People's United Telephone system, a co-operative company, was incorporated, and within three years it had extended its lines into practically every section of the county, with instruments even in log houses situated far from the ordinary course of travel. Weston now had three systems, the Beeghley still predominating, but the others having a considerable number of subscribers. Early in 1917 the Bell company absorbed the Beeghley lines, to the great improvement of the service.

Several other improvements accomplished during the period deserve mention. The Machpelah cemetery was laid off in 1882, the earlier burying grounds being no longer sufficient. A library was established by the women of Weston under the leadership of Dr. Harriet B. Jones about 1891. The Australian ballot was introduced in the election of municipal officers in 1896. The old covered bridge across the West Fork at Weston was replaced by an iron bridge in 1890. The footbridge across the river opposite the entrance to the hospital grounds was completed in 1897. Main street was extended from First street to the electric light plant, thus vindicating, after three-fourths of a century, the wisdom of Edward Jackson in laying off the town.

Weston had aspirations to become the seat of a college when the West Virginia Conference of the Methodist Episcopal church voted to establish the West Virginia Conference Seminary. At a public meeting in 1887 the advantages of securing the college—that it would enable parents to educate their children near home, increase the local demand for goods, bring in professors and students, and augment the population of the town by at least two hundred people—were pointed out, and committees were designated to solicit subscriptions. Weston offered $3,000 and a site; but Buckhannon, which offered twice as much, secured the institution. The action of the board is said to have been influenced also by the large number of saloons in Weston, while Buckhannon had none.

In 1894 the Weston College of Commerce and School of Shorthand opened its doors to students. Buchanan White was president; D. M. Willis, principal, and Miss

Lela Dew and Miss Gertrude Randolph, teachers. The existence of the school was very brief.

A little progress was made in the public schools of the town. In 1885-6 a new building, known as the "Annex", was erected. Ten years later the city schools were completely divorced from those of the country by the passage of a special act by the Legislature forming the Weston Independent District as it now is.

The old courthouse, built in 1856-7, was destroyed in 1886 by a fire commonly thought to have been of incendiary origin. Fortunately most of the records of the county escaped injury.

Beginning about 1890 there was a remarkable change in the agricultural interests of the county. Wool growing, which had occupied the attention of the majority of the farmers from the period of the Civil war, began to be unprofitable about the year 1886 owing to the competition of growers on the western ranches and in Australia and the Argentine. Appeals for a protective duty by the wool growers of America were unsuccessful until the passage of the McKinley bill in 1890. In order to bolster up the declining industry, Andrew Edmiston, then representing Lewis County in the House of Delegates, secured the passage of a stringent dog law. It was soon repealed on account of the storm of opposition which it evoked from the owners of dogs. The price of wool dropped quickly after the passage of the Wilson bill in 1893, and farmers in Lewis County lost interest in sheep raising to a great degree. The breeds of sheep became badly mixed and the quality of the wool deteriorated. Wool growing never recovered. Though many sheep are now kept in the county, the principal object is to sell lambs rather than wool.

Cattle raising became easily the leading agricultural industry of the county after 1892. The breeds were improved somewhat, and greater attention paid to the selection of stock. Dehorning was begun about 1894. At first considered as a harmles craze, taken up by farmers who wished to improve the appearance of their herds, it gradually made its way into universal favor. The feeling that dehorning was cruel, and the fact that cattle lost weight after the operation was one of the causes which led to the introduction of Aberdeen-Angus cattle into the county. They have found favor among farmers because they mature quickly. At present they are about one-half as numerous as the Herefords.

Interest in better farming methods was increased by farmers' institutes which have been held annually in the county since 1890. The first institute was held in Weston under the leadership of D D. Johnson of the state board of agriculture. The officers elected were: President, A. W. Woodford; vice-president, Jasper Peterson, secretary, G. M Chidester; and treasurer, W. B. McGary.

The completion of the narrow gauge railroad to Weston was the signal for redoubled efforts in lumbering. Much of the poplar timber of Court House and Collins Settlement districts was cut, sawed and hauled to Weston for shipment. Some of the lumber was hauled a distance of twenty-five miles. The construction of the railroad toward Sutton greatly increased the exploitation of timber in the upper end of the county, and completely changed the character of that section.

A railroad construction camp on the farm of A. A. Brown became a rather important shipping point for lumber from Skin creek. In 1891 it had become known as Brownsville, and had a store, a postoffice and six residences.

Roanoke became the center for the shipment of lumber from Sand fork, Canoe run and even from upper Skin creek. Thomas Feeney established a store in the village in order to share in the increased trade. David B. Cook began the publication of the "Willing Worker", a paper devoted to the interests of prohibition. In later years Roanoke became the shipping point for all the live stock of Collins Settlement district, due to its superior facilities.

Arnold Station, near the old "Indian Carrying Place," became, next to Weston, perhaps the most important shipping point for lumber in the county. There George J. Arnold established a store and the last of his chain of hotels, "The Indian Farm Hotel." At the point where the river approaches nearest the station, Presley Beach and others constructed a boom in the river and established a mill which sawed several hundred thousand feet of lumber from logs floated down the river.

Farther up the stream sawmills moved from farm to farm sawing all the available timber to be hauled on wagons at Arnold. Near Bunten's mill at the mouth of Laurel run, a large sawmill was established which continued in operation for several years. The village which grew up about the mills was called Millville by its inhabitants, though residents of Walkersville called it "Pinhook". Millville citizens retaliated by dubbing the rival village "Slabtown". The name of Millville was later changed to Crawford in honor of Presley Crawford. On the right fork, a sawmill gave the first real prosperity to Ireland, which had previously consisted of a store and postoffice. Duffy, on Glady fork, was founded in this period.

The construction of the railroad caused a town to spring up at the mouth of Clover fork. The location was recognized as of strategic importance in gaining the trade formerly enjoyed by Burnsville, and by the time the railroad was completed, it had three stores, two in Braxton and one in Lewis.

Though Freeman's creek district did not secure a railroad, it shared in the general development which the better means of transportation brought to Lewis County. Perhaps the most ambitious improvement was the village of Franklin, now Churchville, which grew up in the early eighties around a store at the mouth of Isaac's fork of Fink. Its promoters declared their intention to make it the business center of the district and of a much wider territory as well. For a time it seemed as though the dreams of the founders would be realized. By 1891 there were four stores, operated respectively by Bond and Company, John Hushion, G. A. Kemper and Company and Lovett and Flesher; a blacksmith shop, a wagon shop, a mill, a saddler's shop, and a printing shop, which published the Churchville Hustler. Members of the Baptist, United Brethren and Methodist Protestant churches, eager to place their denominations first in the field, established congregations and erected churches. The name Franklin was already borne by another post-office, and when an office was to be established there, the most appropriate name seemed to be Churchville.

Farther down Fink creek the undeveloped territory began to come in touch with the world through the construction of a road along the creek, and through the establishment of two stores around which villages grew up later—Vadis, named for Sienkewicz's masterpiece, and Hurst, for the earliest settler on the creek.

On Leading creek the old centers were overshadowed by Alum Bridge, which in 1894 was said to have "more improvements and fewer inhabitants than any other village in the district." It had three stores, a flouring mill, a sawmill, a wagon shop, and telephone and postal service.

CHAPTER XXIX.

OIL AND GAS DEVELOPMENT

The presence of oil in Lewis County has been known for many years. The earliest explorers who traversed Oil creek discovered oil floating on the surface of the water and named the creek in consequence of the phenomenon. After the great oil excitement at Burning Springs in Wirt County just before the Civil war, some attention was given to other territory in northwestern Virginia. The name "Oil creek" and the story of how it got its name led to an investigation. A story has been circulated to the effect that a barrel of oil was poured out near the head of the stream for the benefit of the prospectors who eagerly leased some land on the stream and even drilled a well at the mouth of Clover Fork with a springpole. It may well be doubted whether the story is true. Oil has been found not only on Oil creek but also in many other sections of the county. On Abbott's run, a branch of Stone Coal creek, surface oil "of better quality than that found elsewhere in the state" was discovered in 1873, and four farms on the run were immediately leased by eastern capitalists. The discovery created considerable excitement among the people of the county at the time.

Dependence on the chance collection of surface oil soon ceased as the great quantities of oil secured by drilling came in competition with it. The haphazard location of wells, which was the only method in use at first, was superseded by scientific methods based on a study of rock formations. It had been noticed by geologists that most of the discoveries of oil and natural gas were near anticlinals, that is, lines showing where the surface of the ground has been bowed up in long-past ages. One of these anticlinals, formerly known as the "forty-five degree line," had been approximately located through the western part of Monongalia and Marion counties, the eastern border of Doddridge and the western part of Lewis. Developments along the anticlinal to the north of Lewis in Monongalia and Marion counties had proved successful by the early 'eighties, and the area of known productiveness was gradually extended southward by the efforts of development companies until the borders of Lewis County were reached.

In 1886 Henry S. White, a representative of J. M. Guffey and Company, of Pittsburgh, secured leases on the farms of Henry Wanstreet, William Flesher, D. Sweeney, Joseph Droppleman, John S. Tierney, John Keely, John McFadden, N. C. Latta, John Wineberg, Theresa A. Gumm, and others. Most of these farms are situated on Fink creek or its tributaries.

Discovery of the great pool at Mannington in 1890 quickly caused the Standard Oil Company to become interested in the development of the oil territory of West Virginia. In preparation for extensive operations, the company sent a corps of engineers into the field to trace the "forty-five degree line" from the Pennsylvania border to the Great Kanawha river. All the farms within eight miles of the line on either side were to be carefully mapped, and the contour of the surface carefully studied for indications. The sixteen-mile belt through Central West Virginia was expected to be the scene of great activity.

Prospectors from the Sistersville pool (opened in 1890) also were led to make investigations in Lewis County through the surface indications of oil and gas. Leasing of lands in several sections of the county was conducted quietly by representatives of large Pennsylvania companies as well as by West Virginia operators. The object seemed to be not to develop the field at once, but to lease some of the choicest locations in preparation for the opening of the field later.

Tired of waiting for development from outside the county, local people determined to begin drilling. In August 1893, the Lewis County Oil and Gas Company was organized with E. W. Boyd as president. The company had leased 3,500 acres of land along the river below Weston, on which they proposed to make a thorough test to discover whether or not oil was to be found there. Operations did not begin at once owing to the fact that the panic of 1893 caused money to be scarce. It was late in 1897 before the first test well was begun on the farm of Colonel A. W. Woodford on the river below Weston. In 1896, S. E. Barrett, formerly an operator in the Sistersville field, proposed to make a test in the vicinity of Weston if financial aid could be secured from local capitalists. He was successful in forming a company at a later date.

Meanwhile tests had been conducted with varying results in other sections of the county. A Pennsylvania company began drilling a test well on a tract of 2,300 acres of land which they had leased in the vicinity of Alum Bridge There was great excitement in that community, and before the rig was up for the first well, farmers had set a price for their lands at least five dollars per acre higher than they had before dared to ask. The result of the test was kept secret by the company in preparation for the further leasing of territory in the community, and the well was reported to the farmers as a dry hole.

Toward the end of 1894, the South Penn Oil Company began a test on the Rastle farm on Fink creek. The well was finished about the first of January, 1895, and was immediately shut in and the drillers sworn to secrecy as in the case of the well near Alum Bridge. The plug failed to hold. Some of the oil leaked out and was wasted; and soon everybody in the community knew that Lewis County was in the oil field. Citizens of upper Fink creek caught some of the oil which flowed from the well, and placed a sample bottle of it on exhibition in a Churchville store as visible evidence of the mineral wealth of the county. The Churchville correspondent of the Weston Independent, in a guarded statement, wrote, "The sample of oil which escaped from the well on Mr. Rastle's farm looks very suspicious of oil in this neighborhood. It is said that upwards of seventy-five gallons run away daily. We understand that the oil company is preparing tanks. It is believed that they'll open up an oil field in the near future." Farmers were not so conservative as the correspondent. Land owners in the vicinity went wild with excitement. Land values rose until they were out of sight. Farmers offered to sell their lands at from $250 to $300 per acre—more than ten times the amount they would have dared to ask before the oil excitement.

Developments in the Fink creek valley continued. Further test wells were drilled in different localities by the South Penn Oil Company. In 1897, it was generally known that there were four producing wells in the Fink field, though the daily production of the wells was of course a matter of conjecture. Further development was indicated by the laying of a pipe line from McElroy, in Doddridge County, thirty miles away, to convey the product of the Fink wells to market. The best production in the early wells on Fink creek was said to be in the Salt and Big Injun sands.

The South Penn well No. 5 in the Fink field was drilled in a "duster" in 1897. The Fink Creek Oil and Gas Company located a well on the Back fork of Alum fork in October, 1897, at the same time as the Boyd Brothers' well was located on the Woodford farm. Both wells came in with a strong flow of gas. The Woodford well was drilled to the Gordon sand in hope of finding oil in paying quantities. A little was found in the Gantz sand, but when drilling stopped at 2,400 feet, on 19 April 1898, the well was pronounced a dry hole.

In order that the owners of the well should not lose all their investments it was proposed to pipe the gas to Weston. The well was finally sold to a Clarksburg company. Other local companies were formed soon afterwards which leased farms and made preparations for drilling.

In 1899, S. E. Barrett organized the Lewis Oil Company which drilled in a big gas well near Churchville. The promoters, who were mainly local people, were disappointed at the outcome of the well as there was then no means of marketing the product. It was recognized, however, that the gas could be piped to Weston where it would satisfy the demands of the people of Weston to secure cheaper fuel than they were being furnished by the Keener company.

The results of the operations of local companies and the continued development caused the South Penn company to act, and, beginning about 1900, they spared no effort to gain complete control of the territory in the vicinity of Weston. Below Weston on the river and on Gee Lick run, they offered one dollar an acre rental per year, and most of the territory in the vicinity was leased at that figure. Most of the farms around Jane Lew were also leased at about the same time by the South Penn Oil Company and by "wildcatters". By the middle of the year 1899 there were few tracts in the vicinity of Weston and Jane Lew, with the exception of church lots, which had not been leased.

The drilling in of the Hushion well on Fink creek, 3 December 1898, with a capacity variously estimated at from 10 to 35 barrels a day, dispelled every doubt that the northwestern part of the county was a rich oil field. In order to delimit the oil field already known, and to discover, if possible, other pools of paying production, tests were made on Hacker's creek, on Canoe run, near Arnold station, near Burnsville and several miles above Weston on the river, but no information was given out by the oil companies as to the results of the tests. In

THE COPELY WELL

August 1899, the Sparling Oil Company drilled in a test well on the W. K. Wilson farm on the Little Kanawha river, in the southernmost extremity of Lewis County, from which it was reported that oil flowed at the rate of sixty-five barrels a day. In consequence most of the territory in that section was soon leased. The well on the Tom Harrison farm on Stone Coal creek was drilled in with a light production of gas at about the same time. The pertinacity of S. E. Barrett was finally rewarded by the coming in of the "Big Barrett" near Churchville, with a strong flow of oil.

By far the greatest excitement of the year 1899, centered around developments on Polk creek. The Camden well No. 1, at the mouth of Dry fork was started as a test in the middle of the year. In September, so much gas was encountered that operations were suspended for a time. Then on October 5th, it came in a gusher with an estimated production of from 1,000 to 3,000 barrels a day. The oil was thrown nearly to the top of the derrick and flowed for some distance in the channel of Polk creek. Dams were constructed in the channel to hold it back, and barrels were submerged in the pools to collect as much of the precious fluid as possible. The construction of tanks was rushed with all possible speed. One week after the strike, eight 250-barrel tanks and two 1,200-barrel tanks were standing near the well, at least partly filled with oil. Efforts were being made by the company to confine the output of the well until a pipe line could be laid to the Jarvisville field. A close watch was maintained by the company to prevent other parties from gaining the secret of the amount of production.

It was rumored at the time that the driller of the well had exceeded his instructions by going so deep, and that he was discharged by the company immediately after the great flow of oil was struck. Be that as it may, the strike undoubtedly cost the company thousands of dollars in the high prices which it was compelled to pay to secure leases on the farms adjoining. Almost before daybreak the next morning after the discovery, agents of the company went from farm to farm trying to secure leases. Where, before the drilling, they could have made the leases easily and at small rental, they were now compelled to offer large bonuses in order to secure any leases at all.

The great strike on the Camden farm created the greatest excitement in the county since the coming of the Confederate raiders in the 'sixties. All classes rushed to the scene impelled by curiosity actually to see the marvel with their own eyes. There was a constant stream of sight-seers. Many came from Harrison, from Upshur, and from Gilmer counties. Merchants in Weston left their business in order, if possible, to ascertain just how great the capacity of the well was, and how favorable the prospects for securing leases in the vicinity. The fever of speculation seized all classes. Royalties were bought at unheard-of prices, and farmers were offered fabulous prices for their lands. "Men rushed madly in all directions from the well," says a writer in the Weston Independent, "determined if possible to secure leases at any cost."

Many of the farms in the vicinity of the Camden well were held under ten-cent leases which had been in operation for several years. Owing to the indefiniteness of the tract leased, E. G. Davisson and J. W. Ross came to the conclusion that these leases were not valid, and they therefore leased some land held under ten-cent lease in the vicinity. The South Penn Oil Company determined to secure their title to the oil under the J. W. Taylor farm by right of possession. One Monday morning a small army of rig builders came to the farm and began the construction of a rig for them. It was completed Wednesday evening. That night Davisson and Ross started their teams from Weston with a boiler and a string of tools, arriving the next morning at the South Penn rig on the Taylor farm where they immediately began drilling. The South Penn equipment had been started from Wolf Summit, but it never reached the rig. Davisson and Ross employed one of the officers of the Spanish-American war volunteers from Lewis County to round up the men who had lately been discharged and keep the South Penn employes off the farm. A few days later Davisson and Ross were summoned before the federal court at Parkersburg, with the result that a compromise was agreed upon. The ten-cent leases were proved invalid; and farmers in the vicinity received new leases for much larger amounts and thousands of dollars in royalties as a result.

On 25 January 1900 the Taylor well No. 1 was producing forty barrels a day when it had been drilled only a few feet into the sand. Other wells had already been located in close proximity to the big Camden well, and by the end of January eleven wells were being drilled near the gusher.

Unfortunately nearly all the later wells proved to be either dry holes or light pumpers. Even the Camden No. 1, which was a limestone well, soon blew out the oil which it held in a crevice. The interest of the oil speculators in the field waned, and by midsummer, 1900, most of the oil excitement among the people of the county had died out. Oil companies continued to drill test wells in other fields as they had done before, most of the activity being confined to the Fink creek and Sand fork valleys which, like most of the other lands along the "forty-five degree line", were leased almost solidly. The first tests made on Kincheloe creek had been successful, and it was evident that an important field was being opened there.

The chief new development in the Fink field early in 1900, came from drilling on Straight run, a tributary of Fink. On April 25th, the A. T. Gooden well was drilled in with a production of about 300 barrels daily. The location of other wells followed in the same vicinity at once. The Lowther No. 1 was completed late in August with a production of about 100 barrels a day, and at about the same time Davisson and Ross drilled in their first well on the J. C. Waggoner farm, which showed a production of about 400 barrels a day, and was then regarded as being the best well in the county. The A. T. Gooden Nos. 2 and 3 came in good producing wells. By September 1st, ten new locations had been made on Straight run.

Just when the citizens of the county had come to the conclusion that all the oil fields had been discovered and that no startling new developments would take place there occurred the most remarkable event in the history of the oil boom in Lewis County and perhaps of West Virginia up to that time. On 22 September 1900 the Copely well No. 1, on Sand Fork, on the old Camden-Bailey-Camden tract, was drilled in with a production estimated at from two hundred to three hundred barrels an hour, which rapidly rose to seven thousand barrels a day. According to a Pittsburgh newspaper it was the largest well that had been drilled in the Appalachian region in seven years. The oil spurted far over the top of the derrick and fell in a shower which soaked the ground for several hundred feet around the well. Laborers clad in oilskins worked constantly, making frantic efforts to shut in the oil or at least to reduce the flow. Ten tanks, with a capacity of 250 barrels each, were hastily improvised, but they were filled within a few hours. The oil formed a rivulet flowing into Sand fork, which rose rapidly in the bed of the stream. Fortunately for the owners of the oil, it was a season of comparative drought, and there was little or no water in the stream. Dams were hastily thrown up in the channel of the stream, one below the other, for a distance of eight miles below the well. Laborers who had worked day and night at fabulous wages, fell exhausted, unable to continue longer without sleep. The oil flowed on over the last dam that had been constructed and continued down the channel of the stream, some of it eventually reaching the Little Kanawha river. Thousands of barrels were wasted, though every possible effort was made to save it.

Weeks passed before sufficient tankage could be brought to the field, or a pipe line could be constructed to provide for the production of the well. The tremendous flow continued. At the end of five weeks the Copely No. 1 was holding up to a production of one hundred barrels an hour.

If there was great excitement following the striking of the Camden No. 1, there was a perfect bedlam following the completion of the Copely well. There is no comparison except by multiplication by a large number. Visitors came from far and near, some out of curiosity, some to secure leaseholds if possible. The roads were crowded with people riding or driving to and from the great well, and there was more bustle and stir in the hitherto secluded hollows of Court House district than there had ever been before, or will probably ever be again.

The rush to the field would have been far greater if the strike had been made in territory less fully leased. Around the Copely well when it was drilled in the leaseholds of the South Penn Oil Company and Guffey and Galey covered the country like a blanket. Those of a speculative frame of mind had to content themselves with leasing in other fields or in buying the royalties of the Irish owners of the land, many of whom became rich overnight.

The extent of the pool tapped by the Copely No. 1 was unknown. It might extend from the borders of the Polk creek field and the Fink field south and west for a long distance. With the exception of a light producer, the J. W. Cox well No. 1 west of the Copely farm, there was no other well in the vicinity. In order to delimit the field, and to bring it to its full development, a general rush to get material into the field began. Two hundred teams were employed in hauling engines, boilers, pipe and casings from Weston. Boarding-houses, feed stores and barns sprang up like mushrooms near the Copely well. Within five weeks after the completion of the Copely No. 1, the Reynolds well No. 1 had been drilled into the fifth sand and was making one hundred barrels a day. The J. W. Cox No. 2 was completed and was producing forty barrels a day. Locations had been made on the Peters and Heath farms on Butcher's fork and on the Bennington farm on Oldfield fork. Rigs were being constructed on the Judge John Brannon farm and the Devanney farms on Sand Fork, as well as at new locations on the Copely farm, and efforts were hastened everywhere to drill to the Gordon sand from which had been turned the fluid, stored for centuries, into the single outlet of the Copely well.

On November 8, the Turner well No. 1, a little more than a half-mile above Copely No. 1, was drilled into the Gordon sand by Guffey and Galey. It was declared at the time to be fully equal to the great Copely well. Strange to say, upon the completion of the Turner No. 1, the production of the Copely No. 1 sank appreciably. It was evident that the same pool was tapped by both and that the area of the pool could hardly be extensive, or one well would not have been so greatly affected by the drilling in of the other. Nevertheless drilling continued. Several new wells were sunk all around the great gushers, and within a very short time the limits of the pool had been determined within a few rods. On the Donlan farm, which adjoined the Copely farm on the west, it is said that not a single drop of oil was ever obtained. On farms only a short distance away in other directions dry holes were frequently found. In some locations in the vicinity also, good producing wells were drilled in, though there were none which could possibly be compared with the two great gushers. In most of the wells completed in the Sand Fork field, much natural gas was found, but there was as yet no market for it, and little interest was taken in its production.

The Copely well "disturbed the social equilibrum

for miles around'" The four maiden sisters, descendants of the pioneer Copely, who had taught numerous terms of school, were enabled to retire from the profession in ease and comfort for the remainder of their lives. Their neighbors, most of whom had experienced some difficulty in securing a comfortable living from their rough farms, became wealthy overnight. Men whose sole military experience consisted of watching Grand Army parades on the Fourth of July were soon answering to the title of Colonel. Such prosperity as the first Irish settlers had never dreamed of, came suddenly to the rough hollows of Sand fork. Their descendants were able to sell their land for large sums and take up their abode in leisure elsewhere.

One of the most unfortunate immediate results of the big oil strike was a smallpox scare which caused a panic in all parts of the county. Disseminated probably by the congregation of hundreds of persons of all walks of life, from all points of the compass, the disease soon broke out simultaneously on Leading creek, on Sand fork, at Weston and at other places in the county The county officials maintained a pest-house on Buck Knob for the treatment of those afflicted with the disease and caused a rigid quarantine to be placed on all suspects. The measures taken by the medical authorities proved effective, and the spread of the disease was stopped within a few weeks.

During 1901 development in the Lewis County fields was very active. More wells were then being drilled here than in any other county in the state. Tests were rapidly being completed all over the county. The Right fork of Freeman's creek was proved to be a field of considerable promise through the drilling of the T. Joyce well, which produced about sixty barrels daily. New locations were made in the Fink field, in the Copely field, on Polk creek, on Kincheloe creek and in the eastern part of Freeman's creek district.

New developments in the vicinity of Beall's Mills,

east of the Copely field, made known the presence of a good fifth sand pool. The wells, though not great gushers like the Copely well and the Turner well, nor even large producers like the A. T. Gooden No. 1, were uniform in size and never failed to respond to a shot. The discovery of this pool retrieved the reputation of the region which had been badly damaged by the failures at Sand Fork following the Copely strike. The new pool has proved to be of considerable extent, and many of the producing wells of the county at the present time have been drilled into it. The oil development since 1901 has generally consisted in the completion of wells in the well-recognized fields of Freeman's Creek and Court House districts, and few exciting strikes have been made.

By 1902, Lewis County oil production approached its highest point. More oil was flowing from the wells here than from those of any other county of the state, and the output was of a superior quality. The Sand fork and Fink fields were recognized as being the most prolific fields in a state which then led all the other states in production. There were no great gushers, but the steady flow of several hundred ordinary wells made up an enormous total. Wells continued to be drilled—but the new additions do not compensate for the decline in production of the older wells. The Copely No. 1 is still producing, though the once great gusher is now only a light pumper. Perhaps the most remarkable phenomenon connected with oil development in the county is the staying qualities of most of the wells in the Fink field. Wells that were drilled there twenty-five years ago still continue to produce their five, ten or twenty barrels a day as they did in the beginning. A few wells have agreeably surprised their owners by actually increasing their production. As this field was the first to be developed it still holds promise of being the last to be abandoned.

The oil prospectors opened five distinct fields in

Lewis County. On Fink creek the Gantz sand yielded the production for a great number of small oil wells. None of the wells was very large; neither were there many dry holes; and when oil was not struck there was nearly always a compensating strong flow of gas. The Salt sand in the Polk creek field yielded a considerable amount of oil over a rather limited territory. It was the oil from this sand which had escaped into the limestone pocket and caused the first great excitement at the Camden No. 1. The relatively limited Gordon sand pool on Sand Fork afforded the production of the great Copely and Turner gushers. The Fifth sand pool on Kincheloe creek has been fairly stable and has yielded thousands of barrels of oil, though there have been no spectacular finds. The extensive Fifth sand pool on Sand fork, known as the Beall's Mills pool, which extends all the way from Butcher's fork to Oldfield fork and from west of the Copely well to the headwaters of Sand fork, has been the largest pool in area, and one of the surest. In nearly all wells drilled there a small amount of oil has been secured.

The early makeshift means of marketing oil by pipes to the Harrison and Doddridge county fields was greatly improved in 1900, following the great Copely strike, by the laying of two six-inch main lines by the Eureka Pipe Line Company from the mouth of Sand Fork to the great oil pumping station at Downs, just below Mannington. They connected with a gravity line from the Copely well to the mouth of Sand fork.

Perhaps the most spectacular oil strike in later years was on Polk creek where the first great excitement occurred. In 1912 a well was drilled into the limestone which made 1,800 barrels daily for a time; but as in the Camden well, the drill had merely struck an oil pocket which was soon exhausted.

The tests to delimit the area of oil production in

Lewis County also served to fix fairly well the bounds of profitable production of gas. The Romine well on Fink creek was drilled into the Gantz sand in 1898. It was by far the greatest gas well in the history of the county. On 4 September 1900 the Flesher well on Sand fork was drilled into the same sand. No oil was struck, but it was estimated to be one of the greatest producing gas wells in the state. No pipe lines had then been laid to convey the gas out of the county to market, and the drilling of these wells was doubtless a disappointment to the operators. Negotiations were begun by them to interest gas companies in the Lewis County field, with the result that the following summer the Philadelphia Company purchased for $1,000,000 all the gas interests of Guffey and Galey in the county—a territory covering 75,000 acres in the heart of the gas belt. It was announced that the territory would be developed further and that a twenty-inch pipe line would be laid from Lewis County to Pittsburgh. The gas interests of the South Penn Oil Company, a subsidiary of the Standard Oil Company, were conveyed to the Hope Natural Gas Comanpy. For a long time, however, the gas was allowed to remain in the rock reservoirs until the companies could find a suitable market. Even when forced to drill by the owner of the surface to avoid having to give up the lease, the wells were shut in until such time as the proper connections with pipe lines could be secured.

Many of the home companies and independent operators who had drilled for oil and found only gas in large quantities, faced ruin because they were unable to secure enough capital to build pipe lines to Pittsburgh, Cleveland, Baltimore and other markets. Their holdings were practically worthless. Other independent operators turned to the manufacture of carbon black, thus converting the product of their wells to a form which could be readily disposed of. Two years after the Copely excitement two factories had been constructed near Weston and were in full operation, and others were contemplated on Polk creek, on Stone Coal and below Weston. Many carloads of the product were shipped every month.

The Weston State Hospital had been one of the large consumer of gas near Weston, and during the fluctuations in rates which took place in 1900, it was determined to drill a well on the Hospital farm with a view to securing a supply without expense save for the drilling, pipes and connections. Gas was struck in the Gantz sand, 25 February 1902, and immediately connected. It was estimated that the saving to the state as a result of the drilling was about $5,000 a year.

In 1904 the gas territory of Lewis County was extended to include at least a part of Collins Settlement district. A well which had been drilled on the E. G. Davisson farm at Crawford with disappointing results showed a greater production than had been at first indicated. As a direct result of the well the farmers of Collins Settlement have collected in rentals almost a million dollars. Pipe lines were soon laid to supply the villages of Walkersville and Crawford with gas. The production of the well was always small, and it ceased to flow after about ten years.

For the first few years after the discovery of gas in Lewis County the waste was appalling. Each farmer secured the right to the free use of gas, and fires were kept burning day and night. The connections leaked. There were no facilities for collecting the gasoline in the lines, which was disposed of by blowing thousands of cubic feet of gas into the air. The people of Weston heated and lighted their homes at so much per fire or light, regardless of the amount of gas consumed, with the result that millions of feet of gas were burned that were not needed.

As the Philadelphia Company, the West Virginia Central company, the Hope and the Reserve have extended their main lines to all parts of the gas field, as they have laid mains of ten, twelve, sixteen and twenty inches in diameter to the gas markets of Pittsburgh and Cleveland and Columbus, the value of all the gas wells in the county has vastly increased. Many pumping stations have been erected to take the burden of forcing the gas through the lines and to allow the pressure of the wells to send forth a greater volume of gas. Old wasteful methods of ridding the lines of gasoline have been superseded by the introduction of gasoline plants which refine hundreds of barrels of gasoline every month.

The area of gas production in Lewis County includes all of Freeman's Creek district, nearly all of Court House, with the exception of a strip on the eastern border, and the greater portion of Hacker's Creek. There are also many good wells along Threelick run in Collins Settlement and a few wells in Skin Creek The best producing wells are in Freeman's Creek and Court House districts where the volume is great and the rock pressure heavy. In Hacker's Creek district the volume is usually light—1,000,000 to 10,000,000 cubic feet at the most—but the rock pressure is unusually heavy. As early as 1900 Lewis County was regarded as being the center of the largest gas field in the world. The opinion of experts as to the value of the field has not been changed in the twenty years that has elapsed since that time. Further developments must come; more wells will have to be drilled in all sections of the territory before the supply of gas in Lewis County is nearly exhausted. There is a vast territory which is as yet no more than barely touched. The successful completion of a number of wells at Frenchton and the surface indications farther south and west indicate that all of Lewis County is gas territory.

CHAPTER XXX.

THE TWENTIETH CENTURY

Just as the developments and problems of the period from 1880 to 1900 were largely influenced by the completion of the railroad to Weston, so the developments and problems of the past two decades have largely resulted from the discovery of oil and gas in the county. In some respects the period showed great progress in the social and economic life of the people; but new problems have arisen which are now only partly solved.

The effects of the oil and gas developments upon the agricultural interests of the county were extremely harmful. In 1900 Lewis County ranked as one of the foremost stock raising counties of the state, standing second only to Harrison in the cattle industry. The abundant royalties for oil and the rentals and payments for wells in the gas fields gave the farmers sufficient income to maintain a comfortable existence without the back-breaking labor of cutting briars, digging out hickory bushes and building fences. The well-to-do farmers moved to the towns where they could enjoy the conveniences of better schools, better churches, and comparative leisure. Farmers' sons, who would otherwise have operated the farms when their fathers retired, had found the high wages paid by the oil and gas companies a greater incentive than the opportunities to develop the old farm and keep it producing. Farm labor was scarce and the prices were almost beyond the reach of the farmers owing to the competition of the oil and gas companies. The terrible condition of the roads which came as a result of the oil and gas development made the marketing of produce difficult and spoiled much of the attractiveness of country life. The drilling of a well on a farm was discouraging to the owner of the surface, for the location might be made in the middle of his meadow, and a road, which might be ten feet or a hundred feet in width, led to it from the highway. Aside from the actual damage to the land, fences were torn down, gates left open, and the existence of the careful farmer was in various ways made burdensome.

The result was that many of the best farms in the oil and gas territory were allowed to grow up in briars and bushes. The owners or tenants continued to live in the farmhouses, to cut the hay from the meadows, to rent out the pasture to cattle dealers for what they could get, and sometimes to cultivate a small corn patch in addition to the garden. Little attention was given to improving the breeds of cattle and sheep, to the selection of seed or to other important features of progressive farming which had gradually been built up in previous decades. The acreage in corn in Lewis County decreased twenty-five per cent in the decade from 1900 to 1910.

The farmers who stuck to their business increased their wealth through the ready market for their grain and produce which the oil and gas development created. Court House and Freeman's Creek districts increased greatly in population in the ten years from 1900 to 1910, and the increase is wholly due to the immigration of workers into the oil and gas fields. The country storekeepers and blacksmiths shared with the farmers in the prosperity.

In Weston the effects of the oil and gas development were immediately evident in the larger volume of business, in the increase of population, and in the development for the first time of a really extensive manufacturing industry. By 1902 it was estimated that the oil business had added five hundred people to the population of the town. Twelve oil well supply stores had been established, and an extensive pipe line yard had been set aside. The capacity of the livery barns in existence in 1900 was insufficient for the needs of the hundreds of teams engaged in hauling supplies, and many new barns were built. East of the town the Weston Glass Company was erecting a plant. East Weston had been surveyed and lots were offered for sale. In 1902 the Bank of Weston and the Lewis County Bank were established to share the business which had greatly increased in volume.

The manufacture of glass in Weston began in 1902 directly as a result of the discovery of gas in the county. The location of the glass manufacturing industry depends primarily upon a cheap and plentiful supply of natural gas in the vicinity of deposits of glass sands, and good transportation facilities for the product. Weston is rather well fitted to be a center of the industry.

The East Weston factory was built and equipped for the making of glass tile by a new process. It was claimed that the company was the holder of the only patent for a wholly satisfactory glass tile, because other processes either made an inferior piece of work or there was too great a proportion of breakage in manufacture. The factory was in operation about five years, giving employment to about fifty men, until it suspended operations on account of excessive breakage. In 1912 the company was reorganized for the manufacture of glassware specialties, but about the time the factory was ready to be opened again it was completely destroyed by fire.

In 1904 the Crescent Window Glass Company was incorporated with a capital stock of $125,000. The first plant was erected immediately. A second plant, more complete than the first, was placed in operation in 1907. The old plant was completely destroyed by fire in February, 1913, but it was immediately rebuilt. It has remained the premier manufacturing industry of Weston. The Bastow plant, now known as the Lewis County factory, was placed in operation about 1910 for the manufacture of glassware specialties.

The oil and gas development led to the establishment of other plants not directly dependent on gas for fuel, and to the enlargement of older industries. The Sun Lumber Company, the Weston Lumber Company and the Danser Manufacturing and Supply Company were all incorporated in 1904 or 1905. One effect of the industrial awakening was to increase the population of the suburbs of Weston. Homewood was established near the Crescent plant. The building of houses in the narrow Polk creek valley was begun, which has resulted in the present string more than a mile long. Kitsonville and Haleville were more closely built up. In 1913 the McGary addition was opened. Some of the old houses inside the limits of the town were removed and more modern dwellings or apartment houses were erected in their places. The town soon bore an appearance of business prosperity such as it had never before enjoyed.

A consequence of the oil and gas development which was not so pleasing to the better class of citizens of Weston was the establishment of gambling joints which ran wide open in the heart of the town. "Faro, roulette, craps and poker were in full tilt day and night," and many a man, after he had been made drunk by the free whiskey dispensed in the places, imagined that he could break the game; but invariably he left penniless. Several frequenters of the joints lost thousands of dollars.

Jane Lew became an important shipping point for gas well supplies after active operations were begun in the vicinity. Much of the casing for the wells on Kincheloe creek, McCann's run, Hacker's creek and the surrounding regions, as well as pipe for lines through the vicinity were unloaded in the Jane Lew yards. In 1906 Jane Lew had excellent prospects of securing a glass factory. A lot sale was held to open an important tract almost as large as the area of the town. The village wa incorporated in 1907, for the purpose of forestalling future efforts to license saloons there. The increase in population since that time has justified the move. Street lights, sidewalks and other minor improvements have

JUDGE HENRY BRANNON

been made by the town authorities. At present there is a franchise under consideration by the council for the construction of waterworks. The Bank of Jane Lew was established in 1903, and the Peoples Bank in 1911. The construction of the trolley line added to the prosperity of the town and made certain its future.

Rumors of another railroad to Weston were in the air as early as 1901. A right of way was being secured up the river from Clarksburg as far as Goodhope. Later, surveys were made from east to west—from Roaring creek to the Little Kanawha river, to locate a route popularly supposed to be for the Wabash, which was reported to have purchased the Western Maryland railroad. The route finally decided upon for the western extension of the Western Maryland lines was constructed by the Davis-Elkins interests as the Coal and Coke railroad. It passed through Collins Settlement district from one end to the other. Entering the county from Braxton at Orlando, it followed Clover fork almost to its head, passed through a long tunnel to the valley of the West Fork near Jacksonville, and continued up that stream and its left fork past Walkersville and Crawford to French creek in Upshur County.

The road was 175 miles long in all, connecting Charleston and Elkins, and forming the only north and south line from the Great Kanawha to the Monongahela valleys in the central part of the state. It taps some of the finest timber and coal lands to be found anywhere in the state.

The Coal and Coke railroad has been of great value in the development of Collins Settlement district. The products of the southern part of the county can find their way to eastern markets. Before the construction of the railroad most of the agricultural produce was consumed at home. Dairying and fruit growing on a commercial basis were impossible because the local demand for the products was not great enough to justify the expense. Much timber land on the upper course of the West Fork had remained undeveloped because it was unprofitable to haul the lumber to Arnold.

Immediately upon the beginning of the construction work in the fall of 1903 there was a market for dairy products, poultry and truck in the construction crews along the route. The two tunnels caused two large towns to grow up with hundreds of laborers, doctors, timekeepers, merchants and other hangers-on. Nor was all the sudden prosperity confined to the tar paper towns. Jacksonville, Walkersville, Crawford and Orlando awoke to new life.

After the grading had been finished and the track laid in 1906 the laborers abandoned the shacks which were torn down. Jacksonvile relapsed into its accustomed somnolence. Other communities took advantage of their opportunities. A lot sale was held at Orlando which resulted in the building of homes for a large additional population. Enterprising citizens incorporated a wholesale produce and commission house, and a representative of the new company was soon on the road. Blake and Chapman, both flag stations, afforded a means of travel for the people of Clover fork. Wymer and Jewell were also established as flag stations on the Left fork of the river.

The first extensive development of coal in the county was begun as a result of the construction of the Coal and Coke railroad. A party of Pennsylvania capitalists formed the Jacksonville Coal and Coke Company in 1906 and purchased the farm of R. W. Crawford at the mouth of Indian Cap run, and the mineral rights on the Reger farm farther up the run. A long siding was put in, a tipple constructed, and considerable coal was mined. A mining village quickly grew up in the old meadow, which usurped the rights as a flag station which had been given to a strip of meadow land near Jacksonville. The new village was called Emmart in honor of one of the officials of the company. The Elk Lick vein of coal which the company operated was tilted away from the mouth of the mine, and this fact made the drainage problem one of great difficulty. Some trouble also was experienced in selling the product on account of the extremely high ash content (14.95%). Failure to sell additional stock and to obtain credit to make needed improvements caused the company to suspend operations. The land again reverted to agriculture, though a small village still remains there.

Walkersville, as a result of the building of the railroad, soon entered upon a period of prosperity. The old rivalry between the village and Crawford had continued, the advantage resting now with one now with the other. At the time of the completion of the railroad Crawford seemed the more promising place, and it was selected by the railroad company as the site of the only regular station between Frenchton and Orlando. Walkersville was to be a flag station, the company giving as a reason the lack of funds to build a depot. The citizens of Walkersville raised by subscription sufficient funds to erect a standard station, and the railroad company, perhaps unwillingly, sent an agent there to occupy it. The energy of the people and the superior location soon turned the scales in favor of Walkersville. Besides being the natural shipping point for Ireland, Duffy and all the other territory on the Right fork, it enjoyed a good local trade.

The lumber industry on the Right fork has been exceedingly important. Immediately upon the completion of the Coal and Coke railroad, the sawmill site of W. E. Mick and Son below Arnold was abandoned and the mill moved to Walkersville, nearer the location of the timber supply. Many thousands of logs were brought from the upper valley of the Right fork by means of a wooden tramway until the distance became so great that the wooden tramway was no longer practicable. The Micks determined to build a narrow gauge railroad, and incorporated the Walkersville and Ireland Railroad Company in 1907. The work was partly financed by two Grafton business men who had large timber holdings in the district to be tapped by the railroad. Within a few months the railroad was completed to Ireland and log trains were running.

The people of Ireland, who had begun to receive shipments of merchandise over the new road, looked forward to the time when passenger service would be inaugurated. The owners of the road took advantage of the opportunity to be of real service to the community. During the winter of 1907-8 some mechanical genius of Ireland constructed a passenger car on a lumber truck. The result could hardly be compared with a Pullman, but it served the purpose for which it was built. From the time of its completion it made one or more trips daily. The train stopped wherever there was a passenger to board it or a basket of eggs to be taken to market. Conductor H. O. Wilson obligingly marketed farm produce and executed orders for groceries, delivering the goods at the proper stop and blowing the whistle to announce the fact. The road was a great convenience.

Subsequently W. E. Mick and Son acquired complete ownership of the Walkersville and Ireland railroad. As the supply of marketable trees became exhausted they extended it first to Duffy, then to Bablin, then to Ingo, from which point they "went in" to wildest Upshur. The mill was moved from one terminus to the other following the progress of the road. Walkersville did not suffer from the removal of the mill. It was still the junction of two railroads of different gauges and there was plenty of work for several men in transferring the goods from one road to the other. The narrow gauge railroad has meant much to Duffy, Bablin and the whole "Shoestring". As the heavy timber was removed from the hills along Glady creek and the left fork of the Little Kanawha river, the underbrush has been removed also and farms have succeeded the primeval forest. The lumber jack has been followed by the permanent settler, and the last frontier of Lewis County has been passed. The whole of the county may now be said to have become improved land after the lapse of almost a century and a half from the date of the first settlement in the Hacker's creek valley.

As was expected Arnold lost nearly all its importance as a shipping point for the southern part of the county. The exception is in the case of live stock. The stock dealers of the section regarded the facilities of the Baltimore and Ohio as superior to those of the Coal and Coke, and continued to drive their stock to Arnold and Roanoke.

Plans have been made at various times by the Baltimore and Ohio company to improve the branch line leading into Webster and Nicholas counties. Surveys had been made, both along the old line and from the mouth of French creek to Centralia. The latter route, if adopted, would have eliminated the grades from Weston to the main line. Early in 1917 the Baltimore and Ohio purchased the controlling interest in the Coal and Coke, which thereafter became the Charleston division of the Baltimore and Ohio. The deal has solved many of the problems of the older road. Heavy freight from Richwood and way points is routed over the Coal and Coke from Orlando to Sago, thus avoiding the heavy grades on Oil creek and on Buckhannon mountain. Empty cars are sent from Grafton via Clarksburg and Weston, thus giving what is in effect a double track from Grafton to Orlando. The condition of the old roadbed along Oil creek has led to a proposal to abandon it and construct a short stretch of railroad from Arnold to connect with the Charleston division near Jacksonville.

The purchase of the Coal and Coke has enhanced the importance of Weston as a railroad center. The shops have had rather more work to do. Late in 1919 some of the principal offices of the Charleston division were moved from Gassaway to Weston.

Demand for street car service to Clarksburg followed the oil boom. In 1902 the Clarksburg and Weston Street Car Company was incorporated to build a line from Weston to connect with the Fairmont and Clarksburg lines. Delays followed. Franchises were secured from the Harrison County court for the construction of a track via West Milford. After more delays the company abandoned its intention of building the line up the river, and built a stretch of track to Mt. Clare. In 1912 the Monongahela Valley Traction Company was organized and it took up the work in earnest. Franchises were secured from the county court of Lewis, and from the city of Weston. The route from Mt. Clare via Lost Creek, Jane Lew and Jackson's Mill was determined upon, the right of way was obtained and construction work began immediately. The road was well constructed throughout. The first car arrived at Jane Lew, 26 July 1913, and at Weston shortly afterward. The service rendered by the company was rather poor for some time owing to overloading the wires, but the difficulty was solved by the installation of additional power plants.

The effects of the construction of the interurban line were seen at once. Weston was placed within an hour and a half of Clarksburg and the main line of the Baltimore and Ohio. Many Weston people took advantage of the opportunity to do their shopping in Clarksburg to the great disgust of the business men of Weston. The competition of the Clarksburg merchants was, in the long run, of great advantage to the people of the town and the local merchants as well, for it compelled Weston merchants to keep more up-to-date stocks of goods. The completion of the trolley line to Weston led to the revival of the proposal to connect Glenville with the outside world and in 1915, the Kanawha Traction and Electric company was incorporated by Weston business men. Officials of the Monongahela Valley lines inspected the proposed route, and the extension for a time seemed a matter of course to the people of the western Freeman's Creek district.

The old fair ground owned by Mrs. Minnich was cut up into town lots and sold about the time construction work on the interurban line really indicated that it would be built. The cheap means of communication has made Shadybrook a thickly settled suburb. The broad meadow at Turner stop has also been built up to some extent. The tract of land on which stood the Jackson homestead and Jackson's mill was purchased by the traction company for use as a memorial park. A bridge was soon afterward constructed across the river at that point by the county court. The park has become a favorite picnic ground for the people of Weston and surrounding points. The location has made Jackson's Mill a shipping point for oil well supplies for the Freeman's creek field. Tank cars convey from the siding there the product of the gasoline plant at the mouth of Freeman's creek. Below Jackson's mill the trolley nears the site of Westfield, which may after all be a town. Jane Lew has received a large accession of population as a result of the trolley, and the further growth of the town is assured. Some years ago, when an extension of the line to Buckhannon was being urged by Upshur citizens, the people of Hacker's creek and Jane Lew began a movement to have the line go by way of Hacker's creek and Buckhannon run. All the territory along the trolley line has been built up and the farms have been improved.

The great war led to considerable activity in the development of coal in Lewis County. For the first time since the construction of the Baltimore and Ohio railroad the principal movement of coal was from the county and not to the county. The operations on Stone Coal creek were continued until the close of the war when the mines were temporarily closed. At the close of 1919 preparations are being made by the Coal Land Development Company to open a mine just below Brownsville and to operate it on the co-operative plan. Preliminary construction, including a ventilating shaft, slope, spur track and the surveying of a town site at the mouth of Washburn run, has been completed.

Beginning about 1901, most of the coal lands of the

county available for quick development have passed out of the hands of the farmers. Much of the coal on Fink creek, Leading creek and other sections has been purchased by large corporations.

The chief political movement of importance in the twentieth century was the campaign against licensing saloons. The prohibition movement had been a factor in politics from 1869, when a prohibition ticket was elected to fill the offices of Weston. The victory was not long enjoyed. In the country districts the saloons were gradually forced out of business by the increase of federal and state license fees. The sentiment of the people of the county in 1888, when the vote on the prohibition amendment was taken is shown by the vote of 983 for and 1082 against. In 1890 the conditions following the construction of the railroad resulted in a movement to abolish saloons in Weston. Speakeasies sprang up on all sides, and after a brief period of ineffectual enforcement of the law, the regulated traffic was restored. The oil and gas boom brought another wave of vice and crime. By 1904 prohibition sentiment was shown to be very strong when J. G. Jackson, candidate on the prohibition ticket for county commissioner, ran second only to the Republican candidate. Though the election was hardly a fair test owning to the personal popularity of Mr. Jackson and other issues, yet it showed that considerable anti-saloon sentiment existed. In 1906 J. W. Duncan, an avowed anti-license candidate, was elected on the Republican ticket. A brief period without saloons followed, and licenses were again granted. The election of E. M. Stalnaker in 1908 made certain the triumph of the prohibition forces, and on 1 July 1909 the saloon passed out of Lewis County. The vote of the people on the prohibition amendment submitted in 1912 was 3,264 for and 700 against.

In 1909, following much heated discussion concerning the license question and public utilities, a new charter was granted to Weston by the Legislature. Aside from extending the term of the mayor, doubling the number of councilmen and calling the corporation the "City of Weston" instead of the "Town of Weston", there were few changes from the old charter. It failed to include any of the numerous suburbs or to improve the form of government to any great degree. Sentiment for a new charter which will place the government of the city in the hands of a commission has been increasing. McGary Addition, North Weston, Kitsonville and a part of East Weston have recently been included in the city. In 1913 the people of Polk creek, Shadybrook and Haleville voted on a proposition to incorporate a new town to include all three suburbs. Fortunately the movement failed; all three suburbs are part and parcel of the social and economic life of Weston, and should take part in the political life of the city.

Though Weston has always been one of the most progressive communities in the state, though it has many modern improvements, yet the municipal government has not approached the limit of service to the people. The fire department should be reorganized; the flood waters of Stone Coal and Polk creek should be controlled in some way; a garbage reduction plant and refuse crematory plant should be built; a sewage disposal plant is a pressing need of the people; aid should be given in the establishment of a hospital; and better sanitary arrangements should be made in other ways to protect the health of the people. Once these improvements have been taken up, the citizens, by a community effort, will establish a Y. M. C. A. and a public library. One of the business needs of the city is a chamber of commerce. Good work has been done by the Rotary club, but that organization should be supported by an association of business men with an energetic secretary.

The setback in agriculture which followed the oil and gas development was only temporary. A revival of interest took place about 1911, which has increased until farmers in all sections of the county are taking up scientific farming as never before. The passage of the Jewell bill in 1905 which provided that beef furnished to state institutions should be inspected both on foot and dressed, created a home market for Lewis County cattle. Though the act was soon removed from the statute books, its influence continued to be felt for some years. The establishment of a stock farm at Crawford by E. G. Davisson, who kept only purebred stock, gave a great impetus to the pure bred stock industry in the southern part of the county. The Halls, the Laws, C. L. Cookman, W. R. Jewell and numerous others did much to awaken interest in pure bred stock in other sections. The telephone, rural mail delivery and the automobile have made country life more pleasant. The farms gradually came into the possession of men interested in agriculture. The fields which had been allowed to grow up in filth were cleared again, the broken fences repaired and the land was again productive.

The year 1911 will long be remembered in the agricultural history of the United States because of the failure of the hay crop. Farmers, unable to winter their stock, shipped them to markets where they entered into competition with many more than the usual number The result was that prices fell steadily. By fall the live stock raisers of Lewis County faced the alternative of selling their cattle at ruinous prices or having them underfed the next winter. In the emergency several farmers in different sections of the county determined to build silos, and thus secure the greatest possible food value from their corn crops. From the small beginning, the construction of silos has been extended until scores have been built, and more are being added every year. Greater attention to scientific methods of feeding stock and to the use of fertilizers has followed.

One of the first measures taken to revive interest in agriculture was the organization of boys' and girls' clubs by Perry G. Alfred in 1907-08. The work has been continued, largely under his direction until taken over by a paid agent of the government in 1919. In 1914 the Lewis County Agricultural Association was organized with John W. Smith as president and Perry G. Alfred as secretary. The purpose of the association was to remove obstacles to the development of agriculture and to improve conditions on Lewis County farms through united efforts. Co-operative purchasing of supplies was begun. In 1917, as a result of considerable agitation by members of the association, the county court agreed to pay part of the salary of a county farm bureau agent who should devote his entire time to the work. D. W. Parsons was the first agent.

By far the greatest contribution of the agricultural association to the county has been the inauguration of a policy of building permanent roads. In order to avoid the necessity of having to travel over roads which had been condemned in winter because they were unsafe, members of the association secured the passage of a special act by the Legislature enabling the county court of Lewis County to lay a levy of twenty-five cents on the hundred dollars for the construction of permanent roads. The county court, after much consideration, laid the levy, and in the spring of 1916 construction began on the four main roads leading out of Weston. Since that time a short stretch has been added each year. In 1916 it was proposed to bond the county for $1,000,000 for the construction of permanent roads, but the movement failed. Proposals have also been made in several of the magisterial districts to issue bonds for the construction of brick or concrete roads.

In keeping with the educational progress of the state, Lewis County has made improvements in schools. At Weston two small brick buildings on the corner of Court and Third, with the addition of several ramshackle wooden structures, remained the educational plant of the town until 1911. Efforts were made as early as 1904 to provide for the erection of a modern high school building through a bond issue, but the people were apathetic.

In 1910, after the bond issue had been defeated several times, the citizens of the district finally voted to issue bonds to the amount of $75,000 for the erection of a high school and three suburban buildings. Improvement in the instruction of the schools has followed the erection of new buildings.

The board of education of the Jane Lew independent district established a high school in 1912 which has steadily improved both in quantity and quality of instruction. During the administration of M. L. B. Linger as county superintendent, 1911-1915, efforts were made to establish high schools in most of the magisterial districts. The voters failed to authorize the expenditures. The fact that three of the districts meet at Weston and that the railroad connections of the others make for division of territory, has prevented agreement as to the site to be chosen in any of the districts.

Three citizens of Lewis County have recently published books which deserve notice. In 1900, Frances Moore Bland published "Twilight Reveries," a collection of poems which has been favorably received by the critics. In 1915, the history of the settlements in the upper West Fork and Buckhannon valleys was told in an interesting way by Lucullus Virgil McWhorter in his "Border Settlers of Northwestern Virginia." The book is the product of years of patient research and is a very distinct contribution to the historical literature dealing with the American frontier. A scholarly work which is appreciated far more by students of the political history of the country than by the people of the county is Judge Henry Brannon's exhaustive study of the Fourteenth Amendment. It is one of the most important contributions made in recent years to American political thought. Besides the publication of this work, he has also made a contribution of national importance to the development of legal knowledge. The decisions of the West Virginia Supreme Court of Appeals on questions affecting leaseholds, most of which were written by him, have been adopted by the courts of other states where oil development came at a later time than in West Virginia.

Progress was made also in the religious organization of the county. All the denominations represented at Weston have erected new churches within the past generation. Jane Lew has two brick churches which should be the pride of the town. Improvements have been made in many of the churches in the country, and in some of the less well organized communities new churches have been built. Higher salaries are now being paid to pastors in all parts of the county. The organization of the Lewis County Sunday School Association early in the century has caused an increased interest in Sunday school work and has broken down denominational prejudice to some extent.

A student of Lewis County history thirty years from now will probably come to the conclusion that the life of the people of the county in the year 1919 was rather crude and old-fashioned. Though great developments have already taken place, others must come in the future. Lewis County seems now to stand on the threshold of a new era of social development greater than any it has yet experienced.

APPENDIX A

SKETCH OF COLONEL CHARLES LEWIS

Lewis County, whose pioneers made a brilliant record in the Revolution and the Indian wars which succeeded it, was appropriately named for Colonel Charles Lewis. Of all the Indian fighters of Virginia he was perhaps the most intrepid in time of danger, the most tireless in pursuit and the most skillful in planning a campaign. He had no peer among the scouts on the border. Fifty years after his death there were few families in Northwestern Virginia in which the name and deeds of Charles Lewis were not familiar household words.

Colonel Lewis, like most of the people of western Virginia, was of Scotch-Irish descent. He was born in Virginia a short time after the emigration of his parents to the New World in 1730. In 1733 his father settled near the present site of Staunton in what is now Augusta County, Virginia. The pioneer home of the Lewises was then on the most western frontier of Virginia, and the primeval forests surrounded it on every side. Young Charles Lewis during his early life was inured to the perils and hardships of the wilderness. From his earliest recollections he had been taught to fear and hate the Indians. As soon as he was old enough he entered the service of the Virginia colony against the French and Indians, and it is said that from the time of his first enlistment until the date of his death he was never out of the service a whole year. In the French and Indian war, he was regarded as one of the most promising young officers in the Virginia service. When Lord Dunmore led his expedition against the Ohio Indians Charles Lewis was in command of one of the regiments in the army of his brother, General Andrew Lewis.

When the Virginia army was surprised by the Indians at Point Pleasant Colonel Lewis formed his men hastily, and without taking time to remove the red coat which he was wearing, he led his men to repel the assault. His conspicuous dress made him an easy target for the Indian marksmen, and he fell mortally wounded at the first onset. Against his will he was removed to his tent where he expired within a few hours.

Withers, in his "Border Warfare", pays the following tribute to the hero of the battle of Point Pleasant: "Few officers were ever more, or more deservedly, endeared to those under their command than Col. Charles Lewis. In the many skirmishes, which it was his fortune to have with the Indians he was uncommonly successful; and in the various scenes of life, thro' which he passed, his conduct was invariably marked by the distinguished characteristicks of a mind, of no ordinary stamp. His early fall on this bloody field, was severely felt during the whole engagement; and to it has been attributed the partial advantages gained by the Indian army near the commencement of the action."

APPENDIX B

JUSTICES OF THE PEACE UNDER VIRGINIA

Appointed by the Governor

Name	Date of Commission
Philip Reger	13 Jan. 1817
Thomas Cunningham	13 Jan. 1817
John Hacker	13 Jan. 1817
William Powers	13 Jan. 1817
John Bozarth	13 Jan. 1817
Daniel Stringer	13 Jan. 1817
John Jackson	13 Jan. 1817
John Mitchell	13 Jan. 1817
William Hacker	13 Jan. 1817
William Simms	13 Jan. 1817
William Peterson	13 Jan 1817
Abner Abbott	13 Jan. 1817
John Hardman	13 Jan. 1817
George Bozarth	13 Jan. 1817
Elijah Newlon	13 Jan. 1817
Peyton Byrne	13 Jan. 1817
Jacob Lorentz	13 Jan. 1817
Samuel L. Jones	13 Jan. 1817
James Keith	13 Jan. 1817
James M. Camp	13 Jan. 1817
Nicholas Gibson	8 April 1817
Asa Squires	8 April 1817
Benjamin Riddel	8 April 1817
Daniel Stout	8 April 1817
Michael Stump Jr	8 April 1817
John McWhorter	8 April 1817
David Smith	8 April 1817
George Bush	8 April 1817
Joseph McCoy	8 April 1817

LIST OF JUSTICES

Beniah Maze	8 April 1817
David W. Sleeth	8 April 1817
Robert Young	18 July 1818
Aaron Smith	18 July 1818
Edward Jackson	18 July 1818
Weeden Hoffman	1 June 1820
William I. Davis	20 September 1822
Thomas Bland	17 November 1824
Martial Lazell	15 December 1824
Levi Maxwell	9 March 1826
Richard P. Camden	6 March 1828
James Bennett	7 July 1830
John Vincent	1 March 1831
Elias Lowther	1 March 1831
Thomas C. Hinzman	5 March 1833
David Bennett	5 March 1833
Jesse Cunningham	5 March 1833
Alexander Huffman	4 June 1833
Samuel L. Hays	4 June 1833
Simon Rohrbough	4 June 1833
Jacob J. Jackson	7 October 1834
Minter Bailey	6 November 1834
Newton B. Barnes	13 September 1836
James Malone	13 September 1836
David Hall	29 July 1837
Salathiel G. Stalnaker	29 July 1838
Daniel Ayres	9 October 1838
Matthew Holt	8 September 1840
John Lorentz	8 September 1840
Alexander S. Withers	8 September 1840
William A. Lowther	8 September 1840
Currence B. Conrad	8 September 1840
Richard Dobson	8 September 1840
David S. Haselden	8 September 1840
William Bennett	8 September 1840
John Crawford	2 July 1841
George A. Jackson	2 July 1841
William Morrison	2 July 1841

Philip Cox Jr. .... 16 August 1843
Robert S. Beeson .... 16 August 1843
Allen Simpson .... 16 August 1843
Robert Ervin .... 16 August 1843
John J. Burr .... 9 August 1844
Festus Young .... 9 August 1844
George Bastable, Jr. .... 9 August 1844
John F. W. Holt .... 9 August 1844
Blackwell Jackson .... 9 August 1844
James Bunten .... 9 August 1844
William J. Bailey .... 9 August 1844
James N. Norman .... 9 August 1844
Adam Spitler .... 20 July 1846
John W. Marple .... 20 July 1846
David Bennett .... 20 July 1846
Amos Brooks .... 20 July 1846
John White .... 20 July 1846
William J. Bland .... 20 July 1846
Jesse Woofter .... 20 July 1846
Felix L. Hale .... 20 July 1846
Henry Steinbeck .... 20 July 1846
Joseph Darlington .... 9 August 1849
Alexander K. Holloway .... 9 August 1849
Kosciusko Hopkins .... 9 August 1849
George Clark .... 9 August 1849
William Gibson .... 9 August 1849
George I. Marsh .... 9 August 1849
Richard B. Hall .... 9 August 1849
Presley McIntire .... 9 August 1849
Jesse Bouse .... 9 August 1849

LIST OF JUSTICES

Elected by the People Under the Constitution of 1851.

First District (now Collins Settlement)

1852	1856	1860
George T. Duvall	Jesse Cunningham	James Bruffey
John Crawford	John Crawford	Marshall Clark
Robert Clark	William A. Watson	William A. Watson
Porter M. Arnold	Porter M. Arnold	Porter M. Arnold

Second District (now Skin Creek and Court House)

1852	1856	1860
John McWhorter	Thomas S. Wood	Jesse Woofter
William W. Warder	Jacob J. Jackson	William C. Compton
David Hall	David Hall	John W. McCoy
Jesse Woofter	Hanson M. Peterson	Hanson M. Peterson

Third District (now Hacker's Creek with the addition of Gee Lick and Polk Creek)

1852	1856	1860
Allen Simpson	Blackwell Jackson	Mansf'd McWhorter
Blackwell Jackson	John Talbott	Maxwell W. Ball
Thomas C. Hinzman	Philip Reger	Thomas C. Hinzman
John Starcher	Allen Simpson	Isaac P. McBride

Fourth District (Freeman's Creek and Leading Creek)

1852	1856	1860
Vincent Alexander	Vincent Alexander	Henry Steinbeck
Israel Ramsburg	Henry Steinbeck	Thomas Rogers
William Woofter	Reuben A. Kemper	Richard B. Hall
Marcellus White	Isaac Woofter	Jacob Clipstine

INDEX.

Aberdeen Angus cattle introduced ... 377
Abram's Run, settled, 139; development ... 204
Alfred, F. J. ... 314
Alfred, Perry G. ... 410
Alkire, Nicholas ... 201
Alum Bridge ... 379, 382
Andersons come to county ... 204
Anderson, John S. ... 317
Anti-slavery sentiment ... 283
Arms of Pioneers ... 119
Arnold Station, established, 378; decline ... 405
Arnold, George ... 142
Arnold, George J., ... 205, 233, 235, 327, 345
Arnold, Porter M., killed ... 306
Arnold, William E., 233, 235, 327
Asbury, Bishop Francis, quoted ... 114, 120, 126
Austin ... 346
Averill, General ... 313

Bablin ... 404
Bailey House, established, 185; new building ... 226
Bailey, Carr ... 144, 161
Bailey, Minter, establishes Weston Hotel, 185; delinquent lands commissioner, 231; partnership with Camdens. 232; Weston hospital ... 327, 329
Bald Eagle murdered ... 45
Baltimore and Ohio R. R. construction, 352; leases West Virginia and Pittsburgh R. R., 365; absorbs Coal and Coke R. R. ... 405
Baptists, 126; Broad Run. 159; Freeman's Creek, 144; Murphy's creek, 202; Mt. Zion, 263; Weston, ... 344
Barbour Co. formed ... 240
Barnes, Dr. N. B., 194, 202, 331
Barrett, S. E. ... 382, 284
Bastow factory ... 399
Battelle township formed, 317; disfranchisement in, 320; schools ... 350
Batton, Thomas H. ... 180
Beall's Mills, 346; oil ... 391
Beech Fort ... 65
Beeghley, John ... 373

Bendale bridge ... 252, 303
Bennett, Jonathan M., 194; land speculator, 233; Mayor of Weston, 247; president Exchange bank, 257; and state hospital, 260; First Auditor of Virginia, 286; returns to county ... 320
Bennett, Louis ... 351
Bennett, William ... 139, 204
Bennett, Wm. G., ... 358
Berlin ... 345
Big Skin creek ... 134
Bland, Frances M. ... 412
Bland, Meigs ... 351
Bland, Thomas ... 187-273
Bland, Wm. J., 194, 294; at hospital ... 327
Boggess, Caleb ... 289, 327
Bond, Samuel ... 203
Bott, Henry ... 133
Bouse, Isaac ... 204
Bowen, Capt. Lot ... 310, 312
Boyd, E. W. ... 382
Brake, William ... 306
Brannon, Henry, clerk of supervisors, 317; railroad, 357; author and jurist ... 412
Brannon, John ... 225, 327, 363
Braxton Co. formed ... 240
Bridges ... 219, 224, 251, 336, 375
British stir up Indians ... 52
Broad run ... 201
Broad Run church ... 159
Brooks, Amos ... 283
Brown, John ... 284
Brownsville, settlement, 135; postoffice, 377; coal, ... 407
Buckhannon, attacked by Indians, 67, 82; established as town ... 158
Buckhannon and Little Kanawha turnpike ... 250
Buckhannon and West Fork R. R. Co. ... 361
Buckhannon valley, settled, 32; discontent ... 243
Buffaloes ... 19
Buggies introduced ... 264
Bulltown massacre ... 45
Bunten's Mill ... 347
Burnside, John ... 183
Bush, Adam ... 143
Bush, George ... 143, 167
Bush, John ... 76
Bush Michael G. ... 134, 203, 273
Bush's fort ... 55
Bush's Mills, 131; P. O. ... 203
Bushwhackers ... 304

INDEX

	Page
Butcher, Gasper	288
Butcher, Paulser	146
Butcher's fork	390
Byrne, John	139
Cabins	112
Camden	226
Camden-on-Gauley	366
Camden, Bailey and Camden	232-38
Camden, G. D.	232, 347
Camden, Henry	139
Camden, Johnson N.	327, 356, 363, 366
Camden, R. P.	182, 232
Camden, T. B.	331
Camden well	385
Camp, James M.	173, 180, 231
Canning fruit	265
Canoe Run	293, 384
Carbon factories	394
Carnifex Ferry, battle	304
Carouthers, John	205
Catholics	235, 237, 255, 344
Cattle	103, 211, 264, 339, 376, 410
Chalfant, F. M.	291, 317, 338
Chapman	402
Chenoweth, Lemuel	224
Cheuvront, Rev. Joseph	125
Chidester, G. M.	377
Chidester, Phemeno	205
Churchville, settlement	148, 378, 383
Civil War	281-310
Clarksburg P. O., 154; impedes railroad	355
Clarksburg, Weston and Glenville R. R.	357, 362
Clarksburg and Weston turnpike	247
Clawson, Rev. Samuel	209
Clover Fork	198, 204, 402
Coal	402, 407
Coal and Coke R. R.	401, 405
Collins, John	138
Collins, John	138
Collins Settlement, begun, 136; P. O., 204; in war, 294; district formed, 325; gas, 395. See Battelle township.	
Confederates, in county, 294; recruiting, 302; raiders,	308, 313
Conrad, James	321
Constitution of 1870	325
Constitutional Union party	286
Cook, D. B.	377
Cookman, C. L.	410
Copely well	388
Corley, James	321
Corn right	42
County Court, powers	88
Courthouse	173, 259
Court House district settled, 230; formed, 326: population, 398. See Sheridan township.	
Cox, Joseph	81
Cozad, Jacob	81, 127

	Page
Crane Camp	38
Crawford, 378, 395. See Bunten's mill.	
Crawford, Robert	140
Crawford, Robert, (son)	317
Crescent Glass Factory	399
Crook, George W.	350
Curl, Jeremiah	64
Curtis, Henry	131
Danser, George C.	259
Danser Mfg. Co.	400
Davis, P. O.	347
Davisson, E. G.	386, 395
Davisson, George I.	167
Davisson, George I.	346
Dawson, Preston	193
Deer	19
Delaware Indians	26
Democratic party	284, 321, 326
Dentists	341
Doddridge, Joseph	101
Doddridge Co., formed	242
Dorman, Timothy	67
Douglas, Stephen A.	287
Duffy, 404. See Little Wild Cat.	
Dunmore's War	44-48
Duvall, George T.	140
Duvall, John P.	71, 93, 121, 137, 142
Edmiston, Andrew	376
Education	268-280
Edwards, Thomas A.	341
Egan, Michael, quoted, 267; upholds flag, 288; raises company	295
Electric lights	370
Emmart	402
Episcopal church	255
Ervine, Robert	293
Eureka Pipe Line Co.	393
Exchange Bank, branch at Weston, 257; loyalty questioned, 285; funds confiscated,	300, 313
Fair	338
Feeney, Thomas	377
Fetty, Esais	317
Fink Creek, settled, 148; pasturage, 201; villages, 379; oil	383, 393
Fire Department	342
Fisher, Charles	144
Fisher, Elias	329
Fisher, George	202
Flesher, Elijah	193
Flesher, Henry, settles at Weston, 49; Indian attack, 73; shoots Indian 82; still	154
Flesher, Henry, (son)	178
Flesher, James	304
Flesher's Station	80
Flesher well	394
Flesherville	178

INDEX

Entry	Page
Flick amendment	324
Fort Stanwix, treaty	45
Fox, Robert	279
Francis, William	306
Freeman, Mrs.	59
Freeman's Creek, attack by Indians, 76; settlements, 143; expansion, 201; schools, 279; in Civil war, 293; district formed	325
French Creek	156, 283
Furniture of pioneers	114
Gambling	400
Garrett, Anthony	161
Gas, in Weston, 373; wells,	394
Gee Lick, 36; settled, 144; land patented, 198; church	264
Georgetown, 263; township formed	318
German immigrants	233, 236-8
Gibson, Smith	143
Gilmer Co. formed	241
Glady creek	404
Glass manufacture	397
Gooden, A. T. well	387
Goosepen run, settled	206
Granges	339
Guffey and Galey	389, 394
Hacker, John, 33; buffalo hunt, 38; characterization, 39; establishes mill	102
Hacker's creek, Indian remains, 23; settlements, 34; abandonment, 61; return, 63; Indian attacks, 54, 75; expansion, 150; in 1840, 200; in Civil war, 293; district formed,	325
Hale, A. C.	299
Hale, P. M., 261; a Wheeling convention, 291; secures troops, 299; establishes hat factory, 341; contractor	350
Haleville	359, 409
Hall, David	135
Hall, James A.	329
Hall, John S., quoted	270
Hall, Jonathan	135
Hall, Richard	143
Hall, Richard B.	317, 321
Hardman, Henry O.	131, 206
Hardman, Rev. John	133
Harmony church	158
Harpole, Daniel	157, 184, 202
Harrison, M. W.	358
Harrison County formed	85
Hartford	228
Haymond, Ben	305
Haymond, Calder	154
Hays, Perry	305
Hays, Samuel L.	244
Heavners come to county	203
Helmick, Daniel	189
Henry, William Y.	178
Herb Medicine Co.	368
Herefords introduced	339
Hills, Dr. R.	329
Hinzman, Thomas C.	151
Hitt, Robert	143
Hoffman, Weeden	181
Hogs	104, 343
Holden, Benjamin	161
Holt, Jonathan	202
Holt, Matthew	277
Home guards	307
Homewood	400
Hoover, Adam	145
Hope Natural Gas Co.	394
Horner, Charles A.	346
Horner, Seymour	362
Horse run	142
Hotels	185
Hudson, J. W.	291
Hughes, Elias, 37; at Point Pleasant, 49; moves to Ohio,	128
Hughes, Jesse, comes to Hacker's creek, 35; at Bulltown, 46; characterization, 57; wounds Indian, 60; night run to Buckhannon, 63; kills two Indians, 81; moves to Indiana	128
Hughes, Martha	74
Hurst	379
Hurst, John	148
Imboden, John D.	310
Indians, 22; trails, 26; wars	44ff
Indian camp, massacre	47
Indian Camp run	140, 402
Indian Carrying Place	27, 40
Ingo	404
Interurban trolley	405
Ireland, settled, 204; growth, 378; railroad,	404
Irish immigration, 233-238; in Civil war, 294; in politics,	324
Iroquois	25
Jackson, Blackwell, 200; in Virginia Senate	293
Jackson, Cummings	147
Jackson, Edward, 33, 146; candidate for legislature, 163; surveys site of Weston	176
Jackson, George, 33, 62; in Clark's army, 66; night run to Clarksburg, 68; in Virginia convention, 95; Collins settlement	137
Jackson, George A.	340
Jackson, Goodloe	408
Jackson, Henry	95
Jackson, James	300
Jackson, John	33
Jackson, John G.	171, 217
Jackson, S. P.	200
Jackson, Thomas J.	213, 295

INDEX

Jackson's Mill 407
Jacksonville, 138; 262, 279, 306; after war, 346; decline, 402. See also Collins Settlement.
Jacksonville Coal and Coke Co. 402
Jane Lew, surveyed, 200; improvements, 262; Federals in, 300; murder at 307; skirmish, 312; township formed, 317; after war, 345; railroad, 357; gas development, 400; interurban, 406; academy, 279; high school, 412;. See West's Fort and McWhorter's Mills.
Jenkins, A. G. 308
Jewell 402
Jewell, Albert 201
Johnson, Joseph 163, 175, 76, 182, 284
Johnson, Richard 134
Jones, General 310
Jones, Dr. Harriet B. 325

Keith, James 138
Kemper, Reuben 263
Kester, Alexander 184
Kierans, John 278
Kincheloe creek, 147; oil, ...387, 391, 393
Kitson, W. J. 331
Kitsonville 409
Koblegards 367
Ku Klux Klan 323
Kunst, A. H. 331, 358, 362

Landholding, conditions 42, 198, 231
Leading creek, settlement 149
Leatherbark run 139
Leib, Capt., quoted 305
Lewis, Col. Charles 414
Lewis County Oil and Gas Co. 382
Lewis County seminary ...254, 278
Life, John 151
Life, Noah 317
Life's Run 201
Lightburn 373
Lightburn, Benjamin 201
Lightburn J. A. J., at Wheeling, 291; military career 296
Lincoln, election of............ 287
Lincoln, township 318
Linger, M. L. B. 412
Linger, Nicholas 133
Linger, Philip 205
Literary fund 270-272
Little Kanawha 37, 404
Little Skin creek, explored.... 38
Little Wild Cat 347
Live Stock 102, 156
Lorentz, Jacob 153, 282
Lorentz, John 184
Lowther, Robert 35

Lowther, William, 36; appointed justice, 52; organizes company, 63; in Clark's army, 67; sheriff, 71; county lieutenant 80
Lumbering 339, 346, 359, 366, 377, 403

McCandlish, R. J.....257, 300, 327
McCann's run 143
McClellan, General 298
McClellan, J. H. 357
McCann, William 368
McGary addition 400, 409
McGary, W. B. 377
Macphelah cemetery 375
Mack, John 76
McKinley, William 303
McLaughlin, Addison 194
McWhorter, Henry 73, 102, 152
McWhorter, John, raises company, 157; candidate for legislature 163
McWhorter, L. V. 412
McWhorter, Mansfield 317
McWhorter's Mills, postoffice 200
Marsh, George I. 140, 317
Mathews, Stanley 302
Maxwell, Lewis, 176; surveys Jane Lew 200
Medical association 348
Methodists, first church, 124; in Collins settlement, 141; in Weston, 188; Lewis circuit 208, 263
Methodist Protestant church, formed, 208; in Weston.. 345
Mick, W. E. 403
Middle run settled 202
Militia, at West's Fort, 60; new regiment, 200; value of, 213; last muster 287
Minter, Joseph 193
Mitchell, Abner 140, 203
Mitchell, Rev. John.........65, 132, 134
Mitchell, Phoebe 279
Monongalia county created.... 52
Monongalia Navigation Co.......217
Monongahela Valley Traction Co. 406
Morrow, John 369
Mounds 22
Mt. Zion church 263
Mowing Machine introduced.. 338
Murphy's creek, land patented, 198; in Civil war 293
Murrin, Thomas D. 295
Musser, Tobias 349

Newlon, William 158
Newspaper in Weston 254
Nicholas County 239
Nicholes, John 145
Nicholes, William J............ 295
Norris, Richard 144

INDEX

	Page
North Weston	409
Northern and Southern W. Va. R .R.	353
Nutter's fort	49
O'Brien, Adam	40
Ohio Seventh	301
Oil	380ff
Oil creek, settled	204, 347, 380
Oldfield fork	390
Oliver, Geo. P.	191
Ordinance of Secession	290
Orlando, settled, 204; railroad,	378, 402
Owen, Benjamin	254
Peabody fund	351
Peddlers	207
Peoples Tel. Co.	374
Peterson, David S.	247
Peterson, Hanson M.	289
Peterson, Jasper	295, 377
Peterson, John P.	319, 329
Philadelphia Co.	394
Philippi, skirmish	298
Piano introduced	196
Pierpont, Francis H.	291, 299
Pierson, William G.	306
Pittsburgh, trade with	108
Plows	211, 264, 338
Point Pleasant, Battle	48
Polk creek, 145, 400; oil	385, 393
Poor farm	348
Porterfield, Col.	298
Postoffices in 1851	214
Postal service	348
Potatoes, improved	205
Powers, William, 73; opinion of land	98
Presbyterians	209, 344
Preston, town	177
Pringle brothers	31
Prohibition	344, 408
Raiders, Confederate	308, 313
Railroad agitation, 247, 257; construction	352-267
Randolph academy	124
Rastle well	382
Reconstruction	316-326
Reger, John	107
Reger, Philip	167
Republican party, 1856, 283; reconstruction period	319
Revolution, effects on county	51
Rich mountain, battle	298
Riffle, John	205
Ritchie county formed	241
Roads	109, 215, 248-254, 336, 411
Roanoke, settled, 203; named, 346; railroad, 377. See Bush's Mills.	
Roberts, Gen. B. S.	310, 313
Rock Camp run	206
Romine well	394
Rosecrans, General	304
Ross, George	302
Ross, J. W.	386

	Page
Rotary club	409
Ruhl Koblegard and Co.	369
Runyon, John	81-86
Rush run, (Freeman's creek), 144. (C. H.) in Civil war, 293; settled	202
Rushville	345
Salt Lick creek	239
Salt Manufacture	154
Sand Fork of Kanawha, first settlement, 206; Irish immigration, 230-238; in Civil war, 294; oil	388, 393
Sand Fork of West Fork	140, 204
Schoolcraft, Jacob	143
Schoolcraft, John	49
Schools, 128, 196, 268-280, 349, 376, 411; districts, 274; houses, 270; in Weston, 187; commisioners	173
Secession ordinance	292
Sewing machine introduced	265
Shadybrook	407, 409
Shawnees	26, 53
Sheep	104, 212, 265, 337, 376
Sheridan township, formed, 318; schools	350
Sheriffs, early, 212; elective, 266; office vacant	315
Shorthorn Durham cattle, introduced	212
Silo building	410
Simmons, David	202
Simpson, Allen	193
Simpson, John	31
Skin Creek, 132; land surveyed, 193; development, 205; in Civil war, 294; district formed, 325. See Weston, Georgetown, and Lincoln townships.	
Skinner, Alexander	204
Slaver	206, 282
Sleeth, John, appointed justice, 86; lists tithables,	89
Smallpox	391
Smith, Judge Daniel	171
Smith, Rev. Henry	125
Smith, John	143, 358
Smith, John W.	411
Smith, Mark	131
Smith, Weeden	331
Smith's run	131
Smythe, Rev. T. H.	278
Sorghum introduced	265
South Penn Oil Co.	283, 286, 389
Spalding, Joseph C.	327
Spaur, Anthony	133
Stage line	227, 250
Standard Oil Co.	381
Starving year	36
Staunton and Parkersburg turnpike	220-227, 233, 240
turnpike	220, 227, 233, 240, 285
Stills	146, 184

	Page
Stone Coal creek, explored, 34; settled, 131; growth, 206; first tavern, 222; in Civil war, 293; coal....	407
Straight run	287
Straley, Joseph	151
Streets in Weston, 1844, 192; Paved	370
Stringer, Daniel 167,	183
Stringer, John G.	176
Summers, Judge Lewis	172
Sun Lumber Co.	400
Sunday schools	413
Talbott, John,	188
Tannery	201
Tavenner, Cabell	
Taxation, under Va., 281; reconstruction	319
Taylor, J. W., well	386
Taylor, John	131
Tecumseh, birth, 26; leads war party	77
Telegraph line built, 302; discontinued	356
Telephone introduced	373
Tharp, Hezekiah	144
Thespian society	187
Threelick run,	396
Threshing machines introduced	264
Timber resources	17
Tobacco cultivation begun, 265; market	338
Tobetown	263
Tomahawk improvement	43
Tournament	343
Townships	316
Trans-Alleghany Lunatic Asylum, 251-261. See Weston State Hospital.	
Trapping	106
Tunstill, E. M.	329
Turkeypen run	147
Turner well	390
Turnpikes	318
Turvey, Dan T.	138
Tyler, E. B. 300,	304
Union sentiment 291,	293
United Brethren church	202
Upshur County formed	244
Vadis	379
Vandalia 135, 205,	346
Wagons introduced, 152; shops in Weston	187
Waggoner, J. C. well	388
Waggoner, John, family murdered	78
Waldo, Isaac	203
Walkersville, named, 262; Confederate recruiting, 302; bridge, 336; after war	347
Walkersville and Ireland R. R.	403
Warder, W. W.	187
Washington and Ohio R. R.	353
Waterworks	371
Watson, William A. 319,	346

	Page
Webster County	295
West, Alexander, description, 56; wounds Indian	64
West, Edmund, 37, 56; mill, 102; killed by Indians	75
West Augusta, district	51
West Fork river, improvements	216-220
West Fork Manufacturing and Booming Co.	339
West's fort, built, 55; attacked, 59; destroyed, 64; community center	102
Westfield, established, 158; meeting of court, 167; decline	201
Weston, first settlement, 49; abandoned, 66; site chosen for court house, 169; established as town, 178; population, 185; business prosperity, 246; schools, 276; favorable political position, 285; in Civil war, 291-294; captured by Federals, 299; importance, 301; captured by Confederates, 308, 310, 313; after war, 340; free schools, 350; subscription to railroad, 355; railroad shops, 367, 405; oil boom, 398; trolley line, 406; government	408
Weston Academy	277
Weston and Centerville R. R.	361
Weston and Charleston turnpike	227
Weston and Elk River R. R.	363
Weston and Fairmont turnpike	249
Weston and Gauley Bridge turnpike	251-253
Weston and Lewisport turnpike	250
Weston and West Fork R. R.	354
Weston and West Union turnpike	250
Weston College 259,	278
Weston College of Commerce	375
Weston Democrat, quoted 324, 354,	342
Weston Glass Co.	397
Weston Herald, 254; on slavery, 283; favors secession, 289; abandoned by owner	301
Weston Independent, quoted 383,	386
Weston Lumber Co.	400
Weston State Hospital, site selected 285, 327,	395
Weston township	317
West Virginia and Pittsburgh R. R.	364
Wheat 210, 338,	360
Whelan, Bishop, F. V. 235,	255

INDEX

Whigs 285
White, Buckhanan 351, 375
White, John 144
White, Solomon 202
White, William 144
Wilkenson, J. C..................299, 307
Willey township 317
Wilson, Mrs. Mary A............... 277
Wilson, Samuel 110
Wilson, W. K.............................. 385
Winchester, trade with............ 106
Witcher, Col. W. A.................... 313
Withers, Alexander Scott, writes Border Warfare, 210; teaches in Weston,
  277; slave owner, 282; in Wheeling convention, 291; quoted 415
Woffinden, J. W................338, 341
Wolf farming 212
Woodford, A. W................338, 377
Woofter, George 144
Woofter, Isaac 148
Woofter, Jesse 271, 317
Woofter, Jonathan 144
Woolen mill 340, 369

Yoke, Frank R. 351
Y. M. C. A. 342

www.ingramcontent.com/pod-product-compliance
Lightning Source LLC
Chambersburg PA
CBHW030540080526
44585CB00012B/206